"Through the years, I have seen Jack Porter bring creativity to a number of important fields: Holocaust Studies, Sociology, Politics. A serious and passionate individual, he is resourceful in his research and persistent in bringing to completion whatever task he undertakes.

I have known Jack for years, and I am impressed with his vision, his energy, and his powers of synthesis . . . ."

> Elie Wiesel, Andrew W. Mellon Professor
> in the Humanities at Boston University
> and Nobel Peace Prize, 1986

"Jack Nusan Porter's collection of essays *The Jew as Outsider* is one of the most impressive volumes on so-called Jewish Studies to come along in a very long time. Porter is one of those rare writers who is at home with scholarly treatises as he is with the popular media. In fact, this splendid book represents more than a collection of Porter's outstanding writings; it secures his position as one of the important witnesses of his generation."

> Thomas J. Cottle
> Department of Psychiatry
> Harvard Medical School

"I am impressed and delighted with the easy and spontaneity with which your mind moves outside the stereotypes. I found [your work on Martin Buber and people in cults] fascinating . . . [and] remarkably clear headed—I can see why the latter has gone through a number of reprintings. And your *Notes of a Happy Sociologist* is sheer delight. I doubt whether there is more than a handful of sociologists in the United States who could strike off with such apparent ease a series of aphorisms at once so compact, suggestive, and witty."

> Don Martindale
> Professor of Sociology
> University of Minnesota

"Your name is virtually legendary in regard to what you define as 'Jewish Student / Countercultural / Radical Groups.'"

> Rabbi Benjamin M. Kahn
> Director, Jewish Studies Program
> American University

"*The Jew as Outsider* is a solid collection of interesting, well-written essays which evince a sound sensitivity to the Jewish situation."

J. Alan Winter
Professor of Sociology
Connecticut College

"We are opening a file on your life and writings at the American Jewish Archives. . . . Your file is fattening up nicely. . . . Scholars in the future will thank you."

Jacob Rader Marcus
Director A. J.A., Cincinnati

If Only You Could Bottle It

Memoirs of a Radical Son

Cherry
Orchard
Books

If Only You Could Bottle It

Memoirs of a Radical Son

Jack Nusan Porter

BOSTON
2023

Library of Congress Cataloging-in-Publication Data

Names: Porter, Jack Nusan, author.
Title: If only you could bottle it : memoirs of a radical son / Jack Nusan
   Porter.
Description: Boston : Cherry Orchard Books, 2023. | Includes
   bibliographical references.
Identifiers: LCCN 2022016174 (print) | LCCN 2022016175 (ebook) | ISBN
   9781644698990 (hardback) | ISBN 9781644699003 (paperback) | ISBN
   9781644699010 (adobe pdf) | ISBN 9781644699027 (epub)
Subjects: LCSH: Porter, Jack Nusan. | Jewish sociologists--United
   States--Biography. | Political activists--United States--Biography. |
   Rabbis--United States--Biography. | Radicalism--United
   States--History--20th century.
Classification: LCC HM479.P6677 A3 2023 (print) | LCC HM479.P6677 (ebook)
   | DDC 301.092 [B]--dc23/eng/20220425
LC record available at https://lccn.loc.gov/2022016174
LC ebook record available at https://lccn.loc.gov/2022016175

ISBN 9781644698990 (hardback)
ISBN 9781644699003 (paperback)
ISBN 9781644699010 (adobe pdf)
ISBN 9781644699027 (epub)

Book design by Lapiz Digital Services
Cover design by Ivan Grave

Published by Cherry Orchard Books, an imprint of Academic Studies Press
1577 Beacon Street
Brookline, MA 02446, USA
press@academicstudiespress.com
www.academicstudiespress.com

This book is dedicated to a new generation of responsible radicals.

The title of the book comes from a line in a movie with Charles Bronson called *Family of Cops*, produced by a Milwaukee friend of mine, Joey Blasberg. In it, a character says, as she gets off the plane from Los Angeles, "Oh, Milwaukee, it's so nice; you should bottle and sell it."

I try to take Milwaukee with me everywhere I go.

I also dedicate this book to my wonderful sister Bella, who passed away during the coronavirus plague in April 2020. She will be missed by many. My first cousin Allen Porter also passed away during that time.

Contents

Acknowledgments

I have thanked many people over the years in my other books: my elementary school and high school teachers in Milwaukee, my Hebrew teachers, camp counselors, colleagues, fellow writers, and university professors. But here I will thank some new people.

Writing one's memoirs is a bit like therapy. In fact, back in 1981, I wrote a short essay "Psychotherapy and Writing" for a booklet put out by a Wisconsin writers' club called The Raconteurs and edited by Harold Hamley. So I'd first like to thank my therapists, Dr. Edward Rubin and Dr. Robert Raven, and my last therapist, Gail. (Interestingly, here, too, enters the gender issue: therapists have moved from mostly male to mostly female.)

I also thank Gerry Glazer for his insights into the old West Side of Milwaukee and, of course, John Gurda, the preeminent historian of Milwaukee, for his pioneering work. Also, my thanks go to Marc and Melanie Korman, who brought back some memories of growing up on Fiftieth Street.

I would like to thank my sister, Bella Porter Smith, her husband Mitch, and their son Aryeh for their support over the years. Of course, all of their children—Sruli, Avi, Shragai, Mindy, and their spouses—are great, but I have gotten closer to Aryeh most of all. My thanks as well to my brother, Shlomo Porter, his wife, Shushi, and their children.

Also, I should mention my Uncle Morris and Aunt Betty Porter of Los Angeles and Chicago and their son, Allen Porter, and his late wife, Sylvia, and their children—Marlon, Michelle, and Leah—as well as my other Uncle Boris and Aunt Hinda Porter of Los Angeles and their children—Sam, Abe, and Jack—and their children, especially Adam Porter. I would also like to thank my uncle Leon Puchtik and his daughter, the late Batya Levy, and her children in Israel, as well as our cousins, Idkeh Shuster (Puchtik), her late husband Jacob, her late parents, Avrum and Chava Puchtik, and her children Esti and Arik Shuster, as well as my other cousins on my mother's side, the late Yehuda Merin and his wife, Luba, and their children, Mina and Yossi, plus the George and Leila Porter family and their children of Hyannisport, Massachusetts, and all of our cousins all over the world. We may have lost twenty-five members of our family in the Shoah, but we have come roaring back with many more to replace them.

I would also like to thank my attorney and friend, Jim Kickham; my accountant and friend, the late George ("General" George) Marshall of the Jewish War Veterans, Post 211 of Newton and Brookline, Massachusetts; Ginny Audet of the Newton Free Library; and people in the Newton (Massachusetts) Genealogical Society, all of whom helped me track down information on DP camps and my passage on the SS *Marine Perch* and their manifests that "proved" that my parents and I were really on that ship to America in 1947. The Congregation in Waltham, Temple Beth Israel, receives my thanks for allowing me to use their wonderful synagogue library to write in. Surrounded by "old friends," classic Jewish books, the Morris and Ida Cantor Library was a pleasant environment.

Also, I thank the late Joe Voss of Seattle for his research on Maniewicze, Ukraine, as well as Chana Lorber (wife of the late Dov Lorber), for their insights into the Jewish partisans of Volhynia, Ukraine.

While writing my memoirs I came across Shaul Magid's introduction to his collection of essays *Piety and Rebellion: Essays in Hasidism* (Brookline, MA: Academic Studies Press, 2019), the same publisher as this book. I first met Shaul when he invited me to speak to his class at the Center for Jewish History in New York City in 2017. While his journey was more inward and spiritual, it was a journey that felt very similar to mine, always searching, always changing. I learned much from his book, and especially his introduction, which I urge people to read. It is fascinating.

And, of course, I would like to thank numerous libraries and archives, especially the Hebrew College library in Newton Centre, Massachusetts, and the staff of Robert Listernick and Harvey Sukenic; the Milwaukee County Historical Society; Jay Hyland of the Milwaukee Jewish Archives; the Wisconsin

Historical Society and Archives in Madison, Wisconsin; and Kevin Leonard, archivist at Northwestern University, my alma mater; as well as Todd Larson, my typist and editor, plus the staff at Academic Studies Press—senior editor Alessandra Anzani and marketing manager Mathew Charlton.

As I have noted, Porters spread out all over the country, some to Texas, some to Kansas, some to Missouri, some later to Chicago, and later still to LA, and some to Milwaukee. However, the first Porter to come to America was Ben Porter, and he went to a strange place. When we got letter in Yiddish from him, it came from this mysterious address, almost like one word—"Milford, Mass, Milford, Mass." What was it? Where was it?

Again, our name was obviously not "Porter"; it was "Puchtik" and, in some cases, "Puchtig." The word, as I noted, meant the "down" or "feathers" of a duck or most likely a goose, and it was a Ukrainian word. It meant that our ancestors were feather merchants or farmers who raised geese. Goose feathers were very common, and it took a lot of geese to fill the pillows and mattresses of the *shtetlach* (small Jewish villages) homes. I have a feather pillow I bought in Naples, Italy, and it is the softest and most comfortable pillow imaginable, but today pillows are made of rubber or other material, because, one, there is a shortage of geese, and, two, people have become allergic to feathers. Their loss. I love them, but then again, I am a "Puchtik." The actual word is "Puch," which almost sounds like "feathers" or "down," and the "-tik" is a diminutive, as in "little or short feathers."

As for my first two names: Nusia or Nosson became "Nusan" and Jacob or Yakov became "Jack." (I was named after two deceased grandparents; see my genealogy chart in the appendix.) So "Jack Nusan Porter" became my name, and it is an unusual three-word name, which is good, because if you Google just "Jack Porter" you get a character from the TV show *Revenge*, a professional wrestler, and a dentist from Wichita, Kansas.

Ben Porter, then called Baruch Puchtik, came to America in 1907. Morris Porter, my uncle, came in 1913, so Porters started coming here over a century ago to escape the poverty and pogroms of Poland, Ukraine, and Russia. Some Puchtik's went to South America (Argentina) in the 1930s to escape Nazism. My parents waited too long and suffered through the Holocaust, only coming in 1946. By then, most of the European Puchtik's were dead.

Beryl Porter, known as Barney, the son of Ben Porter, describes the flight he took with his father and mother from Europe to Milford, Massachusetts. (His story can be found in the Milford city library archives). Ben came first, and three years later, his son Beryl (Barney) and his wife Shaindel (Jennie Bard) came. Other sons, Joe and George, were born in America later. Interestingly, Ben

Porter got his start in the shoe business with money from the Italian gangster Lucky Luciano, but that's a story for another time.

One final note: I have written some of these essays over a long period of time, so there may be occasional repetition. But I think it adds to the integrity of the overall story, since, like *Rashomon*, one experiences different views from different people. I see this book as a pastiche, a kind of scrapbook filled with essays, articles, interviews, documents, and photos that combine to make up my wild and crazy life, and, at age seventy-five, there is still more adventure to come.

Preface

So many questions: Is it possible to be a radical Jew? What's so "radical" about Judaism? What's so "Jewish" about radicalism? They should be total opposites, but they aren't. Radicalism (which includes socialism and communism) has often been opposed to Judaism, or even to Jews, yet the majority of Jews are liberals and radical, or, in the words of Milt Himmelfarb, "Jews lie like Episcopalians but vote like Puerto Ricans." Why?

I call myself a "radical Jew," not a "Jewish radical," yet I am both, and it is confusing at times. *Radical Judaism* is what Art Green calls his book. Yet my kind of radicalism is not spiritual like Green's, but political and sociological. As a "radical Jew," I put my emphasis on being Jewish first, radical second. On the other hand, Jewish radicals—people as diverse as Leon Trotsky, Abbie Hoffman, Mark Rudd, and Allen Ginsberg—are radicals first and Jewish a very distant second (but not always; it's complicated, and sometimes they switch from being radical to being Jewish, even Orthodox Jewish). Some were self-hating Jews like Karl Marx or Leon Trotsky. Some started out as radicals but became more "Jewish" over time, like Arthur Waskow. Some find a sweet spot in-between . . . like me. Interestingly, I have been blessed to live at a time when a Jewish "radical," a socialist Jew named Bernie Sanders, came close to being nominated president of these United States of America!

I'm not a liberal, and I'm not a conservative. I am what they call a "progressive," a term Communists used when "communism" was too dangerous a word. But basically I'm a "progressive," or, better yet, a "democratic socialist." Bernie Sanders single-handedly made it okay to talk about socialism with his campaigns in 2016 and 2020.

But who exactly am I? That is harder to define and seems to shift all the time. As Daniel Bell said about himself, I am a radical when it comes to foreign policy, a liberal on social issues, and a conservative on fiscal (money) issues. But that still does not define me very well, because I became, after reading Elizabeth Warren's books, more radical about money matters (like bankruptcy, credit cards, and the power banks have).

In fact, I ran for U.S. Congress in 2012 in the Massachusetts 12th District on exactly that platform. I lost, but it was a fun ride. Not surprisingly, it was Barney Frank's old seat and was won by Joe Kennedy III. (The *New Yorker* did a profile on me on April 19, 2012, about that race, and the profile is in this memoir.)

I would say I am a combination of Barney Frank, Bernie Sanders, and Elizabeth Warren. Some would say this is a cop-out, that one should be a radical on all three issues: foreign, domestic, and fiscal. Maybe I've changed a bit and moved to the center. For example, while I loved Bernie Sanders and Elizabeth Warren, I supported Joe Biden for the presidency in 2020, as I felt that he would be the only one who could beat Trump. Some may call that a cop-out, but I have become a little more practical as I've got older.

Extremes at either end usually lose. Still, if Elizabeth Warren or Bernie Sanders or Pete Buttigieg had received the nomination, I would have supported any one of them. Things move so fast as I write this (February 24, 2020) that, while I shifted to Bernie and Amy Klobuchar, it looks like Joe Biden, a moderate, has overtaken both Bernie Sanders and Liz Warren and will be the Democratic nominee to oppose Donald Trump.

Who were my influences?

First, Morris U. Schappes. If any person personified the "perfect" Jewish radical, it would be Morrie, longtime editor of *Jewish Currents*. A former Communist, Morrie spent time in Dannemora Prison in upstate New York, arrested after losing his teaching job. He once told me a poignant story about being shackled to an African American on a train going up to the prison. The man was squirming all night long. When asked what the problem was, the man said he had to go to the bathroom and would have to "expose" himself to a white man. Such was the racial impact at the time. I never forgot that story. Morrie was a handsome, erudite, and dignified man who never lowered himself to anger or bitterness. He always told me: answer them with scientific and historical fact, not emotion.

Second, Habonim/Dror—Left, Socialist, and Labor Zionist—people like Label Fein, Ilana Berner, Assaf Alterman, Tzvika Gurion, Moshe Kerem, Muki Tzur; kibbutz leaders like Amnon Hadary and Mickey Duvdevani, and later *Machon* leaders like Haim Avni; or *madrichim* in Milwaukee like Lorna and Harry Kniaz; or my leaders at Habonim/Dror Camp Tavor in Three Rivers, Michigan, like Berl Post and Ivan and Malke Frank; or people of my age/generation who influenced me: David Twersky, Al Barland, Danny Kutnick, and Peter Braun—*chalutzim*, all of them.

For some reason these were mostly men, and straight men. Ironically the only woman in Habonim who influenced me was a lesbian, Ilana Berner, who of course was in the closet in the 1950s and 1960s when she was our *madricha*. No openly gay person could have been a *madrich* in *Habonim* in those days. But times have changed radically.

And, of course, we read such Socialist/Zionist thinkers as Ber Borochov, Nachman Syrkin, A. D. Gordon, and later Moshe Kerem and Max Langer. Our heroes were David Ben-Gurion, Golda Meir, Yitzhak Rabin, Yigal Allon, and Moshe Dayan. See Gil Troy's book *The Zionist Ideas* for others, as well as Arthur Hertzberg's classic book *The Zionist Idea* (which deeply influenced me, and also influenced Troy's book), along with Moshe Kerem's book (Murray Weingarten of *Kibbutz Gesher Haziv*) *The Kibbutz Idea*, long out of print.

Later in the 1960s I was influenced by the Chicago Seven (or Eight, if you include Bobby Seale), people like Jerry Rubin, Abbie Hoffman, Tom Hayden, Lee Weiner (who was my graduate schoolmate), and David Dellinger. Arthur Waskow, the Jews for Urban Justice, Breira, the New Jewish Agenda, and many of the people in my now-classic book *Jewish Radicalism* also impacted my thinking—but not Michael Lerner's "politics of meaning," which I found meaningless, so to speak, and filled with psychobabble.

Third, Hasidism. I was influenced by the Hasidic leader in Milwaukee, Rabbi Jacob Twerski, and his sons, especially Michel and his wife Faygeh, and his brothers, Shia (Joshua) and Mottel, as well as Rabbi David Shapiro and Rabbi Isaac Lerer. And also—and they might not believe this—by my brother and sister. I may have rebelled against Orthodox Judaism, but inside me is *das pintelle yid* (that tiny bit of Judaism) that prizes spiritualty and closeness to God. I am neither an atheist nor an agnostic. I believe in *Hashem*, one God. I may have some doubts, but mostly I have faith, *emunah*.

In the late 1960s and 1970s, I was also influenced by a trove of sociologists at the University of Wisconsin–Milwaukee—Irwin Rinder, Lakshimi Bharawaj, Karl Flaming, Hugo Engelmann, Don Weast; and Northwestern University—Howie Becker (along with Erving Goffman), Bernie Beck, Richard Schwartz, Janet Abu-Lughod, Jack Sawyer, and the entire school of participant observation, deviance, and concern for the underdog that they taught us back then. Today, very few sociologists of Jewry do this kind of research, with the exception of Samuel Heilman and some anthropologists; the field of Jewish studies today is dominated by mass survey analysis. I guess that is what the Jewish community wants, not in-depth analysis of Jews in prisons or on opiates.

I organized my second book on Jewish life (my first was *Jewish Radicalism*, which came out in 1973), called *The Sociology of American Jews: A Critical Anthology*, in 1978. Marshall Sklare, the dean of contemporary Jewry, told me that it was the first time that the words "Sociology of Jews" were used in a title. That anthology is still relevant today. Here are the titles of some essays from the book: "*Die Yiddishe Arbeters*," "Democracy in Jewish Life," "Vietnam and the Jews," and "Is Zionism Dead?" I should also add such historians as Louis Ruchames and Howard Zinn; they had an influence on me, as well as former progressives like John Allschuuang and the Raconteur's Writers' Club of Milwaukee.

But in the mid-to-late 1970s, I shifted my research from mainstream sociology to the Holocaust and then comparative genocide. Why? That's a painful question. Maybe sociology left me; I didn't leave it. I just did not find it very exciting anymore. Too many statistics and mass surveys, too much "sociologese," too much jargon, and especially too much political correctness all drove me from my original field, plus my books on Jews were not getting very good reviews in mainstream sociology journals like *Contemporary Sociology*.

So I made my mark in genocide studies—and, ironically, I was influenced by a host of female and marginalized scholars like Helen Fein, the most prominent sociologist of genocide, but also by Celia Heller, Joyce Apsel, and one who wrote about Jewish partisan resistance, Vera Laska. Why are there so many women in early Holocaust and genocide studies, yet so few in mainstream sociology? Maybe because Holocaust and genocide studies were new fields, less traveled, and less prestigious than mainstream areas like theory and methods, so women could make a mark in them. It's an interesting question to ponder—this gender issue—and beyond this short preface.

Arnie Eisen, in his Marshall Sklare Award speech in 2016, discussed the three-legged stool that Jewish studies stood on: Israel, God, and Torah. I rarely wrote or even thought about these three things, but as I enter that last third of my life, I am thinking more and more about them.

I joined a traditional Sephardic *shul*. The people are very warm and welcoming. They are who they are. They don't try to "convert" me, but they accept me as I am and try to get me to go one step further. I go to synagogue nearly every *Shabbat*, and I *lay tefillin*. Now that's a radical Jew for you! My parents would be very proud of me, and definitely my brother, an Orthodox rabbi in Baltimore, and my sister, a modern Orthodox woman, and her husband Mitch and their children, especially Aryeh Smith, their son, are proud of me. I thank Avi Sharouz, his wife Deena, and their kids, plus Dr. David Sheena and others, for welcoming me into the *shul*. I have finally found a spiritual home. It's not perfect—no place is—but it is home.

But what about my children and grandchildren? I love them dearly, but while my two kids (Gabe and Danielle) will remain Jewish, I fear for my grandchildren. How Jewish will they be? That is the big question that all of us sociologists of Jewry grapple with, and the future does not look good, but we will see. (I'll pay for the Hebrew school lessons.)

Who am I, and can I "duplicate" myself? That is, are there others like me in the next generation? And if mine is a form of secular Judaism, does secular Judaism have a future?

Still, *das pintelle yid*, that tiny spark of Jewishness, as the *rabbanim* say, will always sprout upward out of the sidewalk.

Am Yisroel Chai!

Part One

1946–1963—
COMING TO
AMERICA

Chapter 1

From Maniewicze to Milwaukee—the Making of a Writer/Activist

———

The Shoah

I have written extensively about the Shoah, the Holocaust, and its impact on my parents, Irving and Faye Porter. So I will move from the actual Shoah experience of the killings of my family—twenty-five members killed in Maniewicze, Poland, by Einsatzgruppe B—to our leaving Russia and coming to America. But I urge the reader to see the list of my writings in the sources section. Still, I include some rare interviews I had with my parents before they died. It sheds light on what forces formed me later.

Interviews with Jewish Partisans: My Mother and Father

Zalonka: An Interview with a Jewish Partisan Leader

This is an interview with a Jewish partisan leader, my father. Most interviews are carried out with people whom you don't know and with whom it is fairly easy to be objective. However, when you interview your father and when you talk about the destruction of your sisters (daughters) or uncles (brothers), all objectivity is thrown out the window.

It becomes a chronicle of tears and a necessary but painful task. This article is an edited version of an interview that lasted nearly four hours and took place in the living room of our home in Milwaukee, Wisconsin. Several times I had to stop the tape recorder when my father and I broke down into tears. Yet the chronicle continued, because he understood how important it was that people, especially young people, know the true story of Jewish resistance during World War II. It was a story that I had to know. As his son, as a young Jew in America, and as a young adult living in this post-Holocaust era, I, too, had to know.

There are so many myths, falsehoods, and half-truths associated with the Holocaust. One of the most arrogant of these lies is that *all* Jews were cowards and that they *all* walked passively to their deaths.

Raul Hilberg, in his book *The Destruction of the European Jews*, arrived at the conclusion that "the reaction pattern of the Jews was characterized by the almost complete lack of resistance." Hannah Arendt, in her book *Eichmann in Jerusalem*, described Jewish resistance as "pitifully small, incredibly weak and essentially harmless." Psychiatrist Bruno Bettelheim, in *The Informed Heart*, pleadingly asked, "Did no one of those destined to die fight back? Did none of them wish to die not by giving in but by asserting themselves in attacking the SS Nazis? Only a very few did."

The myths continue, but what is the truth? Bettelheim says the resistors were "very few" in number. Arendt calls this resistance "pitifully small" and "essentially harmless."

Yet it was these "very few" who, in the Warsaw Ghetto, held off General Jurgen Stroop and his command of one thousand SS tank grenadiers, one thousand men of the SS cavalry, plus two units of artillery for over two months in the spring of 1943, with only a few guns, hand grenades, Molotov cocktails, and plenty of Jewish guts.

It was this "essentially harmless" nature of Jewish resistance that forced even Goebbels to admit that "now we know what Jews can do if they have arms."

It was this number of over twenty thousand Jewish partisans who fought in the forests and mountains—of Poland, Russia, Hungary, Czechoslovakia, France, Greece, Belgium, and Italy. Some of them formed autonomous Jewish national units—Jewish partisans led by Jewish commanders. However, most of the partisan bands were mixed groups wherein Jews fought alongside Poles, Russians, Ukrainians, Frenchmen, Italians, or others.

Of the twenty thousand or so partisans, there were at least ten thousand survivors. My father was one of them. Irving Porter (Yisrael Puchtik), called

"Zalonka" in the underground, was a sub-commander in the famous "Kruk Division," led by the Ukrainian Communist leader Nicolai Kaniszcuk ("Kruk"). They fought from mid-1942 to early 1945 in the vicinity of Maniewicze, Volhynia, Ukraine, USSR.

This is my father's story. It could well have been the tale of his comrades now residing in America, Canada, or Israel and including such partisans as Berl Lorber (Seattle), Avrum Lerer (Cleveland), Moshe Kramer (Philadelphia), Isaac Avruch (Denver), Moshe Flash (Montréal), and Abba Klurman, Itzik Kuperberg, Vova Verba, Josef Zwiebel, Sasha Zarutski, Avrum Puchtik, and David Bluestein (Tel Aviv).

My father was born in the little town of Horodok in 1906, the same year and a similar *Shtetle* to that of the fictitious Anatevka in the popular Broadway musical and film *Fiddler on the Roof*. In fact, after seeing the film I jubilantly asked my father, "It was a great picture, Dad, no?" He punctured my enthusiasm by saying: "Great? That's the way it was. It was no picnic."

We live at a time when our affluence and freedom lead us to glorify and romanticize the European *Shtetle*, but it was nevertheless a hard and dangerous life. My father was one of eight brothers and sisters; his father was a poor shoemaker. After one major upheaval, World War I, he joined the Polish cavalry at the age of twenty-one, one of the few Jews in that army. After four years there, he worked as a textile worker, saving dowry money for his older sisters.

This delayed marriage to his childhood sweetheart Faygeh (Faye) Merin. They finally married in 1937, two years before the Nazi *Blitzkrieg* into Poland. He later worked for the Russian Communists in a collective workers' union until 1941. The Germans came to the area in that same year, and in 1942 he had to make the painful decision to leave his family, go into the forests, and join the partisans. I was born later in a bombed-out hospital, in Rovno, a small town near Maniewicze, on December 2, 1944, a few months before the war ended.

This interview deals mainly with the years in the partisans and those soon after the war.

* * *

Zalonka: When the Nazis came, I was living in the town of Maniewicze, a town of two thousand, at most 2,500 people. They first came in to kill the men. Later they came in a Friday night to surprise us and took the women, children, old people, and the few men that remained.

We thought they were going to work camps, but found out that they were marched outside the town, told to dig a big hole, and then the Nazis killed and buried them.

Question: When did you escape?

Zalonka: On Wednesday, two days before they came, I decided to escape. I threw away my jacket with the yellow piece of cloth that all Jews had to wear. I tucked my pants into my boots, like a Ukrainian peasant, picked up a pail, and passed by the Ukrainian guards as a farmer—and then ran into the woods.

The Germans first came in the summer of 1941 to take just the men. They killed 375 of them. Later, in September of 1942, they came again—this time pushing women and children into the street. (In total, three thousand Jews of Maniewicze and environs were killed.)

They drove them out on Friday night. They knew the families were together, and they would surprise them. They would kill the Jews, then have an orchestra and a big party, while they took Jewish property. When they finished one job, they'd go on to the next little town.

At this point, I made up my mind that I was not going to go like an animal. I was going to take revenge. [*Nekumah* was the word he used.—J. N. P.] I would run away, even though it meant leaving my family.

On that Friday night in 1942, the Germans killed my two daughters (your sisters), my mother, my father, my four sisters, my grandparents—twenty-five members of my family. [His brothers, Morris, Boris, and Leon, had left home in the 1920s and 1930s for Chicago and Buenos Aires, Argentina.—J. N. P.]

Question: How did you feel about surviving?

Zalonka: To this day, I feel guilty. I don't feel bad about killing Nazis or taking revenge on the Ukrainians (who collaborated), but I do about leaving my family. Am I no different from my parents or daughters that I lived and they died? No, we are the same. I may not have helped them if I stayed, but at least we would have been together.

Question: What happened after you escaped? Did you find a group of partisans right away?

Zalonka: After I escaped into the woods, I hid for a few weeks, with a Gentile friend—a Polish man, a Ukrainian, who lived in a different town. He gave me a rifle and 150 bullets. A rifle was worth gold; you couldn't pay a million dollars for one!

I told him I was not responsible over myself—I wanted revenge. My life was worthless. I would burn his house and kill him if he didn't give me a gun. He was scared, so he gave me the gun.

I soon found a group of about fifty people who had just two rifles among them. Within three months, this group grew until it included two hundred "fighters" (about 180 Jews and twenty Russians or Poles), two hundred men who guarded the others, and between five and six hundred women and children. We had a big job—to find food for nearly 1,000 people and to fight the Nazis.

Question: How did mamma escape?

Zalonka: I found her two months after I escaped. When I was with the partisans I asked all the farmers in the area about my family. Did any live? One said that my sister's husband was hiding nearby. I went there, expecting to see a tall man, my brother-in-law, but it turned out to be a "little man" who weighed only sixty pounds.

This "little man" turned out to be my wife. She was so small. She had escaped by hiding in a stall in a nearby barn. The Nazis didn't find her. By a miracle, she was alive. In the partisan camp, she became the chief cook. A miracle! Her whole family was killed. Everyone. She's the only one who survived. I took her in my hands. She was so light.

Question: Why was the leader a non-Jew if most of the group was Jewish?

Zalonka: It was good to have a Gentile as commander because the Jews lived in small towns or big cities. They were tailors, butchers, business people; they didn't know the woods. Our commander, like other Gentiles, knew how to hunt and fight. He knew the woods. Later we wouldn't need him, but at the beginning he was needed.

Question: What did you do in the partisans?

Zalonka: At first, we didn't do too much. But one day, a captain from a Russian partisan group about twenty miles away came over to us. He had done something wrong, and his "punishment" was to be sent over to the Jews.

This captain—who was later found out to be a Jew in disguise—told us that, when the Germans invaded in 1941, they left behind piles of huge artillery shells, which the captain had found and buried. Each shell weighed over one hundred pounds and was filled with gunpowder. With this gunpowder, we could make mines.

I was put in charge of this project, along with twenty other men. We carefully took the shells apart so they were no longer dangerous, put them in long barrels, lit fires under the barrels, and heated up this powder to a liquid state. With this liquid, we made mines.

I would go out with a small band of men, and we would place these mines under railroad tracks, water or fuel depots, and bridges, and blow them up. All day long we would sit quietly in the woods; at night we would go out to set mines. There was not too much face-to-face contact with the Germans; we could only slow them up and slow down the trains going to the Russian front.

We got food from the Gentile farmers, whom we threatened to shoot if they didn't give us potatoes, flour, or salt in good will. You must be careful in war. One is bitter and a little crazy. You do many wrong things in order to survive.

During the time of the underground, there is no law. It is like the Old West in America. We had to take food or rifles from the farmers. You had to use the gun to get food, to take his boots.

The farmer had enough food and three pairs of boots, and they probably stole them from the Jews anyway. So we had to use force, even kill a few if they didn't give, or maybe burn the barns. Most of them gave. They were so surprised to see Jews with guns. They were scared of us. They gave.

This is what we did for over two-and-a-half years. We survived.

Question: What happened after the Germans retreated from your area (in late 1944 and early 1945)?

Zalonka: After the war, I worked for the Russians for a little while, but I wanted to leave Russia and go to Israel. I loved the Russian people; they saved many Jewish lives during the war. They even honored me with a medal for heroism.

I got forged passports from the *Breicha*, the Israeli underground, and began my journey to Palestine. I'll never forget my leaving. I told a Russian officer, maybe he was even a Jew, that I had fought for Russia and now it was time to fight for my own country, for Jews.

He shook my hand and wished me well, and then he said, "Puchtik, go in peace, but remember, the Russian boot is a big one, the heel of Russia is here in Moscow, but in twenty years, the toe might be in Palestine." I'll never forget that.

I, my wife, and child went by train from Poland to Austria. It took over a month, and it is a complete story in itself. We went as Greek citizens, and it was a long and dangerous trip. [I understand that the present-day exodus from Russia follows a similar route, by rail and the "Chopin Express" from Warsaw to Vienna, but it's much less than a month to travel.—J. N. P.]

From Vienna we went to an American displaced persons camp near Linz. There, we wanted to go to Israel, but it was going to be a long wait because the British blockade was in operation and the illegal *aliyah* was starting. My wife was sick, and I had a baby boy, and the *Hagana* told us that the trip would be too dangerous for us. They were only taking single people or childless married couples.

In the meantime, we met an American captain who spoke good Russian. He asked me if I had relatives in America. I told him I had a brother, Morris Porter, in Chicago. The American had someone who was going to New York put a picture of me in the Yiddish newspaper the *Daily Forward*. My brother saw the picture, got in touch with the Jewish authorities, and sent me money and a boat ticket. I came to America in 1946, first to Chicago, and then moved to Milwaukee. I've been here ever since.

I still want to live in Israel, but my children are unmarried. When they get married, I'll move to Israel.

Question: How can you still believe in God after all that's happened to the family?

Zalonka: I can understand if young people don't believe any more in God, but I have reasons not to give up my belief. In fact, unlike some, I believe in God even more now than when I was younger. I saw miracles happen. Ninety-nine percent of the time my life hung on a hair! Bullets would fly all around me, but my body was never touched. Today, I am a strict Orthodox Jew. I don't work on Shabbos or on Jewish holidays.

Question: Now, let me ask you a few questions about today's generation of Jews. First, what do you think of the Jewish Defense League?

Zalonka: They make mistakes, but they do plenty that I like. They should search out and protect Jews. If an old woman is mugged, show the muggers your fist and they won't bother you again. But they should stay out of Israel's politics. They don't need them there. We need them here in America to take care of Jewish enemies.

America needs Kahane more than Israel does. We need protection, self-defense groups, in the parks and in the schools. People are afraid to talk the streets of the city. There's plenty of work for a JDL here in America, but not in Israel. Israel has its own police and army; they don't need the JDL's protection. And give the muggers a fist in the face. They'll think twice.

Question: What can young Jews learn from the Holocaust and the Jewish Resistance?

Zalonka: First, our most bitter lesson is that a Jew can send no one else to take his place. When it comes down to it, no one except a Jew really cares about Jewish problems.

Second, the Holocaust is our history. Young Jews must know their history. They must know their own history before they learn another's.

Third, they must be proud to be a Jew. We must respect every human being; but first of all we must respect ourselves! Our own dignity and our own self-respect must come first!

1972

Mini-Biography

Another account of my father's exploits can be found in a local paper article "Not to Go like an Animal," *Wisconsin Jewish Chronicle*, December 15, 1972, written by Barbara Fein.

There is a chapter and a picture of both "Kruk" and "Zalonka" in a hard-to-get book called *Heym Hayu Rabim* [They Were Many: The Stories of Jewish Partisans in Russia During World War II], edited by Benjamin West (Tel Aviv: Labor Archives Press, 1968). I am now in the process of getting this translated into English. Another book where the "Kruk Division" is mentioned is in a chapter on Jewish resistance written by Abraham Foxman in Judah Pilch, ed., *The Jewish Catastrophe in Europe* (New York: American Association for Jewish Education, 1968). Pilch's book is an excellent textbook. Two other sources are Yuri Suhl, ed. and trans., *They Fought Back: The Story of the Jewish Resistance in Nazi Europe* (New York: Crown Publishers, 1967); and Marie Syrkin, *Blessed is the Match: The Story of Jewish Resistance* (Philadelphia: Jewish Publication Society, 1947). There are a few others, but most deal with ghetto—especially the Warsaw Ghetto—resistance; there is really very little written in, or translated into, English on resistance in the forests. It is a beckoning field for the scholar and student.

Interview with Faye Porter

by Prof. William Helmreich

WH: You came in 1946 to America on the *Marine Perch* . . . When you came to America, you sailed into New York Harbor. What was it like there?

FP: No one came to pick us up. We have relatives in Chicago. My husband's brother [Uncle Morris Porter], he was sick. He couldn't come to pick us up. And we were there, waiting for someone! And waiting for the HIAS[1] or—I think that time it was not the Federation but the HIAS—so we are waiting, and crying, and the baby was crying. I said, 'What for? We came to America!' We were planning to go to Israel, all the time. Coming up from Russia, our plans were to go to Eretz Israel.

WH: How come you didn't go?

FP: Because that time was hard to travel with a child. With a baby. We have to go underground. If you know the story.

WH: *B'rikha. Aliyah Bet.*

FP: And there they kept you and sent you to Cyprus . . . so it was impossible, and they didn't want to give us [a] certificate, you know, to go straight. So [needs translation] we came to America. Our brother-in-law sent us [an] affidavit. We should come to America. And from America, you can go to Eretz Yisrael. So, and that's how I—so that time, you know, from traveling, and coming out from the forest and have a baby, I was very sick. So, some people suggest, "Go better, go to America. Because in Israel it's too hard, and the climate, sometimes too hard for you. So, go to America." So we listened to people, and we came to America. So, after a while, waiting for HIAS, they came and they picked us up and they took us to a hotel, and we have the dinner. They ask us to stay in New York, the HIAS. After all, our brother-in-law and sister-in-law were waiting for us in Chicago . . . so we came to Chicago. The HIAS put us on a train.

WH: You went right away to Chicago?

FP: The next day they put us on the train . . . so they have one bedroom only, and they give it to us. And they are sleeping in the living room. And my

---

1 The Hebrew Immigrant Aid Society, a Jewish American nonprofit organization founded in 1881 to provide humanitarian aid and assistance to Jewish refugees.

husband starts looking for a job . . . and looking for an apartment. At that time, there were no apartments, not even a room . . . so one day we visit Milwaukee . . . and I fell in love with Milwaukee. It was so quiet. And, and we were so frustrated from being—tired, and, and still, the bombs was in our heads, you know. What we went through. So we find in Milwaukee, on Tenth Street, more *shvartze* [Blacks] was there already, we find two-bedroom apartment. Very poor. Roaches, mice. And in the rear was a barn with ten horses . . . So when the family came to visit us, they ask, "Faigeh, you like it?" I said, "Yes! I like it!" They didn't like it, in this apartment, in this condition . . . So my husband start looking for a job and he find a job . . . in a glove factory . . .

WH: What did he do in Europe?

FP: In Europe he had [?] machine, what make the grain go fine . . . His father was a shoemaker.

WH: Where were you born?

FP: In Horodok [Ukraine] . . . in 1909 . . . in Ukraine . . . close to Kiev . . .

WH: You were married before the war?

FP: Yes . . . we were eight children. I am the only one survivor. Four sisters and four brothers.

WH: Your parents didn't make it either?

FP: No. I am the only one survivor.

WH: Where were you during the war?

FP: In the woods. It is a miracle, you know, to be alive . . . and on Friday, they took us out from a ghetto . . . and they lay us out on the middle of the street and we knew that we are going to die. And, to cry, *Shema Yisrael.* And, Saturday night, Saturday morning, they took everybody.

WH: The Germans?

FP: The Ukrainians and Germans . . . in 1942.

WH: How did you get away?

FP: It's a miracle. That night, when they put all in one street, altogether in the houses, packed. Women and children. Very few men, because the men they killed in 1941.

WH: What about your husband?

FP: My husband, Wednesday, when they start surrounding the city, Maniewicze, he said, when they said it's going to be a ghetto, so he said to me, "I'm not going to stay. I'll try to get out . . ." And he took off his patches, the yellow patches . . . and he looked like a Ukrainian. And he pass by. He passed me, with them, when the Ukrainian walked out. So, a priest said to him, in Polish, says, [needs translation] "You running away, or the devil? The devil will find you." So he runs away, and he runs back to Horodok. And, from there, he was hiding in the cemetery . . . then he find another survivor . . . and both together, they start looking . . . and find a group. The Jewish partisans . . . and with them was a Ukrainian leader . . .

WH: What about you?

FP: . . . so, the last night, so I said to my sister, "I'll go to see Velvel." My cousin was in the same street. And [to see] what they are doing. I said to the people, "Let's make a fire and escape." You know, in a fire, you can run. But nobody wants to, nobody was brave. We were women and children. That's all . . . So my sister was afraid to go, so she went back. So I went into the house, no one was there already. They hiding. Where they hiding? I don't know. So I don't know what to do. I went into an open bottom, where the horses were there. And I hid, under the, where they give the horses food, and I sit in a corner. And then next day, morning, the Ukrainian police, they started looking, and chasing out all the people and I saw and I heard and, and, after a while . . . and right early in the morning, Sunday, I saw my cousin, she came out into the house to take water. And I came up and said, "Pessel. Where are you?" "I am here." So she took me and they stay on the attic . . . and after a while, we crawl on our hands and feet and we have to crawl over the railroad tracks and we went into a forest . . . there was a Polack [Polish man], he was the forest guard, and he took us into his forest. Every Jew who escaped from the dead, he took us to his forest, and he took care of them. Slovik was his name.

WH: Is he still alive today?

FP: I don't know if he's alive. He was not so young. People must know. He must be in Israel in—yeah, he's a popular man.

WH: He saved a lot of people.

FP: He saved a lot of Jews.

WH: Even though they say that Polacks were the worst people, and everything else.

FP: This Polack was exceptional. He used to go out to Maniewicze every day, and to find out what they planning to do. So one day he came and said they planning to make a *bluvada* [encirclement]. You know, to surround. They know that we are in this forest. And he [Slovik] took us, like a good father, he took us out from his forest, and he took us to a different area. And after a while they came, and—all that.

WH: Did any Ukrainians help you during the war?

FP: Very, very few. Just one helped my husband. He gave him a rifle, two grenades, and fifty bullets.

WH: When you came here to America, what was your first impression of Chicago?

FP: Big city. Busy city.

WH: Were you happy to be in America?

FP: From the beginning, no.

WH: Why?

FP: No, no. Because we didn't have where to live. No apartment. To stay with a family, in one bedroom, and couldn't find a job. You know, it was hard to find a job.

WH: How long were you in Chicago?

FP: All summer.

WH: You were religious then?

FP: Yes. Strict.

WH: When you went to *shul* on *Shabbos* when you first came to Chicago, did the people there know what you had been through? Did they have any understanding at that time?

FP: At that time, very little. They were surprised at how we looked.

WH: In what way?

FP: They [our relatives] were surprised, they knew that . . . we were in the forest, and living . . . under this conditions, and they surprised that we looked okay. They were surprised, really. And they said, "You have to kiss the ground." And I, we told them, "We plan to go to Eretz Yisrael. We didn't want to come to America." And they said, "Oh, no, you have to kiss the ground [of America]"

WH: That you're in America.

FP: That you're in America.

WH: And you told them, "What for?"

FP: And I said, "What for?" We cannot find a place, an apartment, it's hard to find a job, my husband start working and he came home with blisters. And when we came to Milwaukee, he starts... this job because I want him not to work on *Shabbos*. So, he started to be a peddler . . . with a partner [a German Jew]. So they bought a little truck, and they went without language, they went on the South Side, there are more Polacks . . . and they started from the beginning, it was very hard. I had to take in, in this apartment, a boarder, to give him three meals a day . . . in Milwaukee. I gave him three meals a day, with two children already. Jack was born in 1944, during the war . . . and Shlomo was born in 1947 in Milwaukee.

WH: Were you in the woods with Jack?

FP: No, that time we were out of the woods . . . in Rovno [a larger city], and the Russians came, and liberated us . . .

WH: And you went to a DP camp[2] . . . to come to America?

FP: Before, when we came out from Russia, we were in Austria in a DP camp called Bindermichel near Linz.

WH: You were under a quota?

FP: . . . they allowed us to go because we were Polish citizens . . . out of Russia.

WH: But to come into America, how did they let you?

FP: Yes, there was a quota on Polish people . . .

WH: So how did you get on this quota?

FP: I don't know, we came very easy. Didn't take too long. We went to the Joint . . . [her husband's brother in America] send us the affidavit . . .

WH: Was this boarder a refugee?

FP: Yes . . . a "greener" from Hungary . . .

---

2   Displaced persons camps were established in Germany, Austria, and Italy after World War II as temporary facilities for refugees and internally displaced persons from Eastern Europe and former inmates of Nazi German concentration camps. Two years after World War II ended, approximately 850,000 people were living in DP camps throughout Europe, including Jews.

WH: How long was your husband a peddler?

FP: My husband worked on this until he died.

WH: How many years ago did he pass away?

FP: Ten years ago . . .

WH: What kind of peddling?

FP: Iron, metal, scrap. Buying and selling. They didn't have a shop . . .

WH: What happened to your dream about going to Israel?

FP: Because we had enough in Europe, and we had enough during the war, and antisemitism . . .

WH: But in 1948 when Israel became a country, you were here. Did you think then you should go?

FP: Well, I'll tell you. My husband was already in business, we had small children in school, so it was very hard . . . so Jack start belonging to *Habonim*, a Zionist youth group; and he was very active. President. He was very active in *Habonim*. After high school, he went to Israel to work for one year on a kibbutz . . . then my daughter was in high school in Chicago, and she was active in *Mizrachi* organization . . . so after high school, she wants to go to Israel . . . so she went . . . [and came back] and lives now in Minneapolis . . .

WH: What does her husband do?

FP: He's an English teacher and a Hebrew teacher . . . at a day school . . . they have four boys.

WH: Where did Jack go to school?

FP: Public school . . . Hebrew school . . . and University of Wisconsin . . . and then got his master's and his PhD . . .

WH: He's in sociology . . . and has written books.

FP: He's looking for work now . . . as a sociology teacher . . . he was in real estate . . . but it didn't work out . . . his wife is a social worker, part-time. He has two children . . .

WH: How come your other son, Jack, went to Israel, but Shlomo, your other son, didn't?

FP: After he went to school . . . a friend . . . Ben, wants to go to a *yeshiva* in Skokie, and I said to Shlomo, "Go with Ben to *yeshiva*" . . . so we prepare him, and from Skokie he went to Eretz Yisrael . . . he works with *baal teshuvas* . . .

WH: What was the attitude of people here, in Milwaukee, towards you?

FP: The relatives was a big help . . . we were the only family, survivors right from the beginning that they [HIAS] didn't help . . .

WH: Later on, many more survivors came in '49, '48.

FP: Some of them, they arrived, they gave them little apartment, yeah.

WH: They did help later.

FP: They did, later.

WH: Maybe they weren't ready for you.

FP: Not for us.

WH: You came too early, probably.

FP: That's true. Now, they didn't help us. Nothing. Nothing.

WH: Later on, did you become friendly with the survivors who came later?

FP: Oh, yeah! We had a club, New American Club, and we went together . . . and after a while, we worked for Israel.

WH: The New American Club, you were active?

FP: Yes, member . . . go to meetings . . .

WH: Did the fact that you were religious, and that most of them were not, make a difference?

FP: No difference. I ate what I can eat. And, that's all. I'll tell you, from my home, we were strict religious.

WH: *Hasidishe?*

FP: No, just strictly religious. My father belonged to the *Stoliner Hasidim* . . . and in the forest, we could not afford to keep kosher, and during traveling, we couldn't keep kosher. To tell you the truth, when we came to America, I said, "Here is a country, a free country. We can find dishes, we can find kosher food, I want to do—like I did before, like my parents were." So, we started to [inaudible] be strict.

WH: Your husband, he came from a religious family, too?

FP: Yeah.

WH: *Hasidishe?*

FP: No ...

WH: And he was willing to be religious when he came here? He wanted to be religious?

FP: Oh, yeah. Oh, sure! Oh, sure. Oh, yes.

WH: Since you suffered a lot, you lost your whole family during the war. And most of the survivors who came here, they don't believe in anything. How come you believe and they don't?

FP: Because I—first of all, my parents were strict religious.

WH: So were theirs.

FP: And, another one, I saw miracles in the forest. I saw miracles ... do you want me to tell you a miracle?

WH: Yeah, sure.

FP: We were together with Russian partisans. You know, when Hitler was in blitzkrieg, and he cut the borders, and some of the Russians, they couldn't go through the line and they have to stay behind. So, all of them went to the forest. And ... we met the Russians in the forest. So, one day there was a commander, and he was a nationalist. And the front was going farther and farther, and he saw that, and said, "What we gonna do with these *bissel yidden* [few Jews]?" So ... our Commander Kruk ... there were about one hundred Jews. And in the same evening ... the assistant ... came over and he says, "Watch yourself, because he wants to come and undermine this camp, your camp *zemlyankas* [bunkers or earth-houses], and destroy it." ... So we didn't go to sleep ... and we were up ... so the next day, it happened in this camp ... They wanted to kill us, this group, partisans, and Commander Kruk took all this group and brought us to his camp. This is a miracle.

WH: A miracle of life.

FP: ... yes, that this man warned us to be aware of that.

WH: What about the fact that your brothers, sisters, that they didn't have such miracles? That they didn't make it? Don't you question sometimes why God took them away?

FP: I question. I'll tell you. They were afraid. [inaudible] And some of them, they didn't want to leave the family. Example, my brother's son-in-law. Didn't want to leave the family. There was opportunity to go. Was opportunity to go. They are afraid. Jews are not used to live in the forest, such a life. And, they were afraid.

WH: But, if God performs miracles, I have to ask, didn't it make you ask the question sometimes, why didn't God save them?

FP: Yeah, I ask that. That's true. A lot of people ask, "Why?"

WH: That's right.

FP: Why have miracles when the Jews came out from Egypt, and . . . there were other miracles . . .

WH: Right . . . so, tell me. So people ask, "Why were their miracles then, but not now, right?" But not during the war?

FP: That's a good question. I don't know.

WH: So, how can you still believe?

FP: I believe, I don't know. Maybe I'm superstitious. I believe in God. And that's all. I believe.

WH: Even though you know that six million—

FP: Yes. Even so, I believe in God, and that's all. Nobody can—can brainwash me.

WH: Well, nobody should, but the only thing I ask is, do you ever have any doubts?

FP: I have doubts. And I have God, and I still believe [inaudible]. I'll tell you. We, Jews, we promised to keep the Torah. And when Yitzchak gave the blessing to Yaakov, so when Esau came, after . . . and he says, "Daddy, stop crying, don't you have a *bracha*[3] *for me?" He says, [needs translation] . . . that means, we should learn more Torah. We should learn our children . . . [inaudible] I'm talking to Jack, "Jack, learn the children. I'll pay for everything. Just send your children to a Hebrew school . . ."*

WH: *So they don't go? . . . He's Orthodox, Jack?*

---

3   A thanksgiving or blessing acknowledging all of God's gifts to us, often recited before a meal, the performance of a commandment or other occasions.

FP: *He is traditional. That's all. He's a sociologist . . .*

WH: *Tell me, isn't it interesting, though, if you ask it from this point of view, you know that most of the Jews who came to this country, before the war, before World War II, they were not frum[4] . . . the ones that stayed in Europe were more religious, right? And yet, if there is a God, the ones that daven [pray], that put on tefillin,[5] and everything else, they got killed. And the ones that came here, that were not frum, they lived. How is there an explanation for that?*

FP: Yes, it's a hard question.

WH: Don't you ask it?

FP: Hard question to answer. That question is very hard.

WH: And doesn't it make you wonder, sometimes, how this could be?

FP: Makes me wonder. There's no answer. It's no answer. And that's—

WH: And yet, you still believe, even though you have all these questions.

FP: Yes.

WH: You still believe.

FP: Yes. I believe.

WH: I met people who said, "When I saw in the concentration camps how rabbis were killed and tortured, I lost my belief. Because, how could God allow that to happen?"

FP: [inaudible] . . . that's true . . . we have to believe blindly, and that's all. Because we know the history. Our history from the ancient history, you know. What's happening in Egypt . . . and what's happening when they came out, and what's happening—this, this gives us our belief in a life.

WH: Do you think that the creation of the State of Israel, that that is a miracle?

FP: Yes, it's a miracle.

WH: Do you think that it's connected in some way with what happened during the war?

---

4   Religiously devoted as Jews; a term generally used in Ashkenazic Orthodox Judaic movements.
5   A set of small black leather boxes containing scrolls of parchment inscribed with verses from the Torah, worn by observant adult Jews during weekday morning prayers.

FP: Yeah, it's a miracle. Such a small, you know. Small nation, without preparing the doubt, it was a miracle to, to fight with so many nations. You now. Egypt, and Syria, and all—and they are the winners. I think it's a miracle. Yes.

WH: Do you think that it's related to what happened during the Holocaust? That the State of Israel came into being after the war?

FP: I think so. Even the prophet said . . . [needs translation]

WH: So, tell me, in America, when you were living in Milwaukee, it's hard to be Orthodox here, right? What's it like to be Orthodox here?

FP: No, no. It's not hard.

WH: You didn't think of going to New York or Chicago?

FP: No. It's not hard. If you want, there is a, a will, there is a way. Oh, yes.

WH: Are you happy that you came to Milwaukee?

FP: Yes, yes. Very happy. Because it is a quiet city.

WH: What accomplishment in life are you most proud of?

FP: I'm proud of my children, *zein gezunt*, that's what we wanted. Shlomo went to a Hebrew school, to a *yeshiva*, [inaudible] and this is an accomplishment, and this makes us happy. My daughter. All this makes me happy. This is why we all desire for *yiddishkeit*, this is the most important for Yiddish, for *yidden*. Now. Right now. To work. The *rabbonim* should work more for *yiddishkeit*. Like my son, Shlomo. And this is most important. Otherwise, you see intermarriages. A lot.

WH: A lot.

FP: A lot!

WH: Well, your children didn't.

FP: Thank God. It's a miracle, too. With Jack, Jack was going out with a *shiksa.*[6] He came once and he said, "Momma, there is a beautiful girl, and she wants to convert." I says, "You know what, Jack, stay single. You better stay single." [inaudible]

---

6   A Gentile girl or woman.

WH: Do you think that what happened in Europe could happen here in America?

FP: You never know.

WH: Do you think there could be a Holocaust?

FP: You never know, because we have to be prepared. Because we have a lot of enemies in America.

WH: Who are our biggest enemies here?

FP: The Ku Klux Klan, the Nazis, and all kind of—there's another, the skinheads.

WH: What about the *shvartzes*?

FP: The *shvartzes* are okay. Even the Ku Klux Klan doesn't like them. The Nazis doesn't like them. [inaudible] Nothing is our friend. No. Let's hope for the best. [inaudible] And to be aware.

WH: You have to be aware.

FP: You have to be.

WH: And in Israel also.

FP: In Israel, also. [inaudible] It's a miracle! You know, such a small Israel, country, which surrounds with so many wolves around, and that's why they are jealous. Because a little Israel and so successful.

WH: Do you think that we should give back . . . the territories to make peace?

FP: They want a country in a country. It's impossible. It's impossible. If they'll give one piece, after a while they'll want more and more.

WH: What are they going to do?

FP: Some people, they say, better give land for peace, and some people says, "No."

WH: Do you think there could be land for peace? Do you think it could work?

FP: I'm not a politician. I'm a plain *Yiddishe* momma. Right?

WH: But you made it here, you made it in America, you have three children, and everything else.

FP: It was a miracle.

WH: Are your friends, your close friends, all survivors?

FP: Yes.

WH: Do you think sometimes that the American Jews that they look down a little bit on the *greeneh* [greenhorns]?

FP: American Jews, there are some of them, they're jealous of the *greeneh*. They says, "They came, they run business, they are successful." And some of them are very happy with—you know, people with sense. They are happy for us. And some of them, you know, they say, "Look at the *greeneh*. They came with nothing." And some of them, they say, "Oh, they brought a lot of money."

WH: Yeah.

FP: Yeah! The *greeneh* brought *gelt*. Yeah. We came with nothing. We came with nothing! And my husband worked very, very hard. To be a peddler, to take out furnaces from the basement, and carry on the truck, and—

WH: How come you don't belong to . . . Rabbi Feldman's *shul* . . . because a lot of survivors, they went there.

FP: We are, we are not Polish. We are more Russian Jews.

WH: Does it matter?

FP: Yeah. [inaudible] No matter.

WH: No.

FP: No matter.

WH: But it's a Polish *shul*.

FP: Yeah, but it's a *frumer shul*, and it's a *Polisher rebbe*, and it's a nice *shul*.

Interviewer (Prof. Helmreich) Notes

It was necessary to terminate the interview because Mrs. Porter had to go to a meeting of Israel Pioneer Women. It turns out that she is very involved; she's very involved with Israel. In that sense, she's a typical survivor.

Mention should also be made of the fact that Mrs. Porter is a woman who also lost two children of her own during the war—children she had had before the war. And there certainly is a feeling of guilt, or whatever, that she didn't save them. Also, the rest of her family, although she has commented on that.

Here is a woman who lost everything, but she still stayed whole because she did not suffer the humiliation that those who were in a camp suffered. She was in the woods in the partisans, her husband was a man who attacked the Germans, who fought against the Ukrainians and who was a fighter. And that partisan experience is a different experience than that in the camps.

Many of the survivors feel a certain amount of guilt. If you talk to them, they always will tell you, privately, that they had to make certain compromises—compromises, things against their will, that they wanted to do in order to survive. And many times they didn't even tell their children. Mrs. Porter's children know what happened during the war. They know. But not everyone can feel that way.

According to one person who has observed the survivors, one person always [inaudible] used to see her parents crying at holidays. When she made *gefilte* fish for holiday and everything, she would cry. And she didn't know why she cried. Because her parents didn't discuss the Holocaust with them.

Some of the marriages that the survivors contracted were terrible marriages. This will, of course, not necessarily come out in a two-hour interview. Especially with both parties there. Many of these marriages are terrible marriages. Contracted in the camps. They lasted, but they weren't necessarily good marriages.

Some of the partisans, some of the survivors, exaggerate their accounts. To hear them tell it, they beat up half the Ukrainians in the Ukraine. And that also is to be expected.

These are just some random notes.

July 26, 1989

The Partisan Baby Photo

This is the story behind this famous photo. The picture has been with me for a long time. A photographer in a studio took it in Rovno, Ukraine, in February or March 1945. I was born December 2, 1944, so I'm about three to four months old. My father, Srulik Puchtik (he was Irving Porter in Milwaukee), known during the war by his *nom de guerre* "Zalonka," which means "green" in Russian, was a Soviet partisan commander in the Kruk Fighting Group in the Volhynia region of Ukraine, between Kovel and Sarny and north of Rovno in the Pripet Marshes area. Some four hundred Jews fought in this fighting group while taking care of a large "family camp" of three hundred-plus civilians, hidden and protected by the partisans. My mother, Faygeh Merin Puchtik (Porter), was a cook and nurse in the Kruk family camp. Kruk (Nicolai Kaniszcuk) was a communist Ukrainian commander who organized and led the Jews into battle. He, and a righteous Polish man named Slovik, helped save many Jewish lives. "Maks" Jozef Sobiesek, a Polish communist officer, also led the group. Thus it was called by their *nom de guerre* the Kruk-Maks Group (Otryad).

After my parents survived the war, they returned to their *shtetl* in Maniewicze, Poland, but nearly everyone had been killed, including my two little sisters born before me. They set up a *matzeva* (a stone memorial) and departed.

I was born in the woods, a partisan baby, and my dad said the Soviet partisans had a big party and got very drunk at my *bris* (circumcision). It was tough to find a *mohel* (ritual circumciser), but a young apprentice *mohel* was found but did a botched job, and an infection set in. My mother jokes about this all the time. But I'm not so sure it was funny, yet I survive. I was a tough baby. God had other plans for me. The Germans shelled the town every night. It was a miracle I survived.

My parents could no longer live in Poland, and so the *Breichah*, the illegal Zionist outreach program, brought them, using forged Greek passports, by foot through Poland and Czechoslovakia to Austria to a DP camp near Linz, Austria, called Bindermichel.

A Jewish GI returning to New York City put my father's name and photo, a photo like this one, in the famous New York City Yiddish newspaper the *Forward*, and my dad's brother (my uncle), Morris Porter of Chicago and later Los Angeles, sent us papers right away to come to America. We believe that it was a Jewish GI physician from Philadelphia who took the photo with him to New York and placed it in the paper for my father. I have yet to track him down. While in Bindermichel, it was HIAS or the Joint Distribution Committee that helped us.

We arrived in July 1946 on the ship the SS *Marine Perch*, but no one came to pick us up at Ellis Island. My father's brother was sick and lived in Chicago. He couldn't come. So there we were, waiting and crying, and my parents were crying, and the baby (me) was crying. My mother cried: "What for we come to America ... for this?" We were so alone.

Finally, someone from HIAS came and put us up in a hotel in New York City for the night. We had dinner, and the next morning they put us on a train with a sign on our clothes: "Take us to Chicago." In Chicago, my Uncle Morris, Aunt Betty, and Cousin Alan recognized us right away as "greenhorns" by our shabby clothes.

Uncle Morris and Aunt Betty had only one bedroom, but they gave it to us and slept in the living room. They were wonderful people. Father looked for a job and an apartment, but there were no apartments ... so one day, on a trip to Milwaukee to visit our cousins, we fell in love with the city ... so clean, so quiet. We were so tired, and the bombs were still in our heads. We moved to Milwaukee to Tenth Street and North Avenue, today a Black area, where we found a two-bedroom apartment, and in the rear was a barn with ten horses. Very poor. Cockroaches. Mice. But it's America. My mother likes it. My dad got a job in a glove factory nearby, and off we started on our American adventure.

We owe it all to that unknown Jewish soldier/doctor and to the *Forward* newspaper. Later, my mother's story of coming to America was retold in two books: Rhoda G. Lewin's *Witnesses to the Holocaust: An Oral History* (Woodbridge: Twayne Publishers, 1990), 167–169 and William B. Helmreich's *Against All Odds: Holocaust Survivors and the Successful Lives They Made in America* (New York: Simon & Schuster, 1992), 240.

THE PRESIDIUM OF THE SUPREME SOVIET OF THE UKRAINIAN SSR

DEPARTMENT FOR DECORATIONS
252019, City of Kiev—19, 5 Kirov Street

No. [illegible]   June 15, 1987
                         THE PRESIDIUM OF THE SUPREME SOVIET
                         OF THE USSR
                         Department for Decorations

Re: No. 221—ON of June 5, 1987

We hereby inform you that the department has records of the award to Puchtik, Srul' Yankelevich, born in the year 1898, of medals "Partisan of the Patriotic War, First Class" (orders of the Ukrainian staff of the partisan movement, No. 83 of October 2, 1944, and No. 125 of February 19, 1946). The medal in order No. 83 was presented on February 9, 1945, with provisional citation No. 30821; the department has no record of the presentation of the medal in order No. 125.

It is noted on the registration form for the award that he was a member of the Kuybysheva partisan unit in the district of Rovenki beginning August 1, 1942, and that his home address was the town of Lishnivka in the region of Manievich.

Copies of the roll of honor and archival references to Srul' Yankelevich Puchtik's participation in the partisan unit will be forwarded to your address upon their receipt from the archives.

Department Chief   V. KUTSENKO
                                (signed)

Chief Archival Administration
of the Council of Ministers [i.e., cabinet] of the Ukrainian SSR

CENTRAL STATE ARCHIVE OF THE OCTOBER
REVOLUTION, OF THE HIGHEST AGENCIES OF THE STATE
POWER,
AND OF THE AGENCIES OF THE STATE ADMINISTRATIONS
OF THE UKRAINIAN SSR (TsGAOR USSR)

252601, City of Kiev – 110, 21 Solomon Street
Telephone: 77-36-66

To the Director of the Department for Decorations
of the Presidium of the Supreme Soviet
of the Ukrainian SSR,
Comrade Kutsenko, V.
252019, City of Kiev – 19,
5 Kirov Street.

ROLL OF HONOR

Re: Fighting man of the Kuybysheva partisan unit, formation No. 1, partisan unit of the Rovenki district
(Service, unit, and formation)

1. Last name, first name, patronymic _____ Puchtik, Srul' Yankelevich _____
2. Which decoration has been presented __ The medal Partisan of the Patriotic War, First Class _____
3. Year of birth _____ 1898 _____
4. Nationality _____ Jew _____
5. Party affiliation _____ none _____
6. When did he join the unit _____ August 1, 1942 _____
7. Place of joining the unit _____ Region of Manievich, district of Volyn _____
8. Injuries or shocks _____ none _____
9. Was he in captivity or under siege _____ no _____
10. Decorations (date of decree and order) _ none _____
11. In the army from what year _____ n.a. _____

12. General education _____ third grade _____
    Military education _____ none _____
13. Place of birth _____ District of Volyn, region of
    Manievich, town of Leshnievka _____
14. Address of permanent residence, and last name, first name and patronymic
    of dependents District of Volyn, region of Manievich, town of Lishnivka

Supplementary account of personal combat feat or merit contributing to the award.
He participated in the breakthrough of 5 enemy echelons, the detonation of 4 railroad bridges spanning 1500 meters, and the destruction of 3 police stations, one estate, one sawmill, and one grain silo. He killed 6 Germans and one Cossack. He took part in 5 battles with German-Ukrainian nationalists and in 3 battles with the Germans.
Chief of staff of the partisan movement in the district of Rovenki,

Major General Begma   signature   (Begma)

BASIS: F.I., op. 24, doc. 223, p. 85.

Deputy Director of the Archive   R.I. Tkach (signed)

Senior Archivist   N.V. Diachenko (signed)

(Official seal)

The *Breichah*—the "Escape from Europe"

I would like to start my history with our escape from Ukraine (Russia) in early 1945. My parents saw no future in a country that had allowed such killings or in fact any economic or sociological future. I am certain that antisemitism was a factor, but more so, a desire to go to the Holy Land of Israel. That was the dream of many survivors—to get out of Ukraine and go to the "West" (Germany, Austria, and Italy) and from there to Palestine.

Having been born in December 2, 1944, my memories of the war and the Shoah are non-existent except for chiaroscuro forms that came out during my many years in therapy. I was less than one year old when the war ended in the summer of 1945. This was good in that I have no major traumas, nor post-traumatic shock that many child survivors have. Yet, as a child survivor, since I was technically born while the war was still on, the war and the flight to safety and the stress on my parents must have impacted me as small child, but overall, I am quite healthy, mentally and physically.

World War II ended earlier in Rovno, Ukraine, than further west, since the Soviet armies liberated that part of Europe in mid-1944; then they moved on to terrible battles on their way to Berlin. I was born on December 2, 1944, when the Russians liberated our state of Volhynia, Ukraine, but the war continued in other parts of Europe. The Americans and their allies fought from the D-Day Invasion in June of 1944, six months before I was born, and met up with the Soviets in Berlin on May 2, 1945. However, the war continued for the USA until August 1945 in the Far East against Japan.

So, while I was sheltered from the trauma of the war, I still felt the impact via my parents. But I was luckier than most survivor children. My parents had an intact marriage, whereas most others had either one partner or another who was killed or who died. There were many second marriages, some of them not very "successful." Also, my parents were fairly healthy, mentally and physically, and they had religion. They were Orthodox Jews—not *farchnuketeh yidn* (fundamentalist Jews), but solid, honest believers in God—they put their trust in Him. That led to a stable home and fewer problems for their children. I say this because I have written about my friends and their parents and the many problems they had.[7]

While my "hometown" *shtetl* was Maniewicze, Ukraine, I was actually born in the much larger city of Rovno, about one hundred kilometers south. My parents moved to Rovno because they wanted to leave Ukraine for Palestine

---

7   See my book *Milwaukee Memories / Small Town Secrets* (2014).

and it was easier to find connections to Palestine via the Jewish "underground," the *Breichah*, in bigger cities.

One way they did this was to have a party, which would actually be a disguise for a Zionist meeting, to discuss the arduous trip to Palestine. Israel was not yet in existence, but there were Jewish Palestinians, *Breichah* representatives, in every major European city and town, herding the survivors together, and trying to help them reach freedom, either to Austria or Italy, and from there to Palestine or elsewhere.

After the killings in Maniewicze, most Jews returned to their *shtetlach*, buried their dead, put up a memorial, and left for Western Europe or Palestine. A pogrom in Kielce, Poland, scared the Jews and showed them that there was to be no return, that no Jew was safe in Eastern Europe, and that it was time to get out.

Surprisingly, this is an era in history (between 1945 and 1952) that I know less about than the actual Nazi killings. Sadly, I did not spend enough time interviewing my parents and their friends about the *Breichah*, the escape from Europe, and their time in the DP camps; so much of my story here is fragmented and anecdotal. (I have tried to compensate for this with a new manuscript called *L'Matara: "For the Purpose of": Jewish Partisan Poetry and Prose from the Displaced Persons Camps after World War II, 2020.*)

My parents—Irving Porter (Srulik Puchtik), who was forty years old, and Faye Porter (Feygeh Merin), who was thirty-seven—and I began the tortuous "escape" around the spring of 1946 when I was a year and a half old. Their goal was Palestine, but we never made it, perhaps because I needed to be a bit older and tougher for the arduous journey. Bringing along an infant on the trip across the Mediterranean was too difficult. That is one reason why we came to America.

After my parents came out of hiding and fighting in the woods of Volhynia and Polessia, they returned to Maniewicze and Horodok to say the final *kaddish* for their parents, grandparents, sisters, brothers, uncles, aunts and, in our case, two younger sisters, Chaya Udel and Pessel, age four and two, who were brutally killed by *Einsatzgruppe B* on or around September 21, 1942, in Maniewicze in a cemetery for dead horses called *Ferdishe Mogiles*. And then they quickly moved to the larger city of Rovno. (I use the Polish version of the name; today it is part of Ukraine and called Rivne.)

The reasons, as I have mentioned, why a large city was chosen were several. First, it was safer than a small village, where feelings were often high and dangerous against returning Jews who may have wanted their homes and business back. Plus, these homes were often looted for gold, jewelry, and money buried in the basement or back yard, and the inhabitants were none too pleased to see live Jews returning.

But the most important reason was that it was easier to organize the *Breichah* in a larger city. Surprisingly, the years between 1946 and 1950 were fluid. Stalin and the Soviet leadership, for their own political agenda—weakening the British and French in the Middle East—supported the idea of a Jewish state in Palestine. True, this would soon change to overt antisemitism, such as the killings of Soviet Jewish intellectuals and the ominous "Doctor's Plot." But in the years 1946–1950, the Soviet Union looked the other way as the *Sheerat Haplitah*—"the Remnants who Survived," as they were called—tried to get to Palestine.

You know the story well: Jews traveling over mountains at night to get to Italy or Austria via Poland and Czechoslovakia, and from there to various Mediterranean ports, and then, from there, trying to sneak through the British blockade to reach Palestine. Most ships were stopped and sent to internment camps in Cyprus. It is the story of the ship *Exodus* that novelist Leon Uris described in his 1960 novel and in the Paul Newman–Eva Marie Saint–Yul Brynner movie of the same name.

I was born on December 2, 1944, in a Soviet hospital on Spitalny Street in Rovno. I have been told there was a great celebration with all the partisans celebrating the birth of a new "partisan child" to replace those who had been killed. Lots of vodka; lots of food; lots of singing. The circumcision was done by the son of a *mohel*, and it was one of his "first jobs." I hope he did a good job, but I didn't feel a thing, thank God.

Under the guise of an *Oneg Shabbat*, a Friday evening party celebrating the Sabbath, these young people gathered to discuss, with representatives of the *Breichah* sent over from Palestine, how to best circumnavigate the "escape." My parents and I were told to go as Greek workers and were given Green *laissez-passer* visas—all forged, of course. They were told not to speak Polish or Russian or even Yiddish, but only Hebrew, which sounds like Greek. Trucks were acquisitioned, and money for bribes was given at all border crossings. To this day I know two Greek words that my parents learned to repeat over and over: *kalimera, kalispera*—good morning, good evening.

My parents told me that those three weeks crossing from Ukraine to Poland through Czechoslovakia to Austria were among the most stressful of all, feeling that they could be turned back to the Soviet Union and the "Iron Curtain" at any moment. But they had good guides and plenty of money supplied by the *Sachnut*, the Jewish Agency of Palestine, to make sure things went smoothly.

My feeling is that the border guards knew that we were Jewish refugees and sympathized with us. Plus, of course, the bribes eased passage and escape. In fact, my father related one story that, before they crossed into Poland from

Russia, one Soviet commissar asked my dad where he was going and he said, "To Palestine." The Russian then replied: "Go, but one day, the heel of Russia will be in Moscow, but the toe will be in Tel Aviv." My dad to this day thinks the commissar was Jewish and probably wanted to leave Russia as well.

Even today, Soviet Jews are envious that we were able to escape the Soviet Union during the "thaw." As I noted, in just a few years the "iron curtain" would fall and Jews would be trapped in Russia until the mid-1970s.

The goal was to reach the American Zone in Austria or Germany. That was the way toward freedom, and my parents eventually found their way to a DP (Displaced Person) camp near Linz, Austria (ironically, Hitler's hometown) around the fall of 1946. And a new chapter in their lives began. They spent less than a year in the camp. In the summer of 1947, they were on their way to America on the SS *Marine Perch*, a US Army transport vessel, and to freedom.

Life in the DP camp was paradise compare to the death camps, the concentration camps, and hiding in the woods of Europe. Plus, there was a huge birthrate, a tremendous desire to replace all who had died. It was truly "life reborn." Morale was high in anticipation of freedom, either to go to Palestine, the USA, or other Western or former British colonies such as Australia, Canada, or South Africa.

For the short time that people were in these DP camps, there arose an active political, cultural and religious life—with the full spectrum of Israel/Jewish parties—from the left-wing Bund to the right-wing Revisionists. Be they secular, religious, or atheist, the camp was filled with commotion, emotion, and activity.

Bindermichel, near Linz, was in a beautiful part of Upper Austria where the Traun and Danube Rivers meet—lovely mountains in the distance, green fields. I have returned there twice. One time, I tried to find the tree where my dad told me he had buried his partisan medal and Soviet documents, but there were many trees, and I did not have a shovel. The place today is an apartment building complex and the home, ironically, of modern-day refugees from Africa and the Middle East. None know that it was previously a DP camp, but the Austrian locals know, and they told me stories.

I have tried to interest the Austrian government in putting up a marker on this DP campsite and others, and I am still trying. It will happen. Interestingly, my passport says that I was born in Austria. My parents put own Austria on immigration papers because of fear of Communism—the same reason why my dad buried his Soviet partisan papers. I have tried to become an Austrian citizen, but you can become a citizen only if you father was a citizen. Still, I have a close affection for Austria to this day.

The story goes that a Jewish GI stationed in Binder Michel who spoke Yiddish talked to my dad and said he was going back to America—to Philadelphia, to be exact—and said that, if we had a photo, he would put it into the Yiddish *Forward* to tell our relatives we were alive. This was very common throughout Europe. Well, this soldier did what he said, and, lo and behold, a friend of my Uncle Morris and Aunt Betty in West Rogers Park, Chicago, saw the photo and told my uncle. He then contacted HIAS, and HIAS representatives in Austria contacted my parents in Bindermichel and put the proper visas together. We had a sponsor! (Sadly, I never knew the identity of the soldier; maybe a reader knows.)

With those papers and a cost of $208 for me and $134 each for my parents (paid for by HIAS) we were able to book steerage from the port of Bremenhaven, Germany, on the SS *Marine Perch* bound for the *goldineh medinah* ("golden land") of America.

The trip itself wasn't so "golden." It was a harrowing voyage. My parents got sick from some contaminated fish and threw up all the time. But people tell me I was a strong kid and didn't get sick. (Interestingly, Golda Meir, in a similar tale decades earlier when she came to America and then to Milwaukee, also ate food on her ship and didn't get sick either.)

My dad told me an interesting story. Crawling around on deck, I found a gold ring. He said, "Yankele, open your hand," but I held tight. He opened my hand and found a diamond ring. He gave it to the ship attendants, and they found the owner, a wealthy Jewish German woman. She told us that when we embarked in New York she would give us a reward, but she never did. This was our first introduction to the *goldineh medinah*—the streets were not paved with gold.

But, in any case, we were free.

SS *Marine Perch* Passengers

Bert Beigel
Ellen and Gerald Beigel
Lester Berke
Elizabeth Berkovics (formerly Elizabeth Israel)
Sally Birnbaum
Monica R. Blumberg
Rose Bochman (former Rose Bajadel)
Leo Brenner
Eta Chinkes
Anna (Warszawski) and Isak Federman

Eleanor Field (formerly Gabriella Klein)
Irene (Silberstein) and Henry Frank (Irene arrived on Perch; Henry on Flasher)
Helen Borkowsky Gerson
Rita Gold (formerly Raja Bajadel)
Edzia Y. Goldstein
Sol Goldstein
Arthur Greenbaum
Philip Greenfield
Ruth (Roza) Israel
Julius Jacobs
Philip Jaget
Herta Helm (formerly Bodenheimer, *née* Moses)
Eric H. Kahn
Dr. Michael Katz
Henry Kellen
Margaret Klein
Maria Kurc
Victor Kurc
Barbara Keitner
Harry Luel
Arek Mandelbaum
Janek "Jack" Mandelbaum
Zygmunt "Sigmund" Mandelbaum
Benjamin and Vladka Meed
Geniek Mittleman
Jerry Nathan
Dr. Stanley ("Szymon") and Edith Ostern
Cecilia Pearlstein
William Perry
Faye Porter-Arenzon (formerly Faygeh Merin Puchtik)
Irving Porter (Srulik Puchtik)
Dr. Jack Nusan Porter (Nusia Jakub Puchtik)
Mrs. Hannah Rath
Ismar Reich
Ursula Reich
Ghenle Romanowsky Richman
Evelyn Romanowsky Ripp
Leo Rosen
David Rosenblum

Salamon and Ilona Rosner
B. Schanzer
Eva Schuster
Jack Schwartz
Dr. Gustave Seliger
Bella Shampan (formerly Jakubowicz)
Irene Shapiro
Arthur and Frances Silverberg
Paula Sokal
Martin Spier
Walker Spier
Richard Stuart (formerly Rudi Studinski)
Irena Urdang de Tour
Joseph and Fay ("Fela") Walker
Aron Warszawski Warren
Sonia Warszawski
Marion Weiner
Sam Weinreb
Frederick Weinstein
Mollie Weinstock
Tobias Weisbord
Lisa Williams (formerly Goldmann)
Paul and Helen Winter
David and Gussie (formerly Gucia Warshawski) Wolowski
Dorothy Yahr
Rose Zolen (formerly Zlotogorski, *née* Rotklein)

Sources

Ainsztein, Reuben. *Jewish Resistance in Nazi-Occupied Eastern Europe.* London: Paul Elek; distrib. by Barnes & Noble Books, New York, 1975.

Bauer, Yehuda. *Flight and Rescue: Brichah.* New York: Random House, 1970.

Dekel, Ephraim. *B'riha: Flight to the Homeland.* New York: Herzl Press, 1972.

Gottschalk, Max, and Abraham G. Duker. *Jews in the Post-War World.* New York: The Dryden Press, 1945.

Life Reborn: Jewish Displaced Persons 1945–1951. Conference Program, January 14–17, 2000, US Holocaust Memorial Museum, the Second Generation Advisory Group, and the American Jewish Joint Distribution Committee.

Porter, Jack Nusan, and Yehuda Merin, eds. *Jewish Partisans of the Soviet Union During World War II.* Newton, MA: The Spencer Press, 2013.

Roskies, Diane K., and David G. Roskies. *The Shtetl Book.* New York: Ktav Publishing House, 1979.

Slepyan, Kenneth. *Stalin's Guerrillas: Soviet Partisans in World War II.* Lawrence: University Press of Kansas, 2006.

Spector, Shmuel. *The Holocaust of Volhynian Jews, 1941–1944.* Jerusalem: Yad Vashem Publications, 1990.

Tec, Nechama. *Defiance: The Bielski Partisans.* New York and Oxford: Oxford University Press, 1993. (Plus see the movie of the same name.)

For background on Austria, see:

Mazdra, Marian. *Austria: Countries of the World.* Milwaukee: Gareth Stevens Publishing, 2004.

Also see my two memoirs:

Porter, Jack Nusan. *Happy (Freilich) Days Revisited.* Newton, MA: The Spencer Press, 2011.

————. *Milwaukee Memories: Small Town Secrets.* Newton, MA: The Spencer Press, 2014.

See also my book in progress:

Porter, Jack Nusan. *L'Matara: "For the Purpose": Jewish Partisan Poems and Prose from Displaced Persons Camps after World War II.* 2020. This book contains rare literature from the DP camps written by Jewish fighters and soldiers, men and women, and gives us an insight into camp life.

Chapter 2

Milwaukee in the 1940s and 1950s / Diary, 1959

——————

From New York to Chicago to Milwaukee

When we arrived in New York, we went straight to Ellis Island, where we were quarantined, examined, probed, and booked. Sadly, there was no one there to greet us. No family at all. I was a little boy, only a year and a half old; my mom was sick and pale; my dad was depressed. They had suffered. We were kept in steerage while the richer folks were on the first-class upper levels.

HIAS officials were the only people to meet us after the quarantine period. Sadly, they told us that my dad's brother, Uncle Morris Porter, couldn't make it. "We'll put you up in a hotel in Manhattan for a day or two, and then the next morning we'll put you on a train to Chicago, where your brother will meet you," we were told.

So, like packages, they put us on a train, the *Broadway Limited*, and placed a paper on our clothes in English telling people where we were going, and off we went on the eighteen-hour trip overnight from New York to Chicago. They gave us some money, and we were well taken care of on board the train. (How different is our attitude and treatment of immigrants today!)

We stayed in Chicago in my uncle and aunt's crowded apartment in West Rogers Park. I remember nothing about Chicago. My mom said that she and

Aunt Betty took me to the lake (Lake Michigan) to get out of the hot apartment and that everybody loved me. I was very cute.

But, again, reality set in: the apartment was crowded, and it was hard to find work, so we moved sixty miles north to Milwaukee. Jobs were more plentiful there, plus we had some cousins—the Liebermans, the Magidsons, the Kaplans—plus a *Tante Rivkeh* Baron, an elderly woman who was my father's great aunt. They sponsored us.

We arrived in Milwaukee by train on August 14, 1947. I don't know who met us, whether it was Milwaukee refugee agencies or some other groups. But the Jewish community did a wonderful job. Hadassah, the League of Jewish Women, Pioneer Women, Jewish Family and Children's Service—I don't know all of the groups who helped us, and continue to help refugees—but they gave us a warm welcome.

Unbeknownst to us, we were given an apartment in what people called the "ghetto" or the "inner city"—today it is called Bronzeville, a Black neighborhood—but we were all poor, so who cared? To this day, I saw that I was raised "in the ghetto" and in the "hood" as a white boy, and I have always been comfortable with African Americans, having grown up with them at 2125A Tenth Street, Tenth and Reservoir, just a block or two south of North Avenue. We lived there from 1947 to 1953.

This was an "integrated" neighborhood long before that word was discovered. Whites and African Americans (we used the word "Negroes" back then, or *Shvartzehs* in Yiddish) played together and worked together and lived together in peace. I roamed the alleys and byways of my ghetto from Tenth and Reservoir all the way south to Lloyd Street and as far north as Twelfth and Teutonia, where there was a playground behind Temple Beth Israel, where I went to Hebrew day school at the Milwaukee Hebrew Academy.

It was a wonderful childhood.

The garages back in the late '40s and early '50s housed stalls for horses, not cars. I still remember the fruit, vegetable and used clothing sellers going through the alleys with horse and cart, yelling for customers. I especially remember Mr. Cohen, who had a stentorian voice (I love that word—it comes from *Stentor*, the name of a loud herald in *The Iliad*), a voice that could blow you away: "Potatoes, tomatoes," Cohen shouted to the housewives. In fact, *The Milwaukee Journal* did a photo essay on him on the front page in the early 1950s with him driving his horse and cart in the midst of traffic, surrounded by cars, with the caption "The Last Horse and Cart Dealer." Talk about technological change!

And there were other changes. A cartoon in the July 26, 1953 *New Yorker* magazine showed a bunch of Boy Scouts in the woods, huddled around a TV on a tree stump. The TV was attached to a nearby house by a very long electric cord, and they were all watching television instead of a campfire. We had the same experience. Since TVs were expensive, I remember us kids sitting on the sidewalk watching a TV in Mr. Babush's grocery store window. A few years later, we had our own TVs.

And what shows! I don't remember the national networks, only the local ones that broadcast shows like *Ding Dong School with Miss Frances* (a kind of early and crude *Sesame Street*), *The Polka Hour* with Yank Yankovic, or some weird show of a guy drawing doodles and other cartoons.

But, on the other hand, I remember a poor, paralyzed Black guy dragging himself across the street. I don't know why that image stays in my head sixty-five years later. (I'll have to check with my therapist.) I also remember throwing a metal train at my brother, causing an injury below his eye (he still has a scar), and sliding into a fence one winter, injuring my forehead. Aside from that, I have only carefree memories of running through the alleys with the "gang," oblivious to everything.

I also remember a terrific snowstorm in 1952. I have a picture of me and my dad sitting in the middle of the street with an overcoat and a hat. I tried to duplicate the same picture decades later with my son Gabe in our back yard.

I had a few friends in the "hood," Jewish and Black. One fellow, a Black boy named Kenny, I remember to this day. He had a striped shirt and curly hair. But when we moved to the west side of Milwaukee, to the Sherman Park area, in 1953, I never saw him again.

But the African Americans I most loved were Mr. and Mrs. Cox, who owned a BBQ sandwich shop. Years later I saw a picture of them in a history book about Bronzeville. We lived in the back, and he had a sandwich shop in the front. I can still smell the succulent and forbidden pork ribs. Later, he introduced me to a new delight—custard—which I could eat but not with meat. But the contrast, Mr. Cox's thick, fat hands, his large black face, his white apron covering a huge belly, the apron smeared with reddish-black BBQ sauce, still spellbinds me to this day. How I loved that man.

Today, in my mind, there are only ghosts, a necrology of dead people, mostly dead white Jewish males: Mr. Cwik, Mr. Levinger, Mr. Bitterman, Mr. Lande, Mr. Banker, Mr. Ertel, Mr. and Mrs. Lewin, Mr. Sztundel, Mr. Tuchman, Mr. Parzen, Mr. Frydman, and Mr. and Mrs. Obar. They were tough Jews who had survived the unspeakable horrors of the Holocaust and had to make new life in this country.

Ghosts and Memories . . .

. . . of driving in a big black car with my *Tante Rivkeh* . . .

. . . of helping my mother make hamburger patties on sheets of cellophane for my "Uncle" Kleiger, a grizzled old relative who smoked bits of cigarettes in a short wooden holder and always seemed to be dressed in pajamas, listening to an ancient upright radio, and always looking angry. But sometimes he gave me a dime for candy . . .

. . . of finding a turtle in the back yard and, with my brother Sol and my best buddy Shelly Banker, tying a string around its leg like a domesticated pet. (Of course, it got loose.) Later, we "got" a pigeon and put it in a cage. These were the pets for poor Jews like us—pigeons and turtles.

But the biggest influence on me was Mrs. Cyla (Tzila) Sztundel and her husband Avrum, and their son Ksiel (variously called Bill Vufkeh, or Wolf). When he discovered his roots, Bill forced everyone to call him the unpronounceable Ksiel, which, interestingly, comes from the Bible; Ksiel was the last son of King David and was called Eketiel or Ekesiel.

I was also in love—and who wouldn't be—with their beautiful daughter, who had a crush on me—and I still do. She, too, changed her name from Gloria to Golden, a name taken from Hippy "Flower-Power" days and as beautiful as she was.

Tzila was like a "second" mother to me and to other single men. Her husband Avrum, called "Abe" in America," was a taciturn man who spoke little and joked less. He worked as—I'm not sure what—a carpenter, a real estate landlord, a driver for visiting rabbis. To add to their meager income, Tzila took in "boarders" (men, rarely women) like Mr. Feiner, Mr. Weinrauch, Mr. Aronin, and Earl Zimmerman (who stayed for ten years). Feiner stayed for seventeen years! Was it the cooking?

People paid thirty-five dollars a month for a room without food and one hundred dollars with food. Given that Tzila was an astounding cook, that was a bargain. Some men cooked for themselves and made soup, hamburgers, and pasta. She also worked for the *frum shul*, the Orthodox synagogue led by Jacob Twerski a short walk away, Congregation Beth Jehudah. Everyone knew and loved Tzila. She also took care of the rabbi's wife, Rebbetzin Twerski, when she aged.

"I needed money to send the kids [Gloria and Bill] to college," Tzila said. "Avrum didn't work so much. He was older. You think life was easy. Thanks to God, he left me a little money, and I divided it up for the kids.

"But Avrum was a hard worker. He worked in construction and then was laid off. Plus, he repaired things. He couldn't work as hard as the *goyim*, the young workers, because by that time he was in his fifties. But he made a living. I had a roof over my house. People needed a mother, like a home. What I done, it was impossible for me. People from Chicago came. Orphans came. Rabbis came. I was their mother.

"I feel good in my heart 'bout all I done for people. It was hard on me, but I done it. I don't know why. I guess I have a good heart."

I still remember Tzila's recipe for *p'shat*, a kind of jellied calf's foot, an acquired Ashkenazic taste.

I miss her very much.

Memories of Pesach Past

Of all the holidays growing up in Milwaukee in the '50s and '60s, I remember most of all Pesach (Passover). The winter was over; the ground was moist from the melted snow; green buds were blooming; spring was approaching. It was a wonderful time.

But every holiday had its specialness, especially the food and the preparations. Rosh Hashanah had its apples and honey; Shavuos, dairy products; Succos, fruits; Purim, *humentaschen* with crushed poppy seeds; Chanukah, potato latkes; and, of course, Shabbes, with *challeh*, *gefilteh* fish, *lukshen*, potato *kugel*, and beef brisket. (I will be using the Yiddish form of words to convey the mood and times, not the Hebrew/Sephardic form.)

But Pesach was the most elaborate. First came the cleanup. Housecleaning started weeks before the holiday: washing all of the baking utensils, cleaning the stove, airing out the blankets and clothes, scrubbing everything. My mother needed help, and she had a non-Jewish woman, an African American woman, who came in to do the heavy lifting.

It was a big job, bringing up all of the Pesach plates and pots, again *milchiks* and *fleishiks* (meat and milk), from the basement. When my brother became super *frum* (observant), we had to fire—yes, fire, to a red-hot flame—all of the cooking surfaces. I can still feel the heat on my face. The pots and dishes were special, and many were gifts; some items came over from Europe.

Everything had to be cleaned, even the car. But that was only the beginning. As the first night approached, we had to shop. In Milwaukee, before there were kosher shops and food markets that had kosher food, there was the Twerski-Richt Passover Store. Every year, they found a storefront on Burleigh Street near Fifty-Fourth and ordered food from all over. I don't know how it all mysteriously arrived—from New York, Chicago, Iowa, and Wisconsin.

Motel Twerski, the Rebbe Jacob's son, was a CPA, the financial guy; and Aaron Richt and his wife, Sonya, were the CEOs, administrating everything. I worked taking orders and packing stuff into cardboard boxes and then delivering them. Each box had the name and address on the flap. My job was to load the boxes into a big station wagon and deliver them. It was a *grosseh* (big) mitzvah. Many of the people were elderly or disabled and unable to come to the Passover store. There was so much joy seeing their eyes light up when I unpacked the food for them—the matzos, the grape juice, the wine, the chocolate macaroons, and especially something exotic called "Hungarian Delight," a mixture of sauerkraut, red peppers, and something green, maybe green peppers or pickles.

Everything tasted better on Pesach. But work was not over. We made our own *chereyn*, bitter herbs, *maror*, by going down into the basement in a tub, near running water. Our eyes hurt so much when we ground the bitter roots, which were grayish white, not the reddish stuff that added beet juice. It was tough. Much easier were the *charoses*. We took a mortar and pestle and crushed chopped apples, walnuts, and wine and we put it aside in the refrigerator.

The night before, my brother inspected by strong light the romaine lettuce, whose root is bitter and is eaten with matzos as a sandwich. He was looking for tiny brown creatures, little worms, that were *assur*, forbidden to eat. In Sephardic traditions, the women also collected eggs and boiled them in onion leaves to turn them brown. This tradition was done by my former wife's family, the Almuly-Ben Arroyos, and goes back centuries to Spain.

By the time we sat down to start the Seder, it was a wonder we had any energy at all! At the beginning we used the old Maxwell House Haggados, which started back in 1934 as a promotional gimmick for the coffee company. Later, we used the striking red, gold and black KTAV publishing house Haggadah, edited by Rabbi Nathan Goldberg and published by Asher Scharfstein starting in 1949.

My dad, from the old country, used an old *siddur* that had the instructions in Yiddish.

Then came the ceremonies: lighting the candles; showing the plate with the egg, shank bone, bitter herbs, parsley, and *charoses;* the *Kiddush* over the wine, a special Pesach *niggun*, different than for Shabbos; then *HaLachma Anya*, the ancient Aramaic—"Behold, the bread of affliction which our ancestors ate in the land of Egypt. All who are hungry, come and eat; all who are needy, let them come and celebrate; now we are here; next year may we be in the Land of Israel; now we are slaves, next year may we be free men and women."

Ah, the memories.

Characters

For some reasons, Milwaukee was very tolerant of "characters," whether oddballs or just eccentrics. For example, there was an old guy in Rabbi Twerski's *shul* who had a goiter, a disease due to lack of iodine so that a huge pouch grows out of your neck. He sat in *shul* with his grandson, and nobody ever said anything, but it fascinated us little kids.

Then there was a *gabbai*, a prayer leader who had a crooked finger. In Judaism you use a *yad*—in Hebrew, a "silver finger"—to point out the words to the Torah. We could not tell the difference between his crooked finger and the *yad*—very scary. Plus, the bathrooms had a distinct smell of old men and urine mixed with cleaning solution that I can sense to this very day.

But the most interesting characters were guests, who either lived in Milwaukee or were visiting men (rarely women) who came to collect money for themselves or for their *yeshivot*. Our home was open to everyone. It must have been a strain on our mom, but she never complained. They not only ate here but also slept downstairs in a special room that my dad built.

There was a strange guy, a non-Jew, a Polish man, who did errands and drove people around (kind of like a modern-day Uber driver), plus he taught us how to drive a car. His name was Joe, I think, and he also was a boarder somewhere.

Some were very nice, like Jake Itelman, who worked as a bellhop at the Wisconsin Hotel downtown but came by every Sunday morning with bagels and lox. He was a bachelor; there seems to have been a lot of single men who were lonely and who came over or who stayed with Mrs. Sztundel as "boarders." In fact, there is a funny Yiddish song called "By My Wife, I am a Boarder." For more on these guests, see the story "The Last of the Big-Time Collectors" in this book.

Ziggy, Elvis, and Frances

Tateh (dad) worked in a factory making shoes and in a tanning factory, but, like many of his generation, he wanted to be his own boss. So he became partners with a German Jew named Sigmund Singer, and thus began the start of the Singer-Porter Scrap Metal Company. (Such a big company—two naïve greenhorns and a pickup truck.)

Ziggy, as he was known, had lost both of his sons to the Nazis, as well as his first wife. He soon married an American woman but had no children from her, so he kind of "adopted" me and my younger brother Sol. He gave us presents of silver dollars, chocolates, even took us to a German *kino* (cinema). I think

Milwaukee had the last of the German-speaking *kinos* in the country until the early 1960s.

I also remember staying over at this house on Thirty-Eighth and North Avenue (a very German American neighborhood) and taking early morning cold showers and tough calisthenics. Very Germanic! But I loved the old guy. I still remember driving around in his roomy Buick Road Master with the four decorative "holes" on the side and huge bumpers and hubcaps.

Dad worked very hard gathering scrap steel, copper, aluminum, smashing furnaces for parts, selling them to other Jews who owned scrap metal shops— my dad only owned a truck or two—and they in turn sold it to Jews who owned bigger shops but had access to railroad cars who in turn hauled the steel and "metal" to ports along the Great Lakes and Canada for destinations in Japan or Germany or Gary, Indiana, or Bethlehem Steel to make girders, auto parts, and other material. It was what today we would call "recycling," and Jews invented it. Some, like the Peltz brothers, worked with paper and cardboard, and decades later they sold their "shop" to the giant Waste Management (WM) company for twenty million dollars.

Some of the scrap metal or auto parts guys had their wives work with them. I remember Mrs. Karsh working like a man, all dirty and sooty from grease and oil, working the yards.

Mom (*mameh*), on the other hand, was a housewife, as most wives were back then. But that was a tough job, too—cleaning the home, especially for *Shabbos* and holidays; shopping for food, and cooking. I don't know how she did it—she never got a license to drive a car, so how did she get around to shop? Later, she hired Frances, a Black cleaning lady, to help her on Fridays right before *Shabbos*.

My dad also hired a Black person—Elvis Tarkington (love that name), a burly, jovial young man who drove for him. In fact, I still remember both Frances and Elvis having breakfast with us early in the morning before starting work, so not only were we integrated as a neighborhood, but also our home was "integrated" in a normal, casual long before the civil rights marches.

The Milwaukee Hebrew Academy

Even though I spent only six or seven years (1947–1953) on Tenth Street, they made a tremendous impact on me. The first school I attended was not the Milwaukee Public Schools but the first private Jewish day school in Milwaukee— the Milwaukee Hebrew Academy. Today, Jewish day schools are divided into Conservative, Reform, non-denominational, Chabad, Modern Orthodox, and Hasidic, but in those early days all of the Jewish denominations banded together to form this academy. There is a famous 1956 picture in John Gurda's 2009 book *One People, Many Paths* (page 171) that shows all three major Jewish movements represented in a photo, showing that one could work together to make "Jewish Milwaukee a community of interest" despite "profound differences in doctrine and practice." This collegiality continues to this day in Milwaukee.

The small Jewish community of mostly German Jews was greatly expanded after the war by people like us: Russian, Polish, and Hungarian survivors of the Holocaust. We brought religion and a desire to blend both cultures, Jewish and American, and not assimilate. So in 1948, an all-day Hebrew and English school was established, which was to last for about ten years.

My parents went to Congregation Beth Hamedrosh Hagadol, a traditional *shul* of which I don't remember very much. There were several other small *shuls* in the area, but they soon moved out of the Tenth Street area as Jews moved up the social ladder toward the west and north sides of Milwaukee. They began moving in the early '50s, though they still returned for the High Holy Days to the inner city. I remember when me, my brother, Benny Lande, and others would go down to Congregation Beth Israel to be in the all-male choir under the direction of Cantor Moshe Sorenson. We even had a picture of us in the *Milwaukee Journal* one year. Those services were highly emotional and evocative, since we knew they would be the last ones in that neighborhood.

Some Jews moved even further northwest and east along the lake (Shorewood, Whitefish Bay, and Fox Point) where the wealthier, more Reformed Jews lived; some, like Beth Hamedrosh Hagadol, changed their name to Temple Menorah, and their location from Fifty-Third and Center to Seventy-Sixth Street, and from traditional to Conservative. Yet others remained firmly Orthodox: Cong. Anshe Sfard under Rabbi David Shapiro; Cong. Anshe Lebovich under Rabbi Solomon Shulson; and Cong. Beth Jehudah under Rabbi Jacob Twerski.

Our family moved from Tenth Street to Fiftieth Street and Locust in 1953 and shifted from Beth Hamedrosh Hagadol to Beth Jehudah. I still remember my bar mitzvah teacher, Rabbi Greenman, and the *gabbai* (sexton) at Beth Hamedrosh with his crooked finger that looked like a *yad*. It was really scary—his hand "came alive"!

My brother Sol tells me that, when the synagogue turned from Orthodox to Conservative, my dad left Beth Hamedrosh Hagadol for Congregation Beth Jehudah, and Sol became more Orthodox under the tutelage of the Twerskis.

My bar mitzvah in December 1958 was a lively affair held at the Beth Am Center at Fifty-Fifth and Burleigh, which was also the home of the United Hebrew School. Cantor Moshe Sorenson led the ceremony with singing and a four-piece band. We had huge *challahs* and a white-and-blue cake. Guests came in from as far away as Cleveland, Chicago, and Israel. I still have black-and-white pictures of the affair. Sadly, my parents ran out of money, so my brother Sol had to have his celebration at home.

The largest congregation—which was then Orthodox, now Conservative—was Beth Israel on Twelfth and Teutonia under Rabbi Harold Baumrind. I became close friends with both Hazzan Moses Sorenson, the Cantor and Musical Director, and Isidor Anschel, the *shamosh* (an untranslatable word that means caretaker and right-hand man to the rabbi, which today we would call the "executive director"). Today this grand temple, built in the style of Moorish Spain, is the home of the Greater Galilee Baptist Church and a protected historical site. I had something to do with getting it categorized historical and saved. It is the last remaining synagogue structure in the inner city.

The Milwaukee Hebrew Academy was dedicated, as an early ad book said, "to the spirit of our Torah and the strengthening of traditional Judaism in the American Jewish Community" and was housed in the back of the congregation. We studied Hebrew lessons in the morning, had a kosher lunch in the cafeteria, and then had English subjects. Hebrew meant courses in the Hebrew language and grammar, in Bible, in Jewish history, and in Jewish customs; English was language, mathematics, US history, music, and art. We had strict teachers, but we were a pretty rambunctious bunch of boys. They rapped our knuckles with a ruler, and they washed our mouths out with soap if we swore; it was a tough private school. It was no wonder that I ran away once or twice.

The principal, Manfred Pick, had red hair, a red beard and a white face and was lean and distant but very nice. Mrs. Wolfe, Ms. Renee Goldman, Mrs. Shmotkin, Mrs. Evelyn Raskin, and Mrs. Winninger were the English teachers. I loved Mrs. Wolfe; Raskin and Goldman were strict and not so nice. The Hebrew teachers were Rabbi Pick, Rabbi Harold Winninger, and Hillel Horowitz. Sarah Volk was the "dietitian" (which meant the "cook").

We had no more than eighty to ninety students, and many were to become lifelong friends: Shelly Bankier, Joey Blasberg, Arnie and Harry Peltz, Al Rabinoff, Michael Marks, Freddy Geller, Carl Kupersmith, Jay Milan, and Rabbi Baumrind's son. I still have a great photo of all of us on his playground. That was our "physical education program"—running around and playing basketball. We had no sports teams and no coaches.

The 1953 "yearbook"—actually an ad book to raise money—showed a total of $3,810.20 collected from the various Orthodox *shuls* and groups like the Women's Auxiliary. Wow, can you imagine what the teacher's salaries were like in the '50s—$1,500 per year, pre-inflation dollars!

The school was the first of its kind in Milwaukee. "Modern educational psychology theories" were applied to Jewish education. (Did that mean to talk to the kid instead of hitting him?) The goal was to develop into eight grades with students then going on to secular or other religious high schools in other cities. It received official recognition from the Milwaukee Public School Board and the Board of Jewish Education.

As noted, most of the more affluent Jews had moved out, leaving us poor immigrants and African Americans. I hung out with the Black kids on the street. Some of my friends, who didn't go to the private Milwaukee Hebrew Academy, went to a public school, Twelfth and Lloyd Street School.

The Hebrew Academy was founded by Orthodox rabbis: Rabbi David Shapiro, the alter Rebbe Jacob Twerski, Rabbi David Becker, and Rabbi Harold Baumrind. Moses Wolfe was honorary president, and David Siegel and Sol Blankstein were co-presidents. Other founders were a fiercely devoted group of parents, and they were not all *frum*. In fact, most of them were either not *frum* or just tangentially *frum*. They were the Peltzes, the Kupersmiths, the Milans, the Gellers, and the Trushinskys.

But the driving force may have been the brilliant yet tempestuous Rabbi Baumrind. I was a student at the Hebrew Academy from September 1950 (age five) to June 1953 (age eight) in grades one to three. The Academy was years ahead of its time, predating by a decade the Hillel Academy, and its demise was sudden. Some say it collapsed because it was not supported by the entire community. It's true that orthodoxy was not as strong in the 1950s as it became a decade or two later, and it was also true that the neighborhood was changing. Eventually, a move to the West or East Side was inevitable.

But, the school did not last. I don't know why, but rumor had it that a rabbi (not Pick) absconded with the funds and fled to Canada, and the school closed. But that seems too simple a reason. One version is that a new principal took the money. He forged Rabbi Shapiro's signature on the checks and stole some fifteen thousand dollars, a huge sum at the time.

The money had been allocated for salaries. No money, no teachers. The IRS investigated, but the matter was kept hush-hush, and it destroyed the school. People knew about it but kept silent. Mrs. Milan, the school secretary, Mrs. Vinarsky, Sol Blankstein, Mr. Polacheck, and Mr. Sampson—all insiders, all knew.

The school lasted from September 1948 to August 1958, but we left in 1953 and bought a house on the West Side, 2912 North 50th St. at the corner of Fiftieth and Locust, between Locust and Chambers, a block from St. Joseph's Hospital. That ended my Hebrew private school days, and I started secular public schools: Sherman Elementary a block away, Steuben Junior High School about six to seven blocks away, and Washington High School, also six to seven blocks away. In those days we walked to school, rain, snow or shine; there were no buses and no school crossing guards. We were a hardy crew and we survived.

In any case, in 1953, I started fourth grade in a secular elementary school named after General Sherman of Civil War fame. I continued at Steuben (another general) Junior High and Washington (another general) High, and then, after a year-long trip to Israel, to the University of Wisconsin–Milwaukee. So all my formal education from kindergarten through undergraduate college, 1947 to 1967, took place in Milwaukee.

A grand experiment had failed, but only temporarily. A new Hillel Academy on the West Side would be established in 1960. My sister Bella was in the very first class of Hillel Academy in 1960.

While on Fiftieth and Locust, life continued as usual: school, homework, baseball, basketball, and drive-ins, though I had no car. A new community of Orthodox Jews and survivors formed on the West Side, and the *shuls* quickly moved to join their congregants. That was the pattern.

I lived in two worlds: Jewish Orthodox and American secular. Often the secular won out. This conflict was best epitomized by Gerry Glazer in his essay in our book *Happy (Freilich) Days Revisited* where he noted:

> I was bombarded with a dissonance of conflicting messages.
>
> The message of Beth Jehudah was:
> > *BE a good Jew.*
> > *BELIEVE that Man was created by G-d.*
> > *LISTEN to rabbinical lectures.*
> > *LEARN the Torah.*
> > *OBEY Jewish law.*
> > *COVER your head with a hat or yarmulke (skullcap).*
> > *DO NOT touch girls.*
>
> The message of Steuben Junior High School was:
> > *BE a good student.*
> > *BELIEVE that Man was descended from apes.*
> > *LISTEN to announcements on the public address system.*
> > *LEARN the material in the textbooks.*
> > *OBEY school rules and your teachers.*
> > *HATS OFF in the school building.*

DANCING with girls at supervised dances is OK.

The message of teen culture was:
> *BE a rebel.*
> *LISTEN to rock-and-roll music.*
> *LEARN to fight.*
> *OBEY no rules or authorities.*
> *COVER your head with grease.*
> *TOUCH girls as much as you can.*

Of course, there was no way to reconcile these mutually contradictory viewpoints and imperatives.

The Old West Side/Sherman Park Area and "Happy Days"

Why did we move? It's complicated. Jews are mobile, and as they made more money they wanted nicer neighborhoods. The Sherman Park area had nice green lawns and beautiful homes and crime was nearly absent. First the Jews moved and then the synagogues followed. As they say, the "neighborhood changed." Whites moved out; African Americans moved in. Sadly, Milwaukee is one of the most (de facto) segregated cities in the country. But we stayed in Milwaukee. We did not move to the suburbs.

While many synagogues like Rabbi Isaac Lerer's Temple Menorah and Rabbi Switchkow's Temple Ner Tamid moved to the suburbs or the further edges of Milwaukee County, my mom and dad's *shul*, Temple Beth Jehudah, stayed. True, it moved a little north from Center Street to across from St. Joseph's Hospital at Fifty-Second and Burleigh, but it stayed, and today it is the only synagogue in Sherman Park; all the others have left. Led by the venerable Rabbi Jacob Twerski and his sons Michael and Motel, and for a short time Avraham Yehoshua (Shia)—the rabbi said "stay"—where else could we find large, roomy, affordable homes? And so they stayed, and the community remains as one of the last "white" (Jews and non-Jews) enclaves in the city.

After my dad died in 1979, my mom continued to stay at our home at 2912 North Fiftieth St., corner of Locust and Fiftieth, and stayed there until she was eighty-five in 1994, when she moved to be closer to my sister Bella in Minneapolis. My sister was born in November 1953 a block away at St. Joseph's Hospital, and my brother Shlomo (Solomon) was born at Mt. Sinai Hospital near downtown Milwaukee in November 1947 soon after we arrived in this country.

I was about eight when we moved to the Sherman Park area in June 1953, and I lived there until I left for graduate school in August 1967. Those fourteen years made a listing impact on me and led to several books about growing up in La-La land: *Happy (Freilich) Days Revisited, Milwaukee Memories / Milwaukee and Hollywood / Small Town Secrets,* and *21 Screen Treatments for Hollywood.*

While my brother Sol (Shlomo) was born at Mt. Sinai Hospital on November 17, 1947, my sister Bella was born on the West Side at St. Joseph's Hospital on November 14, 1953, soon after we had moved in. My mother was forty-five, and my dad was forty-eight. They had wanted a girl for a long time. She was born nine years after me and six years after Shlomo. My mom walked to the hospital in the early morning to have Bella. I have a memory of it.

The West Side had a continuously Jewish presence for ninety years, since the 1930s, according to Gerry Glazer, long-time resident. Even Max Kohl of the successful Kohl's food and department stores fame lived there at 3259 North Fifty-First Boulevard in the 1940s through the early 1960s when they moved to the East Side. Today, Rabbi Michel and his wife, Faygeh Twerski, live in the same home. The area was a haven for prosperous businessmen, doctors, and dentists. I remember Dr. Erwin Teplin, for example, and playing with his sons, especially Bobby Teplin, who lived a block away on Fiftieth and Chambers.

The West Side, especially Fifty-First Boulevard and some adjoining streets, has some of the nicest housing stock in the city. Jews like my parents left the "inner city" to live here for the ambiance—air, green lawns, and large, spacious homes—yet to remain close to the old neighborhood, but that ended very soon. All of the institutions and stores in a few short years in the 1950s moved west—the *shuls* and the delis, including Guten & Cohen at 5008 W. Center Street, which sold corned beef at seventy-nine cents a pound, tongue at ninety cents a pound, and hot dogs (wieners) at twenty-eight cents each!

Hebrew School at Beth Am Center

My Hebrew school was the old Beth Am Center at Fifty-Fifth and Burleigh. It was a multipurpose place which housed an afternoon Hebrew school, a banquet hall, and home to the local Farband-Pioneer Women Labor Zionist organizations. My life from 1953 to 1963 revolved around the Beth Am Center, Hebrew school, Habonim, going to *shul,* and secular public schools:

We started Hebrew school after regular school in the afternoon for two hours. As noted, the school was once a secular Jewish stronghold that was not Zionist but Yiddish-oriented. So for a year or two we used the books *Berele* and *Shmerele,* a kind of Jack and Jill in Yiddish. I don't remember any Jewish history, Bible,

Torah or even Jewish customs in Yiddish classes. But soon—actually, gradually in a way—about six or seven years after the State of Israel was established in 1948, a Hebrew and Zionist approach took over.

The youth organization Habonim, now called Habonim/Dror, held its meetings there (I will discuss them in the next chapter), and the Beth Am Hebrew School opened. Our teachers were either totally secular, like Mr. (or *Mar* in Hebrew) Schwartzman or Mr. Melrood, or mildly traditional, like Mr. Herman Pais. Pais led Sabbath service on Saturday morning. We used the venerable Shiloh Prayer Book, first published in 1932 by Zevi Scharfstein of the Shilo Publishing House. I liked the book, even though it had no English, because of its bold, easy-to-read letters and layout. I still use it to this day. Later, when I was a Hebrew teacher at the Conservative Temple Menorah under Rabbi Isaac Lerer, I used *Siddurenu: Our Prayer Book*, edited by Rabbi Sidney Greenberg and Rabbi Morris Silverman. This was a useful prayer book for kids, since it could be used as a textbook, containing explanations of the prayers in English.

Jewish history and customs were taught by Schwartzman and Melrood. If Pais was mild-mannered and "nice," Schwartzman was strict and "mean," but a brilliant and knowledgeable teacher. (Interestingly, his two daughters, Varda and Hasia, were excellent students. Hasia [under the name Diner] became a well-known and prolific Jewish historian and is at New York University. Varda lives in Washington, DC. Note: Both had Biblical names.) The books we used for history were the classic three-volume *The Jewish People* by Deborah Pessin (a rare woman writer) with illustrations by Ruth Levin. They were published by the United Synagogue Commission on Jewish Education of New York in 1952. Written from a Conservative point of view, again they were easy to read and nicely illustrated.

The presence of Labor Zionism and Israel was everywhere in the center. There were large photos of Theodore Herzl and David Ben-Gurion, and we met in the Golda Meir Room. Golda was not only from Milwaukee but also the fourth prime minister of Israel, and its first and only female and American-raised prime minister to boot. The Hebrew lessons and history laid a good foundation for me later in life. To this day I can read Hebrew fluently (but not Yiddish), and I can speak Hebrew and Yiddish and understand both languages at a basic level.

The Germans: Ziggy Singer and My Dad

Milwaukee was first an ancient Native American village or series of villages containing such tribes as the Potawatomi, Sauk, Ottawa, Ojibwa, and Menominee families. In 1679, a Father Zenobius Membre visited a village of

Fox and Mascouten Native Americans at the mouth of the Melleoki River, the present side of Jones Island.

The original form was lost, but Milwaukee was variously known as Mahnawauk, Melleoki, Milouakik, Meneawkee, Milowages, Meolaki, Minnwack, and a personal favorite of historian John Gurdas—Milwacky. It means variously "good land," "gathering place," "wetland," "medicinal plant," and even "stinking river."[8]

And it was always a city of immigrants. One of the largest immigrant waves to come were the Germans in the mid-nineteenth century, who were escaping the revolutions of Europe. They brought with them culture, music, efficient government, good roads, and, most of all, beer. With these Germans came the first Jews—German-speaking Jews who made up the elite of the Jewish community. The Polish and Russian Jews came in several waves, first after the pogroms in Russia in 1881, then after World War I and before World War II began, and then my parents, who came to Milwaukee with the large number of refugees, in the late '40s and early '50s.

Along with Russian Jews came German Jews such as Sigmund Singer, who was a business partner with my father in a scrap metal company. The German Jews had an advantage, since they could speak to the often German-owned "heavy metal" industries in Milwaukee in their own languages. My father, being younger, drove the truck that picked up the barrels of steel, copper and brass turnings and took them to often Jewish-owned dealers. It was hard, backbreaking work. Often I remember my dad coming home with slivers of steel in his feet or fingers, which I had to learn to carefully take out with a needle. Singer had the easy job of lining up the customers; my dad had to do the tough job of hauling away the scrap metal.

Everybody had a role. The German Americans owned the factories. The earlier Jews owned the big scrap-metal "shops." The later Jews found a niche in-between, with smaller shops that either fed the big ones like Afram Brothers or Grossman's or had trucks, like my dad, who picked up the scrap and sold them to the big boys.

Later, my father broke with Singer and hired his own driver as he got older, and the driver did the dirty work. I remember the driver very well. His name I will never forget—Elvis Tarkington—a large, jovial man who came to our house for breakfast and then went out to the truck to start work. Thus our home was "integrated" long before civil rights marches, with a Black worker like Elvis and a Black maid like named Frances who also came in the mornings to housekeep,

---

8 John Gurda, *The Making of Milwaukee* (Milwaukee: Milwaukee County Historical Society, 2018), 6-7.

since my mom had a heart condition called angina pectoris. (Ironically, she lived to be nearly 101!)

Even though my father and Ziggy Singer may have quarreled, he liked me. I think it was because he had lost a son in the war, and he and his second wife—who was also a distant relative—never had any children. I remember the cold showers and early morning exercises at his home near Thirty-Eighth and North Avenue. In true German fashion, we started the day like that. His wife Sonya made great German food, and she gave me chocolates and other candies. I liked them.

Robert M. Gates, who held the Secretary of Defense and other positions for eight US presidents from Carter to Obama, wrote the following: "My life growing up in 1950s Kansas was idyllic, revolving around family, school, church, and Boy Scouts. My brother and I were Eagle Scouts. There were certain rules my parents insisted I follow, but within those bounds, I had extraordinary freedom to wander, explore, and test my wings."[9]

My life in the Midwest was similar to his. If you substitute Milwaukee, Wisconsin, for Wichita, Kansas, or the Bronx or almost anywhere, this could be describing my life in the late '40s and '50s. I, too, was a Scout, a Webelo, a rank between Cub Scout and Boy Scout. I wanted to continue on with the Boy Scouts, but maybe Hebrew school and sports distracted me. I still remember Mrs. Krug, our Scoutmaster—yes, women were Scoutmasters, too. I remember the badges, the secret handshakes, and especially the camping, one time in winter. Wow, that was fun, making a tent from a blanket and string right on top of the Wisconsin snow.

Later, I would hone these skills at Camp Habonim, where I headed the camp craft program, in which we would tie knots—especially square knots, half-hitches, and all-important bowlines—and, using the first two knots, you could build anything, and we did. In fact, we built an entire "city" with towers, gates and tables; with enough wood and twine, you could build anything. To this day I know enough Scout craft to survive in the woods or in any dangerous situation.

Another book that describes the idyllic '40s and '50s, about a decade before me, is Avery Corman's *The Old Neighborhood* (New York: Bantam Books, 1980). He also wrote a sequel, called *My Old Neighborhood Remembered: A Memoir* (Fort Lee, NJ: Barricade Books, 2014) Corman, who wrote the original novels that were adapted as the Best Picture Academy Award-winning 1979 film *Kramer vs. Kramer* with Dustin Hoffman and Meryl Streep and the 1977

9 Robert M. Gates, *Duty: Memoirs of a Secretary at War* (New York: Alfred A. Knopf, 2014), 14-15)

film *Oh, God!* with George Burns as God, wrote a memoir of his growing up in the Kingsbridge Road–Grand Concourse section of the Bronx in 1944 (when he was ten years old) and later. This was a time of collecting scrap paper for the scrap-paper drive, saving Minuteman war stamps and memorizing the silhouettes of enemy aircraft.

My memoir takes place about a decade later, since I was born in 1944, but the feel of the book and the characters are the same as Corman's. Just substitute a small Wisconsin town for New York City. It was a great time to be a kid, and I'm glad I had the chance to be a child. If we look at Corman's book, we see categories that would fit my life. For example:

Street Games

While in New York, the streets belonged to the kids in the '40s and '50s. Cars were rare; gas was scarce. People roller-skated on the smooth black asphalt, which was also perfect for drawing pictures or hangman games on in chalk.

Variations on Stickball and Baseball. However, on the old West Side in Milwaukee, we had wide lawns and a huge playground near Sherman Elementary School at Fifty-First and Locust, so we rarely used the streets. Yet I did play a game similar to New York stickball in front of my house, but instead of a stickball I threw a tennis ball against my wooden porch. If I happened to hit the rise perfectly, the ball flew across the street for a home run. If it landed in the street (Fiftieth Street), it was a triple. If it landed just over my head on the sidewalk, it was a double. If it dribbled past me, it was a single. If I caught a pop fly or a grounder came to me, it was an out. Thus I had an entire "team" and "ball field" at my fingertips at any time, day or early evening.

I could also play a variation on the game in our alley against our garage, but because the distance was so much shorter, I had to bounce the ball against the alley so that it would hit the wall and then fly up. I could also throw it at an angle and practice running to get it and "throw" the imaginary guy "out."

I fantasized that I was Johnny Logan, the great shortstop of the Boston Braves and then the Milwaukee Braves in the 1950s, or second basement Danny O'Connell. I became quite skillful at chasing down ground balls; even to this day I can impress youngsters with my adeptness. Decades later, I had the opportunity to meet Johnny Logan and Alvin Dark, two of my heroes, and I was astounded at how huge Logan's hands were; they were as big as ham hocks. I was also pleasantly surprised to learn that, like me, he was of Ukrainian descent and had changed his name to Logan to hide that fact, just as we had changed our name from Puchtik to Porter. We were both Ukrainians!

Baseball. And, yes, I did play baseball—not football, because my mom said football was too dangerous (especially after my dear friend Norm Schumacher died from being kicked in the kidneys during a game), and not soccer, which was considered a European game and was not widely played in the United States at that time. Therefore, only basketball and baseball were played on my playground.

I was lean, wiry, and very quick. As you will see from my 1959 diary, I played many games and sports; no wonder we were so tired out at the end of the day. I played both softball and hardball plus two variations of baseball if we did not have a full team or playing area: strike-out and porch ball.

Strike-out. Similar to these games was strike-out at the playground. In this game, you could get an actual team. It was played this way: Sherman School had a solid wall of bricks, so we marked on it in chalk a strike-out zone from the knees to the shoulders, and we set up teams. First, one team would come up to bat, and again, depending on how far they hit the ball, it would be a double, a triple, a home run, or a single if it was on the ground. If the ball bounced back to the pitcher or your mates in the outfield caught the ball, you were also out, or you could be struck out. The beauty of this game was that you could imagine yourself a great pitcher like Warren Spahn (a lefty) or Lew Burdette and try curve balls, sliders, knuckle-balls, or steamers (fast balls). If you hit between the chalked-up rectangles, it was a strike. If you hit outside the chalk, it was a ball.

At nearby Sherman School we had a great playground. I would mark in chalk a strike zone, a vertical rectangle, on a brick wall. A batter would face a pitcher and usually one or two outfielders, and they could strike out or ground out to the pitcher. If he hit the ball by the pitcher on the ground, it was a single. If he hit a fly ball that dropped beyond the pitcher, it was a double. If the ball went further out, it was a triple or rarely a home run. After three outs, the next team played. We used a tennis ball.

Porch-ball. Porch ball was similar to strike-out, with similar rules, grounders, fly balls, and so forth, but instead of a wall we used a porch. This game was mostly used as a warm-up for other games but not a real game. The trick was to hit the edge of the porch step; then it would fly across the street.

Marbles. Corman talks about marbles in his book. I still remember my cat's eye marbles (ones with a colorful, feline swirl inside). The goal was to take turns flicking your marble so as to hit your opponents' marbles. If you did, you got to keep the marble you hit and take another turn. If you missed, your opponent got the chance to hit your marbles. We kept our marbles in small felt bags.

Flipping. Similar to marbles was flipping for (baseball) cards. One person flipped a card. If you flipped and it was "heads up" (that is, the picture of the player facing up), you got the card. If not, you lost your card. This was, by the way, not very good for the cards; if they were bent or rounded at the corners from being flipped so much, they were not worth much. But years after we moved out of our house, I returned to it and, with permission of the family living there, went into the basement to recover anything we had left behind.

I found a blue gym bag with all kinds of ephemera: tickets to games, bus tickets, school notes, and, yes, an old Mickey Mantle card—and I hated the Yankees! But I guess I knew a good card even then. I sold it at Swann's Auctions in 2008 for five hundred dollars! Had I had Mantle's rookie card, I could have gotten twenty-five thousand dollars!

Bottle Cap Hockey and badges. When it rained, we had indoor games like Bottle Cap Hockey. You built a rectangular wooden box with three partitions, each with two small holes on the bottom, but at angles so you could not push a bottle cap directly into them. You started by flicking your bottle cap (those were the days when soda pop had bottle caps of metal outside and cork inside) from the top of the box into your opponent's side and then hitting the cap with a Popsicle stick through your opponent's hole to win.

We were very poor and had little metal, so we made do with things at hand. To make a badge, someone would remove the cork from a bottle cap and press it back into the cap with his T-shirt in-between the cap and the cork, so he had a badge to wear.

Scooters and wagons. Nor did we have money to buy fancy bikes and scooters, so we improvised with whatever wood and odd pieces of metal and other things we had to make our own scooters and wagons. To make a scooter, we took a flat piece of strong wood to rest a foot on, attached rollers from skates to it with short nails, then attached a vertical board from the front and a short horizontal bar for a handle. We could then add bottle caps, maybe a flashlight in front and red back-up "lights" for scootering after dark, and then we would paint our creation. It was neat. Similarly, we could build a wagon with small tires from a bike.

Ringers. This more adult game came later. On a school's brick wall, hidden from view and protected from the rain by an overhang, was a ringer board. It was numbered one to thirteen, I believe. Ten was in the middle, thirteen on the bottom, six on top, seven on one end, eleven on the other. We had to reach fifty to win. We certainly learned math quickly. We had five rubber ringers, and we threw them, either one at a time or as many as five at a time. So, if one of us was a hotshot and threw all five at the ten and they all hooked, he won on one magnificent shot. Plus, if he got two or more on a hook, he got them back to shoot again. We would get fancy, trying to get three thirteens—thirty-nine—so we would have to hit only an eleven to win again. Ringers was fun, but I have never seen it played outside of Milwaukee. I'd love to buy one of those ringer boards . . . or make one.

Other games. We also loved to play Capture the Flag, Ringolevio (a variation on tag originating on the streets of New York City in the nineteenth century, requiring two teams with "jails" and near-military strategy), kickball, and tetherball, a game against an opponent in which we pushed a ball attached to a pole with a rope and we had to wrap the ball all around the pole. It could be very humiliating when you lost.

Kids played until nightfall and, then exhausted, came home to eat, watch a little TV, do homework, and go right to bed. Today, the parents are afraid let their kids play outside by themselves and so they stay inside watching video games or TV all the time. So sad.

The Milwaukee Braves

The most exciting event in the '50s in Milwaukee, sports-wise, was the rise of the Milwaukee Braves. They were brought here by the Perini family of Boston, owners of the wealthy construction company Perini Corp. because the Boston Braves could not compete with the Boston Red Sox, and baseball was beginning to expand out of the East to the West, the Midwest, and eventually the South, which offered brand-new stadiums, cash and tax incentives, and other inducements.

They called us "hicks," wondering how a small town like Milwaukee could ever go up against the great New York Yankees, but we did. In October 1957, the Braves beat the Yankees in the World Series! As *The Milwaukee Sentinel* wrote:

> They did it! And just about all the world rejoiced in its new champions. They were heroes . . . in the pennant drive and the Series as well. But as Manager Fred Haney [shown with President Joe Cairnes, General Manager John Quinn, and a new contract] said . . . "It was team effort all season long!" . . . it will be a warmer, happier winter [here in Milwaukee].

We were ecstatic. Who were our heroes? Of course, Lew Burdette, Warren Spahn, Eddie Mathews, Hank Aaron, Joe Adcock, Bob Buhl, Jim Pendleton, Sid Gordon, Vern Bickford, Dave Jolly, Sam Jethroe, George Crowe, Sibby Sisti, Charlie Grimm, Chet Nichols, Bill Bruton, Frank Torre, Wes Covington, Lee Maye, Tommy Aaron (Hank's brother), Gene Conley, Johnny Logan, Danny

O'Connell, Red Schoendienst, Andy Pafko, and on and on. I can recite from memory 65 years later the entire starting lineups. And there were at least four Baseball Hall-of-Famers (Aaron, Spahn, Mathews, and Schoendienst) and near-Hall-of-Famers (such as Adcock, Covington and Logan). It was an unbelievable team. The Perini brothers and their staff were awesome in their ability to acquire and groom talented players. And, unlike the Red Sox, whose owner Tom Yawkey was a racist, there were at least eight Black players on the Braves!

I loved taking the old trolley car to Milwaukee County Stadium. Sadly, in 1963, the team moved to Atlanta, and a new team, the Brewers, replaced the Milwaukee Braves. But my team will always be the "Milwaukee Braves," a team that lives on only in my memory.

The other pro sports team that influenced me was the famous Green Bay Packers, but they played mostly in upstate Wisconsin, but I remember their winning the first Super Bowls with players like Paul Hornung, Zeke Bratkowski, and Bart Starr, and well as their phenomenal coach, Vince Lombardi. Surprisingly, I don't remember any basketball team; I know today they have the Milwaukee Bucks, but I don't remember the basketball team back in the '50s. As for college ball, the University of Wisconsin Badgers were a great team, as well as my own UW–Milwaukee Panthers.

Candy and Things

Again, I took this category from Corman because he had such a good memory for these things. But what kind of candies: naturally Baby Ruth (named after Babe Ruth) candy bars plus licorice sticks, weird things that were juice in a kind of wax form, or pins of sugary stuff on long rolls of wax paper. But what I remember most was ice cream, called "custard" for some reason back then. Milwaukee had the best custard, and I ate it at Mr. and Mrs. Cox's BBQ stand.

Going to the Movies, Watching TV

We went often to the Uptown Theater on Fifty-Fifth and North (where Gene Wilder hung out) and the smaller Sherman Theater at Forty-Seventh and Burleigh, plus, of course, the huge extravaganzas and blockbusters like *The Ten Commandments*, *The Sound of Music*, and *South Pacific* at the Riverside, Wisconsin and Oriental Theaters. For some crazy reason I made a list of theaters as a kid. I was always making lists. Nearly all of those theaters are gone now.

We used to watch TV sitting on boxes in front of Morry Babush's grocery store in the late '40s and early '50s when we lived at 2125A North 10th St. His store was a block away. I think this had an influence on me subconsciously and led to my love of movies and Hollywood, which was reinforced when my parents and I went to Los Angeles by train quite often.

Sources

Cohen, Sheila Terman. *Jews in Wisconsin.* Madison, WI: Wisconsin Historical Society Press, 2016. This contains some photos of our family's extended relatives, Harry Sokol and Bess Klieger, and various Liebermans (p. 49), as well as "newcomers" like Mr. and Mrs. Nate Pelz (p. 91) and labor Zionist activities, including Golda Meir (p. 48).

Greene, Paul H. *Milwaukee's Bronzeville, 1900–1950.* Chicago: Arcadia Publishing, 2006. This contains the pictures of Mr. Londy Cox and his wife, Anna, plus photos of young guys in the 'hood standing outside their Northside Sandwich Shop, which was in front of our house (see pp. 18–19).

Gurda, John. "The Exploding Metropolis" (chapter 8). *The Making of Milwaukee.* Milwaukee: Milwaukee County Historical Society, 2018.

———. "Triumph Out of Tragedy, 1945–1967" (chapter 4). *One People, Many Paths: A History of Jewish Milwaukee.* Milwaukee: Jewish Museum of Milwaukee, 2009. See pp. 145–200. A picture of me teaching at Rabbi Isaac Lerer's Temple Menorah Hebrew School in a suit and tie in the early 1960s is on page 173.

Hintz, Martin. *Jewish Milwaukee.* Chicago: Arcadia Publishing, 2005. This has pictures of my dad in a group picture of the Milwaukee Fruit Peddlers Union (p. 81), Golda Meir (p. 101), my sister in a large crowd greeting Meir (p. 101), and actor Gene Wilder (p. 115).

Kann, Bob. *Lizzie Kander and Her Cookbook,* Madison, WI: Wisconsin Historical Society Press, 2007.

Porter, Jack Nusan, with Gerry Glazer, and Sandy Aronin. *Happy (Freilich) Days Revisited.* Newton, MA: The Spencer Press, 2010. Also see its extensive bibliography on Milwaukee's Jews.

Schlichenmeyer, Terri, and Mark Meier. *The Handy Wisconsin Answer Book.* Canton, MI: Visible Ink Press, 2019. This new book contains a wealth of information.

Traxler, Ruth. *The Golden Land: 150 Years of Jewish Life in Milwaukee.* Milwaukee: The Milwaukee Jewish Federation Sesquicentennial Celebration, 1994. This is a nice overview with lovely photos. Mention of my family is on p. 13 and of me on p. 60. The old West Side days are mentioned on pp. 52–54 and 86–99. It is based on a Milwaukee Museum exhibit that showed pictures of my family and my books; photos of my family and I are also on display at the Jewish Museum of Milwaukee on 1360 Prospect Avenue.

Zeitlin, Richard H. *Germans in Wisconsin.* Madison, WI: Wisconsin Historical Society Press, 2000.

Diary, 1959

This is the diary I kept from January 1, 1959, through December 12, 1959, when I was age fourteen. It marks the end of the innocence with the last year of junior high school, before Washington High School.

Thursday, January 1, 1959

Dear Diary,

I can start writing for the first time now. Went to Habonim's New Year's Party at Gingi Safer's house. Had a lot of fun. John Gilman took pictures, played charades. At about 12:30 went to Ed Norin's house. Sheldon, Steve Cohen, and Al Rabinoff were there. Talked about books and I lent one to Ed's sister. We went crazy when Ed and Al started to fight. Stayed at Ed's until 4:30. Real "gone" evening.

Happy New Year!!

Friday, January 2, 1959

Dear Diary,

Today we went to Lande's house for a party. We had a lot of food and I played ping-pong with Benny and Jerry Ertel. Beat 'um. Also read comics and looked at their Bible. Saw "Bandstand" and heard all hit songs of 1958, also saw Connie Francis. Later at night, went downtown and got my American Album at Northwestern Stamp Co., met Steve Levin's father, and also went to see the stamps at Boston Store.

Saturday, January 3, 1959

Dear Diary,

Went to temple at Beth Hamedrosh Hagadol Anshe Sfard. At 1:45 went to basketball game for Optimist Club. Forfeited and are in last place. Stayed and played in game room until 4:30. Went to Sherman Theater Show with Mom. Saw "Marjorie Morningstar" and "Vertigo." Both good. Got in for half price (25¢). One of them, "Marjorie Morningstar," could possibly win an Oscar award.

Sunday, January 4, 1959

Dear Diary,

Went to Habonim meeting.

Monday, January 5, 1959

Dear Diary,
    School started. Christmas vacation is over.

Tuesday, January 6, 1959

Dear Diary,
    Went over to Norman's house. Did homework there, we later played pool at pool table down in basement. After doing homework we went to some fancy restaurant where he treated me with his mother to their Big Boy hamburgers. Mrs. Schumacher drove me home afterwards to my house. Had a real fine time there at Norm's house.

Wednesday, January 7, 1959

Dear Diary,
    Can't remember.

Thursday, January 8, 1959

Dear Diary,
    We had puppet show at school. The players from Marquette University gave it. It was called the "Nutcracker Suite," about a little girl in fantasy land. At the end they, the 2 boys who worked it, took off the top and showed how they work puppets, also answered questions about puppetry. Most kids did not like the show.

Saturday, January 17, 1959

Dear Diary,
    Went to Temple. Then went to Clark Street Social Center. Forfeited game. Later went to Larry Trogun's house. Beat him once in ping-pong, also beat his father. Talked, played darts. Forgot them in my pocket, returned them later. Later on went to show. Saw "Gigi" and "Houseboat," both real good pictures. Got in by free ticket Sol got me.

Sunday, January 18, 1959

Dear Diary,
Shaved for first time in life, alone!!

Monday, January 19, 1959

Dear Diary,
Can't remember.

Tuesday, January 20, 1959

Dear Diary,
Today was big day at Steuben. We had dress-up day, and some kids really got dressed up. We later took real big science test about everything we have learned. I learned later that I got about two hundred out of 270 possible right. Even though I finished six of the seven different sheets. Al got 176 right. But I got a B in science, he got an A.

Wednesday, January 21, 1959

Dear Diary,
Today was Athletic Honor Day. Lot of girls went up. I got an award for gym (1) efficiency tests. But mark my words, I will get 5 more awards when I graduate. *Mark* my words. Very few boys got awards. Had guest speaker, Mr. McLoughlin. Also saw movie in Science about floods on the Mississippi and also how it helps us too. Kept after school in Dempsey (paper) for throwing of spit balls.

Thursday, January 22, 1959

Dear Diary,
There was Scholastic Honor Day at school today. Awarded pins to graduates. Miss Holtzhauer gave very good speech. Honor awards were given out. We sang songs to 9A's, they sang them back to us. Very sad. Mr. Veitel led the community singing at school.
After school, was 9A party, had the Silver-Tones. Later on went to Optimist Meeting.

Friday, January 23, 1959

Dear Diary,

Last time for 9A's in our Algebra Class to be in before graduation. (Mike Lipshultz and Henry Hoffman) Later at night, Sheldon came over, had to stay in hall reading comics while I saw Disneyland (John Slaughter). Went to Habonim dancing class. Had a lot of fun. Danced until 11:00. Talked about Paula's party, at her house it will be. Walked home with Sheldon.

Saturday, January 24, 1959

Dear Diary,

Went to Temple. Good sermon by Rabbi Greenman. Went to Clark Street Social Center but only 4 guys came, played basketball. At 7:00, went to Paula's house for Kumsitz. Had a lot of fun. Danced, sang, talked. Went on walk with Arnie. Brought my record. Went on Scavenger Hunt, with Marion Gutman. Harry Kniaz gave me ride home.

Sunday, January 25, 1959

Dear Diary,

Went to show (Sherman), saw "Cat on a Hot Tin Roof," and "In Love and War." There was no Habonim meeting, and I was to give my report.

Got a call from Sheldon and after watching "Maverick" went over to Steve Cohen's house. We talked, Steve gave us vocabulary contests. Also had a history and geography contest. Got home about 9:30, asleep at 10:00.

Monday, January 26, 1959

Dear Diary,

There was only ½ day today. Gave book report. Mr. Hintz gave us dot puzzlers. Lot of fun there in [Room] 307.

After school had snow ball fight with [Allen] Saxe and [Henry] Wolinsky. Ran into St. Cathy's [St. Catherine's Catholic School]—nun or sister came out. Later sat home and at about 3:00 went downtown, got this diary, also a few books (35¢). Did not have money to pay for malt at one restaurant.

Tuesday, January 27, 1959

Dear Diary,

Got report card today. ½ day of school again. Talked about how to improve health, with magnifier set some paper afire. Al burned his comb. John Fischer almost got a D for fooling around. On way home, shot ice at big icicles and knocked them down. Later when Mom and Dad went away, had snowball fight. Later went to Gym at Sherman School Social Center. Watched show about the sinking of the Titanic.

Wednesday, January 28, 1959

Dear Diary,

Went over to Sheldon's and then went to Washington Park to go toboggadning. Lot of fun. Had snowball fight. Missed trees by inches. Went real fast on sled. I crashed into lamp pole head on. Loads of fun. John Gilman got his books from High School. Later went over to Gingi's house for hot cocoa, watched T. V. and talked about camp, sex, boys, and girls. Very, very interesting.

Thursday, January 29, 1959

Dear Diary,

Got our first schedule for 9A. Have to buy *Odyssey* and *Julius Caesar* and $1.50 for new towel system in gym. Also got my job back as Hall Cadet, thank God, by the skin of my teeth. [Ken] Shectman told me he was not my partner anymore in ping-pong. After school went to Sheldon's house to play bowling, tied him. Very close game of bowling. Later at night did homework and listened to radio.

Friday, January 30, 1959

Dear Diary,

Were told today to buy *Odyssey* and *Julius Caesar*. Got a lot of new kids in classes, also got to bring $1.50 for towel service, just introduced. Remember to do history. Also got an eighty and one hundred on Algebra homework. Nothing much happened in study hall. Am not Shectman's partner anymore. So I got Larry Trogun and went over to his house to practice in the doubles tourney. Will come again tomorrow.

Saturday, January 31, 1959

Dear Diary,

Went to Willy's Bar Mitzvah. Got ride there, forgot suit jacket, ran back, got ride from Mr. Felder. Willy [Rosman] said very good speech. Talked with all the guys there a lot. Afterwards practiced ping-pong with Larry Trogun. Dave Lew was there, and we played doubles there. At about 8:00 went over to Sheldon's house and with Al went to the show. Saw "Geisha Boy" and "Seventh Voyage of Sinbad."

Sunday, February 1, 1959

Dear Diary,

Was supposed to be picked up by Mr. Trogun, but went to Center by myself. Saw a few AZA [the Grand Order of the Aleph Zadik Aleph, a Jewish boys' organization] games there. Practiced for a time. Forgot gloves. Went home with Willy Grossman. Then went to Habonim meeting, gave speech to younger girls' groups. Then went home, got dressed up for Willy's Bar Mitzvah. Real good party. Lot of fun. Gave my report for older groups. Danced hora before people. Got home 12:00.

Monday, February 2, 1959

Dear Diary,

Did not go to school because got home late and also did not have History homework done. But went to school later in the afternoon. After school went to Basketball School at Sherman School. Got spanked by coach but liked it a lot. Also very lucky, no ping-pong tournament, so I can practice more with Larry. Did homework late at night.

Tuesday, February 3, 1959

Dear Diary,

Snowing outside when I went to school. Bought *Odyssey* by luck. Read it in English. Got new seat in homeroom. Gave report in History room. Got towels and wrote names on gym clothes. After school went to Sherman gym, also to game room. Then did homework. Went to Larry to practice ping-pong. Heard that the Big Bopper, Buddy Holly, Richie Valens died. Met cute chick at Larry's house.

Wednesday, February 4, 1959

Dear Diary,

We had test on Health about the body, got 88 (B) on it. After school had no homework, so went to Larry Trogun's house to practice ping-pong. Have a 5 to 3 edge in small tournament of ours. Also helped with his homework. Afterwards went to special meeting of Habonim. Used mimeographing machine and talked on how to improve club.

Thursday, February 5, 1959

Dear Diary,

Mr. Seppanen (Seppy) got real strict. After school, would like to make the gymnastics team. So went to gymnastics. Have to do a cartwheel and bricks on the rings. Afterwards went to gym at Sherman School. Also stamp club. Then went to Optimist Club. Had to have locker room, Boy Scouts had our room. Played basketball before game. Meeting was uproar with Hamon. Later played Pom-Pom.

Friday, February 6, 1959

Dear Diary,

Got my lab books today. 8 mine, 5 Don Kendall's. Real good books. When got home, had to get washed up, [Sigmund] Singer [my father's business partner] came over. After eating, Harry Peltz came over with Sheldon. We went to Habonim dance group but walked to Wilbur Wright Jr. High for Wright Night. Danced. Met Brent Ghent. Then went to Pizza Wagon for pizza. Then hitchhiked and got picked up at 1:00 A.M.

Saturday, February 7, 1959

Dear Diary,

Today I didn't go to Temple because I got home late. Talked to Mrs. Bankier about the last night. Then went to Steve Cohen's house. Al, Ken, and Shel were there. Talked, sat around. I beat Steve 24–22. Listened to records. Might go to show. I went to show with Steve Cohen. Shel and Al couldn't go. We saw "Tunnel of Love" and "Man of the West." Strip-tease act in "Man of the West."

Sunday, February 8, 1959

Dear Diary,

Today I slept late. Then my homework in Health. I went to Bazaar of Farband's [a Zionist group] at Beth Am Center. Looked around. Bought some potato chips. Had fight with Barry Ellman with peas. Afterwards went to Habonim meeting, practiced our play for this coming Friday, Oneg Shabbat coming up. Also were asked to dance at Jewish Center for pay and will practice.

Monday, February 9, 1959

Dear Diary,

Today had test in History, got o on it. Might have one in Science. We've had bad weather, lot of snow and slush. After school, went down to B. A. A. [Boys Athletic Association] But there was not any. Ping-pong was postponed. During school, guy had a rubber band, and he was taken down to principal's house. At home, didn't have nothing to do, so I fixed up my room.

Tuesday, February 10, 1959

Dear Diary,

There was no school this afternoon because there was a snow emergency. No gym either. Went over to Steve's house, but he wasn't home. So, went over to Eddie's house, with Sheldon and Alan, shot pennies to see who could hit a piece of paper. Played radio real loud, played with the hula hoop. Made a lot of trouble for Ed. Boring day, didn't do much today anyway.

Wednesday, February 11, 1959

Dear Diary,

We had a contest in History. Very close game between a boy and girl. The boy won. Going to have test in Health. After school went home and then I returned books to library, got a book on Abraham Lincoln. His birthday is tomorrow. Then I watched the new program on Project 20, called "Meet Abe Lincoln." Had a lot of pictures, no acting. Then I did my Algebra homework for tomorrow.

Thursday, February 12, 1959

Dear Diary,

We had a test in English on the Greek Gods and Goddesses. Got a 90 on it. Talked to Bernd [Davidson] about Judaism. After school, saw how they divide the gym. Also got into snow ball fight. They shot at buses. Will not shoot at cars anymore. Went to Optimist Club. Larry Poll beat me in checkers. Practiced basketball, shot 13 free throws. Met Mr. Bureta. Had snow ball fight afterwards near school.

Friday, February 13, 1959

Dear Diary,

Got to get soap for Tuesday in gym. Also after school we had our Habonim Oneg Shabbat. I didn't go to Math Club and later they asked me why. At the Oneg, we rehearsed our short skit on newcomers to Israel. Had to pay 60¢ for the dinner. Before dinner we danced, talked, ran around. Girls started giggling when saying prayers. Harry [Kniaz, our youth leader] told us facts of life.

Saturday, February 14, 1959

Dear Diary,

I didn't go to temple today because Daddy was sick. Read in the papers about the vandalism at Steuben Jr. High at about 3:00 in the morning, Saturday. Both were 16 years old, neither were from Steuben. One was from Washington. 25 days below zero so far. Later went over to Steve's house. Played records, ping-pong, wrestled, had fun.

Sunday, February 15, 1959

Dear Diary,

Went to sleep late last night, so I woke up at about 12:00. Found out that my diary was missing. Looked all over the house for it. Sol found it later behind some books in my collection of them. Went with Steve to this teenage dance and get-together. Owe him 15¢. Danced, then went over to his Grandma's house. Later went to Habonim meeting.

Monday, February 16, 1959

Dear Diary,

Today we had big lecture on the vandalism done to the school Saturday morning. He (Mr. Clark) told us about school conduct. It was in the papers the next day. Must have had a reporter of the [Milwaukee] Journal paper there. After school I went to practice ping-pong with Larry, there was no tournament today.

Tuesday, February 17, 1959

Dear Diary,

Today nothing much happened at school.

After school we had gymnastics. Mr. Grollo got mad at me, me and him don't get along very well together. Am on the gymnastics team. Class three, some of the guys did not believe me. Today was very cold, and afterwards I went to Sherman School to play there and practice shooting basketballs.

Wednesday, February 18, 1959

Dear Diary,

There was no school today because of Institute Day.

Went on hike with Sheldon, Al, Sol Lewin. Walked up to 70th and Burleigh when Sol and Al went back home. Had a little fight with Sol because of Al. After they went, me and Sheldon went to Arnie's house. Played ping-pong. Listened to Rock and Roll and Israeli records. Harry Peltz also came over.

Thursday, February 19, 1959

Started to read *The Iliad* in English today. Took shower in gym. Got real many exercises in gym and a few days later, legs got real stiff, muscles tightened up. After school, went to B. A. A. Played a practice game of basketball. Scored 9 points. Then said *Mincha* and *Maariv* [Jewish prayers] at our temple. Later on in evening, went to Optimist Club, played basketball, might go swimming, party on Monday.

Friday, February 20, 1959

Today there was an auditorium program. A Mr. Claver from the Audubon Society gave a film and talk on animals at night. Very funny and very interesting.

During lunch girls gave birthday party for George Washington. Had tablecloth-cake. Have to make a health chart of the skeletal system for Wednesday.

After school there was no Math Club, so walked with Jim Bocher home.

Saturday, February 21, 1959

Went to Rabbi Twerski's Temple today. Mike Maimon's Bar Mitzvah was there today. Later went to Beth Am Center to practice our dancing. We sure need it. Explained to Marian Gutman about the Kumsitz at about 7:30, left for Harry's house. Mixed up address, went from house to house asking to use phone. *Crazy.* At Kumsitz talked about Jackie Faber [a sexy girl with big breasts], ate, and listened to records.

Sunday, February 22, 1959

Did sleep late today. Then I did my homework, which was to make a drawing of the skeletal system, but I can't draw too well. Also I did my algebra homework, which was hard. Later on I went to Habonim meeting, came early, we talked about an Oneg this Friday, where we will dance before people. Discussed about Israel. Also I got ride home.

Monday, February 23, 1959

Today we were supposed to have a program, but we didn't. Returned to almost go home on way to school because of so much slush, which I walked through. Had contest in history, had no homework in algebra. Today we had ping-pong tournament, my partner, Larry Trogun, was not there, so Sol and Ken won the tourney. Drat it!! Later at night went to Steve, borrowed paper to draw on.

Tuesday, February 24, 1959

We had an auditorium program today called "Day Called X," picture about what happens when a bomb warning is heard. Afterwards we had an election of Student Council President. Dave Midland, Ingrid Metzner, Nancy Wittman ran for this office. We also had real hard assignment in algebra. After school I went to practice basketball for game and then went to gymnastics with Mr. Grollo.

Wednesday, February 25, 1959

We had election of president. Ingrid has a great chance to win, it will be the first girl president in a long time. We had a test in English, History, and Health. For talking, we had extra assignment in Health. Got 85 on Algebra homework. After school went to Sheldon's house to play bowling there, then went home and did homework, later in evening went to Beth Am Center for a short walk.

Thursday, February 26, 1959

Today I got a ride to school from Gingi's father. In English, Miss Dempsey gave 5 minutes to do the test again. I knew the answers by that time and got 100 on it. In Health, got 100 on test and a check-plus on my drawing. After school there was no basketball game between us and the teachers, so we practiced. At night I didn't go to Optimist Club, had homework.

Friday, February 27, 1959

Today I saw Gingi's father but I didn't get a ride. We also had a real funny algebra teacher. He was a lot of fun. In History got a 100 on test and A on essay. Boy! Was I lucky. After school there was no math club, so I went to the barber, got haircut, and took bath for Oneg Shabbat. We saw slides of a kibbutz, girls from group and Arnie and Jackie danced. We later did hora, got home 11:30.

Saturday, February 28, 1959

Today I walked Aunt Rifkah to temple and got home at 12:00 noon and didn't do anything much, so far as I'm writing. I didn't do much this afternoon. Got call from Harry Kniaz saying no dancing practice because there will be no debut for the whole deal was called off. Later at night, went to Uptown show to see "The Buccaneer" and "I Want to Live!" The latter has 6 Oscar nominations.

Sunday, March 1, 1959

Today I got call from Arnie, saying to go to Teen Age Club, Steve and Eddie and Shel came to pick me up to go. Danced, joked with Harry, Arvin, and others. Then went to Bazaar, at Rabbi Shapiro's temple, almost won basket of fruit. Did homework afterwards. Then went to Habonim meeting. Had Young Judea visitors. Danced. For Harry wrote down my 6 best friends.

Monday, March 2, 1959

Today we had to write what we wanted to be in future life for English. Steve Cohen was made Red Cross representative because Joanne Leifer works at bookstore. After school, there was a teachers' meeting, so there was no B. A. A. Today was a good program on television, about Jazz, Classical, and other kinds of music on "Bell Telephone Hour" today.

Tuesday, March 3, 1959

Today was very beautiful day, just like spring. At school, some girls were asked to go to Longfellow Jr. High for a swim and volleyball games. Also got in trouble for not taking down someone's name. After school I tried to practice basketball for game, but there was no gym for us, so I went down to the auxiliary gym and practiced for the gymnastic meet.

Wednesday, March 4, 1959

Today we discussed about Comparisons test we'll get tomorrow. Also had Health to study, for I finished my heart picture. We didn't have test in Algebra that we thought we'd have. Today after school met Emmy Ertel's sister, Jennie, whom I didn't see in 3 years. We talked about each other and my work at school. Afterwards went to play baseball with Sheldon for first time.

Thursday, March 5, 1959

Has been snowing for the first time in a long time. Today we had a test in History, about comparisons. Today also we had test in Algebra. After school, waited for Sheldon in Miss Froelich's room, finished all my algebra homework. On way home, got chased by guy I knew at Academy. Basketball game with teachers was postponed. We might play them sometime in the future.

Friday, March 6, 1959

Today we had a community sing, all kinds of songs we sang. Had own little quartet with John Casanova leading us. We had a substitute for History, fooled around the whole period. Also we had a test in algebra. Remember to study for test in science and do chart of feudalism. After school went to Math Club, almost forgot boots in school. Afterwards went to library, very snowy out. Dad mad for going [out in the snow].

Saturday, March 7, 1959

Today I went to temple, got called up to put gold and silver crown on Torah. Afterwards looked at records at store where they were selling them for 5 for $1.00. Later I went to Steve's house with Al, played Easy Money, and watched television there also. Didn't go to show but watched television, Felders came over. Saw "Pillows of Death" and "King Kong" on T. V.

Sunday, March 8, 1959

Got up at 12:30 because I went to bed at 12:30 too. Watched television and prayed afterwards with *tefillin*. Later did algebra homework. Lande came over, went to Steve's house to look at his history book for chart. Then went to Lande's house, read comics at 7:00, went to (rode to) Habonim meeting. Their meeting was in disorder. Wabyck got slapped by Sandy. Walked with girls home.

Monday, March 9, 1959

Today we had Mr. Flaschberger come into our English class and discuss what we will take in 10th grade. I am taking geometry and biology but am not sure what to take, Spanish, Latin, or French. In history had to make chart for tomorrow. Got 86 on Science test on machines. Had substitute in algebra, easy assignment. Watched Ringling Bros. Circus after school on T. V.

Tuesday, March 10, 1959

Today got a B+ on history chart because it was not short and did not look like chart.

In gym, we played with the girls for first time. Some of them are pretty good. Got 100 on algebra test also. After school I went to gym, learned some new stunts in gymnastics with Mr. Lencer. Also I got my Tab books, also walked with Sheldon home. Watched T. V. and listened to radio later.

Wednesday, March 11, 1959

Today got a ride to school by Gingi's house by father. Going to finish *The Odyssey* by Friday. Saw movie in Science on sound. Also going to have test in Health Monday. After school I went to gymnastic practice today. Nobody believed I'm in Class 3. Then I went to Sheldon's house, ate dinner there, Eddy Norin came over, went to library. Then went to Steve's house, played Sorry.

Thursday, March 12, 1959

Today we made out our 10B program and also our entire stay at Washington program. Mrs. Kral is getting mad because of our conduct in homeroom. After school we started our mixed homeroom volleyball with girls. We played 2 games and won both, they were against 9B's. Scores were 30–6, and 28–12 massacres. Later went to last Jr. Optimist meeting, because Mr. Bently is going to Ohio.

Friday, March 13, 1959

Mr. Flaschburger came again and talked to us about our 10B programs. After school did not go to gymnastics or Math Club because Mom wanted me home. At night went to Habonim Dance Group, talked with boys, danced, sang. There'll be no N. F. [(Jewish) National Fund] Collecting. At this time the Optimist Party where they won't let you join in without a girl, but a good party it will be.

Saturday, March 14, 1959

At temple wrapped up the Torah while Dad held it. Also I might say the Haftorah next Shabbat. In the afternoon, I went by bus to the Berger Social Center on 3rd and Burleigh. There was the ping-pong tourney there. My first game was with the champion of last year and winner this year. Drat it!! Later I went to show with Shel and Al. Saw "Some Came Running."

Sunday, March 15, 1959

Got home late from movies I saw with Al, Shel, at the Sherman. Today, this morning, got a phone call from Harry, who told us no meeting because there had been a storm that morning, it sure changed before. Today it was like a spring day, but now a snow storm came out. Later did homework at Sheldon's house, played games of baseball and called Harry about meeting tonight.

Monday, March 16, 1959

Today made out typed program for high school. Got test in Science, and could get 100 on it. Not sure. Got 90 on Health test. Also took Algebra test, which was easy. Found out that Bernd [Davidson] is going to Conservation Shindig. After school went to shuffleboard practice, played doubles against Dennis Williamson and Lyle Lipscomb. Later watched television. Got books from Arrow Book Club, Sol's club.

Tuesday, March 17, 1959

Today was St. Patrick's Day, and everyone was dressed in green who was Irish. Am going to get test in History Thursday, tomorrow they will mark report cards. Played volleyball in gym. After school I went to gymnastic practice, tried out a new gadget to help you make handsprings. Then with Sheldon went to drugstore near library, then went to library. Came home, think I lost a dollar on way.

Wednesday, March 18, 1959

Today we marked report cards, I got a double A in History and also in Health. Paid for Tab Books. Got first 100 on Science test this year. Boy!! Got an 80 in Algebra test. After school went to Al's house, talked to his sister about what I'm going to take, Spanish or French, talked about fishing with Al, lit off some gunpowder, then went to drugstore, afterwards went to library to finish homework, then watched T. V.

Thursday, March 19, 1959

Today we in Science took apart a telephone and talked about telegram service and about the telephone. In gym we played volleyball. In English we wrote a theme on a modern Odyssey. Mine was one in space. After school we played volleyball, won all our games, now have 6 and 0 record. Afterwards, there was no Optimist Club, so watched T. V.

Friday, March 20, 1959

Today we got Algebra tests corrected, got 80, 100, 96, and 88 on them. Today also was day to hand in conference's sheets and if you want your mother to talk to counselors. After school I went to Math Club, had math contest. Will do a chart of big numbers for club. Also I did some of my homework there. Books are due today. Talked to Mr. Felder tonight on talking machines.

Saturday, March 21, 1959

Today was Arnie's Bar Mitzvah at Achudas Achim. Mom said it was not good to go there since I wasn't invited. So I went to Beth Am for the little services, got called up to the Torah there. Later Sheldon came over and we played games such as Parcheesi and Anagrams. Later at 6 o'clock, me and Sol went to Sheldon's house, afterwards with free passes went to Sherman show to see movies.

Sunday, March 22, 1959

Today I got up early and went with Sheldon at about 9:00 to Beth Am. There Lorna gave us instructions about collecting for J. N. F. Then me, Sheldon, and Joey left for the blocks of 54 to 57 and Keefe. The people were real nice, and we collected $19.00. While we collected we played basketball with Norman Cohen and friends. Feyge Tussman, a big person in Habonim, came and we danced for her and played charades.

Monday, March 23, 1959

Was very beautiful day today. Got report card, got 8 A's and the rest B's. Very good. Also got school scribe today. Got a lecture in History about the struggle between Pope and King. After school I went down to girls' auxiliary gym for shuffleboard practice. Afterwards played baseball on playground of school, got 2 hits. At night watched a 90-minute picture, "The Green Pastures," real good.

Tuesday, March 24, 1959

Today finished the questions in *Odyssey*. In gym, practiced medicine ball throw, and hop, step, and jump. In study hall, went to all men teachers with slip, to see if they're going to a bowling tourney. After school, went to gymnastics practice, afterwards went to baseball game again. Didn't play too much. At night I did homework and watched T. V. ("The Perry Como Show")

Wednesday, March 25, 1959

Today we had a 9A class meeting of all the homerooms of 9A for the 9A's. We talked about what to dress up in, what the cost of the party was, etc. This took up most of the 1st hour. Went outside after lunch. In algebra, got 100 on 1 test. In Health, got 2 100's on 2 tests. 7th hour was eliminated, we had auditorium program on underwater animals for Audubon Society group.

Thursday, March 26, 1959

Was also late today. In English took big test on *The Odyssey*. Might get about 94 on it. In History took test on pope and king struggle, got 100 on it. Went outside today and got in a fight, the little shit wants to fight me. In Algebra also got hard test. After school played volleyball in tourney, where we won 2 games. Big storm came up, helped Mrs. Rice out of snow, got ride home (girls).

Friday, March 27, 1959

Today Easter Vacation started. I slept late, till about 12:00 noon. Then I went to play outside, I shoveled snow, and saw the pine tree all bent over backwards. Then afterwards I got ready for the Bar Mitzvah. At about 7:30, Mr. and Mrs. Kaplan picked us up and went to Beth Shalom. The first time I had been in a Reform Temple, had organ, choir, could not wear kepah [skullcap] different.

Saturday, March 28, 1959

Today Sheldon picked me up and we went to Harry's (Peltz) Bar Mitzvah. Said the services and Haftorah, real nice job. Had a lot of fun walking with the girls around. Then Sol and Shel came over, and I showed them my scrap book of pictures. The I watched television. Didn't go to show since I have to get up early for collecting paper with Harry Kniaz on truck.

Sunday, March 29, 1959

Today Sheldon came over and we went to Beth Am to get on the truck for the paper drive. We started at about 9:30. We went to Arnie's father's shop, found pornographic (dirty) magazine. Then at about 12 went back to Beth Am for lunch. Then I went on the afternoon load [of papers] with Paula White. At night I went to see the 2 movies "Tonka" and "The Perfect Furlough," saw them twice.

Monday, March 30, 1959

Woke up very late because I went to bed at 12:30. Got call from Henrietta Galina and went to Sol's house, from there, went to Sherman Boulevard and met everyone. We were supposed to go to Whitnall [Park] but played baseball at Townsend. Afterwards we went to Shel's basement, talked about kumsitz, and smoked. Afterwards, went to Joey's house, ate supper there, then went to bowling alley.

Tuesday, March 31, 1959

Today Shel came over, we played catch. Then he went to eat and came back and we both went to Arnie's house to play basketball. Were supposed to go with Sol and Joey. But they weren't there. Sol and Wabyak opened the kitchen door at Beth Am and committed vandalism. At Arnie's we played basketball, beat Arnie in ping-pong. Went to Paula's house. Jackie Faber came over, and played basketball with us.

Wednesday, April 1, 1959

Today it started to rain, and Lorna [Kniaz] called up to get the younger group of boys to go to the center. Only me, Sol, Marty Rabinowitz came. I sneaked into the gym. Played basketball. Got blisters all over feet. Put salve over it. Bowled 114, got 2 strikes, 2 spares. Played basketball against Neil Pollack, friend of Arnie. At home watched Braves on T. V. Got telephone calls from Shel and Joey.

Thursday, April 2, 1959

Today my blisters were better and I went to Townsend Playground and met the younger boys, Shel, Sol, and others to play baseball. When I got home, I went to the shoe store, got new pair shoes. Then I went to Jackie Faber's house for big party. There I danced, had lots of fun. On way to Arnie's house, the boys kissed Faber. [She was very attractive and "built."] We waited at Arnie's house for Marlene's mother.

Friday, April 3, 1959

Today I mostly slept in bed. Al came over, so did Sol and Shel, played "catch," I went to Friday night dance and song group. There we sang and then learned new dances from Lorna's sister. From there we went to Marlene's house. Were scared to go in, but watched Arnie's Bar Mitzvah movies through window. Then came in and were welcome. Saw movies of West Indies trip, also we danced.

Saturday, April 4, 1959

Today Sheldon came over with Ruby [his brother] and we went to Rabbi Feldman's temple. There we prayed with Harry, Arnie and Joey. Later got ride from Harry's mother. Then ate, went to Klause's bowling alley with Joey. Bowled 135, excellent ball I found. Later played ball at Sherman Park, then came home for drinks, then I won basketball game. Later on night went to see movies.

Sunday, April 5, 1959

Went to bed late, so I got up late. Went to Sherman School to play basketball there. After that didn't do much. Read about fatal stabbing and kidnapping of little boy who lived near Stzundel's house. At night brought $2 for dues, and went to Habonim meeting. Saw movies on Israel and Jerusalem. Also talked about vandalism and about Oneg Shabbat coming up.

Monday, April 6, 1959

Today vacation was over. We had auditorium program today, a magician named Mr. Young. He was also a ventriloquist. I went up there as a helper. Got nice applause for it. Was real nice up there in front of everyone. Miss Karagunis told us about trip to Florida. Had no homework today. Saw picture of self in volleyball tourney. Watched Oscar awards tonight.

Tuesday, April 7, 1959

Today it was snowing outside on an April day!! Today Science was omitted because of conferences, we went (our homeroom) to the library. Finished all my homework, don't have any homework. Missed part of gym also. After school went to gymnastics today, but mostly played basketball the whole time. Then afterwards went to playground to play a little basketball at Sherman School.

Wednesday, April 8, 1959

Today it continued to snow, at school got 93 on *Odyssey*, 2 90's on History tests, A and 100 on Health test. Have number contests in History, which you say a group of numbers backwards. Also told some jokes. After school did not go to gymnastics but went home. Got book on Don Quixote of the Mancha. Went to the store, got pizza, had some that night, very good, yum!!

Thursday, April 9, 1959

This morning the snow was melting from the trees. We had an auditorium program about snakes. A man, Mr. Johnson, brought a tarantula, python, rattlers, and other snakes. Told interesting stories about snakes, and some girls came up and put them around her neck. After school was a dance for needy clothing. Danced 5 dances, did sherele [a Hasidic dance] after, went to playground, played ball.

Friday, April 10, 1959

Got 100 on History test. Got homework to do, eye ball drawing and questions on eye. Classes change tomorrow when we get [our new schedule]. After school walked Sheldon and Jack Wendorf home. Jack picked me up at 7:00 to go to Habonim dancing group but there was none, walked for nothing. Then went to Steve Cohen's house, played cards, and records, read magazines.

Saturday, April 11, 1959

Went to Achudas Achim, Sheldon picked me up. There Arnie said Shachris and we talked about the show at the Riverside (movie theater) with guys like Frankie Avalon, Bellnotes, and others there. We met at Sherman playground. Had baseball game there with Arnie, Joey, Harry and Sheldon. Watched Dick Clark, then went to movies. Saw "From Here to Eternity" (excellent picture) and "Seven Brides for Seven Brothers."

Sunday, April 12, 1959

Went to Hebrew Class at Rabbi Feldman's temple with Sheldon. Fooled around a lot there. He showed us the purpose of Pesach, which is coming. Then went to playground to play baseball and basketball games. Then went to Habonim meeting. Talked about going to camp. Hope I can go. Then did homework later at night until about 10:10.

Monday, April 13, 1959

Today went back to school over short weekends it seemed. Got Tab books today. Got 100 on History test on Crusades. Also got 76 on Science test. Bought bleacher seat ticket from Jackie Wendorf for opening day tomorrow. Also won first noon-lunch game today over Stroiman. Had substitute in Algebra, a Mr. Buechner. After school, went to Sheldon's to pick up glasses, did homework.

Tuesday, April 14, 1959

Today I walked with David Midland home 'cause he got a job a St. Joseph's Hospital delivering papers. Got ticket from Wendorf. Went down to Mr. Aylward's room, got O.K. to go down to ballgame. Walked to Jim Stark's house, got ride there from his father. Braves won 4–3. Aaron got 3 hits. Got bleachers. Walked home. Along river walked. Stopped at filling station, very tired when I got home.

Wednesday, April 15, 1959

Today in English we started *Julius Caesar* with a little reading. Today in gym I did 92 sit-ups, jumped 7 feet, and did 8 pull-ups. Real hard, had pain in stomach afterwards. After school the playground was open and Merrill Grant is coach. Went to Gymnastics and about April 24, the meet will come to Wilbur Wright [jr. high school], it will be held. Practiced for records by exercising.

Thursday, April 16, 1959

Today got up real early. Took Health test from Miss Karagunis. We had auditorium program on Bell Telephone discoveries in science (transistor-solar battery). Very boring. Had test in History. Then at 11:15 had very first fake attack [fake atomic bomb attack]. All people hid in houses, got off streets. We hid in basement until over. After school, we lost the volleyball tourney to [Room] 321. Well, we can't win 'em all.

Friday, April 17, 1959

Today we were to have a band presentation but had a play. Leroy Port was M.C., and had parts in the play. There were also monologues. Hasia Swartzman and Annette Emanual were in the play about the "Missing Bookend." After school, fooled around in homeroom with Bernd and John Fisher. Then went to Math Club. At night had Oneg Shabbat on camp. Had talk on different special camp days, then danced.

Saturday, April 18, 1959

Today Sheldon came to pick me up and we went to Achudas Achim (Rabbi Feldman's temple). It was Ben's (Lande) cousin's Bar Mitzvah. We stayed for the Kiddush, then I walked Benny home. He went to ball game (11–5, we lost). I stayed, read, played with a ball and jumped rope with Sarah. After that I went home and at about 6:30, Sheldon came over, went to show. Saw "The Trap" and "Rally Round the Flag, Boys." Very funny.

Sunday, April 19, 1959

Today Sheldon came over, and we went over to Rabbi Feldman's temple for a class (Hebrew). We learned something about Passover. But the class was in an uproar. Joey was sent out. Arnie's back was hit by the teacher. We then went home for lunch. On way home played "Strike-Out" ball. Went to dancing group. Saw camp pictures (1957). At night Habonim meeting was Pesach discussion.

Monday, April 20, 1959

Today in homeroom, I saw graduation pictures. Read part of Brutus in English in *Julius Caesar*. Got B and B on Health pictures of eye and ear. Did 100 sit-ups, jumped 8.3 in broad-jump in gym. After school, went to practice gymnastics and then went to shuffleboard practice. Got Grolier Yearbook today. Also called on Jackie W. for game of strike-out.

Tuesday, April 21, 1959

Today we had an auditorium program on Venezuelan plants and animals by a Mr. Hermes. First hour was eliminated. Mr. Hermes was here before. Won baseball game at noon. Went to gymnastics practice. Boys did not believe I'm in

Class Three. Took practice meet. Need some practice on certain exercises. Later went to get a haircut. At night washed floors for some money.

Wednesday, April 22, 1959

Today got 80 on History test given by Arlene Gernstein. In gym had substitute teacher, fooled around so much, talked back to teacher. In Algebra, Mrs. Donovan's friend, a woman doctor from India, came in and talked to us. After school, practiced for meet, Friday at night. Had first Seder. Mr. Felder and family came over. Very nice.

Thursday, April 23, 1959

Today took off for school and went to Beth Hamedrath Agodol with Dad. At lunch time (5th hour) went back to school and go admit pass in office. Saw Marian and Clark (Mr.), talked to me. Then went outside, lost to Williamson's team. Had test in Algebra (100). After school went to mixed badminton and practiced gymnastics. Went to temple. Had 2nd Seder.

Friday, April 24, 1959

Went to Twerski's temple for service. Afterwards went home and then waited till about 2:30, then went by bus to Wilbur Wright Jr. High for gym meet. Did very well at meet. Met Paula, Arnie, and Joey there. Went to Arnie's house. Then took bus for going to Beth Am for dancing practice, which will be at the Jewish Center, Sunday.

Saturday, April 25, 1959

Went to Rabbi Feldman's for Saturday services. Then went home. After lunch, played a little baseball against the steps of the house with Sheldon. Then both of us *walked* to Arnie's house. There we practiced singing the songs for that ice-cream party. Played ping-pong. Then went to show, saw "Separate Tables" + "These Thousand Hills."

Sunday, April 26, 1959

Daylight Savings Time comes today. Got up later. Went to Jewish Center. Didn't dance in group because didn't change clock, got there later 1 hour. Was in

Samson auditorium and not many people were there. Then went bowling. (132 score). Did homework later. Saw my name in [the *Milwaukee Journal*] paper because I came in 10th place in a gym [gymnastics] meet. Had 84.6 points.

Monday, April 27, 1959

Mr. Hintz in History was surprised to learn that I went to gymnastic meet at Wilbur Wright and was absent the same day. Today Arlene Gernstein gave her report in History on pg. 600–610. Got 100 on test she gave yesterday. After school went down to the employment office, made out slip there and got instructions to get to Brynwood [Country Club—golf caddy]. Afterwards, went to Woolworth's, got ice cream, saw Pocket Books there, then went to museum library.

Tuesday, April 28, 1959

Today on Tuesday got 97 on Science. After school went to Brynwood with Jackie Wendorf. Took bus to 64th and Silver Springs, then hitch-hiked to Brynwood. Got ride from a somewhat loony character. Had shabby clothes and we were scared. At Brynwood got slip there. Will practice on Saturday. On way back walked back to about 64th and Florist and got ride. Before that, put rock on railroad track and was smashed to dust. At that street above got ride home from college student.

Wednesday, April 29, 1959

Went to temple, then went to Rabinoff's (Al's) house, had badminton game.

Thursday, April 30, 1959

I went to temple. Yizkor was said there today, but after school we went to playground to play baseball. Got home and ate, went to Steuben [Junior High] Spring Festival at 8:00. The band, orchestra, and all the glee clubs performed. Very good, talked to glee club performers. Was up in front row. Paula White was there. Afterwards, walked the girls home.

Friday, May 1, 1959

Had auditorium program on trained dogs, very good. There was a German Shepherd, a real tiny little dog, they were very good. The man also showed how to train a dog. Guy came up there and trained a dog with a few lessons. Tonight there was no dancing because Harry (Kniaz) was tired. They are going to go to New York.

Saturday, May 2, 1959

I went to Rabbi Feldman's temple today and there met Arnie only, Harry and Joey were too lazy to come, I supposed. After temple, went to do my homework, which was plenty. Finished it except for history. Went to Laura Melrood's house for party. Was lot of fun. Had peanut hunt. Danced, pantomimed rock 'n' roll songs, couldn't dance Israeli dances because of a slight stage down in their beautiful basement [the basement was split-level]. Went to Petroffs [Drive-In] afterwards, saw Harry and Lorna Kniaz there.

Sunday, May 3, 1959

Today spent practically whole day doing history chart. It's pretty good and I'm glad I was finally through with it. At 7:00 went to Habonim meeting, discussed Laura Melrood's party.

Monday, May 4, 1959

Today we did our history charts in History today. Got B+ on it. Won bet from Jim Kearnen, when I said Don Kendall wouldn't get an A on his chart (he got a B+, though). After school I went to B. A. A. and played baseball. We won the game. Beat Carey's team during lunch. At night, did homework and then went to playground.

Tuesday, May 5, 1959

Today in school discussed about narcotics in Health. In Algebra, we are 20 pages behind Sheldon's class. In History, we started explaining our charts and got marks on it. After school, played baseball at Sherman [Playground]. I am trying out for traveling team [a baseball team that traveled to other playgrounds] this summer. Starting seeding the lawn today.

Wednesday, May 6, 1959

Today in History got double A and B-A in gym. Got History assignment on inventions during the Renaissance with David Wabyak. Listened to records in English about Julius Caesar's tragedy. Won a baseball game at lunch time against Stroimon's team. After school, went to the playground to practice baseball and a little basketball.

Thursday, May 7, 1959

Today they marked report cards. Got double A in English and Health. A-B in Science, B-A in Gym, and B-B in Algebra. After school, went to B. A. A. in badminton tourney, won first game against Leroy to Port and Janice Niebler, lost second to Kenny Shectman and Jane Stauss. Pat Oppitz was my partner. Then went to office to see about work permit. Went to playground later at night.

Friday, May 8, 1959

Was almost late today again. We had an auditorium program today. It was a play about a girl who most of the girls think stole a beautiful formal dress. The play consisted of 8 girls, no boys. Took hop, skip and jump test and broad jump, jumped 8'2" and 21' on skip after school. After school, waited for Mr. Clark's signature and got too late to go to Industrial Commission.

Saturday, May 9, 1959

Today went to Rabbi Feldman's for Saturday services. After temple, ate dinner, and went to Arnie's house. Took the bus there. At Arnie's house, talked, listened to records, and then for supper, Shel and Arnie went to Mama Mia's. I went to a drive-in afterwards. Went to Arnie's house again. Saw and met Neil Pollack. Had a ball there.

Sunday, May 10, 1959

Got up very late today because got home late from Peltz's house. At noon, after lunch, we went to playground, me and Joey Blasberg played a little catch. Then while listening to ballgame, took bus there. Got to see 2nd game free of double-header. Then walked home, was really adventurous, had fun and experience doing it. Got home at about 8:00.

Monday, May 11, 1959

Today went outside and took basketball throw. Shot 95 ft., though. Saw a friend of mine, Kenny Maters, during Study Hall. After school, didn't go to the Industrial Commission, for it closes at 4:30. During lunch, we beat Williamson's team 7–0. Have to beat them 2 more times. During playground tourney, a guy pitched a no-hitter.

Tuesday, May 12, 1959

Got ride from Lyle Sussman, saved from being late. Had auditorium program, the band played. They (the trumpet players) really stunk. Had test in Health. Were shown slides on pond water, bits of wood and cross-sections of plants. After school, went to play basketball in B. A. A. At the night league, won our 1st game. I got two hits in the game.

Wednesday, May 13, 1959

Finished *Julius Caesar* in English. In English also went to library. In Science, were shown films on plants. In gym, shot softball 185 ft. Got no homework today. After school, got bus right away to downtown. Finally, after lots of looking around, found Industrial Commission. Didn't get work permit. Looked at bookstore afterwards.

Thursday, May 14, 1959

Today we had [UNFINISHED]

Sunday, May 17, 1959

Got up late and went to the show in the afternoon.

Monday, May 18, 1959

Today I got up late and did not go to school, but stayed home and did my homework. Also watched Television Science class to make up and see what I missed in Science. Later in the day went to the playground. It's funny, but I was supposed to be sick but went to the playground. There, played some baseball.

Tuesday, May 19, 1959

Today it rained by about 8:10 and I thought it would rain out our ball game with Williamson would be cancelled, but it wasn't. We whipped 'em 15–0. Boy! Had a test in History and took the hard part of an algebra test (Part B). Had to memorize lines in *Julius Caesar* for Miss Dempsey after school. Went to B. A. A. baseball. Then went to playground. Got in a game.

Wednesday, May 20, 1959

Today we had an auditorium program, a community sing. A topic on Lutheranism was given in History. In gym we went outside, and I ran the 75-yard dash in 9.3 seconds. In Algebra I had a test out of a special booklet. In study hall, made a phone call for Mr. Hintz for the first time. Also wrote article on gymnastic meet for *Scribe* [school paper] went to play.

Thursday, May 21, 1959

Yesterday had nutty weather. Today the same. Had a test in English about all we learned in *Julius Caesar*, also had a test, an easy one, in Health. We played softball during lunch hour, and we won. After school, went to B. A. A., played badminton with Charles Hellman, beat him 2 games. After B. A. A., went to Galina's house and talked about being in talent show.

Friday, May 22, 1959

Today in English, corrected test we had yesterday. Got 54 out of 57 questions correct. In Science, didn't have test which I studied for last night. In gym, ran 600 yards, ran and walked in 1 minute and 57 seconds. In Algebra, had no homework, had a substitute for Mrs. Donovan. Williamson team rained out after school, talked to Galinas and Marcy. Am not in talent show. Went to Shel's house.

Friday, May 29, 1959

Today we had an auditorium program on a Civil War story about a parasol. Joann Leifer and Leroy Port were in it. We also had the girls' glee club sing. In History, report on law was given. In gym, went outside and played baseball.

Took gym clothes home for latest gym period. Won baseball game during lunch. After school, went to playground and played.

Friday, June 5, 1959

Today there was an auditorium program in which there was a community sing and all the 9A's were honored. Boy, it was a big thrill, the whole school singing to you. All the hours were shortened. After school, began seeding lawn, for lawn is getting a little brown. At night, went to Habonim dancing group.

Saturday, June 6, 1959

Wet to Feldman's temple, Arnie and Harry and Joey weren't there. Afterwards met Barry **Ellman** and **friend,** he is a Civil Air Cadet. Then after lunch went to Sherman Park and played baseball. Met Joey there. Played tennis for first time in life. Hit ball over fence on first serve. At night went with Sheldon to Habonim wiener roast at Bradford.

Sunday, June 7, 1959

Today I got up at 1:00 P.M. feeling bad and was hollering at my brother, for he was bothering Bella, and they were making a great racket. Later got dressed and went to Beth Am and was told I'd be a leader of the boy's group of ten to twelve year olds. Later at night went to Habonim meeting. Discussed about full Jewish life.

Monday, June 8, 1959

Today handed in our folder for History. Didn't have [UNFINISHED]

Thursday, June 11, 1959

Today got dressed up and went to school, forgot Mr. Hintz's paper, went all the way home to get it, then was very hot and bothered. Then went to Athletic Honor Day. Got 5 awards, like I said I would. Played charades in Health, real nutty, did nothing in Algebra. Had graduation party after school. Had a good time. At night went to confirmation at Beth El.

Friday, June 12, 1959

Today we had Scholastic Honor Day. Got pin for service and 9th-grade Honor Roll. Algebra and Study Hall was eliminated because of program; after school had sort of party. Got our scribes and our graduation picture. I had everyone I wanted to sign it. Then at night we practiced real hard for Saturday.

Saturday, June 13, 1959

Went to Rabbi Feldman's temple today and talked about the dancing we'll do today at temple to raise funds for Israel. Went to Sheldon's house in the afternoon at about 7:00, left for temple. Waited on pins and needles before dancing. Saw Miss Israel. Wow! *Beautiful!* We danced pretty good. Much money was collected.

Sunday, June 14, 1959

Went to see *South Pacific* at the Strand today. Me, Arnie, Joey, and Harry met and went downtown to see the movie. Paid 90¢. Was very last day to see the show. Was very excellent show. Later went around downtown and at night went to Habonim meeting. It ended early. Went to Gingi's house for great time.

Monday, June 15, 1959

This morning got up sort of early and went to Sheldon's house, then we went to our new school, Washington High. We met at the auditorium and then we went to a study hall to take I. Q. Test. Took two (2) of them. Were hard. After that went home for lunch. At 1:30, went to school to practice our graduation exercises at school.

Tuesday, June 16, 1959

Today we had no school for me in the morning. So I slept late at about 12:00, got ready for graduation exercises. Got dressed up and went to the gymnasium. After talks on Lincoln by Chanita, Howard, Loeb and Kathy, then went up on stage, got certificate. Sandy [Goldstein] and John were there. At night, lost baseball tourney, were beaten.

Wednesday, June 17, 1959

Today was the first day of summer vacation, but I was at school, Sherman School for the graduation exercises for Benny Lande. They also presented Mr. Ulrich [the principal] a picture to be hung up because he is retiring. After that, relaxed, went to Sherman Park to play tennis with Arnie and Sheldon. Joey at night went, Chanita Stillerman's graduation party. Got ride from Bilansky.

Thursday, June 18, 1959

Today, because of party which was last night, got up at 1:30 as usual, ate and went to playground, coach told me not to play strikeout with Norman Shumacher. Played basketball and football later. Heard later that Henry Wolinsky broke shoulder during my game. At night, went to Gingi's party. Danced and played records till late.

Friday, June 19, 1959

Today went down to Harry's house, and with money I got from graduation from Mrs. Sherman and from Mom, put in order for a tennis racket at a wholesale house called Milway. Afterwards listened to Harry's records, played badminton, and were bothered by a neighbor of his. At night went to Beth Am. Got there a little late. Practiced dances [Israeli].

Saturday, June 20, 1959

Went to [Joe] Teitelbaum's Bar Mitzvah. Saw Arnie and Harry there. Sheldon and his cousin, a nice guy from Green Bay [Wisconsin], picked me up. Afterwards went to Sherman Park, played scrubs and tennis. Then got washed up and ate. Got ready for Jack Wendorf's Graduation Party. At the party, ate, danced, forgot present, had a good time.

Sunday, June 21, 1959

Slept real late until one in the afternoon. After that, Sheldon called up and came over. We went to the show to see "Compulsion" and "Alias Jesse James" starring Bob Hope and Rhonda Fleming. "Compulsion": Diane Varsi, Brad Dillman, Dean Stockwell, at about 7:30 went to Sheldon's house for a talk about Habonim's future. Watched his T. V.

Monday, June 22, 1959

Today got up a little unusually early, for we played today. Took bus to Merrill Park and won on forfeit. Was the pitcher on Key Baron's team. Had a practice game. Got 2 for 3. Batted against Reeves (Gary). Later, went to Harry's house, but he was not home. Went to playground and played a little ringers.

Saturday, June 27, 1959

Today I went to Rabbi Feldman's temple. There we talked about the party and tried to shut up Harry, who was swearing in the temple!! Later stayed in house mostly, but played strikeout with Benny and Sol (15-0). Had supper, then with Sheldon and Lyle Sussman went to Wendorf's party. Was very hot and crowded. Went to Petroff's.

[Sunday, June 28, 1959, through Monday, July 6, 1959: empty.]

Tuesday, July 7, 1959

I've just got over a bad cold, still can't swim or play baseball. Since I stopped writing until up to the 7th day of July [probably due to the cold—J. N. P.]. Last night went to party given by Marlene Blyweiss. Shel, Peltz's were there. Had kissing games, got slapped. Was good party. Got ride from Mrs. Blyweiss. This night, I went to Washington Park Blatz Theater. Heard concert there. Was good. Went with [Willie] Stzundel. Saw Howard Barlow.

Wednesday, July 8, 1959

Today with Willie [Stzundel] went to McKinley Beach to see Marine Invasion, met Marty and Carl Shimon. It was real crowded and by pushing got good seat. Was great show. Saw tanks, amphibians, Marines, saw Mayor Zeidler. Then afterwards went to see the tanks and copters, guns, boy it was great. Then I went to swimming party (Habonim), didn't swim, for I was still sick.

Thursday, July 9, 1959

Today I started to write. It's been a long time. I haven't been faithful, but I will. Got up early and waited for Mom to come home. When she did, I picked up Willie Stzundel and then walked to Capitol Court with Al Rabinoff. Saw circus there, it stunk. Saw Marlene and cousins. At night went to barbecue at Varda's [Shwartzman] house, walked and talked with Sandy and Joe Gingrich.

Friday, July 10, 1959

Today slept through the whole morning. Got a call from Norman Shumacher. He came over, and we went to Sherman Playground to practice baseball. Then at night went to Emil Blatz Theatre at Washington Park. Was a salute to the St. Lawrence Seaway. Sat in special reserved seats. Met friends there. Got under tree. Saw Steve Lawrence and band (Marine). Got all wet; it rained.

Saturday, July 11, 1959

Sheldon picked me up today and waited some time for me to get ready. Nice friend. At Feldman's, saw Rabbi. (He just got over a bad illness.) Then had lunch with Jakob Bronstein, who is going to Israel to visit. Then after lunch went to Sheldon's house to read some of the Pocket Books he got at his dad's junk shop. Later at night went to Wendorf's party.

Sunday, July 12, 1959

Today Dad and Sol came from the resort they went to for a week. Rabinoff called and we went downtown to see parade. Tried to get in line to see boats in harbor. Went to Jewish Center after parade, which featured bands, soldiers, etc. Bowled 98, and played 2 pool games free with Jay Lederman. Then I found a good seat for the biggest fireworks display I ever saw near McKinley Beach.

Monday, July 13, 1959

This morning went down to the baseball field at Merrill Park and played handball there. Jimmy Wegner, our pitcher, pitched a no-hitter, and we won our 7th game. We're in 1st place. Got one clean hit and drove in 2 runs and one disputed hit. Then Joey came over, and we played 2 long sets [in tennis], in which I beat him 7–5 and 8–6, in which I came behind and won 5 straight.

Tuesday, July 14, 1959

Got up at about 12 noon as usual, and then Mrs. Gutstein came over and asked if I wanted a job gardening her yard. She's the mother of Debbie and beautiful

Sherilyn [she was a Miss Wisconsin contestant]. Dug around her nice bushes and pulled weeds. Got paid 2 dollars. Went to playground and heard that we are in last place, because we forfeited games, guys were over age. At night, Arnie called for clothes list for camp.

Wednesday, July 15, 1959

At 8:30 went and played hardball against which should have been closest guys. Lost by forfeit. Played in choose-up, got 2 hits. Then played baseball at Sherman Park with Joey and Johnny Wegner, then went home, ate, then Joey and I went to Sol Lewin's house, met Marlene Blyweiss, Essie, her cousin, and Rosa Lewin, went to Washington Park to go boating. I rowed a little bit, Joey showing me. Then I played tennis, then went to playground, missed ride to relay at Lapham Park, so I went to Habonim meeting. Got Harry mad. Went to Petroffs, met guys who did go to the baseball game.

Thursday, July 16, 1959

Went to the playground to practice baseball. Had contest how many times per minute could throw around bases. At night, got call from Harry Peltz, who wanted to know what to wear to camp.

Friday, July 17, 1959

Today went to playground and borrowed Benny Lande's bike, went to Enderis for exhibition game. Beat them 7–5 in extra innings. Got 3 doubles in 5 times at bat. At night went to Beth Am to practice dancing with Joey, Shel, Fred Geller and Lyle Sussman. Are planning big Oneg Shabbat. At night everyone came over to see dog Sheri Shrinsky gave to me.

Saturday, July 18, 1959

Today went to Feldman's temple. Afterwards ate, went to Sol's house, where I found Marlene, Essie, Rosa and Paula White. We went to Washington Park. I rowed most of the time when we went boating. Paula kept hitting me and acting like a baby because she and Essie wanted to row. Got caught in rain on lake, got out of it fast. Went to Paula White's house for a party there.

Sunday, July 19, 1959

Today got up late as usual and then with family and Lande's went to Lake Park to New American club picnic there. Played tennis, again girls were very stubborn and wanted to play. Hit us again. They're nuts, crazy. Didn't take cute little dog named Andy along. Braves lost sixth straight game today. They must get going to take pennant again.

Monday, July 20, 1959

Today didn't go to play hardball because we're in last place and not going to play anymore. Went to get check-up for camp at Dr. Zubotsky. Then went to different stores downtown looking for a sailor hat. Found one for $1. Bought Pocket Book and stamps and pens, ball-point. Met Billy Rossman downtown. Got home tired. Exercised Andy, our dog, till about bedtime, outside.

Tuesday, July 21, 1959

Today went to playground and played against Townsend guys and we won 7-2, I played second base and I also hit a home run with a guy on and walked. Batted 1 for 3 and altogether am batting 4 for 8. Afterwards we went to the beach and there I went swimming and my sailor hat shrunk because I swam with it on. Later at night ordered a pizza from Marco's new pizza place at 48th and Center.

Wednesday, July 22, 1959

Today told myself I was a fool for buying the pizza. Played tennis with Joey today. The guy would like to go to camp but can't. So would others. Am sorry for them. [Why not? Good question—money? Fear of going to a "strange" place?—J. N. P.]

Thursday, July 23, 1959

Today I was awakened by the barking of my dog, Andy, who stays in basement, for he makes poop in the house. Today practiced a little baseball and then played 31st Street. Beat them 13-9, and we showed how good we were. Got 1 for 3 in that game.

Sunday, July 26, 1959

Today Sherri Shrinsky came and picked up her cute little puppy. I wasn't too sad to say goodbye to him. Later went to Lake Park and was a guest at a birthday party there. Ate a lot of food. Then got ready for Heber's Bar Mitzvah at the Wisconsin Hotel. There we had great [time]. Met cute girl whom I danced a lot with. Did kazatzka [a Russian dance] when hora was played. Got home at 12:30. Got to get up early tomorrow for camp.

Monday, July 27, 1959

Today we left at 7:00 for Beth Am Center and at 8:00 got on Greyhound bus to Chicago, picked up some kids at Max Dolnick Center at Stoney Island Avenue (on South side). At Camp met old friends, met some new ones. Great to be back. Ate lunch and then played baseball. I won 14-3. Got 2-4 (a triple) at night, had a game called Capture the Flag at the sports field. Fun.

Tuesday, July 28, 1959

Today I feel better after the stomach ache that stopped the bus yesterday. The nurse checked me, had 99° temp, and she put some violet stuff for athlete's foot on my feet. Had discussions on different races. Today it rained. Was on K. P. [kitchen patrol] and worked real hard, and after that we took a shower and went to the evening program. We had different races (relay). Later at night we saw girls undress. Wow! Fooled around all night.

Wednesday, July 29, 1959

Today I got up when it was raining real hard, the night before, and I found out it's Segregation Day. Our tzrif [cabin] real wet and my clothes in my duffel bag were wet. Stayed in tent almost all day. Went swimming and am going to swim or bust. Also am in a play. Have a bit part of the person, Peretz [a Yiddish writer] in the Friday night program. At night we had an evening program of movies on Israel.

Thursday, July 30, 1959

Today I was awakened by Shemon Kasdai (the guy who calls "Hitamlut in 15 minutes"). Went to sports field and helped line up new baseball field. Later had

Yom Chof (Water Day) where we had different races in swimming in a volleyball game and in building a sand castle. Our castle won first prize, but we on the whole came in third place. At night had bonfire on beach, sat around and sang.

Friday, July 31, 1959

Today was a big day because Harry Kniaz, Lorna and his brother came from Milwaukee for Shabbat. Also saw Leibel and Zelda Fein. Good to see them. Later, Beersheba, our sports team, won 2 volleyball games. We had practices for the skit on Heaven. I'm Peretz the writer, for tonight. Then we got dressed in white and walked up for Shabbat. Me and Dave Moscow led kids up Shabbat Hill. Had great dinner. Danced and sang till real late, me especially.

Saturday, August 1, 1959

Today got up late, for breakfast is at 10:00. Then we went down Shabbat Hill for services, later we had discussion on Reform Judaism by a friend of Al Ehrlichs. Later we practiced baseball instead of playing in the lake (swimming). Later we played the Madrichim in baseball, we won again 5–3, didn't get hit but fielded great. Later at night had K.P. but finished in time to see part of the Midurrah. Fun.

Sunday, August 2, 1959

Today we put on Tefillin, me and Bruce Kutnick. Got done with it too late for Mifkad but Gerry Ehrenberg didn't do anything. For Avodah cleaned up the grounds around the Torin (flagpole). Later we had a send-off for Harry (Kniaz). Few girls started crying. They're homesick. Then practiced baseball for Camp Avodah, which comes Tuesday. At night we had Bible skits. I was Ramses in the life of Moses.

Monday, August 3, 1959

Today for Hitamlut [exercise] we rubbed shoulders to keep warm. It started raining again. Spent a lot of time in tent sorting clothes for laundry. Played gaga [a game with a ball] in Moadon hall for sports. Had K. P. on lunch, worked hard and took a shower later. Then we had a sicha [discussion] instead of a chug [interest group]. At night, for the evening program, they gave us 5 objects and had us make a story about it. Later had meeting about revolution.

Tuesday, August 4, 1959

Today it rained a little. And about 100 kids were supposed to come from Camp Avodah. They came, and we had relay races, which were silly. Then we played volleyball. Our girls stood theirs (we won 21–6) (Pushover). Then we ate lunch outside. We sang together; after that we played their Madrichim vs. ours in volleyball (21–18) *us!!* Then we played baseball, well, we lost 9–8 (got 3–4). Sorta sad to say goodbye. At night had treasure hunt, was very crummy.

Wednesday, August 5, 1959

Today at breakfast, complained because the food was bad. This was the beginning of the start of revolting. During swimming I am learning how to swim. At lunch, Lisa, the cook, said we'll have to pay for the meal ($30). We didn't have money, so we worked to make up the money. We revolted when supper cost $50. We carried Madrichim, kicked 'em in butt, marched around triumphant. Then elected Rosh Merkaz; it was fixed, but I almost won an election. Then were assigned cabins (I had Ivan Frank's). That night slept outside with Mike Cember and John Gilman. It's fun.

Thursday, August 6, 1959

Today we led camp for 1 day alone. Made meals, had Avodah [work], everything without counselors. I even led a sicha. In the afternoon, went on tiyul (hike). Went on farmer's field, saw pigs, had snack, played a little baseball. Was very tired after it all. At night we tried all Madrichim [counselors] and M. I. T.'s [counselors-in-training] and sentenced them.

Friday, August 7, 1959

Spent the day in the regular order. Cleaned cabins out for Shabbat during Avodah, played basketball during swimming. Had a bad cut on palm so I got tetanus shot from Stella the nurse. After lunch, rested, then learned a little Hebrew. Got ready for Shabbat. The meal of chicken was delicious, and then we had Oneg Shabbat program, after which we danced and sang till late.

Saturday, August 8, 1959

Today almost missed breakfast, got up so late. Then went down Shabbat Hill for services. It started raining, and I got caught in it, ran to A. B. K. Later we practiced dancing for Sunday—Parents' Day program. It rained for a while. Later in day played basketball on just-finished court. At night, parents started coming in. We had Midurrah [campfire] inside, since rainfall. Sat with Laurin Miller [my girlfriend at the time].

Sunday, August 9, 1959

Today was Parents' Weekend. We got all set for them. I was so glad to see Mother and Sol, Bella, and Dad couldn't make it. It was great to see them. I showed them around the camp after they had lunch. Then I went swimming. A lot of people came. Then gave program for them. People liked it. I danced in the program at night after game of ringolevio, had pizza. Had party for Bruce Kutnick (he's leaving).

Monday, August 10, 1959

Today Bruce Kutnick and his brother, Danny, missed bus, so stayed till 12:00. For Hitamlut we did Israeli "bulldog." We had a very regular order of the day. During Avodah, slept. Sue Ehrlich gave sicha about how Habonim started. Learned a little Hebrew in Sammy Kelman's class. Later played basketball during sports. Had K. P. for dinner. At night, finished K. P. fast. Had a cartoon and the picture: "The Return of Monte Cristo." (Very good.)

Tuesday, August 11, 1959

Today got up tired. It rained so didn't have exercise. Louie Yeidel set up his hammock—*Neat*. Made torches in Avodah. Went swimming, got a little better in crawl. After lunch, since I'm the kupa representative, picked mail up, also gave Dave Levitan glasses to fix. Played basketball a little. Then in sports, played baseball. At night for program, went on hayride. Sat with Laurin, was fun.

Wednesday, August 12, 1959

Today got up to Shimon Kasdai's voice, "Hitamlut." After breakfast, I worked making wood for Tisha B'Av bonfire. Then had sicha on holiday by Sue. Had K.

P. for lunch. Worked hard, so took shower. I am torch-bearer for our ohel (tent). At night after supper, had beautiful Tisha B'Av program. Held torch, had fire display. Then had shadow play in Moadon [Auditorium]. Very good.

Thursday, August 13, 1959

Today slept late, and I am going too fast for as long as I can. [One is supposed to fast on Tisha B'Av.] There was no breakfast, and lunch for those who wanted to eat. I read in library a few books, and missed little hike our tent had, so I went boating around Kaiser Lake with Mike Cember and Esther Reuter. When supper came, I ate a lot. For program, went to town, played in park for a while, saw movie, it was very good, with Laurin ("The Five Pennies").

Friday, August 14, 1959

Got up late so I slept a little longer. For exercise we had push-ups, others like that. Went swimming. Dave Sarnat taught me a little bit. I went in deep water and swam. During rest period, Berle and Esther Post came in—great to see them again—played a little basketball with Berle. Had K. P. tonight, missed program but danced and had kumsitz later.

Saturday, August 15, 1959

Today got to bed so late, I missed breakfast and Shabbat Services, I was so tired. After lunch, swam, practiced crawl, and then we were challenged to a baseball game by the Stzofim [a group of campers]. Us K. M. Bets, beat them 16–11. Then got in game with Berle. Saw Adra Horpy off. She's leaving for Canada. At night had Midurrah down the hill, I was in a skit. Had to leave early because I had to organize dessert (ice cream).

Sunday, August 16, 1959

Sunday is like any other day. After breakfast, Al gave discussion in Marpeah [Infirmary] because he sprained his ankle and he can't walk.

Monday, August 17, 1959

Today began Kachol-Lavan [Blue and White] Day—day of competition. Had different mifkads [flag-raisings], ate a very quiet and funny breakfast. Had different Hitamlut and Avodah. Then had volleyball games. Our girls lost 21–7 by a slaughter. We also lost 21–17. I can't understand it. Lavan had lunch on a heavenly theme. Had baseball game (lost again, 6–5). Won a grand relay. Supper was done up in night-club stuff. Kachol (my team) lost.

[Summer camp over; high school starts]

Wednesday, September 9, 1959

First day in Washington High School. Went to Washington's cafeteria with Sheldon. Then to assigned homeroom. Had trouble finding rooms. Filled out many forms and slips. After school, went to Gilman's house. Sherilyn and Sandy were there. Told about my first day—they promised to help.

Saturday, September 12, 1959 (written later, in 2004)

We played football, and Norman got injured today. He's in hospital for 4–5 days.

Thursday, September 17, 1959

Today Norman Shumacher died. It's a great shock—He died of complications resulting in a football game when his kidney was ruptured.

My friend died!!

I still have his glove and bat. [This was one of the most shocking events in my young life—my first introduction to death.—J. N. P.]

Friday, September 18, 1959

His funeral was today. I went, was a pall-bearer—took off from school, many people went.

Saturday, September 19, 1959 (written later, in 2004)

Tonight—or today—Mrs. Fink brutally killed [a second shock].

Sunday, September 20, 1959

Mrs. Sylvia Fink, mother of Susie Fink, long no see friend, was brutally murdered by a Negro. Haven't seen Susie in school, was shocked for her.

Monday, September 21, 1959

So 2 unhappy happenings have happened: Norm and Mrs. Fink. As Mike Marks, the guy who accidentally hit Norman, says, "There is no good news around." Braves falling [losing games] for pennant.

Sunday, September 27, 1959

Went to baseball game with Joey, Arnold and Harry, got ride from Harry's mother. Was a record crowd. Braves won the game.

Friday, November 27, 1959

Today was the day of the Chicago-Minneapolis-Milwaukee Habonim Seminar. They came in . . . [UNFINISHED]

Saturday, December 12, 1959

Put in my first points in sophomore [high school basketball] game. Free throw and 1 field goal (3 pts.) at Rufus King High School. Got ride home from Mr. Trogun. [This was my first basketball game in high school. I was on the sophomore team—a kind of junior varsity. Life goes on.—J. N. P.]
    [[With these deaths, the diary ends in tragedy]

Sources

For more on these deaths and other tragedies, see my memoir *Milwaukee Memories* (Newton, MA: The Spencer Press, 2011).

Chapter 3

LA in the 1950s and 1960s

My Love Affair with LA

Because my dad didn't like to fly, we often took trains to LA (Los Angeles). I use the word "LA" instead of "Los Angeles" (see the essays in my book *21 Screen Treatments for Hollywood*), because "LA" implies a "state of mind," while "Los Angeles" is just a congeries of villages and towns connected by a freeway.

In the summer of 2019 I went back to LA. I rented a car and drove around. I was shocked how it had changed. I was also amused to learn that, had I moved to LA in the '60s as many of my friends had done, I would have had the same life, the same marriage, and the same career!

I would have started off in academia teaching sociology at a "second-tier" school (not UCLA), not received tenure, married an LA girl (maybe my childhood sweetheart Eileen Ross), maybe stayed together, maybe not, would have drifted around, then entered into the hot Los Angeles real estate market, made a million dollars, lost it, started a real estate school, remarried and lived happily ever after. Now, how's that for a Hollywood story!

I would have tried to get "into" show business like my Milwaukee friends Joey Blasberg, Stu Chapman and Herschel Weingrod. What's so weird is that I would have duplicated the career I had in Boston except the weather would have been warmer! That's eerie.

So LA and Los Angeles have been on my mind my entire life as the place "I could have been." To be honest, after that trip, I'm glad I stayed in Boston. LA had changed so much, and people were leaving in droves due to fires, earthquakes, high housing costs, and just general weirdness. So I'm glad I stayed in more "stable" Boston (though I do miss the lovely LA weather).

In my trips out West in the 1950s with my folks, I remember, as a young boy, the "Hollywood" of LA, "the Valley"—Knott's Berry Farm, Disneyland, the beaches, Olivera Street (we forget that part of southwest America was under Mexican rule for centuries), Capistrano monasteries, the film studios, the palm trees and orange groves. I ate my first avocado, which grew right outside my bedroom window on South Curson Avenue. I reached out and plucked it. I ate my first orange, my first grapefruit, my first tacos, and my first deli (at Cantors).

LA has been a "moveable feast," to use Hemingway's words, ever since. As a young immigrant boy to America, Hollywood has fascinated me, and I have described this fascination elsewhere in several books: *Happy (Freilich) Days Revisited, Milwaukee Memories, Milwaukee and Hollywood,* and *21 Screen Treatments for Hollywood.* I went out there once in the 1970s with my sister Bella to movie studios to pitch my stories about Jewish partisans and other family tales.

Back then, you could actually walk into a studio or an office building and talk directly to a studio head or a producer. It is so different today. You need an appointment now. I also got on several popular LA TV shows that were local but soon went national: Regis Philbin, for example, and another guy whose name I forget, a kind of Michael Savage tough guy. People tended not to talk about politics in those days but about sociological or cultural issues. On one show, I got to ask a beautiful Black model a question to about racism in her field.

I went to UCLA in the summer of 1966 and stayed at my Uncle Boris and Aunt Hinda's home on South Curson Avenue near Fairfax and Pico, a palm tree-lined neighborhood with solid middle-class homes. I took three courses, and each one was memorable: cultural anthropology with Marshall McLuhan's co-author Edmund Snow Carpenter; Middle Eastern politics with Malcolm Kerr, later president of the American University in Beirut, sadly killed by Muslim militants years later; and a course on collective behavior (riots, mass movements, fads) using the famous Turner and Killian textbook and taught by a female sociology professor. I loved the courses and the campus.

On my days off from school, I worked as a landscaper for wealthy Beverly Hills people, mowing their lawns and trimming their bushes. It was kind of like a combination of the movies *Chinatown* and *Once Upon a Time in Hollywood.* All of the weirdness and the sub-surface menace (think: the Manson cult) of

"Hollywood" would transfer itself into my subconscious later as a writer. I used to ride the buses at night to pick up dialogue. I found out that other writers did the same thing, but I could never write screenplays well. It takes a special talent. But I could write nonfiction, and that's what I did.

I met strange, half-forgotten characters such as comic Ben Blue, and I think I even saw Marilyn Monroe. I met Joan Collins on the train ride out from Milwaukee to LA, and she was very gracious and lovely.

Uncle Morris and Aunt Betty moved out there in the late '40s for the weather. The winters were harsh in Chicago, plus Betty had been paralyzed in a freak accident and couldn't get around in the snow and ice. Their son, my cousin Allen, moved with them and set up one of the first postwar design studios. He was influenced by the Chicago Bauhaus school of design, and he influenced my interest in the sociology of design and architecture.

Later he moved back to Chicago, but I remember his studio at 7777 Sunset Strip, which inspired the name of the well-known TV detective series *77 Sunset Strip*, starring Efrem Zimbalist Jr. and Edd "Kookie" Byrnes ("Kookie, Kookie, Lend Me Your Comb"). Life was always imitating art out there, and vice versa. Sometimes it was confusing.

Allen Porter's LA in the '40s, '50s, and '60s

I had the pleasure of knowing Allen for a long time ever since I was a little kid in 1948 when he visited my parents and me in Milwaukee with his parents, my Uncle Morris and Aunt Betty from Chicago's North Side. Soon after that, Allen and his folks moved to LA for the weather, and because his mom contracted a form of paralysis due to a botched-up operation near her spine. Many Jewish people could no longer stand the severe cold and winters of Chicago and Milwaukee and left for Florida, Arizona, and California, especially after World War II.

While in Chicago, Allen was a child actor, but his mother's inability to properly take care of him led his folks to do a most un-Jewish thing: they sent him to the Howe Military Academy in Howe, Indiana. You can still see pictures of this tiny guy in his tiny little military uniform. It probably wasn't the most pleasant time for him, yet he persevered. Also, as an only child, he had to endure trips to Gary, Indiana, to visit his mom's parents, along with her sister Jeannette. They quarreled a lot; Jeannette was not that attractive; Betty was the more beautiful sister. Yet out of this tension came great art and creativity.

Later in the 1950s, my folks and I often raveled by train to LA via the California Zephyr. So I got to know LA and Southern California. I still remember Uncle

Morris driving me around the citrus groves—I can still smell the oranges in the San Fernando Valley—while he plied his merchandise in children's dresses, shirts and toys that he kept in the trunk and back seat. (In Chicago, he was in the cigar business.) My uncle Boris, Morris's brother, who came from Argentina in 1955, was also in the clothing business, selling to Latinos and LA's rundown downtown. So I absorbed the sights and sounds of Olivera Street, Sunset Strip, Hollywood, and Malibu. This would help me later in my writings and in my love for all things Hollywood.

It would also influence me when I wrote about "LA Noir" and LA architecture. I was always intrigued about the contrast between rich and poor, between color and noir, and how Hollywood (color) masked the darker side of LA (noir), but especially the space between the dream (Hollywood) and the reality (LA).

Later, after I watched the Quentin Tarantino film *Once Upon a Time in Hollywood*, those memories would return, especially when I remembered the "underbelly" of LA, the beautiful flower children that turned into Manson killers. Did I meet people like Manson? Maybe. Did I meet those beautiful flower children? Yes, I did. Was I "this close" to getting murdered? Maybe.

Further Reminiscences

Allen bridged the gap between the Berlin Bauhaus of Moholy-Nagy and Gregory Kepnis, the Chicago Bauhaus School of Design, and the LA Modern School. And he knew everyone, from actors to comics to Scientologists to artists, designers and architects. In an interview I conducted with him in 2013 when he was eighty-five years old (he was born in Chicago in 1926), he remembers:

> On Sunset Strip, we had Cyrano's, Poopies [also a bakery], and the Brown Derby; went to Cyrano's for lunch every day. Lots of people there—Mort Sahl [political], Shelly Berman [cerebral], and Lenny Bruce [angst], even Hedy Lamarr. Also, went to The Troubadour [a folk-singing lounge].
>
> Met Rita Moreno, who went out with Marlon Brando. She was a smart lady, knew her architecture. I also knew Julie Newman [who studied dancing] and Stella Stevens.
>
> The *Casablanca* [the famous movie] crowd—Paul Henreid, Ingrid Bergman, and Claude Rains—all ate at Cyrano's. The owner was Charlie Peet and another fellow.
>
> Poopies was owned by Marge Drury [Neimis]. She took pills and died young. Jim Baker owned the first organic restaurant

in the country, the Aware-Inn, and the Aware-Burger. He later became a cult leader named YOD.

Knew Barbara Clowden. She was L. Ron Hubbard's secretary and mistress. Cults were very popular in Southern California, and Dianetics was no exception. I graduated high school with Barbara. She became a sociologist. I helped design the Scientology symbol.

I met Sylvia [his wife] when she was married to Art Gould, whose wife was Martha Gould. Art made commercial and industrial movies. They had a daughter, Leslie [Leah Urso today].

My office was owned by Sara Taft, an actress who made a lot of movies, fifty of them, mostly silent. Later we moved to 7777 Sunset Strip, later memorialized in the famous TV series starting Efrem Zimbalist Jr., Roger Smith, and Edd "Kookie" Byrnes and called *77 Sunset Strip*.

Remember that famous song, "77 Sunset Strip (snap, snap), 77 Sunset Strip (snap, snap)"?

I was friends with Ross Martin [of the TV series *The Wild, Wild West*], met comic Lenny Bruce and his mother Sally Marr. My wife Sylvia was an "exotic dancer" in her youth and knew Lenny and Sally Marr, his mother, very well.

Later, Allen and I reunited when I attended Northwestern from 1967 to 1971. Allen had opened up Porter, Goodman & Cheatem in LA, but they wanted an office in Chicago, so since Allen was from Chicago, he returned with Sylvia, his bride, and her two children from previous marriages, Leslie (Leah) and Michelle, plus Marlon (named after both Morris Porter and Marlon Brando), their own son.

Leah Urso lives in Israel with her husband and has a grown child. Michelle lives in West Rogers Park with her husband and two daughters. Marlon lives in Australia, where he became a recognized hip-hop artist and social activist. Leah was also a Nashville singer and musician and teaches music in Israel. Michelle's husband, Gerald McClendon, is an accomplished blues singer. So musicality and artistry thrive in the Porter family.

When I left the Midwest in the mid-1970s and moved to the Boston area, I returned often to Evanston to discuss art, design and sociology with Allen. He and I shared an interest in sociology. In fact, he introduced me to what could be called "the sociology of space," that is, how space influences people, and how people influence space. This was the time in the '60s and '70s when people like Vance Packard, C. Wright Mills, Alvin Toffler, and Jane Jacobs were all writing about the city, its social classes, racism, sex and gender rights, and the "built environment." Whether it was a Helena Rubenstein perfume bottle or an office building they were discussing, they all needed to take into consideration human values and concerns.

This was the Bauhaus influence:

1. Learn everything, from sociology to geology.
2. Learn to design anything, from book covers to "high art."
3. Learn to make this world a better place to live in (probably the Marxian influence in Europe).

The Bauhaus was concerned with philosophy and ideology, with progressive issues. That is why it was opposed by totalitarian forces in Europe and the USA. It was people-oriented, not money-oriented. Today, in the design world, it is not easy to balance the two. Your client wants something fast, quick, and cheap. There is little room for art, yet there must be room. That was Allen's message as a designer, a photographer, and a teacher. You can be good and commercial; you can do good and do well; and you can be creative as well as pragmatic. But you have to fight for it. That was Allen's message to artists.

Sadly, Allen died of the coronavirus at age ninety-four on April 28, 2020.

Sources

Chicago Bauhaus and Beyond (www.chicagobauhausbeyond.org) material; also see Allen's material at the Bauhaus-Archiv | Museum für Gestaltung in Berlin.

Kahn, Ava F., and Marc Dollinger, eds. *California Jews.* Foreword by Moses Rischlin. Hanover, N. H., and London: University Press of New England, 2003. An excellent series of articles. See especially the essays on Venice, California, the San Fernando Valley, the Jewish leaders of the motion picture industry, the LA counterculture, and Shlomo Bardin's Brandeis Institute.

Marling, Karal Ann. *As Seen on TV: The Visual Culture of Everyday Life in the 1950s.* Cambridge, MA: Harvard University Press, 1994. Marling is an art historian and tells an entertaining tale about how TV reflected the lifestyles of the '50s and how in turn it influenced those very lifestyles.

Moore, Deborah Dash. *To the Golden Cities: Pursuing the American Jewish Dream in Miami and L.A.* Cambridge, MA: Harvard University Press, 1994. Moore, a professor of history and American culture, explains a great deal about how and why my uncle and aunt left Chicago for California.

Morris, Wesley. "Intoxicating Documentary Tells a Cinematic LA Story. *The Boston Globe,* March 25, 2005. This is a review of the movie *Los Angeles Plays Itself* directed by Thom Anderson in 2003.

Porter, Allen. "Los Angeles: Modernism and the Creative Fervor of the 50s/60s." Video presentation at the third annual meeting of Chicago Bauhaus and Beyond conference, February 1, 2007. See www.chicagobauhausbeyond.org.

Porter, Jack Nusan. *21 Screen Treatments for Hollywood, TV or as Graphic Comics.* Newton, MA: The Spencer Press, 2018.

———. *Milwaukee Memories: Milwaukee and Hollywood and Small Town Secrets.* Newton, Mass.: The Spencer Press, 2011.

———. "LA Plays Itself" and "Allen Porter: A Brief Biography." In *21 Screen Treatments for Hollywood, TV or as Graphic Comics.* Newton, MA: The Spencer Press, 2018.

———, with Gerry Glazer, and Sandy Aronin. *Happy (Freilich) Days Revisited: Growing Up Jewish in Ike's America.* Newton, MA: The Spencer Press, 2010. What it was like growing up Jewish in the Midwest.

Schulte-Peevers, Andrea. *Los Angeles.* Melbourne: Lonely Planet Publications, 2001. A guidebook.

Tigerman, Bobbye, ed. *A Handbook of California Design, 1930–1965: Craftspeople, Designers, Manufacturers.* Los Angeles: Los Angeles County Museum of Art, and Cambridge, MA: MIT Press, 2013. This is a wonderful and colorful compendium of artists and designers. Allen is not mentioned, but many of his friends are. Tied to this book, see the *California Design 1930–1965* exhibit at the Peabody Essex Museum in Salem, Massachusetts, March–July 2014 and its catalog.

Ukrainian Institute of Modern Art. *Chicago's Bauhaus Legacy.* Exhibition. August–September 2013. See also the catalog: *Chicago's Bauhaus Legacy.* 2 vols. Chicago: Ukrainian Institute of Modern Art, 2013. Allen and all of his friends and teachers are in this book.

Chapter 4

Habonim/Dror, 1956–1964

Habonim is the Hebrew word for "builders," and my parents, being staunch lovers of Israel, wanted us to join a Zionist youth group. It was actually a movement, not a "group." A *madrich* (leader, guide) of mine told me, "Jack, the difference between a movement and a ;group' is that a movement wants to change the world; a group just wants to change its organization." In short, we were revolutionaries for Zion and for the Jews. It is no surprise that the fighters of the Warsaw and Lodz ghettos and most of the fighting Jews of the Nazi era were movement people like Habonim, Dror, the right-wing Betar, or the non-Zionist Bund or non-Jewish and non-Zionist socialist and Communist youth movements.

Habonim was founded in England in 1929 via the influence of the charismatic Lord Baden-Powell, the founder of the Boy Scouts movement. Essentially, Habonim was the Jewish/Zionist equivalent of the Boy Scouts—only Jewish, Hebrew-speaking, and devoted to self-realization and working the land. Many of the concepts and activities we did in the city or at summer camp were taken from the Boy Scouts: *tzofiut* (scout craft), hiking, physical workouts, helping others, building one's own environment, self-reliance. Another thing: like *kupa*, the socialist concept from each according to his ability, to each according to his need, was a basic socialist creed. We were more political and radical than the Scouts, who tend to be apolitical, even conservative.

We even had uniforms similar to those of the Boy Scouts. While theirs were blue and gold, ours comprised blue shirts with red ties and khaki pants for work and every day, and white shirts and pants on *Shabbat*. Even today in Israel you can tell each youth movement by its colors, with the Israeli equivalent, Hanoar Haoved v'lomed, wearing the same colors as Habonim/Dror.

But Habonim had two other interesting yet conflicting influences. One was the Wandervogel (German for "wandering birds"), a pre-Nazi German and Austrian youth movement that honored the environment, health, exercise, and camaraderie. They were later co-opted by the Nazi Youth Movement. The other was the Komsomol Communist youth groups.

I lived in two worlds: Jewish Orthodox and American secular. I was a Boy Scout but also a member of Habonim and a secular Jewish youth group called the Grand Order of the Aleph Zaddik Aleph (AZA), an international youth-led fraternal organization for Jewish teenagers founded in 1924 and now the male wing of the B'nai B'rith Youth Organization (BBYO). At thirteen I rebelled and decided not to go to the Skokie (Illinois) *yeshiva* like my brother, but to become active in the Labor Zionist youth group known as Habonim/Dror today and its summer camps. I thus became a Labor Zionist, not a *Yeshiva bucher*, a seminarian. I was not to be a rabbi-preacher-teacher but a secularist-radical preacher-teacher.

After school, came sports and then Hebrew school four days a week, first from 4–6 p.m.; and then later, as I got older, 6–8 p.m. at the United Hebrew School. At first, I learned Yiddish. The Beth Am Center, where we met for classes, was home to the Yiddish (and socialist) Workman's Circle, but later the Zionist forces of the Farband-Pioneer Women forced out Yiddish (and the venerable *Berele* and *Shmerele* textbooks), and we were taught only Hebrew.

I'm sorry about that. My folks spoke Yiddish to me, but I answered in English. To this day, my Hebrew is better than my Yiddish. Though I understand Yiddish perfectly, I read Hebrew flawlessly, but I have trouble reading Yiddish. As the twig is bent . . . Theodore H. White, in his memoir *In Search of History*, tells the same story.

The Milwaukee *Ken*, Camp Tavor, and the Urban Kibbutz

What we called *Ken Lachish* (*ken* means "nest" in Hebrew) was the youth arm of Habonim/Dror in Milwaukee. While we had great leaders like Harry and Lorna Kniaz and Ilana Berner, plus some Israeli *shlichim* (emissaries), we ran it ourselves in a way. That is how a "movement" differs from an "organization." (I was subtly becoming a sociologist at an early age.) A movement has an ideology; it wants to change the world, and being a socialist movement, it gave us "children" (the youth) much greater power in decision-making since we were being trained to be leaders, not followers.

I have written about Habonim, both in the city and at camp, in my other memoirs, especially *Happy (Freilich) Days Revisited*, and I could write an entire book on what I learned and experienced as a leader, and I was a leader very early on. I was *Rosh Ken* (kind of a president of the local Milwaukee youth group) at age sixteen. At age seventeen, upon graduating from Washington High School in June 1962, I was sent to a special program for budding youth leaders called the Machon L'Madrechei M'Chutz L'Aretz (Institute for Youth Leaders from Abroad) for a year in Jerusalem, studying, and then on Kibbutz Gesher Haziv working the land.

When I returned to Milwaukee, I had to promise to work in the movement in Milwaukee and at camp for a minimum of two years. But, as *Rosh Ken*, I was responsible for organizing meetings and events. We had a big *Oneg Shabbat* on Friday nights with chicken dinner and singing and dancing and skits. We had meetings on Sundays for various age levels: *Amelim* for eleven to twelve year olds, *Chotrim* for thirteen to fourteen year olds, *Bonim* for fifteen to sixteen year olds, and *KM-Bet* for those aged seventeen and older, who themselves would become leaders to the younger sets. So we (me and the others leaders plus the adult leaders) had to train the younger leaders in how to lead a *sicha* (discussion) on Zionism, Jewish History or civil rights, how to teach Hebrew by using every day words (soap, dining hall, etc.), how to teach *shira* (singing), how to teach *rikud* (Israeli dancing), and how to uphold such principles as *kupah* (communal sharing), *chalutziut* (pioneering), *ahavat avodah* (love of work and the land of Israel), and *hagshamat-atzmi* ("self-realization"), a complex concept that meant to realize your highest potential by doing good to others and building a better world.

But the programs during the year really set the stage for encouraging as many people as possible to go to Midwest Camp Habonim / Camp Tavor. The camp was an extension of the city group, the *ken*, but even more intensive. Studies have shown that Jewish camps impart more *Yiddishkeit* into young people than either Hebrew school or synagogue. The more you attend such camps, the more your commitment to Jewish continuity grows. But at camp, it was even more intensive: it set the stage for moving to Israel and joining a kibbutz.

At a very young age then, we were becoming "intellectuals." We knew more about ideas, literature, poetry and culture than most adults. It was a heady experience. No wonder—many Habonim/Dror graduates went on to high political, cultural or academic office: thinkers like Label Fein; political leaders like Avraham Harmon; historians like Hasia Diner (Schwartzman); even comics and actors like Sacha Baron Cohen and Seth Rogen.

But the real aim was *aliyah*—moving to Israel, to kibbutz, not to the city for a personal career. No, it was to a communal setting: either to the kibbutz (Urim, Gesher Haziv, Tel) or to a new concept, the *irbutz*—a combination of the Hebrew word for city (*ir*) and kibbutz—a kind of urban collective, like a commune where the people (from eight to fourteen) would rent an apartment building with one room used for community meetings and dining and other rooms used either for married or "common-law" marriages or for single men and single women separately. People would work outside the commune and share their incomes. Some worked in the commune as day-care workers or as typists or research workers. (This was years before the computer and working from home with a laptop.)

The largest, most well-known, and most successful *irbutz* was *Garin* (Hebrew for "seed") *Sha'al*, a commune in Carmiel, near Haifa. But such communes are difficult to last. People grow up and sometimes marry a spouse who does not want to live communally, some have sick parents in the USA or Canada and need to return there, or there can be internal squabbles. The Carmiel commune no longer exists except in the minds and hearts of the "survivors," people like Habonim leader Gary Bennet.

I almost joined this commune. In some ways I wish I had, but I think that, being an academic, I most probably would have left, either for Tel Aviv or Beersheba University or back to the United States. I would have married either a Habonim woman or an Israeli, and I would have had Israeli American children, and they might have stayed in Israel, or not.

Of course, I might not have received tenure, and then I would have gone into real estate, so I would have mirrored the same pattern I have today. It's interesting to ponder what my life would have been in Israel. I really think it would have been the same as here in America. I would have had both an academic and a business career. I would have run for Knesset (Israeli parliament) with a Labor or left-wing party, and I would have become an Israeli. Maybe I would have been happier.

Sources

"Habonim Dror." In *Wikipedia.* Last modified December 27, 2021. https://en.wikipedia.org/wiki/Habonim_Dror.

Hertzberg, Arthur. *The Zionist Idea: A Historical Analysis and Reader.* Rev. ed. Philadelphia: The Jewish Publication Society, 1997.

Jeal, Tim. *The Boy-Man: The Life of Lord Baden-Powell.* New York: William Morrow, 1990.

Troy, Gil. "Labor Zionism" chapter 8). In *The Zionist Ideas.* Lincoln: University of Nebraska Press, 2018.

Also see various Habonim/Dror pamphlets and its magazine *Haboneh,* as well as the magazines *Furrows* and *Jewish Frontier,* the works of Moshe Kerem, David Twersky, Label Fein, and J. J. Goldberg, and the many volumes on youth movements, the German pre-Nazi Wandervogel, and similar groups.

For Socialist-Zionism, see:

Porter, Jack Nusan, and Peter Dreier, eds. *Jewish Radicalism: A Selected Anthology.* New York: Grove Press, Inc., 1973. Especially see the articles by Tsvi Bisk and Moshe Zedek (87–110) and the article by David Mandel on the *Irbutz* (111–118).

For American Labor Zionism, see:

"A Moment Interview with Marie Syrkin and Trude Weiss-Rosmarin." In *Jewish Possibilities: The Best of Moment Magazine,* edited by Leonard Fein, 235–242. Northvale, NJ: Jason Aronson, Inc., 1987. This is a rare interview with two female Labor Zionist thinkers.

Breslau, David, ed.. *Adventure in Pioneering: The Story of 25 Years of Habonim Camping.* New York: Chay Commission of the Labor Zionist Movement of New York, 1957.

———. *Arise and Build: The Story of American Habonim.* New York: Ihud Habonim Labor Zionist Youth, 1961. ("Arise and Build" is *Alei U'vnei* in Hebrew—Habonim's motto.)

Gal, Allon. *Socialist-Zionism: Theory and Issues in Contemporary Jewish Nationalism.* Cambridge, MA: Schenkman, 1973.

Gelb, Saadia. "The Founding of Habonim." In *Arise and Build: The Story of American Habonim*. David Breslau, edited by New York. Ihud Habonim Labor Zionist Youth, 1961.

Katzman, Jacob. *Commitment: The Labor Zionist Life-Style in America*. New York: Labor Zionist Letters, 1975.

Kover, Simon. "A Confession of a Left-Wing Zionist." *International Jerusalem Post*, June 24–30.

Raider, Mark A. *The Emergency of American Zionism*. New York and London: New York University Press, 1998.

Chapter 5

Israel, 1962–1963 /
Diary, 1963

Israel in the '50s and '60s

I'm glad I saw Israel in 1962–63, thus I was able to see it as it was just a decade and a half after its founding in 1948 and less than twenty years after the end of World War II in 1945. In the years 1962–1963, I was on Machon L'Madrechei M'Chutz L'Aretz (Institute for Youth Leaders from Abroad), or Machon for short. The June 1967 Six-Day War was just four years in the future, and the Yom Kippur War was about a decade into the future. Israel was a very different country in the 1950s and 1960s, especially when compared to today, 2020. I'm glad I witnessed those years.

A few movies caught the essence of those magical years. One I especially liked was *The Matchmaker* with Adir Miller as Yankele Bride, a mysterious matchmaker and Holocaust survivor and Tuval Shafir as the sixteen-year-old teenager growing up in Haifa in the summer of 1968, working for Yankele, learning from the confusions of first love with Tamara, a spoiled America-Israeli-Iraqi young woman, as well as the mysteries of the human heart from a beautiful female dwarf, a librarian, and a young religious woman.

Directed by Avi Nesher (*The Secrets, Turn Left at the End of the World*), this movie, though set in Haifa, a city I did not live in (unlike Tel Aviv and Jerusalem), catches the flavor of those early years where everyone was poor but didn't notice it and everyone seemed happy to be alive. Israel was a truly socialist country; everyone shared the good and the bad without the huge economic gap between the rich and the poor that we have today.

Another film about those days is Amos Gitai's *Allila* with Joel Klausner and Yael Abicassis. An Israeli version of *Cinema Paradiso*, it follows a common theme in Israeli and world cinema—the coming of age of a young teenage boy.

If I had the talent of an Amos Oz, I would write a poetic story about Jerusalem in the early '60s as he did in his book *A Tale of Love and Darkness*. (For a glimpse into the social, political, and even sexual life I led in those years, see my diary that follows this essay.)

My year in Israel as a *madrich* representing Ichud Habonim was formative. It consisted of five months studying in Jerusalem in the Katamon section, Rehov Hazkiyahu Hamelech, and later in *Bayit Sheni* a few blocks away, in a beautiful home once owned by a wealthy Arab or Turkish landlord who had fled to Lebanon.

There were classes in Hebrew, Jewish and Israeli history, arts, dancing, choir, and some free time for soccer and "gaga" interspaced with hikes and trips and meetings with political and literary figures. In return, we had to go back home and give two years of our lives as youth leaders for our respective movements (Habonim, Dror, Young Judea, B'nai Akiva) back in American or other countries—this was truly an international program—with young people from England, Ireland, France, Scandinavia, and Morocco.

That was followed by five months on kibbutz for the *chalutzic* (pioneering) movements. In my case, that was Gesher Haziv in the western Galilee, near the Mediterranean Sea, at the corner with the Lebanese border. That, too, was interspersed with *tiyulim* (hikes) throughout the country. I saw more of Israel than most tourists would see in a lifetime and places that only young people or very healthy elders would march through—desert, mountains, sleeping out in the open at night.

And the last two months were filled with more discussions in the Petach Tikvah area (near Tel Aviv) with specific study geared to our movements. It also included meetings with Labor and Socialist leaders like Golda Meir, Yigal Alon, and Jacob Barzilay.

It was quite a year. I was a bit young at seventeen, probably the youngest person on the Machon, but I was a fast learner and matured quickly. (I even had my first sexual encounter in Israel, and I describe it briefly in my diary.) It was also a chance to see for the first time my Israeli cousins, Yehuda and Luba Merin, and their children, Mina and Yossi; Avrum and Chaya Puchtik; Idka and her husband, Yaakov Shuster, and their children, Esther and Arick; plus other survivors and partisans: the Volpers, the Blausteins, and two young people who my parents "adopted" after the war but sadly had to be separated from in the DP camps (they wanted to go to Israel to be with an uncle while my parents went to America): Yechiel and his sister, Razzele Gittleman, their wives/husbands, and small children.

Also, by chance, I met another relative, Ben Porter (1887–1966) from Milford, Massachusetts, founder of the Milford Shoe Company and father to Barney, George, and Joe Porter. He was by then an old man (seventy-five years old) but still tough. I was only seventeen and a bit intimidated by him, but I am glad I met him when he was visiting Yehuda Merin at the Tel-Hashomer Hospital, where Yehuda was head of the Beit-Yoldot, the infant and children's section.

I also met the husband of Uncle Leon's daughter Batya—Shimon Levy, a Sephardic Jew. He was a bus driver in Beersheba, and we drove around on his route, and he told me the story of his wife. It's a strange story. Uncle Leon Puchtik had left for Argentina in the 1920s; Uncle Boris came later in 1937. Aunt Hinda, Boris's wife, came in 1939. They initially settled in the Chaco region in northern Argentina, and then in 1950 moved to Buenos Aires, the capital. Argentina wanted a middle class and invited many people from Italy, Germany, and Eastern Europe to come and settle. America was difficult to enter due to quotas.

While there, Leon and Boris got into the dry goods business, selling shirts, trousers, towels, sheets, and so forth, to the Spanish-speaking Argentinians. (Boris would later use these same skills to sell dry goods to Mexicans and other Latinos in Los Angeles.)

Leon had one daughter, Batya. Boris and Aunt Hinda, his wife, had three sons—Sam, Abe, and Jack—who eventually came to Los Angeles in the 1950s. All changed their name to "Porter" from "Puchtik." Why did Boris' Jack have the same name as me? I was born in Rovno, Ukraine, while the other Jack Porter was born in Buenos Aires (or possibly Chaco) at about the same time. My father, Irving, and Uncle Boris were unaware that each of their wives were giving birth at the same time but on two different continents. We were both named after a deceased grandfather named Jacob/Yaakov—"Jack" in English. That's the Jewish tradition: to name a child after a deceased relative.

But let's get back to Batya Puchtik. It seems that Uncle Leon, if I have the story right, had married a strange Jewish woman and she put Batya into a Catholic convent. Leon was very unhappy about that, and so he got Boris and Hinda to get Batya out—she was only thirteen years old. Batya eventually moved to Israel at age nineteen. There she met Mr. Levy, married him, and had several children.

Decades later, I met not only her but also her two sons and some grandchildren. Batya spoke only Hebrew and Spanish. At first she thought I was the "other" Jack

Porter, Boris' son. Sadly, she died in 2019, and I never got the entire story from her. Maybe she wanted to forget a painful episode in her life. Her sons, however, were grateful to have met me and to hear all of the Shoah and American stories from their newly discovered cousin.

Sources

Interestingly, there are few books or reminiscences of my kibbutz, Gesher Haziv. There is, however, a song composed by the late Sam Flesher of Pittsburgh called "Splendor Bridge." Achziv, the ancient Canaanite name for the nearby site, means "Splendor Bridge" in that language. It's a good song, and Sam is surely missed.

Several biographies of Arik Sharon have brought back many memories of my life on kibbutz and in Jerusalem: David Landau, *Arik: The Life of Ariel Sharon* (New York: Vintage Books/Random House, 2014) and Sharon's own memoir (written with David Chanoff), *Warrior* (New York: Simon & Schuster, 1989).

Why Sharon? Why has he captured my imagination as I write this at age seventy-five, and not David Ben-Gurion, Gold Meir, Yitzhak Rabin, or even Moshe Dayan or Abba Eban? Israel has been blessed with many charismatic and outstanding leaders, yet all have been flawed. No one has avoided scandal, loss, or defeat—not one. And Arik, even more so.

However, the Jerusalem of that time in the first decade and a half after World War II, 1945–1960, also has few memoirs, but Amos Oz's book *A Tale of Love and Darkness* (and the movie of the same name starring and directed by Natalie Portman, which did not do very well at the box office) echoes the Jerusalem of the early 1960s that I remember. Perhaps readers will fill in the lacunae here with other books and movies.

And now, my diary.

Israel Diary, 1963

I kept diaries, one when I was a teenager in Milwaukee (see chapter 2), and this one while in Israel. I think diaries are usually signs of a budding writer. They were some of my earliest writings. Sadly, I have only half of my Israel diary, dealing with my time at Kibbutz Gesher Haziv; the many *tiyulim* (hikes) we took (and will never take again) to parts of Israel one rarely sees; the four-day *Tza'ada* march, a kind of a "walking marathon" that involves the entire country (I can't believe I survived it), and trips to Galilee, Tiberiusm and Nazareth, culminating in seminars in Tel Aviv and Jerusalem. What a trip—but I am so upset I lost part 1.

Thursday, Jan. 31, 1963

This was the last day of the tiyul [hike] to Eilat and the Negev. We got up at 6:00, and packed, ate breakfast, bought some postcards, picked up more beautiful rocks, took pictures of the harbor and the bay and then continued upwards to the Wilderness of Zin (Midbav Zin) to see the Wadi Zin, Ein Avdat and Ein Mar. A beautiful wadi—with waterfall and pool amidst wall-like cliffs of limestone and flint—Climbed up the steep wall and to the buses which then took us to the fortress of Avdat, an ancient Nabatean, then later Roman, Byzantine, and lastly Moslem city. A Roman gate and wall-courtyard remain— Byzantine church with baptistery, Moslem temple, and Nabatean conduit and water systems—all beautifully constructed; ancient altars, tombs with Greek inscriptions and potsherds with Nabatean writing, Roman bath house. A most beautiful reconstruction. Ate lunch there and picked up more rocks and pottery handles—Saw the house and fields of Prof. Avi-Jonah from H. U. [Hebrew University] who lives on a nearby hill and is growing fruit trees and vegetables without irrigation water, just run-off water (This year is terrible—a great drought throughout the Negev—and floods in the upper Galilee; his experiment might die on the vine this year) and dew. Left from here to Kfar Yerucham to get gas and then to Beersheva, where we had an orange and tomato fight between the two buses (inside them). The ruach (spirit) was great on the buses—Did the twist, sang, and made a fool out of this girl, Elisha, who came along for the ride.

Great tiyul. Came back to Jerusalem at 8:30 and went for mail (got letter from Sandy [probably Sandy Goldstein, a Milwaukee girlfriend] and ate supper. Tired and dusty, took a shower and went right to sleep.

Friday, Feb. 1, 1963

Days are flying fast. It's been exactly 5 months in the country and only 6 more remaining. Had classes from 9:30–12 on the tiyul, given by Menachem—showed us film strip and talked about the human problem in the Neger. After lunch, we (Chevreh Habonim) found out that a decision from the maskirut [headquarters] in Tel Aviv that the Americans must go to Gesher Haziv for the entire period— entirely break away from the others who will go the B'ror Chayil 3 months and to their respective kibbutzim for the other months. I, personally, want to be at B'ror Chayil for the greater part and be with the Ichud [the Habonim people], as do all the Americans, but this Monday night—will be a meeting with Max Mader and Ephraim Bariach, the Mazkir Kupa of Ichud Habonim, and we will present our complaints to him then. This, plus our problems, have caused much distress on the part of the chaverim here, and I hope solutions can be found soon for both of these dilemmas. Tonight—I wrote in the diary and did map work.

Wednesday, Feb. 6, 1963

Today was our last day of the period of studying at the Machon. In the morning, at 9:30, we had a party in Bayit Sheni for our Hebrew class. We had games, singing, and food. Took some pictures, Drora was there, was a good party—even though the North Africans and the French had some troubles getting along. Afterwards, we had our final test in Zionism by Haim. After lunch, I packed my luggage to go to Gesher Haziv, which all the Americans are going to, except for Rivkah from Canada, who's going to B'ror Hayil to be with her boyfriend from Morocco. Tonight, our chavurah meeting was in Bayit Sheni, and first we had the serious part, which everyone gave their impressions of the country and the other part—consisted of Sibyl, dressed as me in my clothes and I in Sybil Lamb's (she's English) dress and sweater and bra, singing as a duet on a farewell note. I sang [Joan] Baez's "Silver Dagger." Good show. Handed in my paper on "Jerusalem" [on the water system of Jerusalem].

Thursday, Feb. 7, 1963

Today, last day before our Hofesh [free time] starts before Kibbutz begins. (For me—a week from tomorrow) Went into town to buy some film (b. & w. 36 shots) and make a call to Tiberias about my sleeping bag, which wasn't there. I also got a tape from home.

This evening was the grand finale of the   classes. Called Ben Kaiser to come, the Workshop (some) were there, the African students from the H. U., guest and friends and teachers. Crowded to the hilt. First, Haim [Avni] taking the place of Moshe Levin, who has pneumonia, gave a talk, a farewell address. Then the *makela* performed very well with drum, guitar, and accordion accompaniment. A skit by the dramatics class with Shir, Sammy, and Steve Rosenblum. Dances by the rikud group, a very funny skit on married life by the French—all in Hebrew—and afterwards, a lot of dancing and singing outside.

Ben and I went back to Bayit Sheni and found my beds and other [things] wet—raid by the girls—sang and he played a guitar. Took the doors apart from ours and others' rooms. Had a blast. Hit the sack at 2:00 a.m.

Friday, Feb. 8, 1963

Got up at 9—went straight to the American Consulate in Jerusalem to get my draft release—signed by Consul Henderson. (It was 2 months late.) Returned to the Machon, handed in my utensils and sleeping gear and went to the session of the "complaints and changes-to-be on the Machon." Talked about some (1) poor teachers, (2) more direction in chugim, (3) better psychology classes, (4) better selection of candidates, (5) and better tiyul prep. Ate lunch, packed, took 2:00 train to Tel Aviv to [my cousin] Batya's house. Ate something, relaxed, and went to Avrum's [Avrum Puchtik, another cousin] house for Shabbat—showed them pix—Left kids at Avrum's house, went back to Batya and then listened to radio, took shower, read. Jacob and Batya went to play cards at [Ata's] friends' house. I stayed home to relax and listen to the Voice of America program. Hit the sack at 12:30.

Saturday, Feb. 9, 1963

Got up at about 10:00, went with Yakov and his wife out to visit—first to the Hatikvah section of Tel Aviv to see the Volpor family. His son is going into the army on Monday. Went to soccer game nearby—Beitar vs. Hapoel—Tel Aviv. (1) Took pic of the family on a vespa—from here. Yakov took me to Jaffa—where I took pics of the (2) old port, (3) the view to Tel Aviv, (4) old church and mosque. We went to [my cousin] Idel Merin's house next, and I said good-bye to them. Returned to his home—where I ate and rested—played with little Esther. At night, took his BMW for a bar mitzvah party in Holon—Very nice affair—The boy gave speech. Had combo—drummer (sang also), accordion, violinist—played and sang Russian, Yiddish and Hebrew songs. The family, the Maliks, are related to the Landes [friends in Milwaukee]. Got home at 11:00.

Sunday, Feb. 10, 1963

Left, after breakfast, for downtown Tel Aviv, paid one [Israeli] pound to see Van Gogh's paintings at Helena Rubenstein pavilion—met Billy, Judy Lubitz and her boyfriend from Spain, Michel Ben-Tata. Bought book (2.50) on Van Gogh's works—very interesting. Rushed to train station—just made the station—took the train (12:30) to Jerusalem. In Ramla, saw many Bedouins and their flocks. In Jerusalem, rushed around—got my laundry, sent a package off (3.80) by regular mail to parents (gifts), packed, and bought some 20-Gevacolor film (7.50)—went to Ben Kaiser's house—talked, ate, and went to the Chen movie theater—"Taras Bulba"—exciting, but by far a childish show. Went back to Machon—waited for Arnie to come with the key, and when he came (12:00), went right to sleep.

Monday, Feb. 11, 1963

Got up at 6:30—ate breakfast, and waited around for the truck to load. Loaded the truck of luggage for Yehi'Am, Tirat Zvi, Gesher Haziv, and Maayan Baruch. I, Steve Leon, Arnie Geffman sat in the back—slept and talked 'til we got to Gesher Haziv—to drop my luggage off. Ate something there and put the luggage in the workshop's storage area. Yoel from Holland and Stu Simmons from California were both going to the Hashomer kibbutz (Yehi-Am) after my stop at G. Haziv. Said "shalom"—The maskir of the kibbutz showed us the place. I went right to sleep—slept right through dinner.

Tuesday, Feb. 12, 1963

Got up at 9:30, washed, and started tramping to Nahariya—lost my wallet— had no money for bus, no luck in tramping—started to walk, met a worker from Europe, Moshe Zuckerman (13 years in country)—we started talking, and he gave me 23 agorot to take bus. Landed in Nahariya, was very cloudy and rain- filled day—there was even some rain (4 mm) in Eilat. Saw the Canaanite (1800 B. C.) temple ruins on the beach, took pic no. 1 on new roll of Gevacolor. Went to beach, and wrote this diary. At 3:45—started for the city proper to cash my traveler's checks, eat, and get a haircut. Saw the town a little. Took bus to Haifa, went to Soeurs de St. Charles, 105 Rechov Jaffa Roman Catholic Hospice. Couldn't get in, went to Israel Hotel—paid 3.50 IL. for room. Took walk, paid 30 ag. for coffee at kiosk, returned and hit the sack at 10:30.

Wednesday, Feb. 13, 1963

Got up at 10:30 and started looking for the Maritime Museum on 2 Rehov Ha-namal. Found it in sailors' home at entrance to the port. Interesting replicas of Phoenician, Egyptian, Crusader, and modern-day ships. Also—the section of the captured Egyptian ship taken in Haifa in 1956. From here, went to the old Technion building and to the government tourist office to find out which buses go to places of interest and of cheap hotels. Ate breakfast (1.15) and then took bus to new Technion buildings, quite far removed from the city proper. Took pics of the buildings and views of Valley of Zebulan. Then went to the

Gan Hazikaron [Garden of Remembrance] for a pic of the harbor and Turkish cannon. Then took bus 25 to the Western Carmel to see the Carmelite Monastery for a look at the cave of Elijah and the beautiful murals painted in the apse (at the Technion—Turk came up to me for money)—Took pic of the monastery. Had talk with the monk there on how the meaning of Zionism has changed since Herzl's time. Returned, after taking some pics of Haifa and coast and of an iron cross marking the graves of Napoleon's soldiers, who used the place as a hospital (1799) on his way to Acre. From here to the Aliya hotel (3 IL), went back for my bag at other hotel, got haircut, and rested 'til about 8:00. Went out to a movie—"Escape from Zahrain"—filmed in [Saudi] Arabia or Jordan—a lot of the scenery was similar to the Judean desert and the southern Negev. Bunked with 2 army boys—Hit the sack on about 11:30.

Thursday, Feb. 14, 1963

Got up at 9:00—Checked out at about 9:30—Went to Bahai temple to see the gold-domed tomb of their late leader and founder, Bahua'allah—Had to enter without shoes; the lady in charge was from Milwaukee, and she gave me her father's address there. From here, I took a bus to see the Carmelite monastery of Elijah—beautiful interior—rich collection of artifacts from the time of the Greeks to the Arab conquest. Got into discussion with one of the monks there on the "supposed" change of Zionism since Herzl's time—He was quite interested. Saw the tomb for Napoleon's soldiers in 1799. Returned to the bus station and took it to Acre—Entered the old city on a road built right through a Crusader[10] moat and then proceeded to the museum of Akko—a Christian Moslem and later a French guy showed me around the museum—beautiful replicas of Arab life—Saw 12th-century St. John Crypt-church. Then I paid a little Arab boy 12 ag. to show me around, he was bothered by his friends, to see Pasha al Jazzar Mosque and minaret—Saw the interior of the Moslem house of prayer—sanctioned by the government as a Makom-Kodesh [a Holy Place]. Went to the Citadel—a Turkish building surrounded by a moat—a prison, the strongest in all the Mandate—the place filmed in the movie "Exodus" where Dov and Barak escaped—although this is a bit untrue because they were recaptured and executed. Saw the execution room—the rope, trap door, red "death" shirt, cement weight used to test the rope, map of the Irgun's Israel draw by a terrorist, Dov Grunner—8 men died here in all—now it's an insane asylum. Took pics of

---

10 The moat belongs to Monfort Castle.

the Akko wall to the sea, the mosque—etc.—etc. Then boarded bus to Gesher Haziv to end my interesting trip.

Ate supper—found my room, and I'm bunking with Karl from Buffalo, maskir now.

Dave Scheiderman from Brooklyn—ex-Sadran Avodah [work organizer], and Alan Feldman, ex-maskir—good group of guys—Too early to know, but I think I'll do all right here. Hit the sack at 11:00.

Friday, Feb. 15, 1963

Got up at 8:30—ate breakfast—finished packing and then lolled around the kibbutz a bit. Did my laundry—marked my no. 42 on all my clothes. Will pick it up in a week. At night—at the Kabbalat Shabbat—sang Kiddush and had supper. Had meat—beef. Good. After supper—went to my "parents"—Chaya and Zvi Baer—Americans—with Billy and Marsha. Had coffee and cake—good time—Then saw the movie in the dining hall—"A Summer Place"—a real blast to the Israelis and Americans.

Tomorrow, a tiyul—went to sleep at 12:00.

Saturday, Feb. 16, 1963

Got up at 5:45—washed and went to eat breakfast. Started on our practice tiyul to Yichiam, a Shomer Hatzair kibbutz where Yoel and the French are. He has my wallet, and I thought I'd get it, but it was impossible this time—They were at a seminar in Tel Aviv. The walk was fairly hard—rested in many places—Ga'aton and ½ hour at [. . .]. There was a well-preserved Crusader fortress there—Took pics here—Had to be careful of falling walls and caverns, the ticks which cause a type of Rocky Mountain fever. Also saw the bunkers and graves of some members who fell. Returned in the rain—ran under some elephant grass, surrounding the banana groves. Muddy, tired, and legs painful, we returned to Gesher Hazir. Ate lunch, slept 'til 5:30 (from 2:00), ate supper—potatoes, herring, and eggs—at 7:00. Had discussions on our joining the workshop's Kupa [collective money dispersal]. We'll decide later. Found out, I will work in the lool—turkey runs.

Hit the sack at 11:00.

Sunday, Feb. 14, 1963 to Saturday, March 7, 1963

My work has taken me to weeding and cleaning plots of ground—By working with Yehuda Lehr, I've gotten to know him pretty well. Even had coffee at his house during work. I've also worked in the dining room, washing dishes and setting tables, shalchin—sorting potatoes, weeding strawberries, and in the banana fields, where they've planted a new grove—hard work, carrying banana roots to the place.

Had some problems with classes because some guys—Billy, Phil Saffir, and Danny Gabler—have fooled around and Geula, our Hebrew teacher, almost quit. But she's back, I hope, for good. All those that miss class can't go to work. That's the "punishment." Menucha Kraines teaches us Tanach.

Our practices for the Tza'ada [a national four-day march] have included a run to Rosh Hanikva and the Sasa Crossing and back. Had a walk to Matzuda also on a Saturday.

Friday, March 1, 1963

Had movie in dining hall—"Fortunat"—French movie, good. Spent some time at Tzvi and Chaya's house. Listened to "My Son, the Folk Singer" record by Allan Sherman.

Tuesday, March 5, 1963

Today, after work in bananas—It was raining off and on the whole day. Today, I decided to take a bike ride into Nahariya and Yehi'am (to see the Hashomer Machon kids). Borrowed Miky's bike and, in Nahariya, bought color film and a wool cap (2 K.). Then, started to bicycle up to Yehi'Am. Started to rain, ducked under Egged bus station. Got so hard to pedal. I stopped—got a hitch from a kibbutznik of Yehi'Am to the place. Found Sabbetai and Joel from Holland, got my wallet with the 10IL., saw Stu and others, ate supper there, saw their Bet Tarbut [cultural house]. Got a ride from pickup truck (tender) to Nahariya— pedaled back to Gesher Haziv.

Friday, March 8, 1963

Purim! A mixture of Halloween and New Year's Eve. Everyone dressed up as a bathing beauty, Larry Stoller and Steve Ornstein as "queens," I as a Cossack— "Indians," spacemen, and so forth. Had program of skits by the *chevreh*, hillbilly band and "flappers" by workshop. Drank wine, whisky—didn't get drunk, just dizzy. Hit the sack at 5:30.

Saturday, March 9, 1963

Got up at 12:30—ate lunch with Mrs. Shanfield, Mel's mother, who had come in last night on Hadassah tour. Spent afternoon with Mrs. Shanfield and Billy Hammerman. At night, packed for Negev (7 days) and saw movie "The Last Angry Man."

Sunday, March 10, 1963

First day of tiyul was mostly riding down to Be'er Sheva—passing kids dressed up for Purim, to pick up Rami Pellowski and Myron Seifer. Went to new town of Arad—looked around—Has changed a little since I was last there. Had talk by town planner on its development. Continued to Rosh Zohar—to sleep there—outside—dew got in—slept well anyway. As rosh tiyul [hike leader] got toranut [cleanup], etc. ready. We carry our own food and water all the time. Cans of sprats, eggs, etc., for breakfast. Hash—chicken soup for supper. Sausage and beans for lunch.

Monday, March 11, 1963

Got up at 4:30, wet, freezing cold, drank tea, and started to march to Masada (28 km) through the beautiful, rugged terrain. Hot, thirsty—got to 8th Roman camp on hill higher than Masada, which overlooks it, but is too far away to do anything to it by warfare. Climbed down—helping the girls and finally got to youth hostel—made my sleeping bag—got some beer—ate supper—wrote diary—went to sleep at 10:00.

Tuesday, March 12, 1963

Got up at 3:45, packed food for breakfast and walked up Masada. I was tired (5 hours of sleep) but made it. Saw the storehouses, walls, ramp the Romans built to get to the zealots. After another walk down the bank path on the western side, we ate lunch and went to Ein Gedi. Saw the kibbutz, swam (floated) in the Dead Sea. Saw the Maayan-Nahal David. Ate supper. Group of Tel Aviv students were there also. Slept in wadi under stars. Had shmira [guard duty] from 2–3. Got up at 5.

Wednesday, March 13, 1963

Walked through Nahal Arugot near Ein Gedi. Swam in spring at end of it. Ate breakfast there. Took buses to S'dom. Ate lunch. Saw potash, bromine dredges of Dead Sea. Took new road along Arava border past Beer Menuha to Yotvata. Was exciting because of nearness of [Jordanian] border and grave danger along the way. Our guns were ready at Yotvata, ate in dining room, took shower after long ride. Slept on grass. Went to sleep at 12:00.

Thursday, March 14, 1963

Got up at 5:30 and went into Eilat. Ate breakfast at Yotvata (peanut butter!). South of Eilat, took tiyul to a wadi near Nahal Shlomo, saw Eilat and Aquaba from a high hill. Ate lunch at *Tnuva* [dairy] restaurant. Went swimming in the Red Sea, found coral and shells. Slept on beach near Eilat Coral Beach (Hof Almogi). Ate supper there. Slept well except for the sand that got in the sleeping bag. Had middurah [campfire] on beach—stories about Mt. Shasta by the Californians.

Friday, March 15, 1963

At 5:30, got up and packed and went to Amud (Pillars of) Amram, to get the beautiful colored sand there. I got some cans to hold the sand. From here to Amudei Shlomo to see Solomon's pillars and mines. Picked up some slag [copper remains] and pieces of copper around the smelting pits. Ate breakfast here. The *ruach* [spirit] was great in our truck—singing all the way. Traveled the long road to Avdat after passing Mitzpe Rimon to see the Machtash [the crater] (all foggy) and buy a print in the Nabatean Inn there. At Avdat it began to rain and got very foggy. Saw the antiquities on the high hill but rain cut it short. Ate a delicious Friday meal—veal, rice, etc., at the restaurant there. Raining and lightning got harder as we took the long ride up to Gesher Haziv. Tired, hungry, dirty—got there as movie was showing in the dining hall—ate something and slept 'til 12:30 next day. Got letter from Ronny Laux and a note to pick up package of film that John [Gilman] sent me. Also a tape that Moshe Ezry sent to record dances and songs.

Thursday, March 25, 1963

Practice for the Tza'adah [march]. Walked to Akko—32 km, and the next day to Atzmit, a Hashomer Hatzair kibbutz on the border of Lebanon and Israel.

Last part of march was uphill and hard. Ate lunch at kibbutz and marched back, passed Shlomi and Metzubah. The marches were very hard, worried about making the Tza'adah, which is in about a week.

Monday, April 1—Thursday, April 4, 1963

Didn't work Sunday. Took a truck with about 18 guys and 10 girls. Got to Kibbutz Hulda, got our numbers [for the four-day march] and our tents. What beautiful soldierettes! What guns! Met Doug Renk and that night went to the Kibbutz to see the Y.J. [Young Judea] kids. Howie Druch was at Hazerim. The next morning got up at 3:00. Went over to girls' quarters and ate breakfast. Got a little lost and couldn't find the group—walked the first 10 km with the Bodidim. At the first rest stop—marched together with them through the crowded streets of Lod and Ramla—returned to Hulda to spend the night. The next day got up at same time and went through Nes Tziona and Rehovot—which was the biggest town. We were wearing khaki pants, blue shirts, and red hats. Really looked good!! Finished O. K. except for bad blisters which worry me. At night—went to the grandstand to see the talent put on by the people on the Tza'ada, which included 16,000 people (8,000 soldiers). The next day—Got up at 2:30 A.M. for the 3rd day—which was to be the hardest of all. Left Hulda for Bet Shemash, passing Kibbutz Nachshon, where in 1948, operations began to free Jerusalem from Arab strangulation. Was hamsin [dry, hot desert wind] out—very hard—3 girls had to turn back. Finally made it—and found there was no water to take a shower—so I had a couple of Artic "popsicles." Bet Shemesh, as the name implied, is hot and humid. Was it ever! Ate and slept sound with my blisters aching. The last day—marched—didn't feel a thing on the way to the Kastel [a hill], and then to the airport outside where we got our medals, pin, certificate from an army officer. We made it!!

Got off the windy field and ate with the Machoniks from Bror Chayil. We got ready a couple of hours later and after discussion on marching—Some didn't—but we went and then had bickering with the Machoniks on our different outfits. Some name-calling. But entered Jerusalem in cheers and sang well—Was tremendous. Yom Tov's mother kissed him in the street and gave him a wreath. Found results, we were 9th out of more than 60 groups! The Golani Brigade was first in army units. Got our luggage and left in truck for long trip home. A party greeted us. Geula and Esty were there—coffee, cake, etc. Good night. Slept well.

Monday, April 8, 1963

Seder night

I was glad I spent Seder night here. There were some 700 people attending, including a family from Glendale [Wisconsin]—tourists. A man from a kibbutz near Natanya, brother to Moshe Sharett, Yehuda, directed the choir and wrote the songs for it. Lot of drinking and eating, but I missed home and a simple type of Seder.

Tuesday, April 9, 1963

There was a day of rest for everyone. In the afternoon there was a program for the cutting of the first sheaves. There was dancing and singing and cutting of the sheaves with scythes.

Sunday, April 28, 1963

Today was Memorial Day. But a different one—the President had died—Ben-Tzvi died of cancer in Jerusalem. Big effect all over Israel. Shazar was elected new president. For the memorial day celebrations, the Workshop went to Kibbutz Lochamei Hagetaot for a most thrilling and inspiring dramatization of dance (modern), fire displays, and colored smoke and a 20-gun salute on the ancient aqueduct above. There was also a tour of the ghetto fighters museum, with paintings and pictures of the period of the Holocaust. The only thing that spoiled the effect was the pushing and shouting of the overflow crowd, like that at Ben-Tzvi's funeral parade. I missed it, being on kibbutz. Another sore spot was the selling of ice cream, etc., with screaming vendors, et al. But it was, on the whole, good. Nathan Alterman, Yigal Allon, etc., spoke, and Golda Meir.

Other events in May were as follows:

1) Yom Atzmaut celebration. Workshop and Tanganyikans (African students) went down to Haifa by truck. Saw new tanks and Mirages [planes].
2) Ron and Yael's wedding on *meshek* (farm).
3) Bar Mitzvah of 9 boys and girls.
4) Potato picking 'til Friday, May 31, my last work day on Kibbutz Gesher Haziv.

5) Met Patrick Bouquet from Paris and Mike from Jerusalem (H. U. [Hebrew University student). Went with Patrick to party at Kiryat Hof and met some easy Moroccan girls. Patrick got his already from one. Got permission to go through Europe, will stay at Pat's place in Paris. [Frenchmen were always sexy to the Moroccan women. Morocco was a French colony.—J. N. P.]

Thursday, May 29, 1963

Went to Akko with Pat and Mike to buy a Finjan [coffeepot] set (18 IL.). Saw the mosque and Abu Cristol's café, the usual sites. Pat and Mike went to Jerusalem for a few days. Took bus to Shevi Tzion to see the moshav shitufi, the Dolphin House, beach (4th-century church excavating). Took bus back to Gesher Haziv.

Sunday, June 2, 1963

After saying goodbye and packing yesterday, today went with Workshop to their Tel Aviv seminar, left at 7:30, went to see Technion and Bet Aron kibbutz in the Carmel Mts. where the Palmach struck out from. Past Atlit, witnessed accident on the road.

Arrived in the Pioneer Women center in Petach Tikvah. Ate lunch (2:00). Took bus to Tel Aviv to Sde Dor, came too late to catch flight to Rosh Pina. Saw museum Haaretz and Tel Qacil, the Yarkon river, etc. Slept very uncomfortably in abandoned house near airport. Mosquitoes were terrible.

Monday, June 3, 1963

Took flight (13.50) to Rosh Pina at 6:45. Met rabid anti-US German man on plane. Beautiful flight—Kinneret Lake from distance, Haifa, Galilee wonderful. Got ride (tramp) to Sefad in tender [a truck]. A fantastic city—Artist colony— Kabbalist synagogue. No room at Hostel—Went to Haari synagogue—met Yakov, the guide whom I met 9 months ago on Har Zion. Got me a room—paid 3 IL. for it (Swell!) at the boarding house of the synagogue mentioned above. Shaved, washed up. Was so tired—fell asleep in the afternoon. Ate supper (hummus) and walked around Sefad. Hit the sack around 12:00.

Tuesday, June 4, 1963

Got up at around 8—visited the ancient graveyard—Joseph Caro—Ha-ari, prophet Hosea—etc.—the old synagogues, the Metzuda—the Roman fort and war memorial there. Had lunch of techina and soda. From the Metzuda, one can see an enormous distance—to the east—Kinneret, to the northwest—Mt. Meron and Meron—highest point in Israel. A large group of Israeli students, who filled up the youth hostel where I wanted to stay were there also. In the late afternoon, went to Artists' Colony—bought some lithographs (8 of them—originally 10 IL.) of "Landscapes of Israel" by Zvi Livni, for 5 IL. Best deal of my life. I think they're beautiful!

By the way, also bought a beautiful scarf there also. The tomb of Hosea is also a genizah (an ancient library) and with the caretaker's permission—I took some old parchment scrolls of Megilat Esther.

About 2 or 3, I packed, said shalom to Mrs. Vavik, and walked to the outskirts of Sefad and quickly (couldn't have come sooner—I was almost dying from the terrible hamsin—40°F). Got a lift down the mount to the Rosh Pina-Tiberias road and from there a tender to Kibbutz Amiad to see the British kids. Entered the tzrif [cabin] where Bernie Burns, Frankie Fisher, and Jeff Marks lived. Talked for a while, ate supper—met Sylvie, Judy, Elaine, and others. Joy had returned to England 'cuz her father had died!

Saw French film and discussed the Machon until late.

Wednesday, June 5, 1963

Got up around 8—ate breakfast—and went to the road to start hitching. Before I leave Kibbutz Amiad—a little about it. Founded 1949 as Palmach base, strengthened by British Habonim. Main crops are meat cattle, bananas, and fruit trees.

On the road, met a guy named Alan Dorfman from Kibbutz Hasolilim. Walked a bit and then got a tender ride to Tiberias—saw the sea, old fortifications, Rambam's tomb—Yohanan-ben-Zakai's tomb, the new and old city. Then took a bus (31 ag.) to Kibbutz Lavi. Met Basil Rose, friend (cousin) of Rothman's. Ate supper and went to sleep.

Beautiful kibbutz—gardens—lovely synagogue. Basil seems like a nice guy—wife and 3 kids, 2 of them sick, but he's a bit vague about everything I ask him—and deathly boring to be with, but a fine man, anyway.

Thursday, June 6, 1963

Slept 'til 2—ate lunch and with camera and guide book—went through the prickly weeds to see Karnei Hittin the Horns of Hittin—where in 1187, the

Moslems, under Saladin, defeated the Crusaders and took the entire Holy Land. The fortified walls and towers, fighting areas are still visible—Beautiful vista—Arbel, Sea of Galilee, Kfar Hittim, Mt. Tabor, valleys. Saw monument by church group on way down. Came back very tired. Fire alarm was heard—there was a blaze on the Karnei Hittin—went in sandals to put it out—Very small one. I had seen the smoke that afternoon but thought nothing of it. Got on work for tomorrow. Spent a while at Basil's home—wrote letters at the cultural center

Saw guys playing chess and one sewing up a Torah—Began wearing a yarmulke. Hit sack at 11:15.

Friday, June 7, 1963

Got woken up by the night guard and went to dining hall to have tea. Went down to Yavne'el Valley to work in the cow beets with Aussie, a German man who's been with the kibbutz since its inception in 1949. Great guy. A lot friendlier than Basil and much nicer to be around. Brought up a load of beets—2 Arab workers from Tura there. Asked me the same question—Do I like Israel better than America? Took the beets to the cattle shed and piled them off there. They finish them off fast. Went back for another load and then stopped work at 1:00. Ate lunch and then got ready for Shabbat. Ironed my pants and shirt, polished my boots, etc. Overslept the meal. Talked with Aussie and wife 'til late. Had coffee until bedtime.

Saturday, June 8, 1963

Aussie's wife woke me at 7:30. Got dressed, rested 8:45—Went to services in their lovely synagogue with Basil. Short service, interrupted by exchanging of the Torah scrolls because of a change or omission in a word or letter. Young boy sang the same *haftarah* [Torah portion] I had almost 5½ years ago. Ate breakfast and then went back to room to write letters and sleep a while. Missed supper and then around 9:30—said farewell to Basil and Aussie.

Went to sleep around 10 or 11.

A religious kibbutz is not much different than any other—except that it breeds into its youngsters a knowledge of Torah and Avodah. They're fairly strict, too—no smoking at all on Shabbat. I couldn't even take a picture of Basil's family. Thanks to Basil's help (?), I didn't enjoy myself here as much as I intended, but it gave me an insight into another aspect of Israel.

Tomorrow—Nazareth and its aspects.

Sunday, June 9, 1963

After eating at 8:15, went down to the Tiberias-Nazareth road and began to try and hitch. Even with 2 soldiers and girl, Ginger Golden (from Skokie, Hamlin and Dempster), a good-looking blond with a wow figure, couldn't get a lift—so I took a bus to Nazareth (76 ag.), through interesting Arab towns. In Nazareth, put my pack in a restaurant and went to St. Joseph's church (Joseph's workshop and home was supposed to be here), where a wedding had just taken place between 2 Arabs. Gala affair. Saw the Church of Annunciation and the new basilica under construction since 1955—should be a grand church. Went to see Mary's Well and second Church of Annunciation. Bought John Gilman his two tofim [clay drums] (10 IL. and 9 IL.) to send it, almost broke me. Got into discussion with English-speaking Arab—a teacher—on the military government which he naturally was against and B.G. [David Ben-Gurion] (he's against) and Nasser and Jordan. Very interesting. Went to café, got my bags (pack) and walked to the outskirts of town. Little traffic—I had forgotten Nazareth is a *Christian* Arab town. Got a lift to Afula from a moshavnik from Balfouria—at Afula, met Philly women 27 years in country. From Afula, got lift from a Vatik [a veteran Israeli] from Ein Herod to Geva, to see Tzvika Gurien and his wife. Had coffee, met the kids—lovely kids. Had supper. Discussed the Machon and Workshop, work in the movement, etc. Met Mel Parness from Milwaukee and his Israeli wife. Spent the evening at Tzvika's place with Mel. Saw Tzvika put the kids to sleep. They have the children sleep separately from parents at Geva.

Monday, June 10, 1963

Today, Tzvika showed me around the kibbutz—milking the sheep for cheese-making, the cowsheds, the children's rooms—the pool and B.B. [basketball] court, the members' clubhouse, etc. He went to work in potato fields, and I went to sleep for the afternoon. Dina woke me up—ate, and relaxed at Tzvika's house—It's actually a double-story apartment (Geva has about 200 members—found in 1923). Ate at 8:00 and went to a small Kumsitz at a friend of the Guriens. Sang, had coffee and cake—very pleasant. Met French and British chaps.

Tuesday, June 11, 1963

Next morning—said shalom to the Guriens, went to dining hall to grab a cup of tea. Got a ride all the way to Kfar Vitkin from Tzvika's brother. At Vitkin, found I couldn't stay—so I got lift 'til Petach Tikvah and the Workshop. Stayed here 'til Thursday. On Wednesday, went into Tel Aviv to find Eileen's relatives [possibly my American girlfriend, Eileen Ross]—couldn't—Visited the Dan Hotel—the beach area—new El-Al building. Saw Tel Aviv from above. Magnifico!

Thursday, June 13, 1963

Left Petach Tikvah about 8:30 after breakfast and took bus to the highway before B'nai B'rak and began tramping south to visit Ben on the [Ashdod] archeological site. Got a ride to the Beit Dagon crossroad by Jeep, from there a lift by tender to the Gedera crossroad and from there to the site by car. Went right to place where the archeological building was and found Ben. His girl is coming next week. He looked good. Nice set-up, too. Watched him repair his pottery and walked around the sites—A—B—C—D. There's the main one—"D" and the one below it—"B" and spread around are "X," "A" and "C"—Each section has a leader (director) and workers. They first dig loci in an area and then see what they find and dig more slowly and carefully, leaving big pottery and statues, skeletons, etc., to the expert. All dirt is carted away, and all potsherds, etc., are put in special buckets and marked as to section and place. Met Vivian—sabra—and Howie Druch (this was a surprise!), Jen, and Bernie—from Y. J. [the Young Judea Youth Group]—The excavation wants to put light on the Philistine era of history—it covers early Bronze, Israelite, Persian, Greece, Roman, and Byzantine. Dr. Dothan is the main director. The expedition is funded by the Carnegie Museum and the Theological Seminary of Pittsburgh and Dept. of Antiquities. Went to Ben's room by tender. He lives in an abandoned British army barrack of the 2nd World War. Wrote a letter and then ate supper Kfar Mitzanim—a children's village. Talked and visited and then joined a poker game with Howie and some Israelis. Lost 2 ILs. No cards were coming to me. Lost on a 9-high full house to Howie's queen-high to Moshe's Ace-high. Stopped at 1:00.

Friday, June 14, 1963

Got up at 6:00—ate and went out to the Tel to help. Worked all day on the side of a wall in Section "B." Dug and brushed and carried away dirt. Ate lunch under a tent near the bullet-ridden main building. Accidentally, broke a pot open at the top, left the entire bottom exposed in the hard ground. Helped wash pottery for a while, also work ended early around 2:30. Went and got washed up for Shabbat. Howie and others went to Jerusalem for the weekend. Ate supper and danced a little afterwards.

Saturday, June 15, 1963

Slept 'til 9, ate breakfast and then read, slept 'til supper. There was a movie, "La Nuit" by Antonioni, which I couldn't understand and was way too high for a lot of the youngsters. Played some cards 'til 12:00.

Sunday, June 16, 1963

Got up around 6:30—Howie and the rest returned from Jerusalem. Went right to site with my pack and camera because I'm leaving today. Started right in working in "D," on the top—Working in a little section of the Persian period—found 2 weights and a button-like object used as a weight in spinning and weaving. Ecstatic! Working 'til lunch and said goodbye, filled my bag with handles [discarded jug handles—today you could not do that. Years later, I gave them to the Carnegie Museum in Pittsburgh.—J. N. P.] and went to the road to begin tramping. Waited from 2–4:30 until a moshavnik, driving a horse, a victim of Bergen-Belsen and possibly drunk, raddled on about how great the Jewish race is and nothing can destroy it. Finally a car picked me up, took me all the way, through the modern garden homes (!) of (Savyon), to the outside of Petach Tikvah, took bus to the seminar. Came during sicha and waited 'til supper and met everyone from Dror, Hashomer Hatzair, Ha-noar Hatzioni, Ichud Habonim. The discussion that night was on the history of all the [socialist] youth movements—Wandervogel and Scouts, etc. Hardly understood a word. I hope this doesn't continue. Lights out at 11:00.

Monday, June 17, 1963—Thursday, July 4, 1963

These last 3 weeks have been spent in Petach Tikvah at the Bet Olot. The 1st two weeks for the socialist [pioneering] groups, and the last one just for Ichud Habonim [my group—J. N. P.]. The general seminar had talks all day long. Meals were great. Roomed with Yakov Resnick, a Parisian turned Israeli citizen recently. How happy he is? Some of our speakers have been Moshe Sharett, Yaakov Sharett, his son (spoke on Russian Jewry), M. K. [Member Knesset] Barzilai of Liberals and Azanya of Mapai, Yigal Allon, Minister of Labor. We also took a tour of the Vaad Ha-poel and the publishing house of Dvir, the Histadrut paper. One evening, we also went to Habima to see a play—"Children of the Shadow" ("Yalder Ha-tzeil") or Yaram. Another night we went into Jaffa to see the satirical theater of El Haman—an old Arabic bath house, converted into a theatre and bar. The satire, presented in song and old vaudeville style, was very cutting—especially on the Sephardim vs. Ashkenazim and Shimon Peres, B. G. and relationships with Germany.

Took a walk through old Jaffa before the show—had Scotch before the show also.

Our seminar was good except it wasn't very serious in most cases. Very informal. Roomed with Reznick and Laurie—Played a lot of cards. Heard my second tape at the home Yakov Reznick's relatives for the first time in 5–6 months. Got a check for $200 for Europe, which I promptly put into the bank as Israeli IL. (600 IL.) Took 33 IL. to buy a good Swiss watch. Then, on July 4, the night that fireworks should fire off—we had a quiet party of the Ichud. Mina and Shlomo recently married (she's from Canada—he's from Maroc and later Paris) came to the party. She looked great. She looks more than her 18 years—he, more than his 22. Drank a lot of wine and had a good time generally.

The next day, will leave for Tel Aviv.

Friday, July 5, 1963

Today went over to the Shusters and Puchtiks to visit. Idka and her husband were going to Haifa for a bar mitzvah, so I went to visit Pesel Bronstein—now remarried and called Leiberman. She told me wonderful and sad stories about my brit [circumcision] and how she and her kids and mom escaped the Nazis after they entered the village where they lived. Stayed overnight Friday and next day, went to Yeheil to see his new set of twins—his first kids—They cry, shit, and sleep all day. Yeheil seems a bit tired, yet very happy. Went with him one night to see "Kid Galahad"—fair movie like the lot of them. Took pictures of Yeheil and his wife and of the kids.

On Sunday—have to leave for the z'man sikum [culminating sessions] in Jerusalem.

Sunday, July 7, 1963

From today 'til the 21st—I'll be at the Machon in Jerusalem. Took bus into Jerusalem and met some UJY [Union of Jewish Youth] and Hanoar Hatzioni kids. Got our rooms, which are in a school building; sleeping on cots with mattresses and eating over across the street in the Machon building near the Ulpan Etzion. Right at the Machon mentioned above is a group, ITT, Israel Tour for Teenagers (teen-age tourists). They spend time on Kibbutz and Moshav. Met a girl there—Nancy Goldman from N. Y., quit high school—went to art school—she's pretty good with pen and ink—very lucid characters. Wants to model for some painter in Paris—very mixed-up and neurotic kid. I have a feeling I can go to bed with her if I find the right place and time. Arranged my things that night for laundry tomorrow.

Monday, July 8, 1963

Begin the day with breakfast at 8:00. Sicha [discussion] on various topics at 8:30 and then the methodology of Hebrew, which are very good, given by Ora [a female teacher].

This lasts till lunch at 12:30—In the afternoon—there's the dance and song rehearsals and final lessons and review. At night—took Nancy out to town with Mike Axcen. He was pissed off—I didn't bring a girl for him. The two of them didn't get along well in Bacchus (a joint like the "Unique"); he left because she wouldn't sit by him. I had forgotten my wallet so Mike lent me 5 IL. and left in a fluff and a puff. I stayed and ordered 2 orders each of grapefruit juice and we talked about her art-work and she tells she's been using a diaphragm for the last year, she speaks very candidly and with no embarrassment. I feel now she'll be really easy to go to bed with.

Well, the bill finally comes to 5.50 and I talk the guy down to 4.50—just enough to get home on. She's leaving on a Galil tiyul soon so we make plans to meet again. I come back and meet Larry Stolar, who had something going with a Brazilian girl named Miriam from the Machon. Good-looking—intelligent girl.

Friday, July 12, 1963

Tonight, was the "concluding party," and it was just wonderful, very funny, great. The chorus sang a few songs (I was in it—Malka led it), then some skits and the skit that the 2 North Africans put on—Moshe and Zvi. There were also some very professional-looking dances; Bruce, Dan Shiller and Joel from Hashomer France.

The evening ended with Mach on pins given out by Dov Levin and then some speeches about working in the movement and the need for us, etc., etc. Had dancing and "balagan" afterwards.

Saturday, July 13, 1963

Tomorrow the ITT group was planning a tiyul—so some 7 guys decided to raid the place. We walked around 'til we came to a ditch near the building they were sleeping and crawled through a hole in the fence and then entered the building with not the guard or anyone noticing. We went in—loaded with water and toothpaste—wetted down the floors and put toothpaste on their faces. It wasn't too successful—not everyone got up, some rooms were locked—Shabbeta's rooster yell wasn't coordinated with our movements. It was "chaushis" [Yiddish for "disaster"] but still funny.

Monday, July 15, 1963—Thursday, July 18, 1963

This was our last and supposedly best (?) tiyul. This time to the Upper Galilee. We had Frankel and a "professional" guide—Yehuda along, which spoiled things because he couldn't handle us, didn't know us, and we all wanted someone from the Machon like—Binyamin or Haim Avni, instance. The "pioneering [socialist] movement" kids were in one bus—B'nei Akiva, USY, and a group from S. A. [South Africa] in another.

1st Day

Traveled up to Haifa—to see the Technion and Bahai—than to Akko to see the usual sites, then through Emek Bet Kerem—past Yechiam to Milya—Druze-Christian Arab village. From there—we walked to Montfort—the administration center of the Crusaders around 1270—In 1289—it fell to Saladin and the Moslems.

A very tiring, hot, dusty walk it was. From there, the buses went to Rosh HaNikra and Kibbutz Lohamei HaGeta'ot, *but* I, Bruce, Dorit, Sue and Chaya went to Gesher Haziv, where we visited the Workshop and I went to see Chaya Baer and her new kid. Listened to sicha given by Max Langer.

Walked and got hitch on Vespa to Yad L'yad youth hostel and from there to Moshav Livnon, where we spent the night.

2nd Day

Next day, went to Sassa road to Bar-Am (ancient synagogue) and from there to Nebi-Yesha, overlooking the Hula Valley. Got story on the valley reclamation there. Didn't take boat ride through the swamp but instead went to a place near Kiryat Shmona to swim. From there, took bus to Meiron, walked around Har Canaan, below army base up there, and down to the tomb of Reb Meir Baal-Haness and to Sefad to sleep at the youth hostel there. Ate dinner at very nice hotel (Herzl). Beautiful interior. Broke my glasses (one lens) at youth hospital jumping for a bed. Slept well.

3rd Day

Took tour of the synagogues and sites of Sefad. From there, went to upper Galilee to Rosh Pina and to Hazor—where we got a long talk on the history and devastation of the place. From Hazor went to Tel Chai and then to Tanur, the waterfall (no water) (Lebanese were using it) there. Then to the resort and farm town (500 or 800 people) and saw into Lebanon and the border there. From there to youth hostel at Tel Chai. Had a Kumsitz and dancing after eating there. The S. A. [South African group] put on some very silly, funny acts.

4th Day

Went to see the grave of Josef Trumpeldor and then to the graves of the Hashomer, soldiers in the War of Independence, etc., Went on the way out of the Galil through Afula, and Sefad, Wadi Ara, to Caesarea, where we took a hellish amphitheatre tour of the Crusader moat, the Roman part aqueduct, and warehouses. It was very interesting seeing how the Crusaders, very barbarously, took Roman columns and building blocks and used it to build their own churches and buildings. Returned tired but through Jerusalem—gave the town one last blast with songs and noise: "Ah L'Madrechai Machon" ("Oh, the Machon youth leaders!").

(The next days—up to leaving Israel will be found in another book. Tour of Europe will follow Israel.)

Thursday, August 1, 1963

This morning, I went with Chava Puchtik to visit the Volper family and to pick up the camera in Ramat Gan (cost: 30 IL.). I used the camera to take a picture of Luba Merin (Yehuda was at work and was to be at the station before I leave).

[Sadly, the other "book" (diary) was never found. Maybe it's in some archive in Israel or the United States. It was quite a trip—one year long—and only for the young. It was strenuous, and looking back—fifty-eight years ago—it was a once-in-a-lifetime experience. I hope I run into Nancy Goldman one day . . . soon. Ah, such memories.]

Chapter 6

Golda and Me

Israel's prime ministers are a colorful group. Many books have been written about David Ben-Gurion, Yitzhak Rabin, Arik Sharon, even Benjamin Netanyahu, but works about Golda Meir (pronounced "MY-ear") seem to have surpassed all of them.

She lived in Milwaukee for fifteen years, from 1906, when she arrived at age eight, from Kiev, Ukraine and Pinsk, Belorussia [now Belarus] to 1921 when she made *aliyah* to Palestine with her husband Morris Meyerson, her sister Shayna, and Shayna's two children.

My connection to Golda is manifold. We both lived in the same North Side neighborhood, called the Walnut Street area, and area of first immigration. She lived in a two-room apartment at 615 North Walnut (Sixth and Walnut), and her mother, Blumeh, ran a small grocery store at 623 Walnut Street. Later they lived at Tenth and Walnut, where they ran the Miller-Mabewetz delicatessen. Mabewetz was her original name, sometimes spelled Mabovitch.

She left for Denver but returned to Milwaukee in 1915 and enrolled at North Division High School. Her parents had become involved in local Zionist activities, and after spotting Golda at lecture one day, a young Zionist leader approached her about joining the Jewish worker's movement, the Po'alei Zion (Workers for Zion). In the summer of 1915 at age seventeen, she joined the movement. Golda graduated from North Division in 1916 and then enrolled at the Milwaukee Normal School (now called the University of Wisconsin–Milwaukee) for a career in teaching. She also continued her activism in Po'alei Zion.

I lived with my parents, Irving and Faye Porter, at 2212A Tenth St. (Tenth and Garfield). Golda and I were a short walk away from each other yet thirty to forty years apart historically. We lived on Tenth Street from 1946 to 1954, and I attended the Milwaukee Hebrew Academy, which was in the basement of Cong. Beth Israel at Twelfth and Teutonia. I walked to school.

We were both Labor Zionists, she with Po'alei Zion, I with Ichud Habonim (later called Habonim/Dror). She was motivated to work on a kibbutz (Merchavia); I went to Kibbutz Gesher Haziv in the western Galilee.

I don't think I ever met Golda, though I did hear her speak at Kibbutz Lochamei Hagetaot in the Western Galilee in the spring of 1963 in a colorful pageant commemorating the Shoah. Other Zionist leaders such as Yigal Allon and Moshe Dayan were also there. I did, however, meet David Ben-Gurion a few years later in Chicago on his tour of North America raising money for Israel. It was at a downtown Chicago hotel, and he wanted to meet the leaders of the student Zionist organizations, and so we, about a ten of us, met him and his wife, Paula. It was awe-inspiring. A short man with his wild, fiery white hair, he exuded confidence and energy, and I have a photo with him that is in the Milwaukee Jewish Archives.

Golda had many friends from Pioneer Women, Farband, and Habonim here. Isadore Tuchman was a major influence in her life. Sadie Ottenstein was a fellow Labor Zionist, as was Sara Feder, Nathan Sand, Zelda Lemberger, Sara Lederman, and Regina Zuckerman-Kopelev. Even Rabbi Sheinfeld performed the wedding for her and Morris.

Golda Meir returned several times to Milwaukee to raise funds for Israel, but her most memorable visit was in October 1969, when she visited the Fourth Street Elementary School. There are numerous photos of her with city officials like Mayor Henry Meier—it was funny to separate the two similar-sounding names—and local Jewish leaders such as Mel Zaret, Max Karl, Ollie Adelman, Gerald Coburn, and Marvin Klitzner, along with a young Yitzhak Rabin, Israel's ambassador to the US

My sister, Bella Porter Smith, sixty-four, was only fifteen years old when she and other Hillel Academy students serenaded Golda at General Billy Mitchell Field Airport with *"Hevenu Shalom Aleichem."* There are photos of that serenading, as well as photos and stories of the Fourth Street School event, and the questions the young, mostly African American, students asked her: "What grades did you get?" Golda answered to gales of laughter, "I got A's and B's, but anything lower, I forgot!"

May 3 is Golda's birthday; 2018 was the fortieth anniversary of her death in 1978 and the 120th anniversary of her birth in 1898. There was a movie about her, *A Woman Called Golda* (1982), with Leonard Nimoy, Judy Davis, and Ingrid Bergman, and a successful Broadway play *Golda's Balcony*, by William Gibson.

What made Golda Meir's life so compelling? Women in politics have a double burden. They are seen as mothers and wives first, political leaders second. Thus her life resonates with many women today. And a second reason is that maybe we need her calm, resolute voice today in our complex world. In short, we need another "Golda."

Sources

Agress, Eliyahu. *Golda Meir: Portrait of a Prime Minister.* New York: Sabra Books, 1969. Esp. 8–18. Contains dozens of photos.

Hitzeroth, Deborah. *The Importance of Golda Meir.* San Diego: Lucent Books, 1998.

Martin, Ralph G. *Golda—Golda Meir: The Romantic Years.* New York: Charles Scribner's Sons, 1988. An unusual and surprising take on Golda—her romances.

Schuldt, Lori Meek. *Golda Meir with Profiles of David Ben-Gurion and Yitzhak Rabin.* Chicago: World Book, a Scott Fetzer Company, 2007.

Part Two

_____

1963–1971—THE RADICAL YEARS

_____

Chapter 7

University of Wisconsin–Milwaukee: Becoming an Activist/Intellectual, 1963–1967; the Milwaukee Riots and Father Groppi; the Beginning of the Counterculture for Me; Hippies, Acid Trips, and Communes

---

Fighting the Draft

My biggest concern in the 1960s upon my return from Israel was avoiding the draft in order to avoid fighting in Vietnam. For many, to be drafted into the army was seen as a "death sentence," and to die in an unwinnable war in a jungle many miles away from home was what sociologist C. Wright Mills called "crack-pot reality," meaning if one hundred thousand men die, then throw in another two hundred thousand more.

Some facts:

- About 2.5 million men (all were men except for 7,500 women) served in Vietnam.
- Sixty-four percent were deferred like me.
- 58,200 died in Vietnam; just two percent of all who served.

- The average age of soldiers in Vietnam was nineteen; in World War II they were older, twenty-six.
- In Vietnam they served one-year terms, hence the continual turnover, unlike World War II, where your regiment stayed with you for the entire time in the war.
- There were no welcoming parades for returning Vietnam veterans. You returned alone, you suffered alone.
- Two-thirds of the soldiers were against the war.
- There were conflicts among Black, Mexican, and white soldiers.
- Most GIs hated the National Guard Reserves, even more than the protesters. Those GIs saw the reserves as rich privileged kids who got out of going to Vietnam by serving only four months stateside.

My parents were so worried about my possible conscription they even thought I should go back to Israel. We already had one scare there: the Cuban Missile Crisis in the fall of 1962, while I was living in Jerusalem. My folks sent me a telegram: "Stay in Israel, Yankele, don't come back; the Russians want to bomb America." Luckily they didn't bomb us, and I continued my trip and returned to Milwaukee in August 1963.

I was active in the Milwaukee Organizing Committee, one of the early anti-draft groups or, as the pro-war people called us, "draft-dodgers." It was 1967 and the beginning of my political awakening. The Committee told us what to expect at the draft board and what to drink: some concoction that would raise my blood pressure; hypertension, they told me, would get me out of the army. It was, of course, dangerous. But I was twenty-two years old; today, drinking something like that would probably kill me.

I remember the day I was called down to the induction center early one morning in downtown Milwaukee. I was one of the few middle-class college "white boys"; the rest were ghetto African Americans and Latinos or rural farm boys, most of them joking around about killing "commies." They were totally clueless about where they were going; in fact, few even knew where Vietnam was.

But I was prepared. The Milwaukee Organizing Committee had trained me about what would happen and how I was to respond.

The induction process took place in several stages:

1. First, we all stripped down to our underpants and carried our papers and clothes in a long line. Then we made a circle, and an army sergeant examined our bodies. Did we have any misshapen body parts—a bent

spine, a crooked neck? Did we have asthma or other ailments? He examined us as if we were animals on display to be sold.

2. Then we were asked a series of questions about "radical organizations" and given a list to check off. Some were organizations going back to World War I and long defunct socialist, Communist, and trade union groups, but also some right-wing Nazi groups. I am certain the FBI put this list together. I wish I could see a copy today. I was told by the resistance movement to mark nearly all of them. But, of course, they did not believe me and immediately sensed that I was a "resistor."

3. Then I was asked if I was a homosexual. I was told again to say "yes," but they had that one planned also. When I said "yes," they called in Sergeant Garcia and told me, "OK, Mr. Porter, go into the next room and have sex with him!" Boy, they really knew all about the sociology of attraction. I demurred, and Garcia smirked and said, "Yeah, I thought so." Bizarre, but such were the times.

4. Then I went to see the army "shrink," a psychologist, and here I was really prepared. I had a letter from Dr. Edward Rubin of Chicago, my psychiatrist, saying that I was depressed and mentally unable to go into the army. But I was also told by antiwar resistors to do something really crazy. So, as soon as I settled in, I jumped on his desk and shouted, "I'll kill myself if I have to go in!" and I rushed to the window to jump out.

Well, I was lucky. I had a doctor who was against the war, and he signed my papers stating I should not be inducted. To show you how lucky I was, my good buddy Shelly Bankier did the same thing a few days later, but he had a *pro-war* doctor who said: "Mr. Bankier, I know you don't feel well now, but the army will straighten you out, and you'll be fine." Shelly went in but had to fake a suicide in boot camp in order to get out.

He told me later that what saved him from getting beaten up (the fate of all draft-dodgers or slackers in boot camp) was that he was an excellent "chicken fighter" wherein two sets of men get on top of each other and they fight to see who can topple the other guy.

Shelly was short but had huge shoulders. It was impossible to get a handle on him. He won all his matches; otherwise they would have had a "blanket party" where they throw a blanket over you (to avoid major bruises, or sometimes to secure you down to your bunkbed) and beat you up. Such are the ways of young men in the army culture. Very mature behavior. (For more on this culture, see the books of my good friend Tim O'Brien: *Going After Cacciato* and *The Things They Carried*.)

Racial and Ethnic Relations

I had wanted to go to Harvard. I always knew I would get there one day. And, two and a half decades later, I was at Harvard, but for now I was living at home and commuting to the University of Wisconsin–Milwaukee (UW–M) campus. So I either drove an old compact car—a Ford Falcon, about seven miles down Locust Street from Fiftieth to the East Side, near Lake Michigan, where the campus was—or I took a bus down Center Street to the campus.

UW–M was a commuter school with very few dormitories. People met for lunch at various tables in the student union; there were separate tables for the fraternities and sororities, for the athletes, for artists (musicians, poets, etc.), and for the political activists/intellectuals—people running for office, against the draft and the growing war in Vietnam, and/or for Black human rights. Some emerged later as state representatives, such as Mordechai Lee (I dated his sister Riva Lee). I think they were originally from Israel but came to Milwaukee in the late '50s.

UW–M was also racially and ethnically mixed. I sat with my friends Bill (Ksiel) Sztundel and Lyle Sussman. Other friends, such as Sheldon (Shelly) Bankier and Harry Pelz, went to the much larger university in Madison, simply called UW.

There were Black friends such as Milt Coleman, who later became an editor at the *Washington Post;* and there were romances. Several I remember had some strange and sometimes sad repercussions. Lyle, for example, dated an Italian girl, Celia Adornato, a graduate of Riverside High, who was madly in love with him. (He was quite handsome.) But since he was Jewish and she was Catholic, they had to date somewhat surreptitiously. When he broke up with her, she was heartbroken.

But Lyle and his girlfriend were useful to another romance. A Black friend Bill Beckett dated a white woman, and she didn't want her parents to know that she was dating a Black guy, so Lyle had to pick her up at her home and drive around the corner, where she would meet up with Beckett, her Black boyfriend, and the four of them would then go out together. This was at the beginning of the civil rights movement, which I will discuss in a moment.

Others at our table included a talented Korean fellow named Juno Kim, a trained violinist. And there were several women: Elaine Seidel, Lyle's sister Jerri, Ayala Karsh, Susie Lerman, and Elaine Shlonsky. At the tables for fraternity members, I remember being pledged by a Jewish frat, AEPi (Alpha Epsilon Pi), but I did not cotton to the hazing or the pranks, such as filling gloves up with Coke and serving it to new recruits, or doing push-ups on an oil slick in a garage.

I thought that it was silly and undignified, and that I was above that stuff, but I had good friends who joined.

I dated several non-Jewish women and considered marriage to one of them. Pam Beecher was a smart, attractive Polish German girl, and those two ethnic groups were anathema to my parents, since both groups took part in killing Jews during the Holocaust. I could never bring her home. It was a passionate affair, and I have never forgotten her, but it ended. The last time I saw her, she was living in Cambridge. Another woman I dated was a tall, statuesque Swedish gal. Again, these were strictly taboo categories. But, as you can see, barriers were falling on all fronts, not just racial.

Intellectual Influences

While I had an enviable high-school record that could have gotten me into any elite school, I had to go to UW–M because my parents felt they did not have enough money for Harvard. (Little did they know—since I had no counselor or mentor to tell me—that Harvard would have found a way to pay for my tuition.)

So I went to UW–M, and I floundered. I really didn't know what I wanted to major in. As a good Jewish boy, my parents wanted me to be a doctor or a lawyer—and so, like a good Jewish boy, I took pre-med courses and hated them. I hated dissecting chloroformed and desiccated frogs and cats, and I was confused by all the chemical reactions in chemistry classes and the body parts in gross anatomy classes.

So I started taking psychology classes. This was the age of Skinnerian stimulus-response analysis, and I remember being shocked when a professor brought in an autistic kid and gave him M&M's and the kid performed like a trained bear. But I didn't do well in those psychology classes either. But when I took a sociology class with a charismatic teacher named Karl Flaming, I finally knew what I wanted to do—sociology.

In Flaming's intro class, he asked about our relatives, and everyone raised their hands about a grandparent, but I was the only one who did not raise his hand. I had no grandparents. When I came to Karl after class, he said: "Jack, maybe you should find out why." That was the beginning of my quest to understand myself as a child of the Holocaust. It was 1965.

I had great teachers at UW–M: Irwin Rinder, Lakshimi Barawaj, Hugo Engelmann, Donald Noel, and Don Weast in sociology, as well as Robert Silverberg and Stan Greenfield in anthropology, plus wonderful English professors, poets and history teachers.

The Death of JFK—November 22, 1963

Everyone my age remembers that day of infamy and where they were at the time of President John F. Kennedy's assassination. I was in the college cafeteria looking up at the ceiling, where the loudspeakers were when they announced the news.

But I had briefly seen Kennedy earlier. I know I did, because I notated it in my calendar book: "On May 12, 1962, I saw Pres. Kennedy." He was campaigning in Milwaukee.

Father Groppi

The biggest issue in the mid-'60s was "open housing" and the discrimination against African Americans in renting or selling homes. A joke in Milwaukee went like this: "What's the longest bridge in the world?" Answer: "The Thirteenth Street viaduct, which separates Poland from Africa." The south side of Milwaukee was mostly Polish, and the north side was mostly Black. The marches that ensued hoped that African Americans and Latinos could buy or rent anywhere in the city. So, when African Americans went north and west into mainly Jewish areas, there was little opposition. Jews simply moved to the east side or the northern suburbs.

However, when African Americans wanted to live on the south side of Milwaukee, they were not welcomed. Surprisingly, Latinos were. So what to do? Well, the process had already started in the South with Martin Luther King Jr. and other Black leaders: nonviolent marches.

A newly minted Jesuit priest, Father James Groppi (1930–1985), had been given a small parish in the inner city, St. Boniface. There he began to organize youth activities. It was very unusual, but here was this charismatic white Catholic priest leading a group of young Black boys and men. The Church was none too happy, especially when Father Groppi decided that they would march into Catholic Polish and German neighborhoods. And march they did, crossing the Thirteenth Street Viaduct every day for two hundred days!

Born in Bay View to Italian immigrants, Groppi was the second-to-last child of twelve in the family. He helped run his parents' grocery store. When he graduated from public school, he took bus-driving gigs to afford seminary school in Mount Calvary, Wisconsin. His first assignment after seminary was at St. Veronica's, but in 1963 he was sent to St. Boniface, which had mostly African American parishioners.

From that point on, Father Groppi became active in the civil rights movement. In 1965, he took a position of leadership—rare for a white man—within the NAACP, where he organized a group of African American males that he called the Milwaukee Commandos, who were tasked with protecting those who marched. For the next few years, he was arrested several times at these civil rights marches. His most important act was a series of marches into the Polish south side that finally led to open housing for all people.

In 1976, he left the priesthood and eventually married Margaret Rozga, an English professor, and they had three children. He continued his activism with work on behalf of Volunteers in Service to America (VISTA). At the end of his life, James Groppi was doing what he started out doing—driving buses—but his leadership was still strong. Two years before he died, he was elected president of his local bus drivers' union.

I was a twenty-two-year-old college student, but to make extra money I drove a yellow cab. On several occasions I joined the marches. I parked my car across the bridge in a safe spot and walked along toward the back. Father Groppi and the commandos plus other priests and nuns marched up front. What I witnessed I wish someone with a camera would have videotaped. The marchers were met with bottles and cans filled with shit and dirt and taunts and screaming that I will never forget: "You nuns sleep with niggers!" "Get the hell out of our neighborhood!" "Kill the niggers!"

Martin Luther King was right. The reaction by whites in the North, like in Chicago or Milwaukee, was even worse than in the South. The police "protection" was minimal. I don't know how we survived without major injuries and no deaths. However, within a year the Milwaukee City Council passed an "open housing" ordinance, and *de jure* segregation was over but *de facto* segregation continues until today. Milwaukee remains one of the most segregated cities in the United States.

The Milwaukee Race Riot of 1967

Along with the "open housing" marches came the sudden and terrible death of Martin Luther King Jr. in May 1968. There were riots in dozens of cities across the country, but cities had riots even before then, starting with the infamous Watts (near Los Angeles) riot in 1963.

This Milwaukee riot had a devastating effect. It drove many whites and many Jews into the suburbs and exurbs, and years later these areas would turn Republican. It devastated inner-city businesses and drove out many (but not all) white and Jewish-owned stores. And it scared the crap out of us. I still remember looking with my friends across the "dividing line"—Sherman Boulevard and Forty-Third Street (we lived on Fiftieth Street)—and seeing in the distance the fires and smoke of the riots. The police kept us back. All traffic was stopped, with no way to get into the city to see it up close. But we were young and stupid, so we went around the city, driving on the expressways, which were totally empty, and found a way into the city to see it a bit closer. It was surreal, like a Hollywood film, but this was real fire, real smoke, and real gunshots!

The Beginnings of the Counterculture

As I have said, the 1960s were the most radical years since the Civil War of 1860–1865 on so many levels. I have briefly described their political aspects. Now I will explore their cultural—or, should I say, countercultural—characteristics.

The 1960s were a time of social experimentation—not just drugs such as marijuana and LSD, but also communes and sexual freedom. There were several quasi-communes: simply four, five or more people living together, sharing food, money and girlfriends, and in general coming together to smoke the weed and listen to the Doors ("Light My Fire"), the Beatles, the Moody Blues or Jefferson Airplane. Their songs were meant to be listened to while stoned or making love.

The Six-Day War, Graduation, and My First and Last Acid Trip

On June 5, 1967, it all came together—academic, political, countercultural, spiritual—on my first acid trip on my graduation from UW–M and the start of the Israel-Arab Six-day War. All in one day! I still remember that acid trip in an apartment on the east side, near UW–M. I was dressed in my hippie outfit, and I wore a long robe and felt like kind of a King David or Solomon. It was a "heavy Biblical trip" with me as head of some kind of harem.

What a way to segue from undergraduate UW–M to Northwestern University graduate school!

The times were moving fast.

Sources

Gurda John. *The Making of Milwaukee*. Pages 365–376.

———. *One People, Many Paths*. Pages 201–254.

The Handy Wisconsin Answer Book. 2019. Pages 81–83

The Milwaukee Organizer, the newsletter of the antiwar Milwaukee Organizing Committee, 1966–1968.

Porter, Jack Nusan. *Radical Writings*.

Stevens, Michael E., ed. *Voices from Vietnam*. Madison, WI: State Historical Society of Wisconsin (Voices of the Wisconsin Past), 1996. These are the voices of Wisconsin Vietnam veterans.

Stotts, Stuart. *Father Groppi: Marching for Civil Rights*. Madison, WI: Wisconsin Historical Society Press, 2013. Addressed to high school students, it is the best biography to date.

Chapter 8

Activism Continued, 1967–1971: The 1968 Chicago Convention Riot; the Chicago 8 Trial; My Relationship to Abbie Hoffman, Jerry Rubin, Paul Krasner, and Lee Weiner; the Black Student Sit-In at NYU; the Founding of the Radical Jewish Student Movement; the 1960s (Civil Rights, Hippies, Grass, Acid, the Israeli-Arab Six-Day War, Vietnam, Woodstock)

———

A famous Chinese curse is: "May you live in interesting times." One interpretation of why it's a "curse" is that you will never live through such "interesting" times again, and so you will be very *unhappy* for the rest of your life. The 1960s were definitely the most interesting and revolutionary times this country has ever lived through. Just think what happened in a few short years—Black civil rights and anti-Vietnam marches, riots across America, assassinations (JFK, MLK, RFK, Malcolm X, and many others, such as Medgar Evers), plus the Watergate burglary, which set the stage for the planned impeachment of Richard Nixon.

Woodstock

There were great cultural and sociological revolutions: the rise of hippies, rock concerts, communes, sexual freedom, and alternative medicines and therapies. Woodstock, for example. I almost went to it. I was a writer for the *Northwestern University Daily*, and I asked my editor Elliot Brown about covering it. He said, "Jack, it's just another rock concert. There will be others." Thus I missed the greatest music event of the 1960s. But I did go to the twenty-fifth, thirty-fifth, and fortieth reunion celebrations. They were fun but could never replace the original.

Among the performers who either played or wanted to play at Woodstock were: Richie Havens, Ravi Shankar, Melanie, Canned Heat, Mountain, Creedence Clearwater Revival, Sly and the Family Stone, Joan Baez, Arlo Guthrie, Joe Cocker and the Grease Band, Country Joe McDonald and the Fish, Santana, John Sebastian, the Grateful Dead, Janis Joplin, the Who, Jefferson Airplane, Joe Cocker, Ten Years After, the Band, Johnny Winter, Blood, Sweat and Tears, Crosby, Stills, Nash, and Young, the Paul Butterfield Blues Band, Sha Na Na, and Jimi Hendrix. Among the personalities who either spoke or were involved in organizing the event were the organizers (Michael Lang, Artie Kornfeld, Joel Rosenman, John Roberts, and John Morris), Chip Monck, Bill Hanley, Bill Graham, Abbie Hoffman, Max Yasgur, and the Swami Satchidananda.

The 1968 Chicago Democratic Convention "Police Riot"

I was there. I got gassed and almost beaten. Luckily I squeezed myself in between some doors at the Hilton Hotel and escaped the batons of the Chicago "police riot." They were totally out of control, not only in the streets but inside the convention as well. For example, Dan Rather, the TV newscaster, was beaten up right in front of his own cameras. Mayor Daley was totally paranoid; he believed the wildest rumors, like the Yippies putting LSD into the waterworks. You'd need a ton of LSD to make an impact, but he believed it, so out of touch was he with young people.

I remember the scenes in Lincoln Park. They started off as a series of speeches by both political and literary lions. I was on the stage, so I had a chance to chat with Norman Mailer, French novelist Jean Genet, Allen Ginsburg, and William Burroughs, as well as national political leaders. Then, suddenly, the police waded in for no reason at all and started billy-clubbing people. I have pictures of it.

The rioting and the clubbing continued into the night. It was surreal. I saw people in wheelchairs, members of the British parliament, and a female bystander being clubbed. The cops did not care. I was lucky to survive.

In fact, many times I came home at night and began writing my doctoral dissertation in sociology "Student Protest and The Technocratic Society: The Case of ROTC." Fighting in the streets during the day, and writing at night. I don't how I had the strength to do both, but then again I was only twenty-three years old.

The Chicago 8 Trial of 1968–69

I call it the Chicago 8 because Bobby Seale, the Black Panther leader, was part of it for a few days, but he protested so much in court that he wasn't even in Chicago at the time he was separated from the trial. So it was called the Chicago 7. I knew most of the 7, but especially Lee Weiner, a graduate student, as well as Abbie Hoffman, Jerry Rubin, Dave Dellinger, and Tom Hayden. Paul Krassner was one of the founders of the Yippies with Abbie Hoffman and Jerry Rubin. They were also called the Revolutionary Youth Party and nominated a pig named Pegasus for president of the United States. Yippies were politicized revolutionary hippies who looked down upon hippies as "stoned idiots."

The Chicago 8 were chosen by the FBI, not so much because they were organizers, but mainly because they represented all parts of the "movement." Lee Weiner and John Froines represented graduate students and professors, Jerry and Abbie represented the Yippies and Hippies, Tom Hayden represented the SDS and the New Left, and Dave represented the "old" left of democratic socialists and by extension the dwindling number of Communist Party members.

The Role of the SDS

The SDS (Students for a Democratic Society) was the major New Left movement of the '60s with chapters on over three hundred campuses across the country. Founded in June 1962 at a meeting of student leaders led by Bob

Haber, Tom Hayden, and Casey Hayden, it produced the famous Port Huron Statement that laid out the nonviolent demands of "participatory democracy" that we requested from the university to be part of the decision-making. It was a modest demand, but it soon escalated into more violent confrontations and revolutionary tactics—blowing up buildings, shooting at cops, and the like. In just a few short years, the SDS like amoebas, divided and subdivided in several revolutionary groups . . . and then destroyed itself.

The Northwestern Black Student Sit-In in 1968: The Role of James Turner

There was a tremendous split between the Black and white students. The administration at Northwestern was much more attuned to give the African Americans what they wanted, either because they were nonviolent or out of white guilt. But NU moved too slowly, so under the direction of sociology graduate student James Turner and some undergraduates, they occupied the bursar's office with a list of demands:

1. More Black students.
2. More Black teachers.
3. More student aid.
4. Plus a separate Black organization called the FMO, For Members Only, which still exists on campus. (However, I am not sure they can allow only Black students to join.)

The takeover took the school by surprise and caused a media sensation. Food, water, and communiqués were brought in through a side window; African Americans inside; white radicals like us outside. James Turner would come out and give their demands. He was very a great speaker..

We became good friends, and he later became head of the Africana Center at Cornell. Years later, we met again when I was invited to attend a special convocation in Little Rock, Arkansas, at Philander Smith College when they installed a new president. Philander was an all-Black college, and I was invited due to one of their graduates, Dr. Marty Grossack. I didn't meet Bill Clinton— he was in the White House—but I did meet many top Arkansas leaders such as Mike Huckabee and Winthrop Rockefeller, who was lieutenant governor.

But, as I have said, Black demands were easy, whereas we in the SDS were calling for "revolution" from top to bottom of societry. That's not easy to understand or to agree with, so they didn't; they just punished us physically or kicked us out of school. However, when four students were killed at Kent State University by the Ohio National Guard in April 1970, we shut down Sheridan Road, the main road in Evanston, and thereby shut down the entire university. Now *that* was truly radical.

The Shutdown of Sheridan Road in 1970

On this particular protest, we had the support of the entire student body and many faculty (except for a handful of conservative students). Why? Because white students were being killed over protesting Vietnam. When four Black students were killed at Jackson State (Mississippi), fewer cared, but when white students were killed, there was much more protest. Ironically, all four of the slain Kent State University students were Jewish, several from the East Coast.

The Decline of the Left and the Counterculture with the Manson Murders of 1969

The Left, especially the SDS, declined quickly. At a crucial conference in Chicago that I attended in 1969, the SDS broke apart into several factions. The Weathermen Underground wanted to continue the revolution violently with terrorist acts and explosions and police encounters. The Progressive Labor wanted to keep to a strict Marxist-Leninist doctrine and work with "workers" in factories, farms, or working-class communities. All the rest of us were simply bewildered and adrift.

Another factor was the split between Black and white radicals. Black power advocates wanted whites out of SNCC leadership and other Black movements so African Americans could gain total control. Some, like the Black Panthers on the Left and the Black Muslims on the Right, wanted no whites at all in their groups.

There was also the split between Jewish and Black/white radicals over Israel and Zionism. Palestinian and Third World theorists had influenced the radical groups and turned Zionism into imperialism or even a form of racist "Nazism." This also divided the Left and led to my co-founding a radical Jewish group. I describe this movement in my classic book *Jewish Radicalism* and in my collected *Radical Writings*.

Culturally, the Left and the counterculture declined in several ways. Cults took advantage of the "flower children" by turning them against their parents and exploiting them sexually and financially. Drugs began to flow into the "flower power ghettos," such as the East Village in New York and Haight-Ashbury in San Francisco. This turned the flower children toward drug addiction and violence. Charles Manson, a vile product of abuse and neglect, took advantage of these lost "children" and led them to commit horrific murders.

Those hippies, flower children, and communards who were able to do so moved out of the inner city to the countryside—Sonoma and Napa Valley in northern California, northern New York, western Massachusetts, and so forth—where they set up peaceful alternative institutions. This saved their lives, and their impact on society and those towns continues to this day.

The best example of these changes came from within my own friends. Tzila Sztundel's two children were so affected by their Holocaust survivor mother and father that they moved to the West Coast, changed their names, and established new lives. Bill changed his name to Ksiel and became a union and community organizer. (Some say he started off as a drug dealer to the Grateful Dead before real drug dealers made him an offer he could not refuse.) He remained a committed socialist/Marxist and activist admired by many for his entire life.

Gloria changed her name to Golden and moved to Napa Valley, married, had two lovely children, worked as a nurse, and contributed to that communitarian lifestyle. She is still a "beautiful child."

Conclusions

Radical movements don't have a long shelf life. Even as 1971 was coming to a close, the movement was splintering into many parts. The SDS divided into radical Weathermen who wanted "revolution" with violence and bombings, while the Progressive Labor (PL) faction wanted "evolution," to work with trade unions, farmers, Black sharecroppers, and other working-class people.

We in the middle were divided over tactics as well, but, with the rise of anti-Zionist sentiment on the Left, I and others started a nonviolent radical Jewish movement. So we broke with the Left and started our own thing. (See the essay that follows on the Jewish Student Movement in this book and my *Radical Writings*.)

By 1973, we were growing up, marrying, raising families, and had to make a living. Would we "sell out" our ideals? That was the big question.

Sources

Richard Leonard, archivist at Northwestern University, was very helpful with leads and sources. I wish I could attach visual videos and movies of that time, including my own, that are in the archives. I learned about a great many radical people active in the 1960s and 1970s in the Chicago area that I had never heard of before. The NU archives have much material on the Chicago radical scene.

Interestingly enough, I wrote the only book on Northwestern University about those radical days: "*Student Protest and the Technocratic Society: The Case of ROTC* (Chicago, IL: Adams Press, 1973). Also see my 1971 PhD dissertation in sociology upon which it is based, as well as a history of NU written by Harold Williamson and Payson Wild, *Northwestern University: A History: 1850–1975* (Chicago: Northwestern University, 1976).

Books on late 1960s radicalism are numerous, be they on the SDS, Black radicals, the Chicago Eight trial, or the hippies and Yippies. See the videos: *Making Sense of the 60s, Growing Up in America,* and *The War at Home.* I also recommend Kirkpatrick Sales's massive tome called *SDS;* William Kunstler's and Tom Hayden's memoirs; and my own book, *Jewish Radicalism.* See also the companion book to this memoir: *The Radical Writings of Jack Nusan Porter._*

While I wish there were an equivalent book for Milwaukee's radical politics, Stuart D. Levitin's massive 525-page book *Madison in the Sixties* (Wisconsin Historical Society Press, 2019) was enormously useful in describing the massive demonstrations on the Madison campus of UW, as was the fiftieth anniversary conference of the 1968 uprisings called "Back to Madison" held on campus in the summer of 2018. See especially the documentary *The War at Home.*

It was a blast to go back, but I did not have the same attachment as UW alumni, because, while I traveled often to Madison, my heart was with UW–Milwaukee.

Books on culture include those on Woodstock: Daniel Bukszpan, *Woodstock: 50 Years of Peace and Music* (Watertown, MA: Charlesbridge Publishing, Inc.; An Imagine Book, 2019. That year was the fiftieth anniversary of Woodstock, and there were many events, talks, and documentaries on the festival. This is one of the better books, telling us about every band that was invited; some did not show up, some were not in the original film, and some were not on the original album. The performers were among the greatest of their generation or any generation.

Here are some historical documents and essays dealing with those tumultuous times. The first one deals with leaving my first professorship job at the State University of New York in Cortland, NY and why I left. Other essays deal with the massive strike at Northwestern University in 1970 and with the rise of the

Jewish Student Movement in response to the rising tide of anti-Israel sentiment on campuses.

Soc. Prof. Porter Quits in Frustration

Last Thursday's mail brought to "the press" office Jack Nusan Porter's open letter of resignation, which appears on this page. When the dust settles, another Cortland faculty member will have left. If the present rate keeps up, by 1980 Cortland College will be a ghost town. Is the situation that befalls Porter unique to him, or are there any common ingredients of pattern to his path as well as his predecessors?

One focal point of confusion that lingers around faculty dismissals and/ or resignations is the job's expectations as viewed by the administration, the students and the faculty members in question themselves. Since no one has come to grips as of yet with establishing a viable job description for a faculty member, the position remains in murky waters to be strained by any ambitious educator like a gold rush man panning for gold.

Unfortunately, too many individuals upon panning the waters of education are shot for trespassing, administratively or otherwise, or for unorthodox methods of panning or for not having a license (doctoral certificate) to pan for gold, as well as for not sticking to their own spread of acreage (getting involved outside of academia).

The teaching position at Cortland is compoundedly nebulous. In the transition from a Teacher's College to a Liberal Arts College, the school's methods have lagged with respect to its new directions. The SUNY Board of Trustees state (*The Press*, Vol. 29, No. 15) that the criteria for promotion are listed as follows:

- Mastering of subject matter as demonstrated by such things as advanced degrees, licenses, honors, awards, and reputation in the subject matter field.
- Effectiveness of teaching, as demonstrated by such things as judgment of colleagues, development of teaching material or new courses and student reaction.
- Scholarly ability, as demonstrated by such things as success in developing and carrying out significant research work in the subject matter field, contribution to the arts, publications and reputation among colleagues.

- Effectiveness of University services, as demonstrate by such things as successful committee work, participation in local and University government, administrative work and work with students or community in addition to formal teacher-student relationship.
- Continuing growth, as demonstrated by such things as reading, research or other activities to keep abreast of other activities in his fields and being able to handle successfully increased responsibility.

Now, as a faculty member tries to exhibit "effectiveness of teaching as demonstrated by such things as . . . development of teaching material and new courses and student reaction" (depending on his approach and interpretation of what the above means), he runs into conflict with administrators, colleagues, and department chairmen for not following policy, etc., because each party has a different interpretation of what effective teaching means. Does it mean produced results from students, administered discipline, applied structure, or does it mean, as Dr. Lickona of Project Change says (*The Press*, Vol. 29, No. 23), "Courses should be action-oriented. Children should be working with each other, experimenting, and testing their ideas, making choices, taking the initiative, developmenting independence. All these things have to be done with college students because you cannot free the child until you free the teacher"?

Dr. Roseanne Brooks, head of the Sociology Department, stated (*The Press*, Vol. 29, No. 15) that: "There are all kinds of ways to be popular without really being a good instructor." Dr. Ted Denno, ex-political science professor here at Cortland, was voted professor of the year by the students the semester he was denied tenure, and "popular professors" Dorothy Gutenkauf, Bruce Carruthers and Charles Vivona (all three from sociology) will not be returning next year; and now the current resignation of Jack Nusan Porter. That comes to one political science teacher and four sociology teachers; a grand total of five faculty members within the last two years getting the axe—all of whom were well received by students.

Porter's Letter

From: Jack Nusan Porter
        Sociology Department

An Open Letter of Resignation
This is a difficult letter to write. Difficult because I have made some beautiful friendships, but I must announce that I am resigning as of the end of this

semester. There are 1001 reasons for this decision, but essentially it breaks down into two reasons: the pedagogic and the personal. Both are ultimately tied to the political because I believe most personal actions are political in the broadest sense of the word. In the style of the late great sociologist C. Wright Mills, sociology itself is the attempt to elevate private experience into public policy. This is the sociological imagination, and this is how I conduct my life.

Pedagogic Reasons

At every turn, at every attempt to innovate in the classroom, at every effort to develop an open and free classroom and to make it a "field of action" as well as a place of learning, I have been thwarted; I have been memoed and subtly intimidated; I have been forced to follow vague and hypocritical standards. Hell, there's more change going on in kindergartens than in most colleges.

I have watched my colleagues (Carruthers, Marciano, Griffen, Vivona, Gutenkauf, Parker, and others) being treated to the same hypocritical and inhumane treatment, whether in their teaching, their promotions, or their politics.

There are a lot of people here at this place that are threatened—they're threatened by students, by "deviant" professors, but most importantly by the possibility of change itself. Yes, people are threatened. That's good. It's also very sad. Because change has already come. More is on the way. After me, there will be others.

Many of the paradigms of the past are no longer tenable today. The contradictions of this system have exploded into the open. America's deeds have corroded America's creed. We know what to do; let's do it. My advice to some people here: adapt to change or get the hell out!

Personal Reasons

One of the major reasons I'm leaving is because I've been in the never-never land of academe either as a student or teacher for nearly 25 years. After a quarter of a century, it's time to get out into the real world for a little while.

I have learned a lot in books; I've taught a bit, some have learned from me; now it is time to go out and learn outside the groves, learn and act, write and do political (community) organizing, and grow as a person.

As I've said, I've met some beautiful people here. They know who they are. I've learned as much from my students and my colleagues as hopefully I've taught them. It's too bad you cannot take your friends with you. Keep up the struggle of that long hard march through the institutions of this society. Our goal: the radical transformation of the country. As an old union man Joe Hill said: "Don't sympathize, organize!"

All Power to You . . . and Shalom,
Jack Nusan Porter

Striking Memories

[*Chicago Tribune Magazine*, April 30, 1995]

By Abigail Foerstner

Northwestern University, Evanston, spring, 1995. Emphasis on careers is on the rise in the pragmatic 1990s. Students, faculty, and even the menu at the Norris University Center reflect a culture of racial and ethnic diversity. A recent demonstration was sparked by that diversity as some 150 students and supporters rallied for an Asian American studies program.

But flash back 25 years—to May, 1970—and the same campus scene erupts into a mass protest, ignited after National Guardsmen gun down four anti-Vietnam War demonstrators at Kent State University in Ohio.

Northwestern joined a nationwide strike in response. The campus closed down. Protestors stalled rush-hour traffic on Sheridan Road and later barricaded the road. Radicals trashed headquarters of the Naval Reserve Officers' Training Corps (NROTC) in a campus building. Clenched fists, a mock burial and a flag burning in Deering Meadow marked the mood of the times.

News of the May 4, 1970, killings at Kent State cut through Northwestern University's Evanston campus like a fire siren. Faces registered disbelief and shock from the caverns of the Grill, Northwestern's alternative student union until 1972, to the ever solemn halls of the Technological Institute.

Rock-throwing Kent State students had been protesting President Richard Nixon's escalation of the Vietnam War into Cambodia when guardsmen fired into the crowd. Northwestern had greeted the Cambodian invasion with relative calm, but the Kent State killings brought Vietnam to its doorstep. Northwestern students galvanized in support of antiwar protests that erupted across the country.

"Northwestern was apolitical in the main," recalls Roland Hinz, vice president and dean of students at the time. Most students shied away from demonstrations but confronted the war and racism with "heightened awareness" because of them, Hinz says.

Then suddenly—spontaneously—5,000 of the 9,000 students on campus gathered in Deering Meadow and voted to join a nationwide student strike.

The meadow became an instant hotbed for an area-wide protest movement involving high schools, other colleges and Evanston residents.

"The young and old came with their dogs, their blankets, their friends and loved ones and their ideals," reported the Daily Northwestern of the Deering rally. Eva Jefferson (now Eva Paterson), student government president, emerged as a national figure who could command protest without violence. University Chancellor J. Roscoe (Rocky) Miller was flashing peace signs.

The turbulent 1968–1970 era, culminating in the strike, changed American culture and politics dramatically. The women's movement that emerged with the antiwar protests opened jobs and careers to millions more women. Environmental activism gave way to mainstream conservation and recycling programs. Even the Persian Gulf War of 1991, with its heavy air offensive, proved that policy-makers wouldn't risk another Vietnam, with images of body bags on the nightly TV new revealing a ground war that was killing hundreds of servicemen a month.

The strike era also changed Northwestern campus life forever. At that time the university was in the throes of rapid-fire social change. Dorms became co-ed, membership in the college's bulwark Greek system of fraternities and sororities was plummeting and the student body had become racially and ethnically more diverse. Demands for new academic perspectives resulted in women's studies, African studies and other, similar programs.

All the changes, monumental then, are as routine now as studying on the beach for spring quarter exams, a Northwestern tradition that hasn't changed.

"I think the larger society became much more tolerant of young people's demands" then, says Thomas Ayers, retired chairman of the board of Commonwealth Edison Co. and, when the strike occurred, a fledgling Northwestern trustee. The board met in the fortress-like Rebecca Crown administration building with its underground garage.

But until the strike, no one expected militancy at seemingly apolitical Northwestern.

Bernard Beck, a sociology professor, recalls, "Anybody who looked at Northwestern [in 1970] would say, 'Here is essentially a quiet, conservative place dominated by apathy, in which there is a small, [politically] committed group of people and a large, absolutely indifferent student body.' Northwestern still looks that way. Notice I chose the word 'looks' because what the strike showed was that Northwestern was capable of instantaneous, very impressive action without the appearance of organizations or leadership."

Rather than protesting, today's socially conscious students volunteer time to soup kitchens, tutoring and other community service projects, says Margaret Barr, Northwestern's current vice president of student affairs.

Still, activism is cyclical, and parents who demonstrated in the 1960s and early 1970s may be sending their teenagers off to college just in time for another round. "There are periods of student unrest about every 30 years," says Barr. "I'm going to retire before then."

Hinz encountered controversy from the time he arrived on campus as director of admissions in 1965 until he left 6 years later.

"There were 26 Black students on campus in the fall of 1965. Twenty-one were athletes," Hinz says. "The university was probably guilty of very controlled bias at the time."

He was given credit for recruiting to achieve economic and ethnic diversity but also was blamed for admitting the students who became activists. About 200 of them were members of the campus chapter of Students for a Democratic Society, says Jeff Rice, who was chairman of the group in the strike era and now owns Great Expectations Bookstore in Evanston.

The strike wasn't controlled to SDS or any other group. It tapped the vast mainstream of Northwestern and radicalized everyone—a little. It shut down the campus for a week while students met in huge rallies, distributed leaflets, canvassed and marched through Evanston in a peaceful candlelight vigil.

The National Guard stood ready at a field house in town just in case, but was never called to action. The guard was gone by the time a group of students trashed the NROTC offices.

While only a few dozen radicals had participated, the attitude of a lot of students was, "Oh, you're in NROTC? Bummer. Is there anything you can do to get out of it?" recalls Chicago media consultant Dennis Frisch, who was a cadet at the time.

The radicals also were credited with barricading Sheridan Road after Evanston police closed the road to prevent traffic tie-ups caused when students lined the street to distribute antiwar leaflets to drivers.

But Rice says the barricade wasn't an SDS project and turned into a Southern California, hippie-style "be-in" that undermined political activities and community support.

"Kids burned fires in trash barrels at the barricade. It was like a camp-out or a Grateful Dead concert," recalls Beck.

The barricade came down without incident a week later and, once the strike ended, many students went home.

Many accepted the university's option of "T grades" giving automatic credits for their classes.

The strike had created a heady sense of a unified purpose that could force political change.

And although the unit didn't last beyond spring, the strike remains a vivid memory for those who were there.

It is the recollections of participants such as those interviewed here, and the effect of the Vietnam era upon them that can help others to understand that time, now history.

THOMAS AYERS, Commonwealth Edison President in 1970 and a Northwestern University Trustee, Now a Life Trustee of the University

Ayers says the strike era opened more lines of direct communication between university students, administrators and trustees. Northwestern trustees organized a committee on student affairs in response to the unrest; Ayers was the first chairman. The committee met with students confidentially—without administration members present—to air concerns on both sides.

Ayers recalls that time: "The kids were making themselves heard and by and large they were right, not so much the way they went about it but the fact that they had a legitimate right to be heard."

Ayers says one thing that hasn't changed at Northwestern is the stress on a good foundation education in liberal arts. "The work force is looking for someone with a good understanding of the world where they live. I think an educated person has to have the wider view of the world (provided by the liberal arts), and Northwestern does a super job of teaching that."

EVA JEFFERSON PATERSON, President of Northwestern's Associated Student Government in 1970, an Attorney in California in 1995

Though Paterson emerged as a charismatic strike leader, Bernard Beck, sociological professor, says it was instinct, not her position as student government president that allowed her to assume that role. Instead of coming up with a strict strike agenda, she appealed to the individualism of students joining forces for the first time. She encouraged people to define their own peaceful activities while the strike steering committee—a coalition of campus groups—acted as a clearing house and drafted demands voted on at the rallies.

Now an attorney, Paterson recently helped coordinate the successful fight against several bills that would have dismantled affirmative action in California. She says she still takes courage from the strike, as her present effort now turns to blocking an anti-affirmative action initiative sought for the November 1996 ballot.

"I'm dealing with a whole range of people on this affirmative action thing," she says. "Similarly in 1970, you had the entire political spectrum that was the community of Northwestern. You had people who wanted to burn down Lunt Hall [NROTC headquarters] and conservative men and women who wanted to protest something they felt was very wrong but who had no desire to smash the state."

Peterson says her moment of truth in the course of the strike came when she confronted the students carrying torches and heading toward Lunt Hall.

"The thought of me telling some people with torches that you're not going to burn that building down and them not doing it is rather amazing, but it happened," she says. "If that building had burned down, the police [and National Guard] would have been there and there would have been a different reality. We were able to be passionate and angry and minimally violent."

Instead, student marshals wearing white arm bands with peace signs backed up Paterson, and NROTC was spared—until radicals trashed the offices the following week.

As for the barricade, Paterson says she dragged the first sawhorse out to build it in response to a police action closing off Sheridan Road to leafleting.

"That's a story I've never admitted publicly until now. We blockaded a [state] highway. I hope the statute of limitations has run out," she laughs. "To be completely honest, I'm a lawyer now and it seems so . . . *rash*."

"Rash" was the last word that would have been applied in 1970 when articles in newspaper and national magazines lauded her. She crisscrossed the country on speaking engagements in the aftermath of the strike and debated Vice President Spiro Agnew on David Frost's television program.

She married her college sweetheart and student government cohort, Gary Paterson, put in a salaried stint at the American Civil Liberties Union and then earned a law degree from the University of California at Berkeley.

She now heads the civil rights division of the San Francisco branch of the public service Lawyers' Committee.

Paterson says the strike solidified her personal decision to become an attorney and she believes it hastened the end of the war, even though it took another five years for a complete pullout from Vietnam. But she also says she believes the strike helped consolidate conservative politics in America as the protests initiated the law-and-order message that has gained strength ever since.

ROLAND HINZ, Northwestern Vice-President, 1970; Retired in 1995

Hinz says he is proud of the diversity he helped bring to Northwestern and of the faculty members that diversity attracted to the campus. But he adds that long hours and no-win situations rove him away from university administration.

"During that time there were bomb threats on my home, threats on my kids' lives" that could have come from unidentified right-wing or left-wing extremists, he says.

He left college administration after the strike, joining the Evanston office of the College Scholarship Service, a testing and financial aid screening service.

Nonetheless, during the strike, Hinz once again pushed his long-standing policy that student discipline should be handled in-house whenever possible.

Evanston police acted with restraint and, by the third day of the strike, Evanston officials had decided to send the National Guard home. Still, Hinz took little for granted. He walked the campus each night until 2 or 3 o'clock in the morning, worried that events still would spin out of control.

"If you didn't worry about those things you were a fool," he says. "Altogether we were very fortunate. It was controlled, but part of the dynamic of the radical students was to get it uncontrolled.

"I think it was the bombing of the math building at the University of Wisconsin [later that year] that caused a very significant change [in the average student's attitude about protest]. It took all of those bystanders who had joined in and left them saying, 'I don't want anything to do with this.' It isolated the more radical elements."

BERNARD BECK, Northwestern Sociology Professor Then and Now

With his wild, bushy beard and flamboyant lectures, Beck symbolized the cadre of young activist professors who appeared on campuses in the 1960s. His beard is gone now, but his witty and irreverent style of speaking remains, and the door to his office still is flung open to a generation of students who were not yet born when the 1970s strike occurred.

"The strike is one of the finest memories of my life. Five thousand students turned out from nowhere. It cheered me that Northwestern kids could organize themselves overnight" when the need arose, he says.

Beck says Northwestern had learned from other campuses that protests leveled at Washington policy-makers could quickly be redirected closer to home toward the campus authorities.

Responding to the Kent State deaths, he says, "The [Northwestern] administration came out with a statement essentially saying, 'We understand that everybody's upset, we're upset too, and we understand that there are certain legitimate actions people may take." The faculty came out with a similarly supportive statement. "At Northwestern, everyone was saying, 'Don't shoot! We're not fighting!' By the time the students came out to the meadow to have their rally, they didn't have any local enemies."

Abigail Foerstner is a free-lance writer.

Reminiscences of the Jewish Student Movement at Northwestern University, 1967–1971: A Taped Interview

This is Jack Nusan Porter. This is December 7, 1979. I'm speaking in Boston, where I am presently a sociologist at the University of Lowell and still continuing my extensive writing and editing career. Still doing a lot of things in the area of Jewish communal life, Jewish students. I'm responding to Rabbi Benjamin Kahn's letter. Rabbi Kahn, I don't think we've met. I do hope that when you do come to Boston, I know you're going there to meet with the great Abraham Sachar and Marver Bernstein (at Brandeis) and Al Axelrod for the history, the beginnings of Hillel. I think Abe Sachar first organized Hillel, didn't he? At the University of Illinois? I hope that perhaps you will let me know when you are coming and we can meet again. In any case, you will find at the American Jewish

Historical Society a great deal of information on the Jewish counter-culture student group movement as well as, of course, material in the Hillel Foundation.

Second of all, I want to thank you for the very nice words you said in the letter when you said my name is virtually legendary in regards to what you define as the Jewish student counter-culture radical groups. That's a nice compliment. It was the nicest thing anyone had said to me all day, and I really appreciate that. In essence, I don't have false pride when I saw that I really felt or *we* felt, because no single person can start a Jewish student movement; we really felt, I really felt, that I and others were among the first people in America to start what we called the Jewish student movement, and that was at Northwestern University soon after the Six-Day War in June of 1967. I recommend you look at an article I wrote in *Jewish Currents* in June of 1970, where I outlined why and how the Jewish student movement arose. And, of course, Peter Dreier and I elaborated that as well in our book, *Jewish Radicalism* (published in 1973).

But it was the Six-Day War and the anti-Jewish position of the Black and the pro-PLO and pro-Arab position of Black and white radicals that prompted a Jewish response to the Third World, Black, White, radical, etc. What we wanted was that we had agreed with the White and Black radicals about civil rights, about Vietnam, but we did not like the position they took on Israel, and it was really the Six-Day War and the aftermath of the Six-Day War, and it was Israel along with other issues such as Soviet Jewry, etc., but it was really Israel and anti-Zionism that touched off the Jewish student movement.

It was in late '67 in the fall the first rumblings of a movement. Of course, you know the June '67 war was in June and in the fall when we got back and it took a little while or organize it, but by the end of '67 and the beginning of '68 three or four people organized the first Jewish student movement (JSM) in the Midwest, and again we thought it was the first in the country. But we did not now that simultaneous to that there were other groups arising in Boston, New York and California. This would give rise to such student newspapers as the *Jewish Radical* and *Genesis II* and various others. Fifty or more others followed, but at the time we did think we were the first, and it was quite a heavy experience to be at the beginning of a movement.

The Hillels played an enormous role. I think if you look later into the role that the Hillel leadership played in Breira, and Breira was in essence the adult or the later manifestation of the earlier Jewish student movement. In fact, if you look at, well, the 10th anniversary issue of *Genesis II* is coming out in January or February of 1980. I've looked at the past issues of *Genesis II*, and there's nothing new under the sun, as Ecclesiastes said. We were discussing the same issues in '69 and '68 and '70 as we are today. The question of the West Bank, the issues of the Palestinians, the question of Soviet Jewry, whatever it is, these things did not change.

So that Breira and you should have a chapter or section on the role that the Hillel Directors played in forming Breira along with other veterans of the Jewish student movement such as Arthur Waskow and Steve Cohen—no, actually, Steve Cohen wasn't as active as we thought he'd like to be—Alan Mintz, Bill Novak and others. But it was the Hillel directors which formed the basis for Breira and became under a lot of attack, I need not have to tell you that, but they also formed the basis, I think, for the Jewish student movement. The Jewish student movement at Northwestern University in 1967, '68 and '69 continued through the early '70s and had its basis at the Hillel Foundation at Northwestern though technically Hillel could not start its own movement or give its name, but it did everything else. It gave us rooms, it gave us support and unofficially the Hillel Directors were active in the organization of such a movement.

The leaders back in the late '60s at Northwestern in the Midwest were Rabbi Boris Rakovsky, who later went to Australia and now lives in Israel. Rabbi Rakovsky, the Northwestern University Hillel Director, was also one of the founders of the Jewish student movement. There were other people. Stan Rosenbaum was another founder, and there was a third fellow who was quite active named Byron Cole, who is today a prominent conservative Rabbi in Canada. And there was another fellow who now is a professor of physics at Loyola University named Jeff Mallow. So, it was Boris Rakovsky, Jeffrey Mallow, Byron Cole, Stanley Rosenbaum and myself who organized the JSM. But essentially the Jewish student movement was organized by graduate students, and many of us either came out of a Zionist background or a Yiddish secular background, and we were in the forefront of several projects.

I remember our first early meetings in these years. We sat down, we laid out an outline of what our tasks would be, and we organized marches and demonstrations, and we were a presence on campus and in the community. We had a place and an address where other groups could refer to us, and we were an organized group which could say to SDS (Students for a Democratic Society) or the Black Student Union, "Hey, we of the Jewish Student Movement as a united front speak this way or that way." In other words, it wasn't just a vague group of individuals, but a group that could speak out and make our voices heard. The major issue was, first and foremost, to confront SDS. For a short time, I was in SDS, and I knew the leadership, and I knew that they could get carried away with a somewhat superficial analysis of the Middle East, so our first task was to try to talk to them, if they were willing to listen to anybody, which they probably weren't at the time, but in some way to hold some symposium to form some kind of counter-balance.

At Northwestern, as you know, as in many campuses, there were many Arab and Third World professors, as well as their Jewish and non-Jewish supporters among the faculty. We had one of the most influential, Dr. Ibrahim Abu-Lughod. In fact, his wife, Dr. Janet Abu-Lughod, was a sociologist, and she was on my sociology dissertation committee but never talked politics. Anyway, Ibraham Abu-Lughod after the Six-Day War was forming all kinds of symposiums and conferences dealing with the PLO, and it was very anti-Zionist in some ways. It was not balanced at all, even though Abu-Lughod was somewhat of a moderate Palestinian leader. Abu-Lughod, I might add, was setting up a Palestinian University with campuses in Paris and in Beirut and possibly other countries. You may want to check out this man. He is still quite active. Anyway, he was at Northwestern, but the point is that our first goal was to neutralize any anti-Zionist or antisemitic statements that came out of the Left, from African Americans, or the Third World groups on campus. That was one goal.

A second goal of the Jewish student movement was to do what we could regarding the Black situation, and we decided to do this as Jews. For example, one big issue that confronted us was the number of Jewish landlords, or what they called slumlords, who were engaging in a somewhat questionable practice in Black neighborhoods of getting people, mostly African Americans, to get a mortgage on a house, but if they missed one payment on that mortgage, then these Jewish landlords could take over the entire house. This kind of cutthroat attitude, really a shady attitude toward African Americans, we didn't think was very Jewish; it wasn't in the Jewish tradition, and it gave us all as Jews a bad name, because a great many of these landlords who engaged in these shady practices were Jewish.

We did research—that was one thing about our group—and we went to these landlords quietly by ourselves, hoping to make them feel guilty about their shady practices both in terms of mortgages and in terms of keeping up apartments and homes, because we didn't want another "Maurice Gordon affair."

You know that was this big landlord in Boston who was told numerous times to fix up his buildings, there was a fire and about 4 or 5 people died in it, and he was sued, and he was a rich man. He was about to give some money to Boston University, and there was such a protest because of the shoddy way he had accumulated this money that in the end they didn't accept it, though at first they wanted to accept it but not put his name on the building.

But we criticized the landlords in a nice way from a Jewish point of view, and I think this had much more of an impact than if some Leftist group or Black group would have done it. And we did convince some landlords to change their politics and to fix up their buildings. We also supported African Americans in terms of open housing.

We organized a Jewish march in Evanston to support integration both in housing and in education, and this presence, I think, was very important, and later spun off into other groups in the Chicago area which are still active: the Am'Chai community, and then there was another group of them that spun off and published a journal called *Chutzpah*. I, just a year or two ago, saw these same people, Jeff Mallow and his wife and other people with similar ideas who have hung around Chicago or have come back marching against the Nazis. What distinguished that particular group is that it's a Yiddish secular Jewish group. It's Zionist, but not ideologically Zionist; it's Diaspora in nature, and it's a socialist Jewish group. Now this kind of group still exists so that you know that's another interesting thing, though they didn't have that much to do, I suppose, with the Hillels anymore. So the Black issues were the second goal.

A third goal was, of course, Soviet Jewry, which was just in its infancy stages, and we were involved with marching and protesting regarding Soviet Jewry. So first, just to recapitulate the Jewish student movement, which at its most may be attracted as many as 25 people, but it was the dedication and the fact that the Hillel Foundation really became the center place for this. This is where we met. This is where we got our support—good support, and it attracted other Jews on campus who then came to Hillel by way of these other political and civil rights issues. So just to recapitulate, there was the Israel issue, Zionism after the Six-Day War, it was the Black situation, it was Soviet Jewry, it was also the war in Vietnam, which we were against, both as individual citizens and as Jews. Some of the people in the group were engineers from the Technological Institutes and were physicists, some were astronomers, like Jeff Mallow, these were people who understood the implications of technology and that we would naturally join the other students in their protest against the way. I'm trying to see what were the other—so we had Israel, Soviet Jewry, Black rights, and, of course, the other major issues such as ROTC and the War in Vietnam. We were also concerned with culture.

I think through Jeff Mallow and others we began to re-introduce the study of Yiddish on campuses which had been in decline. We introduced Yiddish songs. I know Jeff and I and his wife went around and gave concerts in Yiddish. In other words, culturally we activated a Yiddish concern, and an Israeli concern on campus, and it could only strengthen the Hillel environment because Hillel, at least at Northwestern, was in an isolated area. It was a beautiful building; now I went back there, it's torn down and made into condominiums, but it was a beautiful location, but it was expensive to run, and it was right on Lake Michigan and it was out of the way of the campus. It wasn't near the fraternities, and, you know, Hillel and other religious groups were seen as kind of sissy or for eggheads; it wasn't what a lot of students wanted to do. The campuses were a disaster area.

I would say that before the rise of the Jewish student movement the campuses were really a disaster area, Jewishly, and in fact those were the words that were used by people like Leonard Fein and Milton Himmelfarb, there's all kinds of symposia held in the early '60s about: what can we do about our Jewish students? They're not getting involved in things? Well, the Jewish student movement took some of that activism that was going to go into the war and the civil rights movement and drew that activism into a Jewish channel, so to speak, and I think that we've kept alive Jewish traditions, Jewish political points of view, Jewish culture through and working very nicely with the Hillel Directors, because some of the Hillel Directors, we had a Rabbi Robert Siegal who was there after Rakovsky. He had just come right out of the civil rights movements in the South. I think he was from North Carolina, and he was engaged in the sit-ins and the busing and just everything. He was quite a gung-ho character. The Hillel Directors themselves have come out, and I still believe, that is, I'm not surprised that Hillel is at the forefront of social change, whether Jewish or otherwise, because it does attract a person who would not fit in well with the congregation or in any other lace that the Hillels provide places for rabbis and for other activist Jews who wish to lead Jewish students in non-traditional ways and who would be stifled in any others.

So thank God for Hillel. Damn it. Hillel's must take their proper position, not only nationally but internationally, in attracting these kinds of people, giving them an address, giving them a place so that they can be in to reach out in innovative ways. Otherwise we would have lost the students. We'd lose them either to apathy on the one hand or to Left Wing nihilism on the other. I just wanted to recapitulate. I remember again the names: it was Stan Rosenbaum, a psychology grad student, Jeffrey Mallow, an astronomer and a physics graduate student, I and Rabbi Boris Rakovsky, along with Byron Cole. We were the founders of the Jewish student movement.

As I look back, I don't have too much more to add; I think that I just can't say enough for the Hillels. They were a very important center for rejuvenation of Jewish cultures on campuses and allowed Jewish students to make their contribution in the face of criticism both during the early Jewish student movement years in the late '60s and later during the Breira period. My hat does go off to all the Hillel Directors for all the sometimes unpopular positions they take and support that they give to Jewish students, I think knowing full well that no matter how radical or how threatening Jewish students are, many of these people, as Will pointed out, are the future leaders of the Jewish community.

Many of them are going on into the rabbinate and Jewish communal work, into writing, into professions; they could be the ones contributing money. You know, when we talk about Jewish students, we're talking about the Jewish future and future leadership and, yes, the university is a place to test new ideas and is a place to innovate; you don't get much of a chance afterwards outside the university, and so those four years or whatever in college are very important, and the Hillel Directors have to foster that kind of innovation, and they continue to do so.

Chapter 9

My Secret Days and Nights in the Jewish Defense League

Betty Keva, editor, *Boston Jewish Advocate*, Thursday, May 2, 1985

Jack Nusan Porter is a long-time Jewish activist and the author/editor of 18 books and monographs, mostly on Jewish subjects. He is founder and president of The Spencer Group, a Newton-based real estate consulting, development and mortgage-brokering company.

Like a bad penny, Meir Kahane seems to be showing up everywhere. He's a troublemaker, and I'd like to tell you how it was f years ago when I was a troublemaker, too, as a member of his Jewish Defense League.

I've never admitted it publicly, and most of my liberal friends will be shocked. But my involvement in the JDL explains some of the appeal of Kahane. Today, I'm a real estate consultant and developer; back then I fancied myself to be a Jewish rebel.

In 1969 when I was a grad student in sociology in Evanston, Illinois, at Northwestern University, the JDL was organizing the protest the treatment of Soviet Jews. There were legitimate groups like the Student Struggle for Soviet Jewry, but the JDL had made a name for itself by using militant tactics such as chaining themselves to the Soviet consulate gates in New York City, engaging in sit-ins on the streets in front of the consulate, smoke-bombing and stink-bombing Soviet artistic appearances, and eventually escalating to the bombing of Sol Hurok's office.

There is a recent movie called *Kaddish* about a young boy named Yossi Klein who was involved in similar demonstrations. He is a son of Holocaust survivors. I am, too. That movie was my story in many ways. It was that guilt and that confusion that led me to temporarily abandon my ideals that I had learned in Ichud Habonim, the Labor Zionist Youth Movement of my early years, and join the JDL.

* * *

A friend at Northwestern's Hillel told me of semi-secret meetings of the JDL to plan and carry out direct action. Since this was the era of angry Vietnam Vets, fiery SDS radicals, and militant Black Panthers, it was easy to model our tactics on the anti-ROTC and anti-government techniques of the day. The only difference was that this was going to be the Jewish Right using left-wing tactics against the Jewish Left and other targets.

I vividly remember my first late night meeting in the Rogers Park section of Chicago. There were six of us plus several Dobermans. The apartment belonged to someone who loved guns—and a Jew who loved guns was a strange bird indeed. There were guns in special cases lining the wall—shot-guns and even machine guns. I was both frightened and fascinated by the fact that here were armed Jews. It was, in my fantasy world, like the Warsaw Ghetto.

My cohorts included a Jewish soldier direct from Vietnam, a Jewish cop, and assorted other Jewish macho types. There was also my Hillel friend. Coming from a small *shtetl* like Milwaukee, I had never seen such Jews before—so different from my Jewish professors and fellow intellectuals at the University of Chicago and at Northwestern. We thought we were tough but we were powder-puffs compared to these characters.

The Bolshoi Ballet was coming to the Civic Auditorium, and we were going to disrupt it. We knew there would be the usual Jewish, Polish, and Ukrainian protest groups with their placards, plus rabbis and their "Sunday School" students. How could we disrupt the ballet, spilling all those people into the street and into the demonstrations? Now, that would get us not only all five Chicago TV stations but also national media like *Time*, the *New York Times*, ABC, CBS, and NBC. We cackled at how easy it was going to be to get the media out and the Jewish community all worked up. We definitely manipulated the media. They knew it and we knew it and it was quite easy to do.

We wanted people to leave peacefully and safely, but how could we disrupt and still do that? Heckling and shouting would just get us thrown out and the show would go on. We thought of throwing a smoke bomb on stage but felt it might blind or stagger people.

Even worse was a tear gas attack, which would most likely cause a riot. We decided on hydrogen sulfide liquid—stink bombs—and my Hillel friend and I volunteered to do it. Why? Youthful idealism and naïveté? Who really knows?

That evening we dressed up in suits just like any other respectable theater-goer, bought tickets, and went to our seats. In our pockets were small vials of the evil-smelling stuff. In the middle of the first act of the ballet, we were to walk up the aisle in the dark and slowly pour out the liquid onto the carpet, then casually walk out the building, and watch the amusement that would follow.

I saw my friend doing it, and then I did it, but something went wrong. Someone shouted, "Long Live Soviet Jewry" and I just ran up the aisle into the men's room after pouring a little on the carpet. To this day, I'm not sure why, but I smashed the vial against the bathroom wall and ran out the door to the street.

The plan succeeded—finely dressed patrons, many in fur coats, came out calmly but deliberately, swearing under their breath. The performance was ruined. They opened the doors and windows to let the stink out.

It was my first and last act for and with the JDL. I decided then and there that not only was violence wrong but the JDL itself was wrong for deceiving naïve students and confused (and sometimes scary) Jewish tough guys with glib speeches and easy answers. I think the JDL and Kach stink in more ways than one, and I'll explain why.

* * *

There is a crazy irony to this. Several years later, I joined a group here in Boston called *Breira*, and we held a national convention in Washington, DC. JDL members marched, harassed, yelled through the windows, and generally disrupted our peaceful gathering. Once they even tried to storm through the doors.

I went into the lobby to see what was happening, and a man in his 50s—not a young man—ran up to me and bellowed, "You damn self-hating Jew"—"You traitorous pig," and then spit in my face!

I was never so shocked in my life . . . nor so angry. I could have destroyed him right there. Luckily, we were pulled apart by a policeman and several *Breira* people. Since then, I've not only had a disagreement ideologically with the JDL but a palpable disgust.

Kahane may be an engaging man, but he preaches hatred of others, and he attracts, both here and in Israel, the worst hooligan elements of the Jewish community. As a Holocaust survivor, they remind me of the Jewish policemen and the Jewish tough guys who worked with the Judenrat and the SS. We now have our own Jewish fascists and racists.

We live a democracy that does not need such vigilantism. The American Jewish community and Israeli society have overwhelmingly repudiated Kahane's philosophy. Kahaneism is a repudiation of everything our rabbis have taught us about righteousness. It is a disgrace to the memory of our prophets who preached social justice and equality. Kahaneism will pass from the scene, but, like a bad cold, it will linger. It will pass on but not without a great deal of pain and shame.

Chapter 10

Northwestern: The Making of a Sociologist

The following essay, "My Secret Days and Nights in the JDL," written soon after my days at Northwestern, gives a flavor of the wild and dangerous times in graduate school during the radical '60s. But they turned me into a sociologist.

This is an impressionistic memoir of my four years of graduate study at Northwestern University from 1967–1971. It deals with personal and professional conflicts in such matters as academic socialization, sex roles, political tensions, Black-white relations, psychological and sexual tensions, religious ambivalences, and lifestyle conflicts. It concludes with a question that all people, not only sociologists, must answer; to whom do you owe your life? To your teachers? Your parents? Or ultimately to yourself? Hopefully, the essay will also serve two other functions: to formulate policy and encourage more humane means of socializing graduate students; and secondly, to encourage research in the areas raised in this article; in short, to convert these personal impressions into hard data. I certainly hope so, because I believe the issues raised here have not disappeared.

Looking back at those years in Evanston, Illinois, they were not only four very turbulent years in American political history but also four very special years in my social and intellectual growth. These memoirs are really vignettes of a time and place that will never be duplicated again. It has taken nearly a dozen years to cut the so-called "academic umbilical cord" and to gain needed perspective. Yet, when I look back, the memory, while filled with moments of pain, is also permeated with warmth and intellectual excitement. Such intense social, emotional and intellectual excitement rarely comes again after graduate school. For me the sociology department emerges as a relatively humane place despite the personal turmoil, political tensions, and personality clashes. The university has traditionally been a place to shake up preconceived attitudes, and the late '60s was quite a time for "shaking up."

Northwestern University (hereafter NU), the only private school in the Big Ten Conference, is also a relatively small one compared to such academic "factories" as the Universities of Wisconsin, Illinois, Minnesota, or Michigan. This gave us a welcome intimacy. Furthermore, although we sometimes fell under the shadow of our illustrious neighbor down the lake, the University of Chicago (U of C), I remember several Chicago graduate students telling me how they envied the close-knit relationship between faculty, students, and staff at NU. This was missing to some degree at U of C.

In terms of prestige, graduate students from both schools respected each other and sometimes dated each other.[11]

The Faculty and Its Impact

I was blessed with a fine, fairly young faculty at NU, and they did much to turn us into good sociologists. While there were differences of opinion on this issue (as I will discuss later), several important contributions were made by students later. I'd like to briefly describe some of our teachers and their impact.

As in most departments, students gravitated to various sociological styles and methods. For example, if one wished to specialize in the sociology of deviance, occupations, and the "soft" methods of participant observation, one tried to have Howard S. Becker on one's dissertation committee. Becker, to me, was one of the most charismatic figures in the department. A student of Everett C. Hughes

---

11 Several Chicago students did tell me how they envied the close-knit relationship among faculty, staff, and students. Teachers often threw parties for students, and students invited teachers to their parties, and even secretaries hosted parties for everyone. If I seem to emphasize this social side of academic life, it is because it is an important socializing element in graduate school. Such years are filled with pressure, and any way to relieve the pressure and enhance more open and warm relations should be welcome. In other words, what the U of C students were saying was that, even though they may have been going to a slightly more prestigious school, they nevertheless felt deprived of faculty understanding, and that counted higher than any added prestige.

at U of C, he had done work on musicians, teachers, and marijuana smokers that was considered quite radical at the time. If his labeling theory of deviance is now somewhat "old-hat," in the 1950s and 1960s it was innovative and exciting. I still marvel at his teaching abilities in methods class; no notes, cigarette dangling from his mouth, he could make the most insightful comments about the most mundane occupations. His work was theoretical but based firmly on much first-hand observation. He, and his celebrated colleague in labeling theory, John Kitsuse, influenced many of us. Two students in particular who have continued in this sociological tradition are Malcolm Spector of McGill University and Charles Suchar of De Paul University, Chicago.

Becker, a man constantly on the move intellectually, perhaps foresaw the decline of interest in labeling theory (or else he felt "talked out" on the subject), and in my last year at NU began to move in a field that was beginning to attract attention—the sociology of art—and he and his students (Barbara Rosenbloom of Stanford University and Chandra Hecht Mukerji, now at the University of California–San Diego) made initial contributions to this area, especially in the sociology of photograph and theatre. Becker had the gift of knowing when to move on to new and exciting vistas and to take a few students along with him.

Others: In the field of urban studies, one gravitated to Scott Greer, Arnold Feldman, and Janet Abu-Lughod; in the sociology of law, to Richard Schwartz, who later became the first sociologist to head a law school (at the State University of New York–Buffalo); in the sociology of the military and developing nations, to Charles (Charlie) Moskos and Arnold Feldman; in demography, to Allan Schnalberg and Janet Abu-Lughod; in Africa social organization, education and the family, to Remi Clignet; in family studies, to the late Robert Winch; and for social stratification, education, and minority relations, to Raymond Mack.

Bernard Beck, a specialist in many areas (theory, religion, welfare) though not a prolific writer, was important to me and other students, both for his formidable knowledge in the history of sociological thought and for his warm personal style, which attracted many of us to his office for coffee and talk. The late Robert Winch, while older and more austere, taught me quantitative methods, though his real interests lie in survey research on the family. Several of his students went on to make a name: Rae Lesser Blumberg and Louis Wolf Goodman. It was a terribly sad loss when this tall, stately, handsome man died of cancer a few years ago. Richard Berk and Carol Owens were also influential in small ways. They were junior faculty at the tail end of my years at NU. I might add that the chairmen of the department during 1967–1971 were Ray Mack, Robert Winch, and Charles Moskos. Mack did not make too much of an impression on me, since he moved into the administration of NU and was rarely around. Charlie Moskos became a good friend, and while some students disagreed with his views on Vietnam and the military, his courses on political sociology were memorable. In all, we had good young scholars and seasoned veterans, and most were excellent teachers. I might add that NU had teachers in other departments that I took courses with: Donald Campbell and Jack Sawyer in psychology, Edward Hall in anthropology, and several in Africana studies.

Northwestern produced a number of fine scholars active in the field: Ron Edari (social change); Steve Buff, Joyce Kozuch, Arthur Paris (Caribbean and Black Studies); Sam Mueller (sociology of religion); George Kourvetaris (military sociology); Joseph Blake (collective behavior); Margaret Gordo, Paul Lubeck, William Bridges (labor studies); and several others, including some active in foreign affairs: Bic Ijomah, Pasquale Paanza, Jose Gil, and Luis Salces.[12]

Without being overly modest, I too have made a contribution in the area of racial and ethnic minorities, the sociology of Jewry, Israeli politics, and the sociology of genocide; Jewish radicalism, and conflict/conflict resolution. A book based on my dissertation "Student Protest and the Technocratic Society: The Case of ROTC: (1973), and an anthology I edited with Peter Dreier that has become very influential in its field, *Jewish Radicalism: A Selected Anthology* (Northwestern University, 1973), were both published two years after I graduated from NU.

In short, NU graduates have made contributions to the discipline. The faculty, too, has distinguished itself: several presidents of the SSSP have come from NU (Bernard Beck, Ray Mack, John Kitsuse, and Howard S. Becker). Raymond Mack was also an unsuccessful candidate for ASA president but held other important positions in the association. Many of them continue to publish widely, and perhaps in greater quantity than their students. Allen Schnaiberg, Janet Abu-Lughod, John Walton, Scott Greer, Richard Berk, Remi Clignet, and Charles Moskos have all published at least one book since I left NU. Some of them are no longer at NU. Academic mobility has taken its effect. (For some reason, a large number have gone to sunny California.)

Academic Socialization

David Reisman makes an important distinction between sociology and professional fields such as law, medicine, and nursing. In the latter, an early

---

12 Even these students have students now. For example, I have had two students who have gone into sociology, and one of them, Barry Glassner, has gone on to make quite a name for himself at a very young age. In short, the cycle continues.

and intensive form of re-socialization takes place that is soon legitimized at the moment of certification. Such students are treated as adults and as (pre) professionals—in other words, as future lawyers, doctors, and nurses. I am sorry to say that this does not always happen in the social sciences; one is not always treated as a colleague or a professional, and worse, one may never really know when one has been fully accepted into the "club." I know full professors who still feel insecure about their status as sociologists. No governing board, no *rite de passage*, not even one's dissertation committee can give one the peace of mind to say: "Yes, I am now a professional sociologist, acceptable to my colleagues and teachers."

This academic state of limbo can last for many years after the PhD and causes a great deal of anxiety. Eventually, however, one accepts oneself as a professional. Part of the "umbilical cord" problem alluded to earlier is to finally see oneself, not as a student, but as an equal partner in the sociological enterprise. This problem may be even more acute for female sociologists because of the added dilemma of gender stereotyping.

How does one become socialized into a profession? The most common method is to serve an apprenticeship under one or several models, and this is what happens in grad school. The search for a mentor is crucial, but what is really needed is to find one faculty "superstar" and two or three supporting "stars." The problem is the competition. Too often, the "superstar" is so popular he or she may be impossible to "catch."

Pierre van den Berghe points out in his humorous and quite useful book *Academic Gamesmanship: How to Make a Ph.D. Pay* (1970) that "if [the "superstar"] has too many students, his ability to be of use to you will be diluted, and the competition within his coterie of clients will be intense. However, if you feel confident that you can outshine our competitors, then attach yourself to the star anyway" (33).

But this may be difficult, as it was for me, because the "superstar" I wanted (Howie Becker) had too many students. I finally chose a fine PhD committee, consisting of Janet Abu-Lughod, Allen Schnaiberg, and Richard Schwartz. Choosing a dissertation committee in such a highly charged atmosphere as van de Berghe descried is a critical factor in post-graduate school success, as their letters of recommendation are key elements in career advancement, especially for the first job. Usually after that, the young assistant professor is on their own, but those letters from dissertation chairpersons are still important years later. One's career will be followed closely by the department for the rest of one's life. For good or ill, what one does reflects on one's teachers, negatively or positively.

Regarding sex discrimination in choosing the "superstars," there was none that I knew of at NU. The department was seen as quite liberal, even radical, and while the feminist movement had not yet reached its peak there or in the country, there were a good number of women among the grad students. (Out of eighty students in the sociology department between 1967 and 1968, twenty-eight were women, or thirty-five percent.)

Both women and men had equal access to the "superstars"; it all depended on the right combination of talents, interests, and personality mesh. However, I am aware that a major concern of the feminist movement is the lack of adequate role models for women. That may have been a problem back then; there were few women teachers between 1967 and 1971—only three out of some twenty positions, or fifteen percent. But, by 1979, the number of women had jumped to eight out of twenty-one teachers, or thirty-eight percent. Affirmative action was on the move. From 1967 to 1971, there were no full women professors; today there are two in the department (Janet Abu-Lughod and Arlene Kaplan Daniels).

Regarding other minorities, in my graduate days there was only one Black professor (Walter Wallace, now at Princeton); today, there are four, a jump from five percent to nearly twenty percent. As for Asian Americans, there was only one (John Kitsuse) a dozen years ago, and after he left there were none. While Jews are not considered a minority group in affirmative action, professors of Jewish background made up about fifty percent back in 1967–1971, and today that figure is roughly the same. In short, for African Americans and women there are many more role models than there were even a dozen years ago.

Political Tensions

These were years of great student and societal upheaval, and no description can fully describe the power of those times. NU sociology students were right in the center of the action. While politically, they were spread across the spectrum from conservative to liberal to revolutionary, most were on the left-to-liberal side of the fence.[13]

There was a small but noticeable contingent of students who came out of the military (Bob Carroll, Frank Osanka) who were attracted to the military sociology specialists at NU and U. of C.—Charles Moskos and Morris Janowitz. These included several army officers (including one major and a captain), West

---

13 (This is not surprising for sociologists or their grad students, and is backed up by research by Ladd and Lipset (1975): 93-124.

Point instructors, and a CIA specialist in counter-insurgency. Their support of the Vietnam War came under attack by the majority of students in the department.

Our department, it must be noted, was considered one of the most radical on campus, and such student leaders as Lee Weiner, one of the famous Chicago Eight who went on trial for demonstrations at the 1968 Democratic convention, were graduate students. Weiner had the sympathy and respect of several key and influential faculty members and was an enormously charismatic student. Even the faculty was in awe of him and his prodigious mind.

The Black students were also highly politicized, staging a sit-in on campus that received national coverage. One of the key spokesmen at that sit-in, James Turner, was a highly respected grad student in the department. James Pitts, who was to return to NU as an assistant professor, was also quite active. Black demands were more readily accepted than those of white radicals, and out of the sit-in came a Black studies program, more Black students and teachers, and a home on campus called FMO, For Members Only.

The women's movement, on the other hand, had not yet fully broken away from the male-dominated antiwar movement, but this was soon realized, and women have made many strides for equality since then. The local SDS (Students for a Democratic Society) was led by undergraduate students, and they distrusted the graduate students to some degree because they felt they were too moderate. (I would use the term "level-headed" instead.) The SDS was led by a very idealistic yet impulsive and paranoid group of individuals. There were times when we graduate students tried (unsuccessfully) to stop them from committing acts of violence (i.e., attacking a ROTC building) even after they had gotten strong student support for their positions on the war and on ROTC. In that sense, the SDS was often politically suicidal (a term that was also used then was "Custeristic"), and it was ultimately discredited in the eyes of most students.

On the academic level, the graduate students were active in educational reforms and policies. Having had sympathetic faculty members made that task easier. For example: great changes were made in what were called the "qualifying exams"—the exams that one took to pass from stage to stage, from MA. to PhD, for example. Instead of the traditional two six-hour doctoral qualifying examinations, we instituted a series of alternatives that still exist a decade later.

Students now had a choice of (a) the traditional sit-down exams; (b) the same exams but take-home; (c) a qualifying paper akin to a Master's thesis; or (d) the innovative part—a judgment on one's previously published material. Ironically, here was a radical deal that was first taken advantage of by one of those in the conservative camp. The counterinsurgency expert from the CIA had edited a book on guerrilla warfare and had written several important articles in the field, and this made it possible for him to pass what the students called "Check-Point-Charlie"—the set of procedures that enables one to go on and write the dissertation and thereby obtain the PhD. This checkpoint was considered to be the most difficult stage in graduate school. If successfully passed, it almost assured one's getting a PhD.

The faculty was also responsive to new courses and innovative approaches to old courses—especially those that reflected the latest political strife: a seminar on the Black revolutionary Frantz Fanon taught by Professor Remi Clignet; another on revolutionary movements; a class on the sociology of art; and one on the art and science of teaching. I am most proud of the last course because I helped organize and direct it.

As can easily be imagined, graduate school between 1967 and 1971 was a time of great stress. Graduate school is always tension-filled, but those years were especially tumultuous. One's personal philosophy and way of life come under seething attack. Long-cherished beliefs from home and neighborhood are vulnerable to the teachings of sophisticated and secular college professors.

For example, I had entered NU with a fairly secure set of religious and political beliefs concerning Judaism, Jews, and Israel, and I had also come from a very Orthodox Jewish background. All my beliefs came under intense criticism by secular leftists and liberals in the department over the issue of Zionism and Jewish rights. In response, my views changed or were modified. (See section on religious tensions). I had to find some golden mean between traditional Judaism and such modern ideologies as radicalism and socialism.

In 1973, out of my personal and political *angst* would emerge a book called *Jewish Radicalism* (with Peter Dreier) and in 1975 a later evaluation (again with Dreier).[14] It also led to my founding, along with a few other NU graduate students (none in sociology), the Jewish Student Movement in Chicago, one of the first in the country. Such a group would be an activist group in Jewish as well as antiwar and civil rights concerns. It would be critical of both the Jewish establishment in America and Israel and any Black, radical, or Third World group who espoused antisemitism or anti-Zionism. These political and intellectual efforts meshed to help me reorient myself, and are a process that continues to this very day. It is the continuous shifting, adapting, and accommodating of

---

14 Peter Dreier and Jack Nusan Porter, "Jewish Radicalism in Transition," *Society Magazine* 12, no. 2 (January–February 1975): 34-43.

political and religious beliefs in order to fit new realities. The genesis of these tensions in my life emerged out of my 1967–1971 graduate days.

Those years vividly raised an old question in science—the tension between the detached, objective scholar and the involved, subjective partisan. Is it our task to study society, or to change it . . . or both? I have opted for Marx's dictum—to understand and to transform. In the end, many of us at NU tried to do both good scholarly work and good political work. My own way out of the dilemma was to demonstrate against ROTC in the morning and to write my dissertation about the ROTC (1971) at night. I was a kind of "schizophrenic" participant observer. Looking back, perhaps *both* the dissertation and the politics suffered. I had spread myself too thin. Still, to this day, I combine activism and scholarship, and I let others decide what suffers. I no longer worry about this existential question.

In conclusion, I have several regrets about those years. First of all, we did not win all our battles for justice and equality. We had to leave a few things for future generations! But also, another thing stands out in my mind: my moral outrage against the war often stifled effective communication with people who disagreed with me. I now wish I could have had more dialogue with the West Point officers and other military specialists, with the more conservative professors, school administrators, and students, and with the outside world. But we were acting out a huge pageant, and, like puppets, *deus ex machina*, we played out our elected roles with history.

Psychological Tensions

The conflicts of academic training can often lead to acute psychological stress, and this stress can lead to a variety of coping mechanisms. The stress of competition in graduate school can, for example, induce a wide variety of cheating, some of it done at a very *un*sophisticated level—blatant plagiarism, prewritten papers and theses, or simply copying answers from someone else. I knew a student who ripped an exam off my desk in order to copy the answers to an extremely difficult statistics test. In most ways, he was an honest student but for his desperate fear of mathematics. He passed the test and today he is a well-respected sociologist at a well-known university.

The pressures can also lead to more serious problems—to what are commonly called "nervous breakdowns" but are really acute anxiety attacks. In many cases, the faculty and students were totally unaware of these "breakdowns" if the person managed, with great effort and pain, to turn in required assignments. The rationale is that if one can still "produce," if one can still work, that in itself can stave off the realization that one is "totally crazy."

One of the most cruel and least understood tragedies of graduate life is suicide, and it strikes every campus. The only case in our class was a divorced mother of three who had returned to school after long years of raising children. She was also one of the few "flunkouts" in our class, having failed her PhD qualifying exams and was told not to apply again. As a "consolation prize" she was given a terminal master's degree. During the last year or two of her short life, she engaged in a series of highly bizarre acts: she spied on a particular professor; she drove to his home, waited for him to come home to his family, and peeked into his windows. Sometimes she waited for him all night long in her car and then followed him to school in the morning. She also suffered from acute pangs of paranoia wherein she thought everyone, including her friends, were in a conspiracy against her, and she threatened to sue the department for being unfairly dismissed. She was told by the chairman of the sociology department to seek psychiatric treatment, but to no avail. A year after my graduation in 1971, I learned of her suicide.

While there is little one can do for a person bent on destroying oneself, and while there are often telltale signs along the way, most people are still shocked. Most of the faculty will not become involved unless the behavior is truly unusual or if it affects one's work. As Craig Eisendrath and Thomas Cottle point out:

> With the exception of some extraordinary people, faculty find such matters out of line with their own stated careers of scholarly concerns, or they feel themselves unable to deal with what they conceive of as the students' "psychological" problems. Indeed, some will even maintain that wherever these troublesome problems may be, the students should buckle down and get to work.[15]

Even though teachers are concerned with the mental health of their students, they find it awkward to get "involved" in these problems which they see as being outside their realm of competence, and they tend to resist efforts to make themselves more involved. As Eisendrath and Cottle point out:

> It is adult attention, among other things, that these young people seek, but the nature of many educational institutions prevents them from receiving it. (54–55)

---

15 1972, 54.

Moreover, a school's health services can never compensate for a lack of human care of the part of faculty and administration, and for a system of education which fails to nurture the autonomy and competence which students lack when they enter. Most faculty fail to actively involve themselves with the mental health of their students and, in doing so, they exacerbate the health of the very students they are there to help.

Perhaps Eisendrath and Cottle are too hard on faculty. Most are concerned, more are aware of suicide and other psychological problems, and clinics have been set up to intervene. But in the late '60s it was a taboo subject. Still, it is an area that more faculty and students must be attuned to, and in any discussions of academic history or departments, it is a common phenomenon.

Sexual Tensions

If death and mental illness are still "closet" subjects to some degree, sex has emerged out of the dark, and yet we know very little about the sexual problems of graduate students. I am concerned here not with the physical act but with the social relationship. Relationships among graduate students are analogous to sibling rivalry and therefore "incestuous." Each sibling is competing desperately for the approval of multiple father or mother figures. Furthermore, business and pleasure rarely mix, and so I remember that most students sought out students in other departments or in other schools for sexual gratification.[16]

For single and divorced students there is the problem of time and energy needed to search out and find suitable partners. Often, that is why student-teacher or undergraduate-graduate student relations are so common: availability. There is also another reason that is only now coming to light. Teaching, as the late social thinker Paul Goodman has noted, has sexual overtones. A large pool of single men and women (students) and a powerful leader (the teacher) can set us a situation that can lead to sexual favors given or rejected. The teacher, even the graduate instructor, is in a position to seek out attractive partners of the opposite (or even same) sex in exchange for higher grades or simply as a sign of dominance. Examples of blatant sexuality and sexual favors among students and teachers were so common that few considered them a problem if they were carried out with discretion. However, the feminist movement has exposed this practice, and many instructors will think twice about engaging in sex with a

---

16 The sexual issues are sensitive enough without even mentioning homosexual concerns. It was even more of a taboo subject back then.

student today. Still, the practice continues and has ramifications beyond this short paper.

As for the impact of graduate training on marriage, again we need more research. While the common assumption is that graduate school puts a great strain on marriage (and it does) and leads to higher rates of divorce, one should also note, as I have, the number of marriages that *survive* graduate school and prevail. What accounts for this success? What are the stress factors? What can be done to help wives and husbands of graduate students through this *rite de passage?* It would behoove us to formulate humane policies and frameworks to deal with the issue.

Religious Tensions

This issue may seem irrelevant to some readers, but it is important. Sociology continues to attract people from the religious life just as it has eighty or more years ago when large numbers of American sociologists were the sons of Protestant ministers. Could sociology be a secular substitute for the religious life? In any case, our department had a small but visible number of priests, nuns, seminarians, or simply people from an orthodox background, such as myself.

Being young and impressionistic, my religious beliefs were shaken at NU, and there were few role models in the department who were both Jewish and proud of it. As I discussed earlier, this led to a painful reorientation basically done on my own but with the help of the NU Hillel Foundation rabbi and several graduate students who shared a similar anguish. Just as African Americans, women, Asian Americans, and other minorities used role models, so too did Jews. While half the department was Jewish, only a few were willing to discuss my interests in Israel and Judaism. The rest were assassinated Jews or had other, more important interests. Nevertheless, it was a painful process.

I have discussed my own socialization problems regarding religious tensions. There were others in the department—nuns, priests, ministers—with similar tensions. Coming under the stress of the secular university life, some left the clergy altogether or else found some compromise, perhaps a secular substitute for "people-healing" (i.e., social work, counseling). All of them had to modify their own religious attitudes and lifestyles, and usually religious tensions went hand-in-hand with political and psychological ennui.[17]

---

17 For more on this tension, see Kotre, 1978, on the life of Father Andrew Greeley, sociologist and priest.

Conclusions

On a recent visit to my *alma mater* (winter of 1975), one of my professors sadly remarked that so few of the students in our class of 1971 were actually doing sociology. He was frankly discouraged, while other faculty members were angered at the waste of time and trouble. Still others were simply resigned to the fact. As one put it:

> All one needs do is peruse the journals to note the absence of the Northwestern cohort members. . . . Faculty concern with this group (and not just the "rebels") centers on the inability of a large number of these people to engage in quality research, consultation, or teaching. Witness their presence in the job market year after year.[18]

This professor has no firm data to rely on, and neither do I, but a closer look at those who graduated with me does show that a good many are involved in sociology in one way or another. Many may have gone into alternative lifestyles or careers, either temporarily or permanently, but the majority are involved in either teaching sociology or "applying" it as social workers, drug counselors, public health professionals, and similar work. Given the present job scarcity of academic positions, the number may not be at all discouraging. Many are not writing in journals that this professor cherishes or are not doing the "quality research" he desires, but given the economic situation, perhaps other skills should have been taught them so as to better cope with the "job crunch."[19]

Nevertheless, the 1967–1971 cohort is teaching at fine schools; for example: Yale, Stanford, Wisconsin, University of Washington, Amherst, University of Hawaii, Boston College, Rutgers, McGill, Cornell, and several others. Very few graduate students in any case become renowned in their field, and very few even publish books, but NU graduates have published several books; they have published articles in prestigious journals like the *American Sociological Review* and *Social Problems*; and some have even founded scholarly journals (George Kourvetaris set up the *Journal of Military and Political Sociology* and I founded the *Journal of the History of Sociology*; and several are active in professional groups and as journal editorial board members. I don't believe that their output has been minor when compared to graduates of Chicago, Harvard, or Columbia, but in

---

18 Anonymous letter by reviewer, March 1977.
19 See Morrissey and Steadman (1977).

any case, this is all conjecture. Until the NU sociology department conducts its own full-scale survey, we will never know for sure, one way or the other.

Still, the major question, the *leitmotif* really of this article, is: To whom do you owe your life? To yourself, or to your professors? Do professors have the right to mold their students into a model of their own making? Perhaps they do, but should they be disappointed if that mold cracks and another persona emerges? There comes a time when professors too much break the "umbilical cord" with their students and accept lifestyles different from those of the conventional professional scholar. Graduate schools must today present *other* models, give the scarce number of jobs, and they are beginning to do just that today.

Here are some examples of what this 1967–1971 cohort has done:

Item: One student dropped out of training before completing his PhD in order to become director of an African American studies institute at a major university. Years later, he received his PhD, but from another college, and he is still director of that institute.

Item. One politically active student also did not complete his dissertation but went on to teach at a major East Coast university. He lost his job under administration pressure because of an article that appeared in a New York paper regarding his political views and activities. He is today a social worker in New York City and later completed his PhD in sociology.

Item. Another student temporarily dropped out of school to become an organic food farmer on an island on the Northwest Coast. Yet, he too completed his dissertation and now teaches in a large public university.

Item. Another decided to become a medical doctor after dropping out with only his master's degree. He is now a physician.

Item. Another student lived in the Rocky Mountains and supported himself as a musician, but I've seen him recently at a sociology conference, and he has returned to teaching and completing his studies.

Item. Another student has published a dozen books and over 150 articles and reviews in the general area of ethnic studies, but finds it difficult to find a full-time position because of the economic situation. He is listed in *Who's Who in the East, American Men and Women of Science,* and *American Authors,* but it doesn't help. Still, he continues in sociology.

Item. One student joined the Montreal Symphony Orchestra.

Item. And finally, another works in San Francisco for the recreation department and ended his NU studies after obtaining his master's degree. He does no more sociology.

The crucial question remains: To whom do you owe your life? To what use must you make of your education? Is graduate training a complete waste of time if one decides to do something else? These are not easy questions to answer. To continue this line of reasoning, if a PhD in sociology took his skills and joined the staff of a political organization, a consumer group, a religious institution, or community project, and forsook teaching and research, what would his or her professors think? (In today's shrinking job market, they'd be happy he/she is not driving a cab!) But professors are demanding other things as well. Many want their students not only to *do* sociology (research and teaching), and this is a fair and reasonable demand, but to do the *right kind* of sociology.

What if a student did go into research but did it in a very different way—a Marxist approach? A feminist approach? A Jewish approach? A new and vastly critical approach (of their own teacher's, no less)? What then? Alvin Gouldner answers it best: "There is no such thing as Black, white, feminist, Jewish, Christian, radical, sexist, or gay sociology, hard or soft sociology . . . there is only good or bad sociology!"[20]

Yet what is often overlooked is that the vast majority of my classmates *are* immersed in the sociological enterprise in one way or another. Many are in academia, too, or trying to get back in. They are teaching. They are acting as consultants. They are lecturing to community groups. A few are even doing research and trying to get it published. There may not be enough being published to please some of my professors, but there may be powerful reasons besides motivation behind that—lack of research money, lack of time, and difficulty getting into those prestigious journals that their professors are reading.

Epilogue

It has been impossible to summarize in a few pages four of the most tumultuous and important years of my life. Whenever I look back at those years, I feel a tinge of pity for today's students. They are too young to have taken part in the 1960s—Vietnam, the demonstrations, Kent State University, Jackson State College, ROTC protests, hippies; these are just another chapter in history books. Only the faculty remembers and those of us who lived through those powerful years. As one Boston student leader put it:

> The masses aren't marching this year. The masses are in the library. They take school work *soooo seriously* . . . . Everybody's just fuckin' blah. I can't offer any original explanation except,

---

20 Personal conversation with author, August 1975, Boston.

at Harvard, everyone's studying. Everyone wants to go to grad school. Everyone wants to be doctors or lawyers. Everyone wants to make lots of money.[21]

These same views were echoed by a Northeastern University (Boston) student president:

Deep down, the fact is that a lot of kids wish they were going to college in the 1960s when students got together more often and were active. (Quoted in *Span*, 1976:10)

History, however, moves in cycles. The 1970s student lived through a '50s apathetic concern for security, but the 1980s has brought back student protest over the draft, Iran, the economy. Living through the 1960s was not easy. It reminds me of the old Chinese curse: "May you live in interesting times." We did indeed live through interesting times, and as our class enters early middle age, we wouldn't replace those years for anything.[22]

1976

References

Dreier, Peter, and Jack Nusan Porter. "Jewish Radicalism in Transition" *Society (Transaction)* 12, no. 2 (Jan.–Feb. 1975).

Eisendrath, Craig R. and Thomas J. Cottle. *Out of Discontent: Visions of the Contemporary University*. Boston: Schenkman Publishing Company, 1972.

Kotre, John N. *The Best of Times, the Worst of Times: Andrew Greeley and American Catholicism, 1950–1975*. Chicago: Nelson-Hall, 1978.

Ladd, Everett Carl, and Seymour Martin Lipset. *The Divided Academy: Professors and Politics*. New York: McGraw-Hill, 1975.

---

21 *Harvard Crimson*, 1976, 10.

22 This paper was first presented at the American Sociological Association Professional Workshop on "Survival in Graduate School," August 1976, New York City. I have kept anonymous names of students and teachers where such disclosure would prove to be embarrassing or rude. This paper was not meant to appeal to "prurient interests" but to raise issues that are often concealed. My apologies to those who feel otherwise.

Morrissey, Joseph P., and Henry J. Steadman. "Practice and Perish? Some Overlooked Career Contingencies for Sociologists in Non-Academic Settings." *The American Sociologist* 12, no. 4 (Nov. 1977): 154–162.

Porter, Jack Nusan. "Student Protest, University Decision-Making, and the Technocratic Society: The Case of ROTC." PhD diss., Northwestern University, 1971. Micro-film. A shorter version was published by Adams Press, Chicago, in 1973.

———, and Peter Dreier. *Jewish Radicalism: A Selected Anthology.* New York: Grove Press, 1973.

Span, Paula. "We Search for the New Campus Leaders." *The Boston Phoenix* (Special Education Section), April 6, 1976, 8–10.

Van den Berghe, Pierre. *Academic Gamesmanship: How to Make a Ph.D. Pay.* New York: Abelard-Schuman (an Intext Book), 1970.

Chapter 11

Academic Follies

———————

I spent over half a century in academia, from undergrad to grad school to lecturer to assistant professor (I never got higher than that, since I never stayed around long enough), from lowly community college to Northwestern University, and from small liberal arts colleges to a major university like Harvard. While I loved my students and many of my colleagues, I must admit that the overall experience was negative and became more so at the tail end of my academic career.

And I am not alone. I remember the case of the great Harry Zohn, eminent professor of German at Brandeis University, and how his last years were ones of war and strife. Why? Because he supported the hiring of a young female colleague, which was opposed by other professors in the department.

You might ask why. And I would have to answer, as my great psychoanalyst and therapist friend Dr. Robert Ravven once told me, "Jack, it would take a team of ten of us to figure out the minds of academic professors."

Prof. Richard Pipes had the same experience at the end of his tenure at Harvard's Russian Research Center (now The Davis Center), which he describes in his fabulous memoirs *Vixi: Memoirs of a Non-Belonger*, how in May 1995 he was sorely disappointed with his department's refusal to promote to tenure an excellent young specialist on twentieth-century Russian history. Pipes was outraged, not because his judgment was overruled, but because the department did not even bother to read any of his work and rejected him in an offhand manner. This convinced Pipes that his days in the department were over. In his words, the Russian department was

> no longer a cohesive body which treated department interests as the supreme good, but an agglomeration of individuals who pursued their private concerns and careers. As a result, its reputation declined precipitously: traditionally in the first or second place in the national rankings compiled by *US News and World Report,* by the end of the 1990s it had sunk to sixth or seventh place.[23]

Harry Zohn ended his career embittered. I did *not* want to end *mine* that way. So I took the easy way out: I entered the world of business, real estate, to escape academia and to make a living for my family, and I am happy I did. The money I made in real estate gave me the freedom—even if I had a position at a university—not to depend on the whims of a dean or the decisions of my colleagues. I had freedom!

Humiliations

In his book *My Love Affair with America,* the eminent literary and political critic Norman Podhoretz described his humiliation in an encounter with another giant in the field, Irving Howe, whom he met while he was in the army at Fort Devens, Massachusetts, a short ride from Brandeis University in Waltham, where Howe was teaching. As Podhoretz wrote, "It did not go well."[24] Yet humiliations serve a purpose: they spur you to greater heights. Here are some examples from my own life:

1. Charles Moskos was a Greek American sociologist of some note at Northwestern University in the late 1960s. Graduate school is rife with humiliation. You are new; you aim to please; you are naïve. You want to impress, and then you're shot down. Moskos, a popular yet conservative teacher, punctured my enthusiasm when I told him about an article in *TIME* magazine that had impressed me. He said: "Jack, we don't quote from popular magazines." Yet this same guy would have

---

23 Richard Pipes, *Vixi: Memoirs of a Non-Belonger* (2003), 248.
24 Podhoretz (2006): 120-121.

gone gaga if *he* had been quoted in *TIME* or *The New York Times*. In fact, he became famous later in life when, during the Clinton administration, he suggested the "don't tell, don't ask" approach to gays in the military that Clinton adopted, and Moskos was all over the popular press. What a hypocrite!

2. Harry Madison (pseudonym) was a well-known professor of Holocaust literature at a college in Boston. He punctured an early book I wrote on homosexuals under the Nazis, where I mistakenly labeled several concentration camps as "death camps." Not all camps were "death camps" like Auschwitz or Treblinka. He was, of course, correct. I was new to Holocaust studies, but he could have said it "nicely." Instead, he humiliated me. I promised myself that I would "surpass" him—and I did, in a way. I ended up at Harvard, the most prestigious school on the planet. Years later, he also put me down when I told him that *The New Yorker* had done a short profile of me: his acid response was, "Jack, that was not a profile." (That *profile* is reprinted in this book.)

3. At a Harvard cocktail party in the mid-'80s at the home of Richard and Irene Pipes, people were throwing highfalutin names around like nobody's business: Kierkegaard, Schopenhauer, Nietzsche. I stood there like a statue, saying nothing, unable to open my mouth. The next day I was in Widener Library, learning all I could about them. Had I tried to "prove" that I knew these philosophers, I would have ended up like that classic scene in the movie *Good Will Hunting* where Ben Affleck's character tries to come off as a Harvard student when thankfully he is saved by Matt Damon's character, who ends up humiliating the Harvard students plus walking away with the hot chick.

4. Also in the mid-'80s, when I was connected with the Ukrainian Research Institute at Harvard, I hung around the Center for European Studies (CES), and once, after I gave a talk, I was publicly corrected and humiliated. Today I would have taken it with a "grain of salt" or a "pound of anger." Yet I continue to see such acts of humiliation by audience members or fellow associates at the Davis Center at Harvard and at MIT, and I am astounded at the lack of civility I witness at universities, especially elite ones, as well as the restraint often shown by the "attackee."

True, it is just as bad in the political or business world, but, in many ways, academia is worse. Often it is so petty, or, as Henry Kissinger once said, "They fight so hard over things that are so small" (like who gets a larger office). In fact, as I will point out in my chapter on the organization of genocide scholars (the IAGS) that I helped build, the humiliations came fast and furious. Why was that?

One reason is that academics are usually bookish, unathletic (athletes—ironically, despite their image—have superb social and cooperative skills), insensitive, and insecure. I was, on the other hand, a fine athlete with excellent social skills, plus very smart from a young age; but I still had to face older, less secure professors and intellectuals. Again, Richard Pipes superbly describes the ways of academia:

> Academic life is not all sweetness and light. Scholars are psychologically less secure than most people ... a businessman knows he is successful when he makes money; a politician, when he wins elections; an athlete, when he is first in sporting contests; a popular writer, when he produces best-sellers. But a scholar has no such fixed criteria by which to judge success, and as a consequence he lives in a state of permanent uncertainty which grows more oppressive with age as ambitious younger scholars elbow themselves to the fore and dismiss his work as outdated. His principal criterion for success is approval of peers. This means that he must cultivate them, which makes for conformity and "group think."[25]

I was never concerned with approval from peers when I did my groundbreaking research. I cared only for the ideas themselves, and since I was not part of any department or "school," I was never influenced by such "group-think." True, it was a lonely life being an independent scholar and having no colleagues. But it helped me develop original ideas that later were nominated for a Nobel Peace Prize and other awards.

It also brought me to Harvard.

At Harvard, I learned that if they ask you to come, they assume you are one of the best in your field and you will bring renown to the great Harvard name. They will give you little money—maybe not even a desk or a parking space—but just their name and the use of their libraries and facilities. That's all—and, you know, that's enough. The name itself is prestige.

At first, when I started at Harvard in the early 1980s, I did not feel confident, but now I am. Sadly, it took me many years to acquire that feeling.

---

25 Pipes, *Vixi: Memoirs of a Non-Belonger*, 91-92.

Academic Follies

Maybe I was young and naïve (naïveté is good—it protects you), but I feel that my earliest days in academia at Northwestern (NU), at De Paul University, and at several smaller colleges in Chicago were great experiences. In fact, some of my students, including the sociologist Barry Glassner of the University of Southern California, became quite well known.

In turn, at NU I had great teachers and fellow grad students whom I describe in my essay "The Making of a Sociologist." Plus, I was in love with a fellow teacher, and I still remember our making love on the desks early in the morning before classes.

What a time!

But things would change and go downhill quickly.

SUNY–Cortland

The State University of New York in Cortland (famous for its Cortland apples and great skiing) was my first teaching job as an assistant professor right after graduation from NU in June 1971. It was at the height of the anti-Vietnam War movement, and times were crazy—demonstrations and rallies, speeches from famous figures on the Right and Left. I remember asking (I know, as a leftist, it seems crazy) the infamous Rabbi Meir Kahane to campus to speak, and we were very impressed with his radical call for activism to fight antisemitism and to free Soviet Jews. But we also heard from Black Panthers and radical antiwar figures. We had famous poets such as Paul Blackburn. In all, it was a great crew of colleagues, such as Charlie Vivona and Bruce Carruthers. I even had a wonderful girlfriend from New York. People like her were called "Newyoricans"—New York Puerto Ricans.

But I was unhappy, as the enclosed "public letter" points out. I even made the front page of the school paper. It wasn't just the isolation in winter up north or the conflict on campus that made me leave after one year, but I saw up close the politics of tenure in a department. I saw how full professors who had tenure but were so unhappy with their "golden handcuffs" that they took their misery out on new people, meaning they got tenure but were never going to go anywhere else up the academic ladder to more prestigious places.

They were what Alvin Gouldner called "locals," while I saw myself as a "cosmopolitan," a person of the world, a public intellectual, with a vision of going to the very top, even though I wasn't sure where that was; but I knew it wasn't going to be in Cortland, New York.

What I saw was the humiliation of what sociologists call the "degradation ceremony" of acquiring tenure. It's kind of like the abasement you have to undergo to be accepted into a fraternity or sorority or an army boot camp—in short, the hazing and the just plain stupid and degrading acts you have to endure to get in.

What I saw was a youngish scholar, male, married, with children, going through a similar hazing—personal questions about his life, his wife and her personality, all in the name of "will he and she fit in?" It was so humiliating that I decided then and there I would never go through with it, and I never did. I left the school after one year and returned home to Milwaukee to live with my parents, but at thirty I was too old to be a child at home, and so I left for Boston immediately. It was 1975.

What I said earlier about reaching for the top—that was Boston; that's why I chose Boston. I did not have Harvard in mind consciously, but subconsciously I knew I would get there one day, and within five years, I was at Harvard.

Boston College

Mary Daly, Father Daley, and Catholic Church conflicts were all the rage, plus my not being a theologian or a rabbi but a sociologist of religion. I was surprised I got the job in the first place—a Jewish sociologist in a major Catholic university's theology department.

Mary Daly was a radical Catholic and lesbian feminist who refused to allow men into her classes unless she interviewed them first to see if they were "sexist." This was blatantly illegal, but such were the times. The conflict was so deep that she did not attend faculty meetings. It would have caused too many fights.

I got along splendidly with the chairman, Father Daley. I guess Jews were neutral in this internal battle for the heart and soul of the church. But I was not rehired after one year, even though the students loved me. Like I said, they wanted a theologian; they already had a sociologist of religion on staff, and one was enough.

Pine Manor Junior College

My days and nights at an elite women's post-preppie school for very rich girls—I have written about this elsewhere. (See the essay "The Jewish Upper Class," in my book *The Jew as Outsider*) Back then you could sleep with your students, and they were so beautiful. Some even dated Kennedys. We were so young (I was only twenty-seven) and so naïve.

Community and State Colleges (Bunker Hill, Northern Essex, Massasoit, Fitchburg State)

These were totally different places compared to Pine Manor—working class—police, firemen, public workers, tradesmen, recent Vietnam veterans; and I am still in touch with some of them. It was kind of like the scenes (and they were actually filmed at Bunker Hill) from the movie *Good Will Hunting*. I was the Robin Williams-type teacher. Loved the students.

I had the most fun at Bunker Hill; spent less time at the other places. I taught urban sociology, crime and deviance, sociology of death and dying. At Essex I had one bad example of political correctness, which was just beginning to raise its head in the late 1970s and early 1980s.

In a criminology course with lots of police and prison officials, I was discussing the boxer Mike Tyson's alleged rape of a Ms. Givens. A white woman, somewhat older, raised her hand and talked about her own case of being raped by a Black man. I forget exactly what happened, but a week later I was called into the office of the sociology-anthropology department, and the department chair told me that I was "insensitive" to the student's presentation and that I was dismissed!

UMass–Lowell

I had great rapport with the UMass–Lowell students, and I taught the nation's first course in comparative genocide/the sociology of genocide there in the fall of 1977 with the support of Armenian American sociologist Levon Chorbajian. That, plus my love of the evening division adult students, were the high points of my time at UMass–Lowell. I am still friends with some of my students, like George Koumenzelis, to this day.

My courses were: introduction to sociology, urban sociology, social deviance, and, my favorite, the '60s. My classes were Monday and Wednesday from 7–10 p.m., and I was able at night to take my students on jaunts into the city of Lowell and show them the where Jack Kerouac hung out—the huge clock at Lowell High School, the bars—and one time I took them to the Edison Cemetery, where he is buried. As with James Dean, people leave mementos—tobacco, empty cans of beer, little jugs of liquor, and notes. It's eerie. Plus we topped it off with a meal at Cobblestone's, a local restaurant. I loved those classes.

However, like Professors Zohn and Pipes, my final months at the university were not that pleasant, due to the rising tide of political correctness and interference in my classes by deans. Enough said. It is much too painful to even discuss.

Boston University

I had a one-year appointment in 1980 at Boston University's College of Basic Studies (CBS). It was my first and my last stint as an assistant professor—but I was finally a "real" professor. The courses were very exciting yet geared to students who were learning "below their level." In many ways it was like a "Great Books" class: one semester on social science, one on Western civilization, one on science, and one on art. (In fact, I still have the notes for the Western civilization class, and I hope to write a book using them.)

The school was run like a military academy by Dr. John Silber, a very conservative, anti-liberal ruler, very similar to Donald Trump. He hated Howard Zinn, but he loved Elie Wiesel. In fact, he wanted to get Wiesel the Nobel Prize—not in literature, but in peace—and he succeeded.

I was not intimidated by Silber's stump of an arm, and I even worked in his campaign for governor. (He lost, but not by much.) I often had lunch with him at a private club. In fact, I liked him. I also liked Prof. Fred Koss, the chairman of the social science department at CBS. And I liked the students, and they liked me. I was sorry to leave, but all teachers had one-year contracts, and if enrollment went down, teachers were dismissed. I knew then that academia was not a very stable place to raise a family.

Harvard: Round 1—The 1980s

I describe this round in my essay "A Jew at the Ukrainian Institute (HURI)" in this book. What stands out is that I learned to become a Ukrainian. I always thought I was "Russian" or "Polish," but I was really Ukrainian. The reason is that my parents did not sympathize with a group like Ukrainians who were not in power yet were part of the German machine that killed their families while the Russians had liberated them. So I thought of myself as a "Russian."

It was the great polymath Prof. Omeljan Pritsak who recognized my talent and brought me to Harvard in 1982. I loved the guy. He was a large, jovial "old uncle." I was even invited to his home in Wellesley. He wanted to transform HURI and to show the world that not just Ukrainians made up Ukraine but also Jews, Poles, Armenians, Israelis and others. Other mentors included Frank Sysyn and Ihor Sevchenko.

I was given free rein to teach and to study any subject I wished. I ran a seminar on social research methods that were very basic for sociologists but eye-openers for historians, for example, content analysis, participant observation, and techniques of interviewing, especially what we called "unobtrusive measures" in sociology.

Harvard: Round 2—The 1990s

Here again, I have written extensively about my course with Prof. Erich Goldhagen and his son Daniel (Danny), whom I knew when he was in high school in Newton. I loved Erich's course at Harvard "The Holocaust and the Phenomenon of Genocide."[26]

Sadly, it did not end happily for either of them. First, I found Danny's thesis about the Nazis in his infamous book *Hitler's Willing Executioners* (1996) too simplistic. It was not just antisemitism but antisemitism and peer pressure, group pressure, following orders, and other social-psychological pressures that led to the Holocaust. In fact, his own father Erich talked about these things in his course, yet in public Erich had to defend his son against the onslaught of attacks.

But the scandal of Danny's book goes even deeper and will be the basis for a chapter in my forthcoming book *Chutzpah at Harvard*. Briefly, there was a chair in Holocaust studies being prepared for Danny and supported by a group of supporters such as Stanley Hoffman and Charles Meier. Danny was their golden boy. The money was put up by a rich Wall Street investor named Ronald Lipper. Lipper wanted Danny in the chair, not a non-Jewish scholar named Christopher Browning. Neither got the job, because Harvard pulled the plug on the chair for many reasons. The scandal that ensued was embarrassing. The attack on Danny's book came from such prominent Holocaust scholars as Yehuda Bauer and Raul Hilberg, as well as internally from the Jewish Studies Department's Professor Ruth Wisse, who believed that Holocaust studies should be part of general Jewish history and not separate from it. So, for all these reasons—the embarrassment and the attacks—Harvard abolished the $3.5 million chair to be named after Mr. Lipper.

Harvard: Round 3—the 2010s

I was accepted at the Davis Center for Russian Studies, formerly the Russian Research Center, in 2013, and I am here today (2023). I have found a home, and while it did not impact me as intensely as my time at HURI, where the interaction was far greater among associates, graduate students, and faculty, I still felt at home. (The Davis Center has many more associates—over two hundred—than the twenty or so at HURI.)

But here at the Davis Center—maybe because I am aging (or should I say *sage*-ing)—it is harder for me to get to campus, park, and so forth. Thus I am

---

26 See the essays about them both in my book *The Genocidal Mind* (2006), 212-245.

there less often. But still, under the direction of Maxim Shrayer, Rochelle Ruthchild, and others, I feel welcomed.

What I like is that nearly every field is welcomed, especially my favorite—sex and gender issues as well as music and culture. I am not into politics, neither Putin politics nor internal politics. I stay away from both and do my own thing. It's good advice for others to heed.

Sources

Porter, Jack Nusan, *The Genocidal Mind*. Lanham, MD: Rowman & Littlefield, 2006.

Chapter 12

Reunions

Milwaukee, the middle of a Middle America. A quiet and strange city in a strange state. A state with a tradition of progressive political ideals going back to "fighting Bob" Lafollette, going back to socialist mayors like Frank Ziedler and the panjandrum of Wisconsin socialism, Victor Berger. But it's also a state that has produced Senator Joseph McCarthy and gave George Wallace a lot of votes. Figure that out. The contradictions of America are reflected in Wisconsin.

Milwaukee. The city of beer, bratwurst, and the Braves. The Braves moved to Atlanta, the bratwurst to Sheboygan, and the beer moved out to St. Louis via Budweiser. But don't get me wrong; Milwaukee still has beer (and brats). The descendants of the old families—Pabst, Schlitz, Miller—still run the town, but Milwaukee lost the beer-drinking award to Cleveland a while back.

Milwaukee. A beautiful and clean city. Milwaukee. The biggest little village in the world. It's so small that whenever I go downtown, I never fail to meet at least one friend. Try that in New York, Chicago, or LA. Yet it's got nearly a million people. A metropolis with big-city problems and small-town *Gemütlichkeit*.

Like Chicago or Cleveland, Milwaukee is still a city composed of "little villages"—neighborhoods that retain their ethnic/racial distinction. Irish, Italians, Germans, Poles, Russians, Slovaks, Greeks, Swedes, Slovenes, Lithuanians, Jews, Puerto Ricans, Chinese, Japanese, Mexicans, Cubans, and African Americans. During the two decades directly before and directly after the turn of the century, the country filled up with Europeans from the East; Japanese and Chinese from the West; and African Americans ("Negroes" then) from the South. They came to do the dirty work in the tanneries, meatpacking plants, foundries, steel mills, and shoe factories.

There's a railroad line that runs like a thin curved ribbon from Ellis Island in New York north up to Albany, Schenectady, and Syracuse (another ribbon cuts across Pennsylvania and onto Rochester, Buffalo, Cleveland, Toledo, Detroit, Gary, Hammond, Chicago, and on up to Milwaukee). The white ethnics dropped off along the line to find their brothers and sisters and stayed to set up their ethnic villages.

Milwaukee is like Chicago *fin de siècle.* In fact, when Hollywood director Norman Jewison looked for locations of Chicago in 1900 for his film *Gaily, Gaily,* he went to Milwaukee—to "east town," near the river. It's still got an old-world feel to it.

Milwaukee. People keep busy in the summer with Fourth of July Circus Parades, Summerfest, and the State Fair. An old-fashioned town. A good town to grow up in. I should know. I spent a very happy childhood there, doctor, and a miserable adolescence.

This is the tale of my coming back to Milwaukee, the return of the native, back to my junior and senior high school, and culminating in my high school's tenth-year anniversary reunion. It's quite a trip: 1962–1972. Quite a decade. Rivals 1929–1939 for top honors in cataclysmic events. I think it beats the thirties, but I don't know. I wasn't there. To paraphrase Will Rogers, I only know what I see on TV, and I saw about two thousand hours of reality on the "boob tube" during that decade. And, as we used to say in the fifties, I saw some pretty neat things.

* * *

One night in 1964, Earl L. B. Clarke, the principal of Steuben Junior High School on Milwaukee's northwest side, locked his garage doors, got into a car, turned on the motor and killed himself.

The natural question we all asked ourselves was . . . why?

It was like out of Edwin Arlington Robinson's "Richard Cory." Why would this tall, impeccably dressed, self-composed man want to kill himself? I had to find out, and the answer that emerged was a profound statement on the nature of America's educational system.

In a sense, Earl L. B. Clarke was as much a victim of the swirl and madness of social movements in the sixties as were King, Kennedy, and the Kent State Four.

I graduated from Steuben in 1959. Looking back, the fifties seemed like a dream world. Elvis Presley. Dion and the Belmonts. Dick Clark. The Platters.

Fabian. Annette Funicello. Buddy Holly. Davy Crockett. Hula-hoops. Sputnik. Paola. *The $64,000 Question.* Scandola. Sunday afternoon movies with ten cartoons, two westerns, the Three Stooges, and a Captain Midnight serial. Bosco. Howdy Doody, Buffalo Bob, and *Your Show of Shows.*

At "sock hops" and chaperoned proms, we danced the jitterbug and the stroll. At parties we drank Coke, ate potato chips, and played Spin-the-Bottle and Post-Office. At the playground, we shot ringers, played kickball and "strike-out," and hoped to win the city softball championship. (We lost.)

A lot of fond memories. The '50s were great for a thirteen-year-old kid. Too young for politics. I didn't even know who Adlai Stevenson was until my folks said they'd vote for him because he was a nice guy. Lost twice, I heard.

But school was the focal point. We played hard, and we studied even harder. In junior high school, the school was split between the "greasers" and the "collegiates." The latter were getting primed for college; the former were primed for the technical schools. Maybe there was no formal tracking in the schools, but in the end, the results were the same.

The "collegiates" studied their asses off, joined what seemed like an interminable number of after-school clubs, and stood in nice straight lines with polite smiles on their faces. The "greasers" goofed off, got into fights, took most of the mechanical arts classes, and were sent down to the principal's (really the vice-principal's) office with regularity.

Steuben was one of the many feeder schools that supplied Washington High School with students. Just as you can judge a college by the quality of its high schools, so too can you judge a high school by the quality of its junior high schools . . . and Steuben had good quality students.

The "greasers" were a small but exotic group; the majority of students, the "collegiates," came from solidly middle-class Jewish or German families and were, in educational jargon, highly motivated. Or better, they were overly motivated. Both our parents' desires and the post-Sputnik race to outdistance the Russians propelled many, if not all, of us to "make it."

Between 1950 and early 1960, Washington High School was considered one of the finest high schools in the city. After graduating from Steuben, I entered into those final glory years. When I graduated from Washington in 1962, I didn't know it then, but we were to be considered one of the last of the "great" classes. From 1962 on, Washington and, of course, Steuben began to go downhill . . . or so the teachers and administrators told us.

My years at Washington from 1959 to 1962 were more of the same: sports, dating, school clubs, and hitting the books. We all scrambled for the top grades, the top honors (National Honor Society), and the top elected offices, whether in Boys' Club, Tonia Toppers, or the Lincoln Debating Society.

The big men in school were, of course, the "lettermen," with their white sweaters festooned with red W's, gold and silver medals, and other paraphernalia. Next in status seemed to be the cheerleaders. Down the list came the "scholars," the grinds who won top honor awards or got straight A's, and further down were the rest of the students. Holding down the bottom but still well respected were the "greasers"—the sharp, slick, tough (to us) chicks and guys who were, in their own way, the first rebels, the first hippies.

Nearly all of the collegiates went on to college, some even to Harvard or Oberlin. Many went to Madison, and another large portion went on to UW–M. The girls were going on to college to find husbands; some went to work; some were getting married; some (the scandal of it) were secretly married and pregnant. The star basketball player (later to become a Milwaukee cop) was to marry the star cheerleader, have a kid a few months after the ceremony, and supposedly live happily ever after. (They didn't.)

As for the "greasers," some were to go into the army (this was before Vietnam and the draft); or into construction jobs; or get an apprenticeship for a trade; or do other things that "greasers" do. A few, rumor had it, had been in jail; and one or two were being groomed to take over some Mafia position.

Of politics we knew or cared little. The only event even smacking of political was the time that a few of us protested to the principal that somebody was passing out John Birch Society literature in the halls, and we felt that an editorial should be written about it in the school paper.

We meekly walked into the principal's office and began to debate the issue. At first the principal agreed to the editorial and then reneged. As we started to methodically point out the inconsistencies in his argument, he got angry and threw us out of his office! At that time, students, like African Americans, had or knew their place. One didn't argue with a teacher or principal; one just accepted their final decrees like acts of God.

I graduated from Washington in 1962, traveled through Europe and Israel for a year, and in 1963 entered the University of Wisconsin–Milwaukee (UW–M) just as Camelot was about to fall. The Cuban Missile Crisis set the stage of paranoia; Kennedy was assassinated; the civil rights movement was in full swing; Vietnam became more than just a strange name to stamp collectors; the revolt was on.

While I was at UW–M, I heard about Clarke's suicide. It bothered me; I had liked the man. But there were too many other distractions: Watts, Newark, Detroit, the war, women, and, of course, school.

I graduated from the University of Wisconsin in June 1967, a day before the Israeli-Arab Six-Day War, and two weeks before my first (and last) acid trip. Graduate school at Northwestern in sociology began and continued on into the '70s. I had flunked my physical at the army induction center, so I just stayed in school. The tumult of the last decade carried on, but, as the movement quieted down, I had some time to reflect on the past decade and was drawn back to my old schools to see the changes that had gone down . . . the suicide of Earl L. B. Clarke being the touchstone.

I returned to Washington and Steuben during the past year to do some investigating. Things had changed; there were no dress codes; there were many Black and Chicanos (there was only one lonely Black "dude" when I graduated); there was smoke in the johns; and a general aura of paranoia.

In fact, on my first trip back, I had trouble even getting into the school—all visitors' passes were revoked. I saw my old gym teacher and he let me in, but told me I couldn't take any pictures.

I didn't stay long, but from the short time I was there, I noticed the tension and subdued anger on the faces of the teachers. I started rapping with the gym teacher, now an assistant principal.

"You see those kids [pointing to a few African Americans on the sidewalk]? They should be in class. Damn it, things were different ten years ago. The colored come in now, and all the rules have to change just to please them."

I felt sorry for him and a bit angry. In a way, he seemed like Archie Bunker, someone who could have easily become a cop if he hadn't gone into teaching. Ten years ago, he was just a gym teacher; now he looked like a brave warrior holding down the line for law and order. It seemed as if he had learned nothing from the rebellion of the last decade; he understood nothing. It seemed that the students had changed, the times had changed, but the teachers had not; even the school with its rows of lockers and wooden desks had been kept intact, like a museum piece.

He told me of the fires at the school, the false alarms, the drugs, the flexing of student power, the questioning of authority, the breakdown of rules. His world was crumbling around him, and he didn't know how or why it was happening.

I walked into the vice principal's office. To my surprise, he immediately recognized me. After some perfunctory cordiality, he said, "Your class was one of the last good ones; now, there's just trouble."

More sadness, more tales of gloom. I was an outsider now. With me he talked of the old days, the really quiet good old days. But the tension was there in the creases of his face. A month later, I read in the paper, he died of a heart attack. Another casualty.

Not long after my visit to Washington, I went back to Steuben. The Clarke suicide was on my mind.

Steuben was an all-white school a decade or less ago; today there are African Americans, Chicanos, Puerto Ricans, and Native Americans, but then it was predominantly white, maybe seventy percent.

Suddenly, the bell rang and teachers with their students were rushing outside. I thought it was the bell between classes; it was a false alarm. I ducked into the principal's office and looked around. A secretary came up to me and asked if I wanted to see the principal.

I said I'd like to talk to someone and that I had been a Steuben graduate and all. Well, the principal was out (that seemed to be true ten years ago too—the principal was always out—where, no one knew or wanted to tell).

The secretary asked if I would like to see the vice principal. I said sure, I knew him back when he was just a music teacher. He had moved up in the world. I walked into his office.

A replay of Washington. More gloom, more crises, more tension.

"I feel like a cop," he said as he twirled in his seat to answer the phone for the third time in about ten minutes. "No time to teach, just discipline."

"You've heard about the problems at Washington?" I nodded.

"Here it's not that bad, but it's bad enough. We had some disturbances a while back. A lot of broken windows."

He went on to explain that the students didn't like the rules concerning the closed lunch sessions. They couldn't eat their lunch on the playground or go off into the streets and businesses surrounding the playground to eat or just rap, so they broke two hundred windows.

"I may be old-fashioned, but I feel a rule is a rule and rules should be obeyed.

"I put the blame on the parents, the stability of the home. When you were here, the parents complained that we didn't give enough homework. Today everyone complains we give too much.

"We had solid middle-class families here a while back, now there's no stability. I've got a report that shows that fifty-five percent of the families that send their kids here have only one parent at home."

The alcove outside his office was filling up with kids—nice-looking kids who were going to get "disciplined." And I thought, where were the "greasers"? Now, even "nice kids" were rebelling.

"There's been more vandalism in the past six months than in the past ten years combined, and I blame the parents. We shouldn't be doing their job."

More calls. More trouble. I brought up the question of Clarke's suicide. With an unexpected bluntness, he told me.

"Clarke was a good man, but he just couldn't adjust. He couldn't roll with the punches."

The contagion had spread, from the colleges down to the high schools and now the junior highs. The rebellion was against the sense of powerlessness, against the "bullshit" taught in the schools, against the formidable rules. There were new alternatives, alternatives unavailable to us ten years ago. And you had to move with the times or go under the wheel.

I concluded the rap, told him I'd try to come back. It was 10:30. Another false alarm went off, the second of the morning. I followed the merry horde and their nervous teachers out the door and into the street.

I probably won't come back.

*　*　*

Betty Maris was worried. She had put a lot of work into this reunion—Washington High School's tenth year anniversary reunion—June 1962 to June 1972. A lot had happened during those ten years to me, to this country, and to Betty.

Betty, a pretty Greek girl, once a star cheerleader, now a schoolteacher, was disappointed with the group that crowded into a dining room of the spanking-new performing arts center. I didn't think it was a disappointing crowd (maybe because I was too "stoned"), but later I was told that only twenty-six percent of the class had showed up, 138 out of 545 alumni.

Some didn't have the money (cost: twenty dollars a couple, plus parking, babysitter, etc.) or didn't want to spend it. Some lived too far away. Some probably wanted to come, but maybe a spouse objected. One woman, another popular cheerleader, didn't show up because she was too ashamed to admit that she was still *unmarried*. Some were dead. Some were in Vietnam or overseas. Some were taking law boards or final exams. Most, however, might have thought that it would have been a neat nostalgic "trip," but their lives had changed to the point where they had little in common with their former classmates.

While the band played, I sauntered over to the bar and looked around. Our "class" looked good—healthy and well groomed. Not too many had gone to pot. For some, this was the biggest event of the year, maybe of the past ten. Some had little else but fine memories of carefree high school days. Frustrations, dead-end jobs, rotten luck, all would be forgotten for a few golden hours.

The class president, as jovial as a Junior Chamber of Commerce officer, had shed over one hundred pounds. I hardly recognized the guy. Another ex-cheerleader, Bonnie Braun, was the envy of all the women with her sleek figure. She was now a world-hopping airline stewardess and had married well, a wealthy California man ten years her senior.

I began rapping with another ex-cheerleader (I knew them all). Gail, after three children, looked great and was as sexy as ever. Her husband, a former basketball star, was now a crew-cut, tight-lipped, overweight cop. He glared down at me all the while I drank with his wife, jealous that this "pointy-headed intellectual writer" could entertain *his* wife. The more others ogled, the more her husband scowled, the more Gail loved it.

The class had produced about ten marriages, and they were all intact. Two women were still in love with guys they had met during high school days, and ten years later they were still waiting and hoping to get married to them. They're still waiting.

Dinner was served. I sat at a table with the relatively successful—lawyers, doctors, junior executives. We even had a "guest appearance" of a fellow who composed musical scores for TV and Broadway—Dennis Hanley (*né* Hirshbein). A celebrity!

As a writer and political activist, I regaled my attentive audience with tales of publishers, literary agents, and the New York "scene." Mostly, they listened as I described the March on Washington, the "armies of the night," the Chicago "conspiracy" trial, the 1968 Democratic Convention, and all of the other rocking, shocking events of the '60s.

I feared a backlash, but these were the sons and daughters of a "middle America" that had seen it and lived it vicariously with Walter Cronkite and now with me. They added their tales to the memories I spun for them, and we all relished them together.

The entertainment began. The president of the class welcomed us and talked on in clichés—"we were a class devoted to service; we must continue to serve our community." Middle America wasn't listening. The TV composer was asked to sing, and sing he did, in a beautiful, trained voice. The remnants of the football team at the back table weren't listening. Too drunk. An ex-Vietnam veteran now turned "hippy-freak-radical," dressed incongruously in a black-and-green jungle camouflage suit, sang "Oh, Shenandoah." At this point, even *I* wasn't listening.

The crowd didn't want entertainment; they wanted booze. They could watch TV at home. Now, they wanted talk and gusty tales of the Green Bay Packers and their rival gridiron teams.

There were a few prizes. For the most children (six in ten years). The winner waddled up. For the longest hair. The Vietnam vet and I both lost to a "dark horse" candidate. We didn't even recognize the dude. He could have walked in off the street. For the farthest distance traveled. ('Nam and Guam and Laos didn't count.) One guy, a doctor, jumped up and shouted, "Israel!" A girl meekly intoned, "Alaska." Alaska sounded more plausible, but "Israel" demanded an open hearing at this United Nations of Middle America. This dude wanted the award so badly—just like he was sucking for the National Honors Society or student government. He got it—a booby prize—a three-foot-high Styrofoam replica of the Liberty Bell.

After thanking the reunion committee and after exchanging addresses with people we knew we'd never call again, we all stood up to sing the school anthem—with all the *de rigueur* foot-stomping and giggling that goes along with anachronistic cultural play-backs.

It was time to leave. The bar had run dry.

* * *

A few months after the reunion, I went up to talk to Ron Franzmeier, the ex-class prez, now assistant to the president of Manpower, Inc., in Milwaukee, its international center. Ron is really a nice guy, and service to the community is no cliché to him. He lives it.

"You know—reunions are dying out," he told me as he leaned back in his swivel chair. "The change is due to our temporary relationships between people," he added. (Alvin Toffler would call it "modular life styles.")

"Graduates in the '30s and '40s know where people live and how they are. They still socialize. When they travel, they stop for dinner, even from San Francisco or New York, but our class doesn't do this anymore. People just don't develop those lasting relationships anymore."

Sadly, he noted: "We live in a temporary society, and I work for a company that epitomizes all this—temporary work. Our president, Elmer Winter [of Manpower, Inc.], says that very few people receive twenty-five-year gold watches anymore. Young people today don't show many signs of making a career in one company. There's too much jumping around."

"High school played a more significant role in the '30s and '40s. In those days, the senior prom, the yearbook, the graduation ceremony were the highlights of their young lives. Today, with more kids going to college, high school is just a stepping-stone rather than a finale, so it's not that important anymore. Subsequently, reunions aren't so important or successful anymore, either."

It goes even deeper. In a McLuhanesque world, there are a greater variety of stimuli outside the school. As Ron Franzmeier puts it, "How can a school play or a debating team compete with a war in your own living room? Today, there's no debate on capital punishment, you just go out there and picket!"

Ron Franzmeier is now the Director of the Washington High School Scholarship Foundation, which was founded in 1961, and in which he was one of the first winners when we graduated back in 1962. He noted that the "troubles" at Washington made it much more difficult to collect funds, but things have improved.

"The older alumni now understand the school and understand the changes a lot better. They feel relieved that the school is changing in a positive way and not being destroyed. We now give out eight five hundred dollar scholarships a year. They've toured the school, talked to students, white and Black, and while still unhappy with some changes, still, the crisis has rallied them to continue to support us. Their own kids go here too."

* * *

What exactly happened to Washington High School? The scenario is a familiar one. In 1962, there were one or two Black students. Then, busing started. Integration was the watchword in the years 1963–1964. In short, the twenty-five percent middle-class Jewish minority was replaced by a twenty percent Black minority. It was an old story in the 1960s. A clash of lifestyles, of racial strife, and of student power. It's a national phenomenon.

One feeder school, Steuben Junior High, was predominantly white working-class. Another feeder school, Peckham, was mostly Black working class. When they converged on Washington, trouble began.

But as a Washington-watcher for all these years, I'm happy to report that the worst is over . . . I hope. In fact, wherever I went and to whomever I talked, everyone told me to write *positively* of the changes that have occurred.

This past year I've seen how one school coped with change. There's hope. There's a new and younger principal at Washington; there are new and "hipper" teachers; there is stronger community, alumni, and student participation.

Two voluntary associations that have helped are the Parent Teacher Student Association (replacing the old PTA) and a local neighborhood group, the Sherman Park Community Association.

The SPCA's concern goes beyond just school strife, but into action over expressway construction, housing patterns, attempted block-busting and other issues. It even promotes block parties and youth outings. It is one of many such associations springing up across the country. Its major goal: to create a sense of community and neighborhood involvement in order to slow down the rampage of the "temporary, modular society."

Washington has now become more of a vocationally oriented school than in the years I went. It still meets the needs of the college-bound, but, in addition, offers exposure to the trades (electrician, welder, plumber).

One exciting example: a nearby service station owned by the school gives students credit in auto mechanics and business managing. Ex-welders and ex-electricians now teach the kids. Students work on an entire corner of a house in the schools' workshops.

All reports show that vocational-technical training is increasing while college attendance has dipped slightly. A college graduate is no longer assured a job. There are hundreds unemployed, including many PhD's. A voc-tech graduate has a better chance for a job today than his college peer.

The strain has been great on teachers. Many have left to teach elsewhere, seeking the white middle-class students they know and loved in the past. Those that remain and who have adapted to the "culture shock" are now working harder than ever to keep old standards alive, but the interest just isn't there.

Teachers had to be re-educated to cope with Black culture, to cope with the youth culture. Some, like Earl L. B. Clarke, couldn't do it. Others try and muddle through. Still others are bitter, very bitter.

As one teacher put it: "I've become radicalized. I don't believe in integration anymore. Teachers should teach their own kind. If African Americans want Black teachers, a Black curriculum, Black administrators, Black anything—I say give it to them. Let them run their *own* schools in their *own* way. I've had it up to here. I'd rather teach white kids. In fact, I'd rather teach Jewish kids; Africans should teach African Americans; Catholics should teach Catholics; and Jews should teach Jews!" (The teacher was Jewish, by the way.)

Through all the bitterness and chaotic change of the past decade, there is hope. As one teacher put it: "If we don't make it at Washington, I don't know where we will."

Washington in a small way has "made it." The rioting has ceased; the halls are fairly quiet; there are fewer cigarettes snuffed out in the carpet; there is more student power. This could all be reversed tomorrow, but today, it's quiet.

Ron Franzmeier says, "Students may have less respect and less sentimental attachment to a school, but they now have a place that serves their needs."

The long, hard march through the institutions of this society is still far from over, but amidst the cynicism, there's always faith. We've been left with little else.

Amidst My Lai, the Pentagon Papers, the Watergate scandal, and all the rest, Washington High School (and I) survived the '60s. We've made it through, and if we've made it, then there's still some hope for the rest of the nation.

1973

Part Three

1971–1991—THE TRANSITIONAL YEARS

Chapter 13

My Grove Press Days

Recent bios by Barney Rosset (2016), Michael Rosenthal (2017), and George Braziller (2015) brought back many memories of my days "in the big time." My first important book *Jewish Radicalism* was published by a major publisher, Grove Press, and distributed by an even bigger publisher, Random House. I'm not even sure how I found Grove Press, but I loved it, especially that they published the most radical, cutting-edge stuff not just in politics but also in sexology, erotica, and avant-garde literature and by the major Continental writers. To be part of their famous paperback series, their "Evergreen Black Cat Books"—we were #B-360—was a great honor.

Braziller notes that three publishers are considered the founders of the modern radical, cultural and political book industry in America—Tom McLaughlin's New Directions Press, Barney Rosset's Grove Press, and Braziller's George Braziller, Inc.

Barney Rosset, while difficult, abrasive, even abusive, was a major force in overturning censorship and the punishment of so-called obscene literature. First, with D. H. Lawrence's *Lady Chatterley's Lover* and then Henry Miller's *Tropic of Cancer*, Rosset fought against those Puritan forces who wished to ban such works, and not just ban them but to imprison and fine the authors, publishers and distributors involved. We take these rights for granted today, but before the mid-'60s it was a serious problem. Rosset must be given full credit for almost single-handedly making literature and movies available to all and for distinguishing between vile smut and real erotic literature.

But my introduction to Grove was not through Barney but through his esteemed editor, Fred Jordan, a suave, cultured European man with a great deal of patience and probity. You had to have that if you worked for Mr. Rosset.

Fred described Barney as follows: "[He] lived both his professional and personal life at warp speed . . . always on the run, even when he was sitting down."[27] Barney was "scary"; I rarely interacted with him; all my dealings were with Fred or at times with his beautiful assistant Claudia Mazza—and Barney loved having beautiful women as assistants.

To be chosen to be among these great writers even in a small way was a great honor. Again, from the Rosenthal book:

> Barney treasured especially those subversive writers who challenged and irritated, who pushed against the conventional, people like Kerouac and Ginsberg; John Rechy and Hubert Selby; Henry Miller and William Burroughs; Alain Robb-Grillet, Eugene Ionesco, and Jean Genet; Samuel Beckett and David Mamet, Harold Pinter and Bertolt Brecht. In taking forbidden, offensive, and little-known work and finding an audience for it, Barney bestowed gifts on writers and readers everywhere. (9)

Later, Richard Seaver joined Grove Press after working with George Braziller, who lamented the fact that he had mistreated Seaver, was rude to him, and thus Seaver left him and helped bring such icons as Henry Miller and Jean Genet to Grove Press and, later, to an imprint under his own name.

I loved working with Fred. Sadly, it was the last time I had a real-live editor who actually read the manuscript himself, discussed it with me, and improved it. I remember visiting Fred at his lovely home in Croton-on-Hudson, New York, staying overnight, playing chess with his precocious son Kenny (and losing), and meeting his lovely wife. Where can a writer do that today?

Perhaps, an agent like Berthold Fleiss or his lovely assistant (why were the assistants back then always so lovely?) recommended me to Grove. It was at the height of the radical '60s, and Grove was looking for that kind of analysis. They had published the icons—Franz Fanon, Regis Debray, and the Berrigan brothers—and were looking for unique perspectives on the revolutions going on. I suggested an anthology on Jewish radicals as opposed to "Radical Jews,"

---

27 Rosenthal (2017), 7.

meaning a book on Jews who were committed to Judaism but in radical and countercultural forms as opposed to "radical Judaism," which would have been more theological but instead who transformed their Judaism into universalism—Marxism, feminism, and other -isms. In other words, it would be about lesser-known radical Jews and not about more well-known figures such as Noam Chomsky, Abbie Hoffman, Jerry Rubin, Bernadine Dohrn, or Mark Rudd.

I had been gathering Jewish radical papers like *Genesis 2*, *Davka*, *The Jewish Radical*, and *Chutzpah*, and I felt that an anthology of the best of these writings preserved for future generations would make a great book. I was right, but I made a major mistake. I asked someone from the University of Chicago, a sociology graduate student, to help me. The book was my idea and my initiative, but I felt I needed help with the collection. It was a decision I would regret. He wrote an excellent introduction, and then he felt I was not "radical enough" for him. So, while the book was enormously influential (I still get emails from younger activists who find it in "their grandmother's attic," as one activist, Ben Lorber, told me), still it has not been reprinted in forty years since this graduate student, now a professor somewhere, tried to distance himself and cut off all connection to our co-authorship. But since he retained co-copyrights to it, he has not allowed me to republish it.

The book eventually came out in 1973, probably two years later than it should have, and was called *Jewish Radicalism: A Selected Anthology* (1973). A similar book, but one that emphasized cultural and religious transformation, *The New Jews* (1971) by James Sleeper and Alan Mintz, came out earlier. *The Jewish Catalog* series by Michael and Sharon Strassfeld and Richard Siegel also came out around this time. Basically, what we were all doing was applying a Jewish spin to the prevailing cultural and political revolutions of the time.

Our book reflected such themes as a Jewish response to the growing anti-Israel and even antisemitic trends of the New Left and Black Left; the interest in socialism; a response to right-wing Zionism like the Jewish Defense League (JDL); the Jewish counterculture of poetry, cartoons, and communal living; the attack against the "Jewish establishment" of "machers"; Jewish feminist and gay thought; Jewish identity and intermarriage; and the struggle for Soviet Jewry. As Gerald Strober noted, "The American Jewish community is currently faced with critical problems of an international and domestic nature. In a genuine sense, the Jewish community is under siege."[28]

---

28 Strober (1974), 1.

It's interesting that, aside from Soviet Jewry, all these issues are still germane today, forty, fifty years later. Only the JDL has been replaced with more powerful, more sophisticated, more affluent, and therefore more effective right-wing Jewish leadership like Sheldon Adelson, Charles Jacobs, and Avigdor Liberman. I never found a single Soviet Jew who became a Democrat. Not one. They are all Trump supporters.

I wished I had written more books for Grove Press, especially more original theoretical work in sociology, radical thought, or genocide studies, and not anthologies, but still it was and continues to be a great honor to have been part of this major institution in American culture. Those days, those times, with such intimate relations with one's editors, may have passed forever.

Postscript

In October of 2019, I traveled to Frankfurt, Germany, to see for the first time the famous Frankfurt Book Fair (the Messe), and I ran into several editors at the Grove Press Atlantic booth, who knew Fred Jordan and Barney Rosset. I fulfilled Fred's "dream" for me—he always urged me to attend this fair. I wish he were still around. He was the best editor I ever had.

Sources

Braziller, George. *Encounters: My Life in Publishing.* New York: George Braziller, Inc., 2015. He has many interesting anecdotes about Richard Seaver, his many authors, the Frankfurt Book Fair, even Marilyn Monroe and Arthur Miller.

Jordan, Ken. "Barney Rosset: The Art of Publishing." *The Paris Review* 145, Winter 1997, 171–215. This is an interview with Ken Jordan, Fred Jordan's son.

Menand, Louis. "People of the Book." *New Yorker*, December 12, 2016, 78–85. This is a review of several books by editors/publishers of the 1950s and later—Barney Rosset's time at Grove Press and Robert Gottlieb's time at Simon & Schuster and the *New Yorker*. But mostly it concerns the founding and tribulations of Grove Press under Mr. Rosset.

Porter, Jack Nusan, and Peter Dreier, eds. *Jewish Radicalism: A Selected Anthology.* New York: Grove Press, 1973. There are both paperback (B-360 Black Cat Series) and hardcover versions of this book. Sadly, my co-editor Peter Dreier, for personal reason I cannot fathom, will not allow the book to be reprinted. In short, he is responsible for censoring the book for future generations. Luckily, however, there are many previously owned copies available for sale on the internet via Abebooks.com for less than five dollars. Perhaps one day I will be able to reprint the book properly.

Rosenthal, Michael. *Barney: Grove Press and Barney Rosset: America's Maverick Publisher and His Battle Against Censorship.* New York: Arcade Publishing, 2017.

Rosset, Barney. *Rosset: My Life in Publishing and How I Fought Censorship.* New York: OR Books, 2016. His papers are in the Rare Books and Manuscripts section of the Butler Library, Columbia University, while the Grove Press records are in the Special Collections Research Center at Syracuse University Libraries. They even have the royalty statements and other correspondence between Fred Jordan and me in this collection.

_____. *Evergreen Review Reader, 1957–1966.* New York: Arcade Publishing, 1966.

_____. *Evergreen Review Reader, 1957–1966: A Ten-Year Anthology.* New York: Foxrock Books, 1995.

Sleeper, James A., and Alan L. Mintz, eds. *The New Jews.* New York: Random House/Vintage Books, 1971.

Strober, Gerald S. *American Jews: Community in Crisis.* Garden City, NY: Doubleday, 1974.

The reader may also want to peruse other writers and thinkers such as Sheryl Baron, Tsvi Bisk, Everett and Mary Gendler, J. J. Goldberg, Meir Kahane, Jerry Kirschen, d.a. levy, Bill Novak, M. J. Rosenberg, Danny Siegel, Robbie Skeist, Judy Timberg, David Twersky, Arthur Waskow, and Aviva Cantor Zuckoff.

Chapter 14

My Nazi-Hunting Days

_____

Among the many things I have done in my life, Nazi-hunting may come as a surprise to some readers. But it is true. When news that I was conducting research on Nazi collaborators came out, I was inundated with "leads," as well as some threats about such people and their crimes. I would receive addresses of alleged criminals highlighted in yellow from telephone books (remember them?) or gunpowder wrapped around a bullet casing. It was scary.

Here are several articles detailing the three thousand Nazi collaborators who came to America. I was responsible for tracking down a few of them.

3000 Nazis Brought to US, Author Says

[*Boston Globe*, May 19, 1982, 25]

By Judy Foreman
Globe Staff

More than 3000 Nazi collaborators, about 300 of whom were from Byelorussia [now Belarus], came to the United States immediately after World War II, a sociologist and Holocaust specialist said yesterday, and at least one is believed to have lived until recently amidst Jewish neighbors in Brookline.

According to Jack Nusan Porter, a sociology teacher at Hebrew College in Brookline and the author of a two-volume work on the Jewish resistance, this week's disclosure that the US State Department smuggled in 300 Russian-born Nazi collaborators is not only true, it probably understates the case.

According to Porter, the allegations of Boston lawyer John Loftus, who worked at the Justice Department's Office of Special Investigations and who went public with his findings on Nazi collaborators on Sunday's CBS-TV's "60 Minutes," are "not even the whole story because [so much of the information] is classified."

Leonard Zakim, civil rights director of the Anti-Defamation League of B'nai B'rith, declined to give specifics on reported local Nazi sightings out of consideration for the Jewish individuals involved. But he did say that when people report information on alleged Nazis to the Anti-Defamation League, "We refer that information to the Justice Department."

Like other people interviewed, Porter could speak only of "rumors" about the cases of two alleged Nazis in the Boston area, one of whom was said to have been spotted in a dentist's office and the other on a Brookline street.

But Porter, who lost 25 family members in the Ukraine during World War II when Nazi collaborators formed "death squads" in search of Jews, was certain that one Nazi collaborator lived in Brookline until his death a few years ago.

The man was "sentenced to death in absentia in 1962 by the Russian government as a Latvian police official and a Gestapo agent," Porter said yesterday.

Although Porter says he does not want revenge, his own life story is marked by the actions of Nazi collaborators before the end of the war.

Born in Rovno, Ukraine, in December 1944, Porter said his two sisters, aged 2 and 4, were rounded up along with 23 other family members by Ukrainian collaborators known as the *Einsatzgruppen*, special SS death squads who followed the German army and, "with the help of the Ukrainian, or Byelorussian or Latvian police carried out the final solution."

"The collaborators were not forced by the Germans to do this work," said Porter, "but the Ukrainians and the others decided this would be helpful because they did not want to live under Russia, and so they supported the German occupation, sometimes with great glee. They rounded up the Jews, brought them to ditches, shot them, including my two sisters, covered them with dirt and lime and moved on to the next town."

After the war, Nazi collaborators found themselves "persona non grata in Russian-dominated Ukraine—they would be executed as war criminals" by the Russians, he said. "In fact, my father and other partisans [in the Jewish resistance] took it upon themselves to execute the collaborators. But many escaped these reprisals and entered this country as displaced persons between 1948 and 1951—a great many, more than 3000."

Porter's parents eventually escaped through the Jewish underground and settled in Milwaukee.

Porter, who does not consider himself a "Nazi hunter" but who does pass on information on suspected Nazi collaborators to the Justice Department said Nazi collaborators "are literally everywhere. They can be found in every town. I was not surprised to find one in Brookline."

Porter added that under a project known as "Operation Paper Clip," about 1500 German and Austrian scientists were brought to the United States through joint Pentagon-State Department program, and that some of this group were "minimal members" of the Nazi party and some outright "war criminals who were actually requested by the State Department, the CIA, the FBI, the Voice of America and Radio Free Europe . . . and used as propaganda weapons to instill anti- Communist sentiment among Americans."

"The Justice Department," Porter added, "is doing an excellent job and this [furor] is no reflection on them. It takes five to eight years to bring somebody to justice. First you have to denaturalize them, then deport them and only then can you prosecute them. Most of these people will never be brought to trial.

"But this should not be considered a black eye against the Lithuanian, Polish, Ukrainian and Hungarian communities. It's not all Ukrainians who are guilty—our task is to build bridges with the children of Nazi collaborators, to educate them."

War Criminals Found in Hub

By Wayne Woodlief

Nazis are among us in Boston. Two of them have been sighted within the past two years by a concentration camp survivor and an American GI of World War II.

A third Nazi, a Latvian collaborator sentenced to death in absentia by the Russians 20 years ago—under the name of Zigurds Katkins—also reported has lived in the Boston area since the early '50s, according to a local Nazi hunter.

The Nazi sightings since 1980, confirmed by Congressman Barney Frank, D-Newton, involve chilling face-to-face encounters nearly 40 years after the war:

- "A concentration camp survivor was waiting in a Boston dentist's office when another patient came in," said a source in Boston's Jewish community. "The survivor recognized the second patient as one of the officers who had been in charge of the camp."
- "A GI who had guarded some German prisoners of war was on a street in Brookline one day, when he saw one of the Nazi POW's, a former concentration camp guard, who had escaped years before."

Frank confirmed the two incidents, which have been passed on to the Justice Department's Office of Special Investigations (OSI). Their outcome is still undetermined, since OSI refuses to comment on pending cases.

"Apparently, incidents like these are seared into people's memories," said Frank when he was asked how witnesses could be sure of faces from so distant a past.

Jack N. Porter, a Nazi-hunter who lectures at Brookline's Hebrew College, cited the case of Katkins, apparently living now under an assumed name.

"He was sentenced to death, in absentia, in 1962," Porter said, "as a Latvian police official and Gestapo agent."

US Hit for Role in Plot

By Margery Eagan
Scholars of the Holocaust have long known that American intelligence abetted Nazi collaborators immigrating here.

What is new in Boston lawyer John Loftus' research, they say, are his charges that:

- The CIA continued this policy in direct defiance of orders from President Franklin D. Roosevelt and Harry S. Truman.
- Eisenhower administration officials, including [Vice President] Richard Nixon and [Undersecretary of Health, Education and Welfare] Nelson Rockefeller, knew of, and condoned, this policy.
- A cover-up continued through 1978, when the army lied, Loftus claims, telling Congress it did not have files on many of the alleged Nazi

collaborators. The army, Loftus said yesterday, doctored collaborators' files, removing criminal information to aid their immigration here.

All this was done with the CIA's, the FBI's and the State Department's knowledge, Loftus charged.

"The real problem here is the gullibility of the American intelligence services once the Cold War with Russia began," said Professor Dietrich Orlow, chairman of the history department at Boston University and a Nazi expert.

When Germany lost the war, he said, many collaborators who went back to Germany found themselves as displaced persons and "promptly sold themselves to American authorities as experts in anti-communism . . . [Authorities] were willing to close their eyes on Nazi atrocities in hopes of using [collaborators] for propaganda," he said.

Loftus, formerly a Justice Department lawyer, only had access to classified research documents because of his better security clearance, he said yesterday.

But as more information becomes declassified, more will be known about other American intelligence activities after the war, said Norman Naimark, a Russian history professor at Boston University.

Hub Man's Kin Wiped out by Collaborators

[*Boston Herald American*, Tuesday, May 18, 1982, 4]

By Margery Eagan

Nazi collaborators shot and killed his two sisters, his grandparents and 21 other members of his Jewish family living in Rovno in the Ukraine.

Ironically, when Jack Nason [*sic*] Porter and his parents immigrated here after the war, so did at least some of his family's murderers, Porter said.

Like the Russian-born collaborators of Byelorussia—a section of Russia just north of Rovno—these Ukrainian collaborators masqueraded as displaced persons, refugees later to find jobs and security in America among the survivors of Jews they had slaughtered.

"It's absolutely true," said Porter, 37, of Brighton, of charges by Boston lawyer John Loftus that Nazi criminals came here with the help of American intelligence.

"Several hundred came illegally, supported by the CIA, the FBI, the Voice of America and Radio Free Europe," said Porter, a lecturer at Hebrew College in

Brookline. "In America's eyes [the Nazis] were very important during the Cold War. They were so anti-communist."

The son of a Jewish resistance fighter, Porter has edited a two-volume set on Jewish resistance during the Holocaust. He has reported any information of former Nazi collaborators living here to the Justice Department, which tries to deport them.

Dubbing himself a part-time "Nazi hunter," he believes these criminals must be brought to trial.

In the Ukraine and Byelorussia [now Belarus], he said, collaborators joined death squads called "Einsatzgruppen," which shot Jews, dumped their bodies in long ditches and covered them with dirt, making common graves.

"My father and others in the Jewish resistance didn't wait for the trials to start. They killed collaborators during and after the war, surprising them in their homes," Porter said. "He found one or two of them [those who killed his family]. But killing is not very easy . . .

"The right way is not to lower yourself, not revenge-seeking through murder," he said, "but trial . . . We cannot stop looking for every last one of these Nazis."

Chapter 15

My Native American Days and Nights (Sun Dances, Sweat Lodges, Dealing with Death)

Native Americans—or "Indians," as we used to call them—had a profound impact on my life, especially when they helped me through my divorce from Miriam in the period 1997–2000. But my interest in them started earlier, in 1990 or 1991. The Native approach to healing the entire body—physically, spiritually, and mentally—has proven very effective, not just at transitional times, such as divorce, death, or serious illness, but also for returning "wounded warriors" from Vietnam, Iraq or Afghanistan who are coping with post-traumatic shock, mental illness, alcoholism, suicidal thoughts, and opiate dependence. They have a very good track record for healing these problems.

My personal problems led me to the Mashpee Wampanoag tribe, led by their charismatic chief, John Peters, known as Slow Turtle, a tall, handsome man with a beautiful young wife and many female admirers.

I was also influenced by Mashpee Wampanoag Sly Fox (his American name was John Oakley), brother of Drifting Goose, Supreme Sachem of the Wampanoag Nation of Haverhill (Bradford), Massachusetts. I invited Sly Fox and his French American wife, Whispering Tree, to my classes at Northern Essex Community College to speak.

I especially enjoyed his talk about finding dead animals killed on the highway and his skill as a taxidermist to rebuild them or to use their feathers, bones and claws for various purposes. He showed us that the animal and vegetable kingdoms are part of our planet and must be respected and that even after death these animals and plants can be useful to us. He also taught us about the "Talking Stick" that is used like therapy: as long as you hold the stick you can talk and talk and talk until you pass the stick to someone else.

I remember Micmac Native Paul Cloud (Wild Cat) from Rhode Island and his wonderful wife, Whippoorwill (Wikeleek). I learned a lot from him, especially in the sweat ledges. I also learned that he had contracted mesothelioma, a cancer of the lungs caused by asbestos while in the Navy cleaning the hulls of ships. He was a wonderful spiritual man.

Native Americans are given names for animals that represent their skills or attributes. John Peters was—hard to believe—a slow child, hence his name, while Sly Fox was very clever and smart. I received an "Indian name"—John Porter. It was like a new identity. Sometimes an animal will emerge out of an experience in a sweat lodge or other ceremony, and that will be your name as well. I don't remember any animal name for me.

A Native American gathering would comprise a welcoming, an opening circle, and a blessing by the Supreme Medicine Man (often Slow Turtle himself), intertribal dancing, food, and a closing ceremony. If it were an overnight event such as a sweat lodge, then this would take several days on a reservation, and we would spend a great deal of time gathering clean, round stones for the sweat lodge, cutting down green saplings, stripping them and braiding them into a tent-like structures, and covering it with wet blankets. Inside would be a small pit, and the stones would be heated up outside on a fire until they were red-hot and then placed in the pit. Then a large wooden pitcher of water was placed inside. The leader would call the men in naked, while women would be in a separate lodge. We would not carry anything metallic with us, or else we could be burned; only wooden objects were allowed in the lodge.

The chief would do the prayers, and then we would go around taking turns holding the stick. As long as you held the stick, you could talk; otherwise all would be silent except the chief. While holding the stick, people would tell their most intimate stories of love, loss, heartbreak and pain. During this time, water from the pitcher would be poured on the hot stones, and steam would fill the lodge. The steam could be very intense; if you left the lodge, you could not return, but you could get as low as possible to the earth, since it was cooler down there (steam rises). At times I was allowed, as a "white man," to gently lift up the tent flap a crack and breathe some air. At times people would get "visions," and your vision was often an animal, and that animal (a wolf, bear, or eagle) would be your totem animal and sometimes your name. It was a powerful experience.

Even more powerful were the Sun Dances. In one summer in 2000, I went to not one but four Sun Dances, and I was exhausted. What is a Sun Dance? It is an ancient Native American ceremony; they are usually held out West.

I went to one in southern Minnesota; one in Anna, southern Illinois; and two in South Dakota. Hundreds gather to support the dancers. Sun Dancers excoriate themselves and suffer for four days, taking upon themselves the sins of the world. When it is over, we are all cleansed of our sins, and so is the world.

What are Sun Dancers? They are usually males (though I did see some females) who fast all day, but at night are allowed to lick the dew off the grass. Wooden dowels are pierced through their chests or backs, and leather thongs are attached to them, and as they march in a circle in the sun, they are pulled up as high as they can until their skin breaks. The higher they climb, the higher their power to heal us expands. They eventually drop to the ground, first aid is given to them to avoid skin infections, and they are brought to their tents. You can tell how many Sun Dances a person has gone through by counting the double skin scars on his back or chest. One man had as many as five or six pairs of scars.

In Anna, they had to cut a down a tree to place the long leather straps onto the Sun Dancer, and they sent a little child to point out a tree. They had difficulty cutting it down (no power tools are used, only manual saws) and dragging it to the site, since it was very heavy. People were exhausted pushing and pulling this huge tree, so the chief said, "Let us wait until morning," and lo and behold, a miracle happened: all fifty of us were able to carry the tree to the spot. I had never seen anything like it.

At night, while the dancers rest, we feast on food and drink. It is a very strange and fascinating ceremony. We feast; they suffer. The Sun Dance has been controversial and has been banned in some places, but freedom of religion has guaranteed they go on. We had special guards to watch over us, because some local "hoodlums" tried to enter the camp and break it up, but the police came and arrested them. The Sun Dance is also controversial because it is a combination of Christian faith (resurrection, pain, healing) and Native American religion. Every aspect of it is spiritual.

The Sun Dances in South Dakota are extraordinary on the Oglala Lakota Sioux reservations. One popular chief had followers who came all the way from Germany and Poland to his camp. Native American lore—in fact, Western lore—is very popular in Germany for some reason, and dozens come every year to these ceremonies.

What can we learn from Native Americans about our planet, death, dying, and coping with addictions and stress? A lot. So much that I could write an entire book on the relationships between Native religions, Judaism, and Christianity and what they can teach us about living. They healed me during my divorce and continue to heal me. Sadly, most of the leaders I have mentioned have passed away.

Chapter 16

Marriage and Settling Down / The Almuly Family / A Jittery Decade, the 1970s—the First Half of the Radical Decade; the Second Half—We Grow Up, Settle Down, and Get Married

---

Why I Came to Boston

People often asked me: "Jack, why did you leave Milwaukee and come to Boston?" My answer surprises them. It was not to get a job, or to teach at a university, or because of the weather. It was to find a wife! Yes, Milwaukee had only 20,000 Jews, and the pickings were slim. After graduating from Northwestern University in June 1971 with a PhD in sociology, I got my first job at the State University of New York (SUNY)–Cortland in upstate New York, a bit south of Syracuse in the Finger Lakes District.

Jobs in sociology were plentiful at that time. Enrollments were climbing. It was the '60s and '70s, and whenever liberal and radical protests and leaders emerge, sociology goes up; and when more conservative leaders like Ronald Reagan come to power, funding for sociology is cut and enrollments drop. This is a bit of a simplification, but it explains things. I was hoping for a more prestigious university or college, but the top professors, such as Howard S. Becker, had given their imprimatur to other graduate students for other higher level schools.

I would have liked to be in a large city like New York or Los Angeles, but in any case I interviewed with the people at SUNY–Cortland, and they seemed interested in me, so I accepted. Cortland was an interesting place—a school that specialized in physical education teachers for the entire state, thus had a mix of white upstate students and Black and Latino students from New York City. I loved the students; in fact, in those days you could actually "love" your students physically if you were discreet about it. I had a passionate relationship with a Puerto Rican woman from Brooklyn. There really wasn't much to do up there in the winter except to have sex and ski, so I learned to ski at Greek Peak, utilizing the graduate-length method. It was taught by a Japanese American woman, and it was fun, especially at night. I loved skiing.

It was also a time of protest, right and left. One time, Rabbi Meir Kahane, the leader of the Jewish Defense League (JDL), came up to SUNY–Cortland to speak, and as a faculty member I was chosen to introduce him. After his fiery talk about being a proud Jew and fighting for Soviet Jewry, we had a cup of tea in the cafeteria, and he told me something I will never forget: "Jack, if I had just five of you radical [left] professors and students as leaders, boy, what an impact I would have." He respected us on the Left for our organizational skills, knowledge of history, and ideological commitment. He felt he could "turn us around" to his way of thinking. As noted in a previous chapter, his charisma did entice me to join the JDL for a while.

Another issue was the war in Vietnam. We had many rallies and teach-ins, and several professors, such as Charlie Vivona and others, spoke out. I was a speaker as well, but I was becoming uncomfortable in this small-town in this out-of-the-way university. I had also seen how the tenure process worked, and I was not happy with that, either. The full professors, especially a woman who had barely written anything but had received tenure nonetheless, was the main culprit. They asked questions about the man's wife and other personal issues. I said to myself, *I do not want to go through that scrutiny and that control by others.* It reminded me in a way of that kibbutz incident at Kibbutz Gesher Haziv a decade earlier when the kibbutz decided that a member had to teach in a distant city for the income to the kibbutz, even though his wife was having a baby and he wanted to be near her. I never wanted to be controlled by others like that.

I wanted out, so I wrote an "open letter" saying I was quitting, and it was printed in the paper. I knew that this would most likely end my academic career, but I didn't care. I had to get out. I had to go to a bigger town with bigger universities. I was ambitious, and I knew I would succeed. The students were sad to see me leave, but they understood. They, too, had ambivalent feelings, especially the New Yorkers, about living in a small town for the rest of your life. So I left. Where? Back to Mamma and Daddy in Milwaukee.

So, at age twenty-seven, I moved in with my parents in my childhood home and bedroom at Fiftieth and Locust. For work, I was a journalist for the local Jewish paper, the *Chronicle*, and also wrote for the *Milwaukee Journal*. I tried dating the local girls, but they proved too insular. I had to make a choice— Boston or Los Angeles/San Francisco? Boston was one day's drive away (back then I had the strength to do it in one day while sleeping on the road overnight; today it would take me three days). It was closer, so I chose it. I stayed for a few days at the home of Rabbi Dick and Sherry Israel in Newtown Centre, and then I found a large apartment in Brookline at 28 Stanton Road to rent and share with two, sometimes three other roommates, and they were quite a collection of guys: Marty Abramowitz (Yossi Abramowitz's father, going through a divorce); Meir Rosenberg, whom I still see; an Israeli scholar at Brandeis (also going through a divorce); plus one or two non-Jewish guys.

By major luck, I actually had a job waiting for me. I saw an ad in the *Chronicle of Higher Education* for a lecturer in Jewish studies at Boston College, and I applied and I got it. (Gosh, jobs were so much easier to get back in the '70s!) Since I'd had an excellent education at Hebrew schools and the University of Wisconsin– Milwaukee, and was even beginning my "irritably prolific" publishing, as one colleague here at Harvard described another colleague's output, I got the job.

By 1975, I had my dissertation on student protest published, I had edited the classic anthology on Jewish radicalism, and I had several peer-reviewed academic articles published. I was not a rabbi, but I could teach introductions to Judaism and Jewish theology. There were two other Jews in the theology department, both rabbis, one an expert on Job. Father Daly was the chairman, and we got along fine. The students loved me because they were so sick of the Catholic catechism they were getting from the priests in the department. (Back then, it was mandatory for all students to take theology courses and attend Mass.)

So to take a course in Judaism was lovely for them. Alas, my time at Boston College was limited to one year. The new chairman, a German theologian, wanted only theology of religion, not the sociology of religion course, and since I was a sociologist and not a theologian, I was to be replaced by a rabbi or a Jewish studies scholar. Such are the uncertain vagaries of academia. Now you know why I left it.

While I was living in the Boston area, there was ferment in the '70s of freewheeling open marriages, open relationships, open everything. While living at Stanton Road, I met someone across from my building named Irv Doress, a tenured professor at Northwestern University. Irv was a kooky, iconoclastic guy who was living in an open marriage with his wife (of course, it had to be done discreetly), who was also an intellectual and a writer and one of the authors of the famous *Our Bodies, Ourselves* books.

But Irv wasn't having much luck. Overweight and not that attractive, he couldn't get anyone, but his wife was able to. I had a chance to do it with his wife, but I felt uncomfortable doing that and having a friendship with Irv, and more than a friendship. Irv and I wrote a booklet and several articles on cults together. His daughter was a member of the Hare Krishna cult, and he was trying desperately to get her out. Plus, it was around the time of the infamous cult in Jonestown, Guyana, northern South America, where the leader, Rev. Jim Jones, told his followers to drink cyanide-laced Flavor Aid, and hundreds died.

We became "famous," as we were invited to be guests on talk shows, interviewed by *Ladies' Home Journal*, and even NBS and national networks. Everyone wanted to know why kids join cults, why they stay, and why they leave. That was the name of the booklet and later a book.[29]

As I mentioned, Irv was a kooky guy and, way before the #MeToo movement, he was always pursuing women in his psychology classes, asking them out. One was a very attractive student named Miriam Almuly, a beautiful woman with an Italian Yugoslavian background. She rebuffed him. Irv told me that she had, but then he said, "You know, Jack, she may just be perfect for you. She's Jewish." So, when my birthday came up in December, and I was having a party at my Stanton Street apartment, Irv told her about it and gave her my address and told her about the party.

It was getting late, around midnight, and I was high or slightly drunk, when the bell rang, and at the door was one of the most beautiful women I had ever met—Miriam. She said, "Irv told me about your party. I was supposed to come with a friend, but she decided not to come, but I thought, 'Why not?'" We ended up talking for the next three hours. It was love at first sight.

We were married in November 1977, a few months later. She had gotten off a bad relationship, and her parents were very unhappy about it. I was Jewish (the other relationship was not—he was an Arab who secretly had a wife and child that he lied about to Miriam, and so she was ready for a normal relationship). Her parents and family loved me. I loved history and World War II. I listened to her father, Yotza (Joseph) Almuly, and her mother, Reli, and his sister, Lea (Leitza). They were ecstatic; my parents were ecstatic. We had a great wedding in Sharon, Massachusetts, and then drove out to Milwaukee for another celebration at the JCC there.

---

29 Porter and Doress (1977; 2014).

The Almuly Family

The Almuly family and their extensions (Ben-Arroyo, Davico, Alcalay, Eskenazy) were what Stephen Birmingham called "The Grandees" in his book on the great Sephardic families of America *The Grandees: The Story of America's Sephardic Elite* (1977), except that the Almuly-Benaroyo families came from Serbia, Belgrade, and Sarajevo in Bosnia. They could trace their roots easily to Morocco, Spain, Turkey, and the Balkans. One of their ancestors was Solomon (Shlomo) ben Jacob Almoli.[30]

Shlomo Almoli wrote a treatise on dream interpretation three hundred years before Freud did, and it is reputed (though I have not been able to verify it) that Freud quoted from his book. The book has been translated from Hebrew or Arabic into Hebrew and English in several editions. In Hebrew it is called *Pitron Halamot*, which means "interpretation of dreams." However, Almoli and Freud differed in their interpretation.[31]

The Bible has many examples of dreams, most prominently Pharaoh's dream about seven fat cows and seven lean cows that Joseph interprets to mean that the ruler should store the next seven years of grain because the following seven lean years of drought will lead to famine and starvation. Dreams in Judaism mean two things: they predict the future, and they allow one to communicate with dead relatives.

Freud, on the other hand, saw dreams as conflict or as signs of conflict, fears, phobias, tensions, often of a sexual nature. For example, dreams of knives might mean fear of castration, which was based on the Oedipal Complex, wherein one fears the father for love of the mother or the love of any woman, and, in retaliation, the father or husband or some father figure will castrate you. This fear of castration could be the cause of impotence, for example.

Other examples would be fear of enclosed spaces, thus having a fear of flying or being in a casket; or the opposite, fear of open places, agoraphobia, such that one fears driving on an open highway or even leaving one's home. I had a real estate student once who was afraid to come to my school in Newton because she had to drive on Route 128. She could drive on small streets, but that would have taken hours. She had to take the main highway. The solution: I came to her house for classes.

---

30 The 1972 *Encyclopedia Judaica* has an entry on him in 2:663, and 6:211, in a discussion of dreams.

31 Shlomo Almoli, *Pitron Halamot* (Warsaw, 1902).

The Almuly family was an unusual family in that several generations lived under one roof. On 1724 Beacon St. in Brookline, Yotza and Reli lived with his sister Leitza, his brother Dr. Zarko (Jack) Almuly, a doctor, who also had his medical office there, plus Miriam and her two older sisters Ena and Alisa, who lived there until they married. There was a large table in the center of the home, and there were lively gatherings there and in the living room for a growing family. Ena had eventually three children with Charlie Lorant, and Alisa had three children with Saro Palmeri, also a physician.

This was not unusual. Sephardim traditionally have large extended clans, and historically in Europe they have been physicians and businessmen, as well as artists and diplomats. Lonny Davico, a cousin, was a major director of UNESCO at the United Nations and lived near Geneva, Switzerland, its headquarters; and Yotza himself was an executive at Gilchrist's, a major Boston department store. They were a fascinating family.

Yotza was one of the few people I knew who were born in the nineteenth century and lived long enough into the twentieth century for me to interview him. He was born in Sabac, Yugoslavia, on March 14, 1898, and died July 21, 1892, at age eighty-four. I only knew him for five years but learned a lot. He was in the Yugoslavian army and was captured by German troops and interned in a stalag. When the German commander asked that all Jews be turned over to him, the Yugoslavian commander said no. This saved Yotza's life. Later, ironically, he became a favorite of the German commander because of his superb command of the language.

His wife, Reli Benaroyo Almuly, was born in Belgrade on October 21, 1905, and passed on February 21, 1988. His sister, Lea, was also born in Sabac on June 7, 1906, and died October 4, 1995. Yotza and Lea were the children of Kalmi and Reyna (Davicho) Almuly. Brother Dr. Zarko (Jack) was born on September 21, 1902, and died July 28, 1974. Their mother, Reyna, died on July 27, 1953. Ian Almuly, her brother, died during the Holocaust in 1941, and Ella Eskenazy, Reyna's sister, died in Jerusalem in 1951.

Lea was a delightful, iconoclastic person who told me that she had once been psychoanalyzed by a student of Sigmund Freud named Wilhelm Stekel (1868–1940) in Vienna. The time frame fits, since, if she was psychoanalyzed when she was around twenty-five, that would be in 1931, when Stekel was still alive. I wish I had been a fly on the wall at those sessions, but I can imagine what they were about: complaining about a strict father and a distant mother, typical Oedipal Freudian stuff.

Another distinguished relative was the artist Albert Alcalay, who was born in Paris on August 11, 1917, and died in Boston on March 29, 2008. His wife was the daughter of Ella Eskenazy, who still lives in Brookline, Massachusetts. One son, Gingi, is a professor of literature in New York, and the other, Mishko, is a lecturer in mathematics at Quincy College near Boston.

Sources

Aguilar, Manuel, and Ian Robertson. *Jewish Spain: A Guide.* Madrid: Altalena Editores, 1984.

Almoli, Solomon (Shlomo) ben Jacob. *Dream Interpretation from Classical Jewish Sources.* Translated and annotated by Yaakov Elman. New York: KTAV, 1998.

———. *Pitron Halamot.* Warsaw, Poland, 1902. This is a Hebrew version of *The Interpretation of Dreams,* most likely translated from the Polish or Russian. Also see a profile of him in volume 2 of *Encyclopedia Judaica* (1972 ed.).

Costigan, Giovanni. *Sigmund Freud: A Short Biography.* New York: Collier Books, 1965.

De Quiros, Felipe Torriba Bernaldo. *The Spanish Jews.* Madrid: Sucs de Rivadeneyra, 1972.

Freud, Sigmund. *The Interpretation of Dreams.* Translated and edited by James Strachey. New York: Avon Library, 1965.

Friedenwald, Harry. *The Jews and Medicine: Essays.* 2 vols. Baltimore: The Johns Hopkins Press, 1944. Esp. 2:469n5. Friedenwald describes a man named Montalto, a Jewish physician at the court of Marie de Medicis and Louis XIII, whose son republished a book in Hebrew in Amsterdam in 1637 by Almoli on the interpretation of dreams.

Gaon, Solomon. *Del Fuego: Sephardim and the Holocaust.* Edited by M. Mitchell Serels. New York: Sepher-Hermon Press, 1995.

Jastrow, Joseph. *Freud: His Dream and Sex Theories.* New York: Pocket Books, 1955.

Malka, Jeffrey S. *Sephardic Genealogy: Discovering Your Sephardic Ancestors and Their World.* Bergenfeld, NJ: Avotaynu, Inc., 2002.

Porter, Jack Nusan, and Irv Doress. *Kids in Cults: Why They Join, Why They Stay, Why They Leave.* Newton, MA: The Spencer Press, 2014. Earlier versions appeared in 1977 and 1985. This book also includes Porter's booklets *Jews and the Cults* and *Handbook of Cults, Sects and Self-Realization Groups.*

Chapter 17

The Death of a Father

———————

This is arguably the most powerful essay I have ever written. In fact, my own brother has used it in his lectures in Baltimore and even on YouTube on a show about the afterlife. I wrote it in a swoon as we watched my dad pass away. It resonates today in 2020 as we face the coronavirus plague. The articles from the *Milwaukee Journal* and the *Wisconsin Jewish Chronicle* describe this extraordinary man.

* * *

The phone call came on a Thursday night. My mother was crying on the phone for the first time. She could hardly say the words: "He's not talking anymore. He sits in the chair, but he doesn't talk."

My father had been struggling with the pain for nearly four years, first cancer of the prostrate, later cancer of the bone marrow. His doctors were angry at themselves. Not because they couldn't save his life, but because they couldn't stop his pain. The cancer had metastasized into crevices of the body that drugs could not reach. He was on constant morphine.

* * *

My father had been a fairly healthy man, working as he did with iron and steel in his small scrap-metal business. He had the heart of a forty-year-old man. During

World War II, he was one of the few Jewish commanders of a partisan brigade. He had been honored with a medal by the Russian government for valor. After he came to America in 1946, he worked in a shoe factory in Milwaukee to support his wife and two young sons, my brother Shlomo and me. He finally quit factory life because his boss insisted that he work on the Sabbath, and my father, an Orthodox Jew, could not do that. So he went into partnership with a German Jew, Sigmund Singer, and after a few years and many quarrels, started his own business. He worked very hard breaking steel, taking apart furnaces, picking up lathe turnings, and selling them to richer men who owned their own scrap iron and waste yards. They in turn would sell it to steel mills in America, Japan, and Germany.

My father had lost two daughters and twenty-five members of his family to the Nazis, and perhaps work was an anodyne; and a religion, too. My father never lost his faith in God.

* * *

I tried to carry on with my life after the call—teaching, correcting exams, writing, the usual duties of a college teacher, but I knew I would be going to Milwaukee very soon to see my father. My brother and his wife had already flown in from California, where he is a *rebbe* at a *yeshiva* in Santa Clara; and my sister and her husband had arrived from Minneapolis. The waiting began. As I drove to the university, I could not stop crying. I had to pull the car over to the side more than once because I could not see the road.

After two worrisome days, the call finally came last Saturday night. It was my sister. "You better come. It doesn't have to be tonight, but take the earliest plane tomorrow."

Sunday morning, my wife drove me to the airport, and I left Boston on the first flight. A friend picked me up, and after dropping my luggage at the house, I walked to St. Joseph's Hospital, located only a block from my parents' home.

My father was on the cancer war. He was propped up in bed, oxygen tubes in his nose. He recognized me, and we embraced. His face was the same except for dark shadows around his eyes. His cheeks were still a bit pink. Every word he spoke was difficult. My mother, sister, and brother, plus a few close friends were there. All of us knew what was happening. We tried to be brave.

During the day and into the night, we kept vigil. Friends and relatives came and went. My brother constantly chanted the *Tehillim*, Psalms.

The doctor told me that *Tateh* ("Dad" in Yiddish) had contracted pneumonia because his defense against infections had been shattered by the cancer. It was a matter of days now. My response was surprisingly angry: "Your job is over, doctor. Now let God do what He can." He nodded his head in agreement and left.

The next twenty-four hours were unbelievable. We sat around the bed, telling my father news of our lives. We sang some songs in Yiddish, a few Sabbath songs. We could see that he was drifting into another realm. He spoke in Russian, a language he rarely used around us. He shouted, *"Choroshoy!"* ("It's o.k." in Russian). He was dreaming of his youth, of his days in the partisans. Perhaps he was comforting us—*Choroshoy!*

The day before, on Shabbat, when our rabbi, Reb Michel Twerski, came to visit him, my father sag with him, and as Rabbi Twerski left and said good-bye, my father corrected him and said, "Not good-bye, I'll see you tomorrow."

Sunday evening my brother gave my father a new name, *Rephual*. His name was Israel, but, according to Jewish custom, when a person is grievously ill he receives a Kabbalistic name to confuse the angel of death. If he or she survives, they keep that name—*Rephual* ("God will heal"), *Chayyim*, or *Chaya* for the illness, they receive another name, and another . . . The names mean "Health," "Life." My brother told me of a man who has gone through four or five names and is still alive.

My father gave all of us his last blessings. To me, he said: "Mach a leben, Yankele. Es is shver tzu machen a leben in America." ("Make a living, Jackie. It's hard to make a living here.") To my mother, he said: "It's enough for you, Momma. Be strong. It will soon be over."

Each minute in that hospital room seemed like eternity. Night came. We didn't know what else to do except pray and sing. My brother took out the holy *siddur* of Rabbi Jacob Emden, a sixteenth-century German Kabbalist and scholar. The hospital was quiet. We were alone with my father when a most miraculous event occurred.

As my brother Shlomo read from the text, I could almost feel the room fill up with angels. I could hear their flapping wings. My father's soul was in the room and was speeding toward heaven.

> On your right flies the angel Raphael; and on your left, the angel Gabriel. The *Keter* (crown) is at your head and the *malchut* (kingdom) at your feet. Angel wings protect and cover your chest and angel wings cover your feet. You are flying toward heaven carried by angels.

My brother prayed and then translated the Hebrew into Yiddish. We cried. We prayed. We were astounded. We could hear our father saying goodbye. The soul was winging toward the heavens, toward the world to come, to *Gan Eden* or to *Gehinnom*, to heaven or hell, but we knew it was heaven. With tears in my eyes I asked Shlomo: "He's going to heaven?"

"No question about it, Jack. He's going straight to heaven."

* * *

I thought only Christians had an afterlife and Jews did not. Heaven was always something quite vague, something one never discussed in Hebrew or Sunday school. Perhaps the rabbis were trying to tell us something with their reticence. Concentrate on *this* life, don't concern yourself with the world to come. Geoffrey Gorer has called it the "pornography of death"; that is, death has replaced sex as the last obscenity to be kept from the eyes of children and adults. Yet, in Judaism it is not simply fear of death but the assumption that to dwell upon death or the afterlife could lead to madness. Thus, *Kabbalah*, which does deal with these issues, could only be studied by mature, married individuals, steeped in Talmud and Torah. Before you can run, you must first learn to crawl and then to walk. The same with *Kabbalah*. You must first learn the basics.

I am essentially a secular Jew. I live a life based on reason. Never would I have thought that I would so fervently believe in angels or heaven and hell. My brother and I talked about this, at times in earshot of my father. He explained to me that Judaism has a complex map of the afterlife and that Christians took their system from the Jews. Very evil people go to hell; a small number are in limbo; but most people will reside (their souls will reside) at various *madregot* (steps or stages) of heaven. *Tateh* would be at a fairly high level because he was a righteous man, and he would move up the *madregot* as time went by. At the very highest levels are the souls of Abraham, Isaac, and Jacob, Moses, Solomon, David, and all of the great prophets and rabbis of ancient times. To be invited to sit at their table is the greatest of heavenly delights.

I was also intrigued by another thing my brother said. How can a soul move up in heaven after the person dies? The individual is no longer able to carry out *mitzvot* or acts of righteousness. How, then, can he or she be lifted up still higher? The answer is unusually innovative. It is the family and friends of the deceased who, through good deeds and acts of kindness, can lift their beloved higher and higher throughout eternity. The poignancy of this idea overwhelms me at times.

* * *

Sunday night the doctors informed us that *Tateh* was entering irreversible shock. He would live only as long as his powerful heart would hold out, twelve hours, a day, perhaps two days.

We prayed even more. We sang. We talked with Dad. Perhaps he heard us. I'd like to think that he did.

We took turns with the vigil. Friends came. Some were so distraught they had to leave. We waited. My brother slept in the hospital all night. I went home, knowing that in the morning my father might be dead.

I returned to his room in the morning—praying, hoping. I went home for lunch. At 12:15 p.m., Monday, March 19, my sister Bella called: "Jack, it's over."

I would not believe it. I didn't hear it. I would continue life as usual. I calmly finished my soup, trying to ignore the phone conversation. Then, I quickly walked to the hospital. When I entered the ward, I knew it was over when I saw the nurses crying. My father had also touched them deeply.

I walked into the room. My mother was weeping over his body, and she wailed: "You see. This is what your *Tateh* has now become." I went to the bed and embraced my father for the last time, and taking his strong and beautiful hand I said: "Good-bye, *Tateh*. You were the best." I broke into tears and just looked at him, holding his hand for a long time, until it got colder and colder.

The nurses, who had been trained in a special kind of primary care, comforted my mother, giving her a sedative and putting warm blankets around her. She was shivering uncontrollably, and the nurses who knew of her heart condition were worried. I embraced a sad and dejected Dr. Hurwitz, my father's physician. He was totally leveled. To him, death was a monumental symbol of his failure as a healer.

"Be comforted that he is out of his pain, Jack." He was a caring man, and he needed *my* comfort at that moment.

Our rabbi, Reb Michel Twerski, arrived within minutes. Immediately, a new phase began—the mourning process, and this too was ensconced in four thousand years of law and tradition. The first ritual was that of *Keriah*, the rending of clothes. Reb Michel went up to my brother and me, made a small cut in our shirt or jacket with a pocketknife, and we tore it down the size of our fist. We would wear these mourning clothes for the next seven days.

* * *

I never knew how much work would follow a death. The *Chevra Kadisha* (literally "holy society"—a Jewish burial society) arrived soon after the rabbi. They had been well trained and knew exactly what to do. My family and I could go home to begin the *Shiva*, the seven days of mourning.

My father's body would be watched by a guard (a *shomer* in Hebrew) from the moment of his death to his burial, which would take place within 24 hours. I was not allowed to observe it, but my father was taken to the funeral home (it could have easily been the synagogue as well) where the *tahara* would be performed. The *tahara* is the ritual washing and dressing of the body in preparation for the afterlife. A son should not take part unless no one else can do it.

A few years ago, in 1975, I had the honor of aiding in the *tahara* of the great Rabbi Jacob Twerski of Milwaukee, Reb Michel's father. So, I will describe that rather than my father's *tahara*. After immersing themselves in the *midveh* or ritual bath, the men entered the synagogue where Rabbi Jacob lay in state and carefully washing the entire body in the proscribed manner. As Maurice Lam notes in his book *The Jewish Way in Death and Mourning*, the *tahara* is not only the preparation of the body but the reciting of the proper prayers asking God for forgiveness for any sins the deceased may have committed and praying that the All-Merciful should grant him/her eternal peace.

Men do the *tahara* on men, and women on women. After the body is washed, it is clothed in a perfectly clean, perfectly white shroud. Holy soil from Israel is placed on the eyes and upon the forehead. No autopsies or cremations are allowed except under extreme circumstances such as a plague. The body is placed in a simple wooden casket and again guarded by the *shomer* until the funeral begins.

* * *

My brother said that one phone call is sufficient to spread the news. "Bad news never travels fast. Each person will call another." However, it isn't that simple in a complex society. Relatives in other states had to be called, telegrams to Israel sent, the newspapers had to be informed so that the death notice could be inserted. And the mourning had to continue. Mourners, according to Jewish law, should really not do this work. In fact, they should do nothing else except mourn during the seven days of the *shiva*.

Nevertheless, I had the onerous task of calling my father's business clients and customers, of writing his obituary, and of taking care of other minor details. My brother concentrated on the funeral arrangements. This is not the proper place to lament the rising costs of funerals and plots. But, according to Jewish law, a traditional funeral must *not* be ostentatious. One *must* use a wooden casket and a minimum of flowers. Still, even with a simple casket and funeral, it cost my mother about $2,000 (with $750 going for the cemetery plots).

The funeral was set for three o'clock the next day, Tuesday. Since we children were already in Milwaukee, we had only to wait for someone from my Uncle Boris's family in Los Angeles, someone from my Aunt Betty's family in Chicago to come, and for my wife to arrive from Boston. They arrived in plenty of time.

Almost immediately upon hearing of my father's death, people sent baskets of fruit and telegrams and friends started arriving. It was wonderful to have the support of so many relatives and friends at this hour.

We sat on low chairs or on the floor of the house; the mirrors were covered; we wore slippers; we could not put on makeup, shave, or comb our hair for that week. The door was open. Visitors entered and quietly waited for us to greet them. The mourners could either remain silent or initiate conversation. When visitors left, they did not say good-bye but repeated the words, "May you be comforted among the mourners of Jerusalem and Zion."

* * *

The limousine picked us up at 2:30 p.m. to take us to the funeral home. It was a bit unreal. I thought these things happened to other people. We were giddy in the car, awed by the uniqueness of it. Such a fancy automobile.

We were ushered into the side room of the funeral home. I could see the beautiful pine-box casket, the candles, the crowd coming in. People queued up to greet us. Small trays of aspirin, smelling salts, and Kleenex were on the tables to our side. The crowd was large, nearly 300 people. My father was loved and admired by many people, Jews and non-Jews, African Americans and whites, young and old.

The survivors of the Holocaust, old friends, sat with us in the special anteroom reserved for the family. These survivors substituted for the sisters and brothers, cousins and nephews lost in the war.

Several rabbis requested to speak. We chose four, but easily a half-dozen would have gladly eulogized my father. My brother and I would speak after them—giving our own personal thoughts.

I remember only a few sections from each speech. Reb Michel Twerski spoke eloquently of my father's years in the Russian partisan movement and his devotion to his family and the *shul*. His opening lines were chilling: "Irving Porter, an old fighter, has lost his first battle."

The next speaker was Rabbi David Shapiro, who gave a very deep and very poetic interpretation of my father's life, comparing his home with the building of the Jewish Temple in Jerusalem.

Finally, Rabbi Isaac Lerer came up and read a beautiful poem that he had composed on the spot in honor of my father. Then, Rabbi Feldman spoke. All the eulogies were very moving.

Then, I walked forward, saluting my father as I walked by him. I had written the speech last night and that morning a reporter from the *Milwaukee Sentinel* had come over to do a story on my father and took a copy of the speech with him. Here are portions of it:

> My father was an ambitious man. Yes, he was very ambitious, but not for fame, money, or power. His ambition was to help support his family and to help others. His home was always open to any person . . . He was basically a happy, lively man, and this, despite the Nazi hell he had gone through. In fact, he was often amused and sometimes saddened by his American relatives who had all sorts of material comforts yet were depressed. He could never understand that. His advice was always: *"Zei labedik, yidden!"* ("Be lively, Jews!") . . . I often interviewed him on his role during the Holocaust, and he left me with an important legacy: a Jew can send no one in his place. When the time came for him to take revenge, *nekumah*, he left his family and joined the partisans. Not to take another's life, but to regain his dignity and the dignity of his family . . . His role made a deep and lasting impression on me—to fight for Jewish rights throughout the world . . . He is gone, but our memories live on in his essential goodness, his singing, his dancing at weddings and parties . . . He battled the cancer like he battled the Nazis—an old partisan, a fighter till the end. He was even more—a man blessed with *hen*, grave, a righteous man, even a *lamed vovnik* . . . We will never forget you or what you did . . . Goodbye, *Tateh*. I salute you, you old partisan.

* * *

The funeral was a blur, a dream. We arrived. The body was placed into the ground. The prayers were said. The *Kaddish*. The casket hit bottom. Then, all the men took the shovel and threw earth on the casket. When the grave was completely filled, everyone left. It was suddenly over. My wife, Miriam, told me of an ancient Sephardic custom. Take a pebble, throw it over your shoulder, and don't look back.

Every morning and evening, men came to my mother's house and with a *minyan* (a group of ten men) my brother and I said *kaddish* for my father.

We carried out the *shiva* through more tragedy. A few weeks after my father's death, his brother Boris died in Los Angeles, and a week or so later, my mother's cousin, a woman only sixty, died in Florida.

Our friends buoyed us up. One of the most thoughtful cards we received said the following: "Please accept our sincere sympathies on the death of your father and father-in-law, Irving Porter. Losing a parent is a very hard thing to deal with. Doubts, guilt, sorrow, grief, and regrets are all part of the mourning process. There is no magic way to get through this painful time. But somehow, sometimes it helps to know that you have friends who care. Jack, we are your friends and we care. Love, John and Laurie."

My very wise father-in-law, Mr. Joseph Almuly, talked to me about death after the *shiva*. A man in his early eighties, he quoted Cicero to me:

> Why should we be afraid of death? If death is the link with past relatives and friends, then it is a wonderful thing, is it not? But if death is nothing, then why should we be afraid of nothing? In any case, no one has ever come back to tell us if it is nothing or if it is indeed the reunification with one's family . . .
>
> I don't know about an afterlife, but I do know that there was a beginning before my birth and that my death is not an end . . . That is the truth of the matter. All that I know is that life is very precious, very short, and very complicated.

1979

Chapter 18

The Founding of the IAGS / International Association of Genocide Scholars / Trips to Sarajevo, Iraq, and Other Zones of Conflict

---

The Founding

The IAGS (International Association of Genocide Scholars, first called simply the Association of Genocide Scholars, or AGS) was founded in the wake of the famous Robert Maxwell Holocaust Conferences—the first held in London and Oxford in 1988, the second in Berlin in 1993. These conferences were called "Remembering for the Future," and the second one took place exactly 48 years after the end of the war in 1945, which meant the survivors were dying off quickly. Soon few survivors would be left to tell the tale.

Maxwell, a strange and mysterious yet charming rogue, announced that he would spend a million pounds (a huge sum twenty-eight years ago—about five million dollars in today's terms) so that Europe, and especially England, would finally recognize the impact of the Holocaust.

Spurred on by universalists such as Claude Lanzmann and Yehuda Bauer and the recent genocides in Bosnia and Rwanda, a definite tilt was occurring in the direction of "comparative genocide," not just emphasizing the Shoah. (In fact, this conference was the beginning of calling the Nazi Holocaust "the Shoah.")

Helen Fein, Israel Charny, Robert Melson, and Roger Smith met in a café in 1993 and announced that they would create the first professional association in the field—the AGS. A year later, at its first conference in Williamsburg, Virginia, I proposed that it be international in scope and that its name be changed to the IAGS.

Research on comparative genocide had begun about fifteen years earlier in the late 1970s with Helen Fein's classic book *Accounting for Genocide* (1978); Vahakn Dadrian's comparative approach of the Armenian and Jewish genocides (1975); and my work—a review essay called "On Genocide" in *Contemporary Sociology* (July 1976), the mainstream official ASA journal of reviews; a review of Terence des Pre's masterpiece *The Survivor* in *Jewish Currents* in April 1978; and the very first anthology in the field *Genocide and Human Rights: A Global Anthology* (1982), which contained a very influential, oft-quoted introduction,

I was, however, preoccupied with student unrest and political radicalism from the time of my dissertation at Northwestern University in 1971 and throughout the mid-'70s with essays and reviews on a subject that had grabbed this young graduate and budding professor of sociology. When the radicalism petered out, I turned to my own life. I was a child of Holocaust survivors and needed to make sense of my own life, my own past, and my own angst.

Since my parents were Soviet Jewish partisans during the war, I first tackled that subject in a four-part series called "Jewish Resistance During the Holocaust" that appeared not in an academic journal but in my home-town of Milwaukee's Jewish paper, the *Wisconsin Jewish Chronicle*, in December 1972. At the time I was only twenty-seven years old and had just completed my first academic job in upstate New York, SUNY–Cortland, but had returned to Milwaukee in the summer of 1972. (I was unhappy with academia and a bit lonely, so I returned "home" to Milwaukee, only to leave again within a year for Boston in 1973, never to leave that city again.)

In 1979, I also contributed an essay to the anthology *Encountering the Holocaust*, edited by Byron Sherwin, in which Helen Fein published one of her earliest essays, "Socio-Political Responses During Holocaust," which was chapter 5 in the book. My essay dealt with an important social psychological issue at the time: the impact of the "trauma" of the Shoah on survivors and their children. I was one of the first to predict not only a "sociological syndrome," as opposed to a psychological syndrome, but also one that was passed on to the second and third generation: the so-called "survivor's syndrome," akin to the post-traumatic stress disorder of returning Vietnam War veterans.[32]

This was the beginning of the comparative approach in sociology. Thus we saw Helen Fein's "two-case" analysis of the Turkish and German genocides and Vahakn Dadrian's similar analyses even earlier, in 1975.[33] I also tried my hand at this genre by analyzing a class of people who were often victims of beatings,

---

32 See Porter (1982); Sherwin (1979), Fein (1979), and Stevens (1996).
33 Fein (1978): 271-294 and Vahakn Dadrian (1975).

killings, and oppression: urban middleman like the Jews, Armenians, Chinese, Indians (in Africa, for example) and Greeks.[34]

The First Generation (1994–2007)

The first generation of IAGS scholars was mostly Jewish and Armenian, with some Israelis, and, of course, mostly male and all white. Aside from the four founders mentioned above, other "firsters" would include Frank Chalk, Henry Huttenbach, Herb Hirsch, Joyce Apsel, Barbara Harff, Steve Jacobs, Vahakn Dadrian, Rouben Adalian, Kurt Johanssohn, Sam Totten, Mark Levene, Eric Markusen, Ted Gurr, and the present author.

It was a very small group, one that could fit into a fairly medium-size classroom. (In fact, at the very first IAGS conference in Williamsburg, Virginia, at the College of William and Mary in June 1995, all sessions were held in one room, and everyone—approximately fifty people—attended each session.) Though Roger Smith did not mention me at the Williamsburg conference in his tribute to Helen Fein, many at the IAGS conference believed that I was a founder in the field, including Helen Fein, Israel Charny, and Eric Markusen. (From Porter's academic diary).[35]

The inaugural conference was also the first time I gave a paper at an IAGS conference. Not surprisingly, it was based on the introduction to my anthology and was called "What is Genocide?" I also read a controversial paper by my colleague at Boston University, Prof. Steven Katz, a professor of Jewish philosophy and a colleague of Elie Wiesel. It was based on his recent and controversial book *The Holocaust in Historical Context* (1994). It was a very unpopular paper, even booed. He stated that the only "true" genocide was the Holocaust. Everyone disagreed.

What was Katz's contention?

He felt that a true genocide had to be total in scope and geography and inescapable by any means (intermarriage, conversion), and had to have intent (itself a controversial issue). The only genocide Katz had difficulty with was the Armenian, and later the Rwandan. He battled with the former for a long time but still rejected it on the following grounds: urban Armenians in Istanbul could escape the killings; females and some children could escape death via marriage

---

34 See Porter (1981).
35 Smith (2007) and *Confronting History and Holocaust* (2014).

to a Turk and conversion to Islam; and, perhaps most importantly, Armenians outside of Turkey were safe.

Unlike the Nazis hunting down every Jew everywhere in the world, Armenians who escaped Turkey were not hunted down and killed. Katz's views spawned numerous responses and discussions. The most important one was Alan Rosenberg's book *Is the Holocaust Unique?*

The Second Generation (2007–2011)

The IAGS was run by a tight group of insiders (Charny, Fein, Hirsch, and Chalk). While there were many fights among them, Israel Charny seemed to be always the lightning rod for conflict, and so the organization barely survived from year to year. Conferences were held every two years, so there was plenty of time to organize and raise money. Income was based on very minimal dues (about twenty to forty dollars) plus support from the Armenian community, especially the Zoryan Institute of Toronto, which contributed thirty thousand dollars every year, especially for the journal.

There was no oversight over finances. For ten years, Steven Jacobs, a rabbi and professor of Jewish thought at the University of Alabama, was treasurer and often both secretary and treasurer. Money was spent carelessly with no vigilance or transparency. When I took over as treasurer in 2007, an audit was undertaken, and a huge amount of money was unaccounted for—sixty thousand dollars.

So, under the leadership of Greg Stanton, the new IAGS president and the first "outsider," a non-academic lawyer, founder of Genocide Watch, and a US State Department official, a complete overhaul of the organization took place. Every check over fifty dollars had to have two signatures: those of the treasurer (me) and the president (Greg). A professional bookkeeper was hired; the books were carefully managed; and expenses were carefully monitored. Now there was complete transparency.

The triumvirate of Greg Stanton, Second Vice President Alex Hinton of Rutgers University–Newark, and Jack Nusan Porter met often via conference calls and even personal visits and put the organization back on a firm footing. The sixty thousand dollars was eventually returned to the organization.

The Trip to Erbil, Northern Iraq

The highlight of Greg's leadership was a trip that he, Alex, Steve Jacobs, the secretary of the organization, and I took to meet with President Barazani and his staff in Erbil to organize a conference in Brussels on the "Anfal," the genocide of the Kurds by Saddam Hussein. It was one of the highlights of my political and academic career. We were wined, dined and toured. We hammered out a conference, but the Kurds nixed it, because we wanted to mention other victims of Saddam, not just the Kurds. Such are the politics of the Middle East—a puzzle.

Conflict and More Conflict

But conflict within the IAGS would not end. At the Sarajevo conference, Israel Charny, in his farewell speech in Sarajevo, Bosnia, in June 2007, was thought to have insulted his audience by implying to "psychoanalyze" them. His was a brilliant, charismatic personality who felt that we as a group, not individually, should admit that we have "sinned"—a kind of a secular Yom Kippur, a Day of Atonement, but for what? For not doing enough to stop oppression and genocide. Perhaps he meant well but was badly misunderstood.

I remember rushing from table to table, calming our hosts and telling them that Israel meant no insult—he was, well, crazy. I think I helped cool this uproar.

The INOGS Split

However, there were much more serious revolts, again partially instigated by Charny. The most serious was a breakaway group of European scholars who would call themselves the INOGS (the International Organization of Genocide Scholars). They were fed up with two things. One, they felt the IAGS was spending too much time putting out political declarations, protesting every possible mass killing or slight in the world, rather than concentrating on the real work of hard and demanding research. They felt that there were plenty of other groups out there to protest genocide, and that in this context scholars should be scholars, not protesters.

But another factor was more personal: Israel Charny did something that seemed very unprofessional. He openly criticized a fellow scholar personally who had dared to question Israel's past and present. The scholar was the British social scientist Martin Shaw from the University of Sussex. Shaw felt that an incident at Deir Yassin, a village in Israel, was an example of Israeli genocidal actions, a massacre of innocent civilians in 1948, and that Israel's occupation was also oppressive, though not genocidal.

Charny flew into a rage and condemned Shaw publicly. In response, the newly elected IAGS president George Schabas (who had defeated me for the position in 2009) publicly denounced Charny. One IAGS president condemning a former one was unprecedented. With that the European contingent, the INOGS, broke away and started its own organization, held its own conferences, and even took over a journal that maverick Henry Huttenbach, a member of the founding generation, had started—the *Journal of Genocide Research*.

The Zoryan Split

In the same time period, to show how everything seemed to collapse at once, IAGS President Alex Hinton and Vice President Feierstein felt that the official journal of the IAGS *Genocide Studies and Prevention* was too expensive as a print journal and needed to be converted into an online version. This was a common view at the time, but one that pitted older scholars used to a paper version against younger scholars used to electronic Internet culture.

Immediately, editors Herb Hirsch, Nicholas Robins, Henry Theriault, and Sam Totten, joined by other "old-timers" such as Israel Charny, Greg Sarkissian, and Roger Smith, protested and began their own journal with the support of the Armenians and the Zoryan Institute. That journal is called *Genocide Studies International* and has both print and online versions and is the official journal of the International Institute for Genocide and Human Rights, the IIGHR (a division of the Zoryan Institute of Toronto).

Three Groups

This basically split the IAGS into three groups who rarely speak to each other, though INOGS and IAGS have the best chance of coming together. I do not see the IIGHR coming together with INOGS, nor with IAGS ever. I might add that there is a much smaller group, the IGS, founded by Orlanda Brugnola and Helen Fein, but now headed by Joyce Apsel and Edgar Ferreira of Notre Dame University. It publishes a small newsletter and gives the Lemkin Award every year in New York, but it has no major global impact.

The Third Generation and the Future

The sociology of organizations is fascinating. They go through amoeba-like divisions when conflict happens. This is life, an organic growing life. The organization is now fully international and no longer American or European-centered. All conferences since 2011 have been held *outside* the USA, for two reasons: (1) it has become more difficult for foreign scholars and students to obtain visas to come to America; (2) the IAGS has truly become international in scope. The last six conferences have been held in Buenos Aires, Argentina; Sarajevo, Bosnia; Winnipeg, Canada; Brisbane, Australia; Yerevan, Armenia; and Phnom Penh, Cambodia.

Conclusions

I am hoping that one day all three groups will come together, especially the INOGS and the IAGS, but we will see. The major issues persist: What exactly is genocide? Should any and all massacres be labeled genocide? Is the word "genocidal" just a slippery slope that tries to have it both ways? It's genocide, but not quite genocide . . . What other tensions?

First, the field suffers from a great deal of political correctness. One example is the "sins of the white man" syndrome, whereby we make the Anglo-Saxon white male guilty of all crimes of genocide, forgetting that nonwhite tribes also committed genocide. Or, if we include slavery as a form of genocide (which it isn't), then we must note historically that white men usually grabbed slaves within ten miles of the African coast. Beyond that area, Africans or Muslims captured Africans as slaves, not white men. In fact, Arabs, not "white men," continued slavery well into the twentieth century.

Second, the field must decide (if it wants to) to engage in moral criticism or historical scholarship. Will it have a political agenda of activism, or will it merely stick to scholarship? Can you combine both? Yes, I believe you can, but others disagree with me.

Third, genocide has replaced the Holocaust as the major direction of teaching and research. No school can have only a Holocaust center or department; comparative genocide must be included in either. Some, however, believe that this would denigrate the uniqueness of the Holocaust.

Fourth, genocide is a young field, only some twenty-five years old; perhaps forty as a discipline. New fields lack authority, so one condemns others. The field has seen a lot of backbiting and conflict, much of it very nasty, due to the insecurity of the participants. As the field ages, however, it should mellow out.

Fifth, there will always be controversy, because genocide is a sensitive topic. Since the term was first defined in 1944, only two genocides have been legally defined as genocide by the world courts: the Holocaust and the Rwanda-Hutu-Tutsi genocide. So it reminds me of an old Jewish joke:

> Two groups of Jews come to the rabbi and ask: "Rabbi, should we *stand* when we say the *Shema* (an important prayer), or *sit*? We have been fighting for weeks. So what is the tradition, Rabbi?"
>
> "*That's* the tradition."
>
> Puzzled, they asked again: "Rabbi, what do you mean? *What's* the tradition?"
>
> "The *fighting*, my friends. *That's* our tradition."

Humans keep finding creative ways to kill each other. Will the planet undergo cataclysmic seizures that will lead to genocides? Things like famine, climate change, catastrophic weather patterns, and, of course, pandemics? We will see, but the future looks foreboding.

Time Line

1944 The term "genocide" is coined by Polish American jurist and scholar Raphael Lemkin.

1977 The first course on genocide is taught at UMass–Lowell by Jack Nusan Porter, with the help of Prof. Levon Chorbajian.

1980 Frank Chalk and Kurt Jonassohn teach another early course on genocide in Montreal at Concordia University.

1982 The first anthology in genocide studies appears—*Genocide and Human Rights* (*GHR*), by Jack Nusan Porter.

1982 "Sexual" is used in the definition of genocide for the first time, in *GHR*.

1988 The first Robert Maxwell-sponsored Holocaust Conference on "Remembering for the Future," is held in Oxford, England.

1991 The first anthology-style textbook on genocide appears, written by Chalk and Jonassohn.

1991 The first major analysis of the genocide against homosexuals appears—*Sexual Politics in Nazi Germany* by Jack Nusan Porter.

1993 The second Robert Maxwell-sponsored conference on "Remembering for the Future" takes place in Berlin.

1993 IAGS is founded in Berlin at the same time as the "Remembering" conference at a luncheon of Israel Charny, Roger Smith, Robert Melson, and Helen Fein. First known as the AGS, the Association of Genocide Studies, its international focus is now emphasized.

1995 The first IAGS conference held at the College of William and Mary in Williamsburg, Virginia. Helen Fein is elected its first president.

1996 The genocide curriculum guide appears, created by Jack Nusan Porter. Later that same year, another guide appears by Joyce Apsel and Helen Fein.

2006 The first comprehensive textbook on genocide appears, published by Routledge and written by Adam Jones. I am mentioned in the book among the first definitions of genocide.

IAGS Conferences

1995 College of William and Mary, Williamsburg, Virginia (the first gathering).

1997 Concordia University, Montreal, Canada (I was elected second vice president during this time).

1999 University of Wisconsin, Madison (I ran for president).

2001 University of Minnesota, Minneapolis (I ran for president).

2003 National University of Ireland, Galway (I ran for president).

2005 Florida Atlantic University, Boca Raton.

2007 Sarajevo, Bosnia (I was treasurer during this time).

2009 George Mason University, Virginia (I ran for president for my fourth and last time).

2011 Buenos Aires, Argentina.

2013 University of Manitoba, Winnipeg, Canada.

2015 Queensland University, Brisbane, Australia.

2017 Yerevan, Armenia.

2019 Phnom Penh, Cambodia.

2021 Barcelona, Spain (via Zoom)

2023 Barcelona, Spain (live)

Sources

Apsel, Joyce, and Barbara Harff, eds. *Essays in Honor of Helen Fein*. New York: International Association of Genocide Scholars, 2007. This is an excellent overview of Helen's life and of the founding of genocide studies and the IAGS by her colleagues and friends.

Dadrian, Vahakn. "The Common Features of the Armenian and Jewish Cases of Genocide." In *Victimology: A New Focus,* edited by Israel Drapkin and Emilio Viano. Lexington, MA: D. C. Heath, 1975.

Fein, Helen. *Accounting for Genocide*. New York: The Free Press, 1979.

———. "A Formula for Genocide: Comparison of the Turkish Genocide (1915) and the German Holocaust (1939–1945)." *Comparative Studies in Sociology* 1 (1978): 271–293.

International Association of Genocide Scholars website: www.IAGS.com.

Katz, Steve. *The Holocaust in Historical Context*. New York: Oxford University Press, 1994.

Porter, Jack Nusan. "Jewish Resistance during the Holocaust" [Four-part series]. *Wisconsin Jewish Chronicle*, December 1, December 15, December 22, and December 29, 1972.

———. "On Genocide: Review Essay." *Contemporary Sociology* 5, no. 4 (July 1976): 490–492.

———. Review of *The Survivor*, by Terrence Des Pres *Jewish Currents* 32, no. 4 (#351) (April 1978): 32–35.

———. *Genocide and Human Rights: A Global Anthology*. Lanham, MD: University Press of America/Rowman & Littlefield, 1979. Esp. "Some Social-Psychological Aspects of the Holocaust in Byron Sherwin and Susan Ament, 1979, 117–139.

———. "The Urban Middleman." *Comparative Social Research* 4 (Summer 1981).

———. "From Holocaust to Genocide Studies: The Odyssey of a Scholar." Unpublished manuscript (2019). This is an expanded version of this essay on my odyssey from Holocaust to genocide studies and the many influences on my work.

Sherwin, Byron. "Some Social-Psychological Aspects of the Holocaust" In *Encountering the Holocaust*. New York: Hebrew Publishing Company, 1979.

Smith, Roger, "For Helen." In *Essays in Honor of Helen Fein*, edited by Apsel and Harff (2007), 67–69.

Stevens, Michael, ed. *Voices from Vietnam*. Madison: Wisconsin Historical Society Press, 1996.

Chapter 19

A Jew at Harvard's Ukrainian Research Institute

———

VERITAS! This is the motto of Harvard University, and, despite some fumbling and bumbling, political expediency, intellectual, and social snobbism, it has kept to that standard for nearly 350 years.

For about twenty years I've wanted to come to Harvard (who doesn't?). But at Harvard, you don't come: you are *invited*. This is why so few of its graduate students and junior faculty get tenure. First, you must go out into the world and achieve what in their eyes is the "best." Then, and only then, will you be asked to join this most exclusive club. I am only a research associate, the lowest and most expendable run on the ladder.

But first, to understand the Harvard Ukrainian Institute (HURI), one must understand Harvard, and to understand Harvard one must understand a few principles of its culture:

One, Harvard considers itself the greatest university in the world, and it probably is. Therefore, HURI considers itself the greatest Ukrainian research institute in the world, and it probably is, in its own way.

Two, Harvard's departments would rather be deep than wide; that is, they would rather specialize in a few areas or time-frames and be the best in that than spread itself horizontally across many areas. This is as true for the Jewish studies and history departments as it is for Ukrainian studies. For at HURI, it is best if one stops research in 1819, or 1881 at the latest. It is not strong in the modern period, and it does not want to be. These are legitimate claims, even though they grate on some people at other departments, plus many outside Harvard. (This may explain why Harvard is weak in what is known as "Holocaust Studies.")

Three, Harvard is liberal, more liberal than Yale. It is, of course, not radical, but it is liberal. Perhaps too conservative for left-liberals but quite liberal for most people. And it is tolerant of divergent viewpoints. HURI is also considered "too liberal" by many Ukrainians. Of course, all Ukrainian centers are committed to Ukrainian nationalism in the positive sense of that term: they are anti-Communist and devoted to a free and independent Ukraine. HURI, however, is considered liberal because it has Russians, Poles, Jews, Germans, Israelis, and, heaven forbid, even a few closet Communists as research associates. But this is the way it should be everywhere; Harvard is only being an exemplary model to the world.

Four, Harvard is concerned with *method*—excellent research and linguistic skills plus penetrating original research based on those skills.

Finally, it is the emphasis on history and literature that sets Harvard apart from the rest of the pack. It is the *classical mode*. Harvard sees itself as the *guardian* of all that is best and truest in Western Civilization, and it transmits this responsibility not only to its undergraduates (the true "Harvard man") but also to researchers, faculty, and even staff. Sociological and psychological perspectives are taught and respected—don't get me wrong—but are seen as secondary to history and language. The emphasis is on pre-twentieth-century life and lore, or, if twentieth century, then rooted in earlier periods. Thus, to be a sociologist interested in contemporary intellectual and political history at Harvard, and especially at HURI, is to be unique in some ways. In fact, I think I was HURI's first sociologist *cum* research associate.

* * *

I came to HURI on July 1, 1982—so this summer marks my third anniversary. I was invited by HURI's sixty-five-year-old director, the Myxajlo Hrusevs'kyj Professor of Ukrainian History, Omeljan Pritsak, a polymath who has mastered a dozen languages, spanning Finno-Ugaric to Chinese (and he even knows some Yiddish and Hebrew); a man who has almost singlehandedly carved out several new fields, especially opening up new vistas on Islamic and Turkic influences on Slavic countries, especially the Ukraine. He received his doctoral degree *summa cum laude* from the University of Göttingen in Turkology, Iranian, Islamic and Slavic studies.

After some 15 years of almost total absorption in philology, his interest in linguistics waned and Professor Pritsak finally turned his attention, in the early '50s, to his own roots: expanding the source base for Ukrainian history to include data from Oriental materials. This has led to a major study of the relationship of Hetman (Commander) Bohdan Chmelnitsky and the Ottoman Empire; to an analysis of an earlier period—Kievan Rus'—specifically the epic Igor' Tale, especially its Turkic elements; an investigation of the Origins of Rus'; and a recently published book on Jewish Khazar documents, co-authored with Norman Golb of the University of Chicago.

What Prof. Pritsak did for me was not only to help me reclaim my Ukrainian roots, but to help me understand the *universality* of all human history. Research in Jewish history, especially the Holocaust, is often done with blinders. We see only *our Jewish* version of reality and no other. We must see others as well. This has been the most valuable lesson I have learned at HURI and at Harvard.

Furthermore, Prof. Pritsak's generosity and accessibility are phenomenal. Despite his busy schedule, he always had time to attend sessions I organized, and his comments were always helpful. He is the epitome of the word "scholar." And he has always made a point of bringing Jewish and Israeli scholars to HURI. Thus, I find it astounding when I hear that the institute is full of antisemites, and this even from professors at Harvard! If they think there are such antisemites (and there might be some secret ones in the closet, for all I know), they should go directly to Prof. Pritsak and tell him. I am sure he would be as outraged as I would. But I have not found one, and I have not heard a single comment that could be construed as derogatory of Jews. I have found people who I think are very sensitive and very quiet on the subject of the Holocaust; many who are very pained and embarrassed about it; and a few who want to confront the topic openly, but antisemites . . . no! There are antisemites in the general lay Ukrainian community, but at HURI . . . no.

* * *

I was intrigued by HURI for personal as well as scholarly reasons. I was born in Rovno, Ukraine. I was a Ukrainian! But my parents insisted that I was a Polish or Russian Jew. They had repressed the Ukrainian ethnic identity for reasons that I will describe later. So HURI intrigued me—here was a place where I could find my roots—roots that the Holocaust had twisted and transformed. Perhaps, too, being the social activist that I am, I could also help bridge the gap between Ukrainians and Jews, which, as we all know, needs some good public relations. So I sent Prof. Pritsak material on my research on the Holocaust, in particular my two volumes of *Jewish Partisans* (University Press of America, 1982), and a week later, to my surprise, Prof. Pritsak invited me to Harvard. Why did he do this?

First, of course, I hope on the research strengths and interests that I brought with me, but there may have been other reasons. Timing—which is so essential to so many events in our lives—was also important. I think Prof. Pritsak wanted to put more stress on twentieth-century Ukrainian life and thought and especially to cement even more, as I was to learn, ever closer ties between Ukrainians and Jews. But most importantly, I feel that he wanted in a roundabout way to confront the Holocaust and the tense historical ties between these two oppressed minorities—Jews and Ukrainians, who, like Arabs and Jews, have so much in common, and yet are bitter enemies.

I must admit that I was a bit frightened and somewhat defensive, waiting for the least bit of antisemitism to rear its ugly head, but I never found any. In fact, after my inaugural lecture at Harvard on Ukrainian-Jewish relations, Prof. Pritsak asked me to prepare another lecture for the fall—on historical and sociological theories of antisemitism. Now some cynics may ask, "Why in carnation do people need to hear such a lecture? Don't they know what antisemitism is by now?" The sad answer is that . . . no, not even at Harvard do they understand the roots of racism and antisemitism completely.

A relative of mine by marriage who teaches at Harvard told me: "Jack, the place is full of antisemites! What are you doing there?" He was wrong. While to some it might seem like a Turk at an Armenian institute (and vice versa) or an Israeli at a Palestinian research agency, I would describe it as more analogous to a liberal Democrat at a Republican convention.

Of course, there were differences of style and disagreements over perspective, but there were also quite a few pleasant surprises. First, even Prof. Pritsak's secretary was Jewish. There were quite a few Jewish and Israeli research associates there. (Prof. Pritsak has lectured at the Hebrew University and has specifically forged closer ties with Israeli scholars.) Peter Shaw of the Jerusalem campus and now of the Tauber Institute at Brandeis University has been there; as was Prof. Israel Oppenheim and Prof. Gallai of Ben-Gurion University, plus Prof. Joseph Bartal. I think most of the research associates were *not* Ukrainians at all, but Poles, Germans, Hungarians, Russians, Canadians, and Americans.

But most intriguing of all, and least known to most scholars, is that over the past decade a small Ukrainian Jewish study group has quietly met and discussed mutual historical interests. The fruit of that study group will be seen in monographs and books that will appear in the future.

* * *

It is true that the leadership of HURI is nationalistic—in the sense that they see Ukraine as a nation and a state, albeit a captive nation. In a way, they see themselves as Jews did prior to 1948—a people without a free and independent state. Those few periods of freedom, the early Kievan Rus' period, 1648–1664, and 1918–1923 are carefully remembered and cherished, almost like the Jews who remember the periods of freedom before the First and Second Temple eras.

But, like much of Jewish history, theirs is a sad history. Ukraine has been overrun and dominated many times in its one-thousand-year-old history—by Poles, Russians, Germans. And—and this is even sadder—rather than seeing Jews as allies in the struggle for independence (and vice versa), they saw the Jews as aligned with the Polish aristocrats or as a Communist *apparatchik* or whatever, depending on the times. Instead of forging an alliance, they saw the Jew as a threat—and persecuted him/her, and in turn were also persecuted by others.

It is a tragic history, and in this case to understand is *not* necessarily to forgive. But at least to understand is to understand, and that is healthier than to ignore, and Jews have simply ignored the sufferings of the Ukrainian people for obvious reasons. One victim is not going to be very sensitive to the hurts of another, and it is these historical hurts that overshadow the hundreds of years of peaceful coexistence between Jews and Ukrainians. If the Ukraine had *always* been a free nation, not threatened and dominated by others, these two peoples might have been far closer than they are. Look, for example, at the intercultural penetrations in song, dance, food, language (Yiddish), folklore, and even religious customs.

We need scholars to research those areas and to build bridges between a *new generation* of Ukrainians (and other Slavic people) and Jews.

It might entail a *new* interpretation of history going back to Chmelnitsky and continuing on to Petlura and then onto the Holocaust of the Nazi period, and this history is being re-evaluated today right now at HURI by both Ukrainian and Jewish scholars. I think it is important to see the Holocaust as an aberration in European history and not as the culmination of years of hatred. I know this is a controversial issue. Nonetheless, we have no choice. Either Jews continue to see the world—Poles, Arabs, Ukrainians, the French, Russians, in fact most people—as our undying enemies . . . or begin to see that the bonds of hatred can be broken, perhaps not forever but at least for the present. I won't say that all scholars at HURI walk around with such idealistic and loving feelings, but I think that they should. We have no other choice. We must live in this world; we cannot return to the ghetto of fear and chauvinism. There is an inherent risk involved here, of course, for us Jews, but it is a risk I feel we must take.

Chapter 20

No Tenure: The Switch to Real Estate: Hello, Harold Brown and Other Billionaires

———

When I saw in the late 1970s that I was not going to receive tenure at a university and was living from year-job to year-job with a poor salary to boot, I decided to switch to real estate. (In 1976, for example, I received only nine thousand dollars teaching sociology full-time at Pine Manor College in Chestnut Hill, Massachusetts.)

Also, my son Gabe was born in August 1980, and my daughter Danielle came along in December 1982. So I had to make a living to support my family. I continued to teach part-time, but I discovered I could do both: teach and do real estate sales and brokerage. My first job was with Century 21/M&M Homes, the Munsel brothers. In 1984, I combined real estate and teaching and started The Spencer School of Real Estate, which continues to this day, thirty-six years later. Both things, sales and teaching, have sustained me throughout my entire life.

My Dad in the Inner City

I was lucky in two ways. First, I had real estate in my blood, going back to the inner city of Milwaukee, where my dad, Irving Porter, owned an apartment building. Plus, we lived in a two-family home on Fiftieth and Locust, so I saw how my dad handled tenants and collected rents.

Two incidents stand out. The first was the way my dad collected rent on Friday afternoons when African Americans received their welfare checks or regular job payments. Before they could spend their income on wine, women, and song, so to speak, as well as groceries, my dad went door-to-door to collect his rent. Sometimes he carried a baseball bat for protection. I never saw him with a gun, even though he had killed thirteen Nazi soldiers during the war. He was fearless.

The second event was the time my father calmed down our upstairs neighbor, who came home one Friday afternoon from his construction job drunk and demanded a meal from his wife. She was a bit slow preparing it, so he took out his rifle and started waving it around. Her mother, who lived with them, ran downstairs and told my dad. He went upstairs and, in a total reversal of what the guy expected, started yelling at the wife for not having dinner prepared.

This calmed the husband down, and my dad was able to take the gun away from him with no police and no fuss. That was the kind of guy he was: fearless and confident. He was what they call in Russian a *muladetz*, a man who gets things done. It would hold me in good stead when I also owned property in the "inner city" of Boston and had to handle difficult and at times dangerous tenants.

But I was lucky in that it was the beginning of the good years in Boston. As Rich Thompson wrote in *The Boston Herald*:

> At the dawn of the 1970s, Boston was gripped in an economic malaise of post-war stagnation . . . [It] was a house divided over court-ordered busing, and its downtown had become a graying façade of a once prosperous destination.[36]

Rent control, which had locked the city into a case of downward-spiraling rents and foreclosures, was under discussion to be removed, but not fast enough for me. So what developers did was to convert buildings into condos and make quite a profit.

Mrs. Erma Moulton, Our Fairy Godmother

My luck continued when Mrs. Erma Moulton, the owner of the four-family we lived in with my wife Mimi and soon our newborn son and daughter, was about

---

36 April 13, 2020, 36.

to "retire." She sold us her four-family plus loaned us money to buy a nineteen-unit building in Allston-Brighton. We were on our way to riches. She was a wonderful lady, and she had faith in us; she knew she would be paid back with interest. The city was on a roll. Those who bought buildings at this time and held onto them would become multi-millionaires.

I learned from Michael Perry and others how to convert a building to condos. I hired Marc Hershman, an architect, to draw up the plans, submit them to the City of Boston, and get the approvals. But first we had to deal with the tenants, which was not an easy job. Luckily we lived in one unit. In a second unit, again luckily, the tenant, a teacher at The Park School named Eleanor Judkins, died. In a third unit, we induced them to leave by charging them no rent for a month. But the fourth unit was the most difficult to deal with.

Its tenant was a librarian in her thirties, and she hired a lawyer who discovered that, if you didn't put the security deposit in an escrow account and tell the tenant the account number and the name of the bank the account was in, you had to pay the tenant three times the security deposit, in this case $400 x 3 = $1,200. We paid her that amount, and we now had the entire building free and clear of tenants and ready for condo conversion.

The condos, some as large as 1,400 square feet, went for the unbelievably low prices of $150,000 or less, but with that money we could buy not only a house in Newton for $120,000 but also a nineteen-unit apartment building in Allston for $140,000 plus land in Roxbury plus a four-family in Mission Hill and one in Dorchester, and so on.

My students today are astounded at how low the prices were back then. For example, our home in Newton Highlands, which we bought for $120,000 in 1979, is worth $840,000 in 2020, and that apartment building in Allston is worth over $5 million.

But I made a big mistake. I should have kept that nineteen-unit building, but, as I said, rent control was in effect, and rents were very low ($175, $225, $275 per month), so that one could easily go into foreclosure and bankruptcy if a recession came. Plus, tenants were very difficult. I sold the building for $240,000 to investors, and they in turn sold it to Samia and Company for $1.2 million, and they converted the building to condos. Everybody made money back then.

My real estate made for great stories in my classes. For tenants I had prostitutes, drug dealers, gunrunners, thieves, the mentally ill, hustlers, and weirdoes of all stripes (see the story "The Landlord" that follows), but the stress from them put a strain on my marriage and even sent me to the emergency room with Mallory-Weiss syndrome, a case of serious internal bleeding caused by a twisted esophagus caused by stress and vomiting.

Fisher Avenue and Gordon Street

The 5 Gordon St. property in Allston contained nineteen units, but under rent control it was very difficult to make ends meet, plus the tenants were, as usual, difficult. Regarding the prostitute, I had no moral disapproval; I had to get rid of her simply because her customers were making too much noise—both verbally and through loud sexual activity—and my elderly tenants were complaining. The drug dealers were actually the best; they kept quiet, only using the place to conduct "deals." Sadly, one of them, a very nice guy, was shot dead in Roxbury, far from my building. The gun-runner in my building, Steve Butts, was also a charming guy but could be nasty.

One evening he came over to my home in Newton—a taboo—and scared the hell out of my wife. Plus, he brought a strange friend, a "Mr. Sandman." It seems that some thieves in the building on Mission Hill at 19 Fisher Ave. broke into his place and stole his TV. But instead of going after them, he comes to me and jacks me up for a free TV.

"No way, Steve," I said.

"Well then, say hello to Mr. Sandman," he said.

"What do you mean, 'Mr. Sandman'?"

"He puts people to sleep, Jack."

But I was cool; I said, "I'll call you later, Steve."

Instead, I called my lawyer (you could call lawyers at home back then), who said, "He's bluffing, Jack."

"No, he came to my house," I said. "I got to do it."

So I called Steve and told him to come the next morning, and I would have his TV for him. I went out that night and bought him a television set. Do you know the expression "so afraid you could pee in your pants"? Well, I felt that way with this guy. I knew my lawyer was right—Steve was bluffing—but I was not taking any chances. My family was involved. Now you know why I sold or lost some of my buildings to bankruptcy and nearly died in the process from stress.

The Ocean House and the Rivers Brothers

This was my first foray into big-time development, and, sadly, I failed. I had opened a mortgage company in Newton Highlands with a fancy office and desk when one day in walked a strange guy with a curled mustache, a Stetson hat, and a large yellow Rolls-Royce that looked like something out of *The Great Gatsby*. Welcome, Don Rivers!

Don and his brothers owned the Ocean House, one of the last wooden hotels on the Maine coast in York Beach. A hurricane and ocean surge had badly damaged the place, and they were looking for money or partners with money to help rebuild it. They were in a very vulnerable state. Had I had the *cojones* and a lot of money, I would have bought them out. Instead, I went to my private lender, Erma Moulton, and borrowed twenty thousand dollars and took out a six-month option to develop the place or find a bigger partner to buy them out.

I decided that with that money I would hire an architect, Warren Freedenfeld of Boston, and go up there and present plans to rebuild the place into 168 condos plus high-end retail shops such as L. L. Bean. It was a magnificent idea, and today it would have attracted investors, but back then people were wary about Maine and future storms. In any case, we made several trips up to York Beach to present our plans. (See story.)

I needed more money to build, so I had to find an investor/partner. After several unsuccessful attempts, I finally found one in a strange character named Pritham Singh, a "white Sikh" with a white turban and a white gown who was a leader in a Sikh cult and very wealthy. It turns out he was from Portland, Maine, and knew the area. (I would also run into him in Key West, Florida, when I was rabbi there—a small world.)

Well, to make a long story short, it was through Pritham's architect, some German American, that I set up a meeting with Rivers, Pritham and myself in Pritham's luxury condo in Boston's Back Bay. What a place—totally barren except for a meditation mat and Pritham sitting there in the middle. A weirdo.

His architect had warned us: "Just present the plan, and he will decide right there, but don't ask for any partnership or any extras like being the brokers in the deal." I don't know if I decided to break that rule or if Rivers pushed me, but I asked.

Pritham stood up and said, "Are you trying to get into my pants?"

I said, "No, Pritham, I was just asking if we could act as brokers, that's all. You can say no."

"The deal is over," and he walked away.

I learned a valuable life lesson: when someone asks you to do something, listen to them. Don't try to be a wise guy. We lost him as an investor, and I lost my option.

But God has a way of deciding otherwise. As the great Yiddish expression goes: "Mann tracht und Gut lacht," "Man plans but God laughs" (at our plans— only He decides what will happen).

Eventually, the Rivers brothers found a buyer, a company that owned major hotels, and they built exactly according to our plans, except that instead of retail shops they just added more condos, but guess what happened? Not once but twice, someone burned the project down—a townie, no doubt.

Maine, as I said, has lots of weirdoes. Of course, eventually the condos were built, and some company in Medford got the listing to sell them. The Rivers did okay, and with the money from the hotel chain they bought other property and are still in town.

It was a learning experience, and not the first time I would fail as a developer.

Planners Review Ocean House Project

[*York Weekly*, July 25, 1984]

By Christine Redden
The York Planning Board, on Thursday, July 19, examined a rendering of the proposed development of the Ocean House hotel on Short Sands in York Beach. Density, height requirements, parking, drainage and other issues will be considered by the board before approving the plan, which will be taken up at the next planning board sub-division review meeting on Sept. 20.

Land consultant Richard Mabey, formerly the York code enforcement officer, is representing the Spencer Group, a development company from Boston, in its attempts to achieve planning board approval for the project. The proposed renovation of the old hotel would include the following additions—a restaurant, health club, indoor swimming pool, retail stores, and dwelling units to be sold as condominiums. The developers also plan to construct 22 luxury townhouse condominiums behind the existing hotel.

While residents living near the Ocean House expressed their concerns about parking, traffic increases and possible drainage problems, the plan's proponents emphasized their commitment to make the project a quality addition to the town, at Thursday night's meeting.

Although the proposal did not formally exist, at that time, the plan was discussed at the York Planning Board's meeting on July 5. In a telephone interview two weeks ago, Mabey said, "I think it's a very good project. The way it is now it's going to waste."

The hotel, which had fallen on financial hard times in recent years under a group of owners once registered with the Main Secretary of State as Orbust Inc., sits on approximately four acres of land and is in a resort commercial zone which permits 20,000 square foot buildings and up to 50 percent land coverage by buildings. The zoning laws in effect also permit subdivisions and dwelling units, according to Mabey.

Speaking on behalf of the Spenser Group, which is located in Newton, Massachusetts, architect Warren Freedenfeld assured residents and board members that the necessary drainage facilities would be located within the site and that suitable parking would be provided. He said traffic would not be routed onto the small, neighborhood side streets.

The Spencer Group proposed to renovate, but maintain, the existing main structure. Older buildings currently behind the main structure would be torn down to make room for a pool and a health club that would be attached to the rear of the property, requiring some excavation.

The proposed dwelling units would be located inside the main building and behind the structure, with 19 inside and another 22 town house structures in the rear. The zoning ordinance requires a minimum of 600 square feet for dwelling units, but Mabey said the smallest of the proposed dwelling units would be 954 square feet. Although the land consultant said he did not know how many retail stores would eventually be included in the project, he added that each must be a minimum 765 square feet in size.

In a telephone interview on Monday, July 23, York Code Enforcement Officer Armand Tremblay said the group, which had five of its members at the most recent planning board meeting, was mainly introducing itself to the board and asking for "ground rules." The board went over its checklist requirements with the group.

Tremblay said the group did not supply the board with a topographic map, did not have a soil survey, did not have a description of the existing conditions of the site, did not have proposed utilities, did not have a code enforcement officer's sketch and, therefore, did not have a preliminary sketch plan.

Tremblay said the group did provide a description of proposed road connections (in its artist sketch rendering) and because the traffic on Route 1A is directed one way, into the town center, in the summer, the board asked York's new town planner, Anthony Dater, to examine the impact the projected increased traffic would have. Dater said he hoped to have the requested information by the planning board's next subdivision review meeting on Sept. 20.

Tremblay said the board requested figures on the "maximum density" in the area. He said the board has never reviewed any project like this one, citing the density issue and the number of units proposed. Tremblay said the board wants to know whether or not the grassy swamp next to the existing building is wetland, because of drainage concerns, before finalizing preliminary plans and drawings.

The group said they are anxious to get planning board approval for its plans and begin construction as soon as possible, Tremblay said. "They're doing their homework very well, and Mabey is helping."

Tremblay said that, although many questions would have to be answered before approval of the project will be granted, his assumption was that it would be approved. He said, "The big beautiful building by the beach is now almost vacant and is possibly a fire hazard, but has much potential . . . They have got to do something with it."

The Wilson Brothers of Roxbury

This is a wonderful story with a long and convoluted history going back to the early 1980s. I was walking around Roxbury one day as a sociologist. I love ethnic and racial neighborhoods, and I came across a burned-out lot. It seems that three small houses were once on it, but via arson (very common back in the '80s, it seems) they were burned down, not by the owners but, in a bizarre case, by a fireman who felt that if there were more fires then more firemen would be hired. This is Boston logic.

Well, what happened was that the houses burned down, and the owners had to pay the city for the teardowns and back taxes but didn't have the money. I had just inherited some money from my father, who had died in 1979, and I met the guys who owned the homes.

They were a bizarre group of leather-clad gay bikers led by a guy named Larry Loffredo. At the time, 17 Centre St. and 234 Roxbury St. at the bottom of Fort Hill were in an area of Roxbury that was unique. It had a mixture of whites and African Americans, artists, journalists, and even a commune or two.

I offered the boys three thousand dollars for all three lots, plus I offered to take over the back taxes. They immediately accepted. It was the best investment in my life. I immediately began to hire architects and lawyers to develop the land. It was also the first time I encountered my lifelong friend and attorney, Jim Kickham, who handled the deed transfer.

I also encountered a talented but eccentric architect, an African American man named Edward Theodore Johnson. He drew up plans to build six condos on the site. It seemed like a slam-dunk, but, as I said, God laughs. I could not find money from banks. I was so frustrated I decided to turn this valuable land into a "Black-Jewish park" to celebrate my parents, Martin Luther King Jr., and two brothers who had marched with him, Richard and Benny Ollie Wilson. I put up a huge banner (I don't know where it is to this day) and was ready to donate the land to the City of Boston, but, again, God had other plans. The story of Harold and Jameson Brown is next in this strange odyssey.

THE PORTER-WILSON MEMORIAL PARK
ON THE FORMER SITE OF
THE PORTER ESTATE
DEDICATED TO
THE CELEBRATION & PRESERVATION
OF
THE AFRICAN-AMERICAN/JEWISH CONNECTION
from
The Powerful Nubian Empire
(between Egypt and Ethiopia, 6th – 14th centuries)
through
The Onward Crusade for Civil Freedoms:
The Rights of Personal Liberty guaranteed to US Citizens
by the Thirteenth and Fourteenth Amendments to the Constitution
and by Acts of Congress
ERECTED BY
DR. JACK NUSAN PORTER
IN HONOR OF HIS PARENTS
IRVING AND FAYE PORTER
Survivors of the Holocaust
The Systematic Extermination of European Jews in Nazi Death Camps
Prior to and during World War II
and FAMILY FRIENDS and NEIGHBORS
RICHARD and BENNIE OLLIE WILSON
Missionary Christian Allies of, Financial Sponsors of,
Freedom Bus Riders with, Alabama Foot Soldiers for
THE REVEREND DR. MARTIN LUTHER KING, JR.
Drum Major for Justice and Recipient of the 1964 Nobel Peace Prize
for his heroic determination to rid America of her racism and discrimination
Send Park Construction Campaign Contributions to:
THE SPENCER INSTITUTE
ATTENTION: DR. JACK NUSAN PORTER
Conservator/Archivist
8 Burnside Road, Newton, MA 02161
Voice: 617.965-8388
Facsimile: 617.964-3971
Signage & Urban Designers: **ETJ&A ARCHITECTS**
EDWARD T. JOHNSON II, AIA
304 Newbury Street, Suite 162

Boston, MA 02115-2832
Voice: 617.433-7029
Facsimile: 617.437-9655

Landscape Contractor: **RICHARD T. DAVID & ASSOCIATES**
140 Highland Street
Roxbury Highlands, MA 02119
Voice: 617.442-5251

E. THEODORE JOHNSON II, AIA
DESIGN DEVELOPMENT SPECIALIST

PORTER-WILSON PARK: ITS VISION & SIGNIFICANCE
prepared by
Edward Theodore Johnson II with Jack Nusan Porter, Ph.D.
for
THE SPENCER INSTITUTE
Dr. Jack Nusan Porter
Conservator/Archivist
January 29, 1997

The purpose of the Porter/Wilson Park is to highlight and educate the public, especially young people, about the long and colorful history of Black-Jewish relations from the Nubian Empire (between Egypt and Ethiopia, 6th -14th centuries), the Queen of Sheba to Sammy Davis, Jr., with stops along the way during the Civil Rights Movement (Andrew Goodman, Michael Schwerner and James E. Chaney), Rabbi Joshua Heschel and the Reverend Dr. Martin Luther King, Jr.), and today Lenny Zakim, the Reverend Charles Stith, the Reverend Eugene Rivers, Nancy Kaufman, Sheila Decter and Dr. Larry Lowenthal. Recent encounters between Dr. Cornel West, Dr. Henry Gates and Michael Lerner (Tikkun Magazine) are further examples. It is a physical consecration moreover of an old, much-cherished friendship between two former Roxbury Families and next door neighbors the Porter and Wilson families: Irving and Faye Porter, Jewish survivors of the Holocaust; and Bennie Ollie Wilson (Deacon, New Hope Baptist Church) and Richard Wilson (Deacon, St. John's Missionary Baptist Church), Black Civil Rights Freedom Fighters of the 1960s. Conceived as a trellised, garden promontory nestled between two nineteenth century bowfront residences, its featured amenities include a bench-lined square of cut bluestone pavers with bronze inlay, cherry blossom perennials bordered in plush, groundcover carpet of pachysandra, and a Centre Street-side view out over the recently completed Reggie Lewis Track & Athletic Center at Roxbury Community College to midtown Boston's Back Bay. Crafted as an oasis of tranquility, this intimately scaled vest-pocket park within walking distance of the Timilty Middle School and situated in the heart of historic Highland Park is designed to refresh, inspire, and above all else, remind all who enjoy it that Jews and Blacks are venerable, long-suffering friends.

Landowner Planning Race Relations Park

[*Bay State Banner*, March 27, 1997, 16, 23]

By Lynn Granger
The common thread linking brothers Richard and Bennie O. Wilson to Jack Nusan Porter is their working class background. Porter's proposed plan to erect a park dedicated to the celebration and preservation of the African American-Jewish connection will create a tie that is even more binding and long lasting.

The park will be named after Porter's parents, Holocaust survivors Irving and Faye Porter, and his new friends, the Wilson brothers, who were Freedom Bus riders with and Alabama foot soldiers for the late Dr. Martin Luther King Jr.

Porter's parents escaped the German Army during World War II and came to Milwaukee in 1946, settling in one of its predominantly black areas. Of his father and his own life, Porter said, "I remember my father coming home evenings with his hands dirtied from working in the steel mills. He hired blacks and worked with them. The guys I hung around with growing up were black."

The Wilson brothers, who both served in segregated military units in the South, were born in Sawyerville, Alabama, and remember well their own days of toiling in the steel mills and returning home with blackened hands. "I was 14 years old when I began working with my father cleaning white folks' homes," said Richard. "I later worked at a pipe shop in Alabama."

Bennie, 85, moved to Boston in 1946, and eventually settled in a house on Center [*sic*] Street in Roxbury, where he has lived for the past 40 years. His brother, Richard, 74, joined him much later, in response to a call to act as companion and care-giver.

Porter, 52, who moved to Boston in 1974 with a bit of money left him by his father, was a professor of sociology at Boston College and Boston University.

Richard said, "We've been brought together for a higher purpose, since through the park young people will be given the opportunity to learn more about their history and encouraged to work together."

The picture would not be complete without the inclusion of another team player, design development specialist E. Theodore Johnson, whose path crossed with Porter's during a round-table meeting of the American Jewish Committee when Porter made public his plan to donate land for the construction of a park dedicated to Black-Jewish relations. Johnson, in response, offered his services to make such a park a reality.

"This park, when completed, will be a place of spiritual repose where people of all denominations can converge," said Johnson. "It will be a place of elegance, utilizing the best materials, and insignias that will elevate the human spirit."

Plans are now in store for this vacant lot which sits between Roxbury and Center [sic] Streets, a description of which has been outlined in Johnson's mini proposal and reads, "Crafted as a place of quiet repose, this intimately-scaled vest-pocket park, situated in the historic district of Highland Park by nearby John Eliot Square, is designed to refresh and inspire, and above all else to remind all who use it, particularly families with children, that Jews and Blacks are venerable, long-suffering friends."

A fund-raising drive has been launched to raise funds for the construction of the park, and Porter is hopeful that churches and synagogues throughout Boston will rally to the cause. Park construction campaign contributions can be sent to: The Spencer Institute, Attn: Dr. Jack Nusan Porter, Conservator/Archivist, 79 Walnut Street, Unit 4, Newton, MA 02460.

New Private Park in Roxbury Will Celebrate Black–Jewish Relations

[*Jewish Advocate*, February 21, 1997]

By Michael Gelbwasser
Advocate Staff
Learning about the history of black-Jewish relations will soon be as easy as a walk in the park.

Specifically, a new private park in Roxbury.

The Porter-Wilson Memorial Park is being designed to broaden awareness of the centuries of black-Jewish interaction and cooperation, as well as facilitators such as the Queen of Sheba and Rabbi Abraham Joshua Heschel. A 14-by-16-foot banner will be raised over the site, located on nearly one-tenth of an acre between Centre and Roxbury Streets, at noon Feb. 24.

Dr. Jack Nusan Porter of Newton is erecting the park in honor of his late parents, Irving and Faye Porter, and his neighbors, Richard and Bennie Ollie Wilson. The Porters were Holocaust survivors, while the Wilsons were financial sponsors of, Freedom Bus riders with, and Alabama foot soldiers for the late Rev. Dr. Martin Luther King Jr. Today, the Wilsons are deacons, Richard at the St. John's Missionary Baptist Church in Roxbury and Bennie at the New Hope Baptist church in Boston.

The site of the former Porter home, the urban vest pocket park will be "dedicated to the celebration and preservation of the African-American Jewish Connection," Porter says. It may be the first of its kind in the United States, architect Edward T. Johnson II said Monday. Johnson's firm, ETJ&A Architects of Boston, is designing the facility.

"We're trying to build closer ties on a person-to-person level in Roxbury," Porter said last Thursday.

Porter hopes to do this through a three-to-four-page educational module on the history of black-Jewish relations that may be used at local schools. In addition, some of this history will be included in a statement printed on a "weatherproof box on the site," Porter said. Other projects between the neighborhood and the park are possible.

"We hope it accomplishes peace, love and caring," Richard Wilson said Monday. "It will be good for the neighborhood kids around here. They need something like that."

As recently as 1988, Porter planned to construct a six-unit apartment building on the property but couldn't get funding. Since then, he's "maintained" the site and "landscaped it a bit." After the park is finished, Porter will continue maintaining it and paying taxes on the property. He hopes that "upon my death, it'll be turned over to the city."

"The Jewish leaders I've run it by are excited about it," Porter said, adding that he already has municipal approval for the park. "I think they see it as something that could be a model for other cities."

Porter envisions the park will include picnic tables and benches, as well as a trellised garden promontory. The estimated total price tag? $20,000.

Porter hopes to raise the funds through contributions to the Spencer Institute, his "entity for my social action." So far, he's raised $300. Fund raising began over a week ago, and if the target isn't reached, it "just won't look as professional as a park should look," Porter said.

Johnson anticipates that ground breaking will start in March.

Building Common Ground

Planned Park Would Recall Black, Jewish Ties

By Richard Chacon
Globe Staff

At the same time that Irving and Faye Porter escaped the German Army during World War II by hiring in the Ukrainian forests, Richard and Bennie O. Wilson were serving in segregated American military units in the deep South.

For most of the next half century, their distant worlds would move in parallel orbits. Fortunate to survive the Holocaust, the Porters came to the United States and settled in a mostly black neighborhood in Milwaukee. The Wilson brothers left the South and moved to predominately white Boston.

The Porters and Wilson have never met. But their histories, destinies, and legacies are about to converge on a bumpy, sloping vacant lot in Roxbury.

It's on this half-acre rectangle of land, with its sweeping views of the city's skyline, that the Porters' only surviving son, Jack, wants to build a park named after his parents and his new friends, and dedicate it to the centuries-long ties between black and Jewish cultures.

"There was a time, after World War II, when blacks and Jews got along peacefully and those are what I call the glory years," says Jack Nusan Porter, Irving and Faye's son, who owns the lot and who decided last year to turn it into a park. "There was no anger back then and we lived as a community. That will never exist again unless we build it and that's what this is about."

Porter, 52, is a sociologist who teachers about the Holocaust at the University of Massachusetts at Lowell, met the Wilsons, who live next to the lot, soon after he bought the parcel in 1984. His plan is to create a bench-lined refuge in this gritty city neighborhood, which was once a center of Boston's Jewish community.

The design, which is still being developed by Porter and architect E. Theodore Johnson, a Roxbury resident, envisions walkways paved in bluestone and a perimeter dotted with cherry trees with historical monuments that highlight black-Jewish relationships dating back to the Nubian Empire, the alliance formed between Egypt and Ethiopia in the 6th century.

"This will be a 24-hour education center," said Johnson, 56, who sought out Porter after hearing about the park at a community luncheon last year. With all of the building going on in Roxbury, it's important to have demonstrations of African-American self-esteem."

Porter, who also runs a real estate management institute in Newton, admits he originally bought the land as a financial investment. He wanted to build a six-unit apartment building.

But banks refused to loan him the money. As a result, the land sat idle for years while Porter continued to pay taxes and maintained it just enough to keep city inspectors away.

A year ago, Porter finally gave up hope of developing the site, which sits between Roxbury and Centre streets, across from a once-neglected city-owned park that has been razed and covered with gravel. He then approached the Wilsons with his idea.

"It's a strange way how our lives have come together," says Richard Wilson, 74, who served as an Air Corps corporal during the war. "I can only imagine that God had something to do with it, but it's a nice thing to do to bring people together."

Much remains to be done if the lot is to become the park that Porter and the Wilsons wish for. Money has to be raised—as much as $50,000 for leveling the parcel and building the park's amenities.

Bureaucracy also has to be tackled. The Boston Redevelopment Authority must be persuaded to give up a slice of the property that it currently owns. Permits must be secured—Porter got the first one last week to put up a banner proclaiming the park, which he will do with the Wilsons tomorrow.

And the park's décor and accompanying historic symbols must be agreed upon. Porter doesn't want crosses on the site, but is willing to consider Johnson's suggestion for a pyramid, a common icon for blacks and Jews.

If and when the park is completed—a process that could take another two years—Porter hopes to make the park part of the surrounding Roxbury Heritage State Park.

"Not a day goes by when I don't think about the Holocaust and what my parents went through or what I learned from growing up in mostly black neighborhoods," Porter said. "We live in very cynical times today. I want this space to remind people of what we have in common instead of what we don't."

From Radical Sociologist to Real Estate Guru

[*ASA Footnotes*, November 1992]

By Rochelle Cummins
ASA Staff Reporter
From radical sociologist to real estate guru, Jack Nusan Porter remains dedicated to the sociological imagination. Porter is an active and creative sociologist who

emphasizes in all his work the importance of the sociological imagination. He has made both academic and practical contributions to the field of sociology.

Porter is the author and editor of many books and journal articles, a lecturer on college campuses in the U.S. and Israel, a former research associate at Harvard University, and the president of the Spencer Group and the Spencer School of Real Estate. Recently, he was nominated by the American Library Association for an award from their Gay and Lesbian Caucus for an essay entitled "Sexual Politics in Nazi Germany: The Persecution of Homosexuals during World War II, An Introductory Essay and Bibliography." Moreover, he has prepared and contributed three syllabi sets to the Teaching Resource Center of the ASA. They include: *The Sociology of Genocide / The Holocaust: A Curriculum Guide*, *The Sociology of Jewry: A Curriculum Guide*, and *The Sociology of Business: A Curriculum Guide*.

Porter defines himself as a "Renaissance man." He has studied the Holocaust, sociology, politics, and real estate. In spite of his diverse training, he considers himself a sociologist. His sociological training has influence and guided his real estate career and continues to impact the real estate training of others.

Born December 2, 1944, in the Ukraine, Porter is a Holocaust survivor. He was one year old when he came to Milwaukee, Wisconsin. In Milwaukee, he lived in a predominantly black neighborhood, where he was a minority. Despite his minority status and the trauma of the Holocaust for him and his family, Porter earned his B.A. at the University of Wisconsin–Milwaukee in sociology in 1967. In 1971, at 26 years old, he completed his Ph.D. in Urban Sociology under Howard S. Becker and Bernard Beck at Northwestern University.

Believing that academia was too narrow in scope to accommodate his philosophy of change, Porter decided to leave the tenure track in academia and enter into a real estate career. His decision may have resulted from the influence of his father, who owned property in Milwaukee. In addition, as Porter notes, "It is surprising how many sociologists are in real estate or associated fields (e.g., Peter Dreier and Henry Tischler)."

Nevertheless, Porter needed action and desired social change. He believed that progressive people should have money. He had the idea that he could make a difference by becoming an entrepreneur and a philanthropist. His goal was to make money and donate it to various charities. Porter could not miss the opportunity to achieve his goal and meet his philosophy of change through real estate development in the early 1980s when the Massachusetts market soared.

"Although training in sociology is not a direct preparation for a career in real estate or business, it sensitizes you," Porter argues. Porter's sociological training sensitized him to the small town and the needs of different groups. For example, in Roxbury, Massachusetts, and Brighton, Massachusetts, Porter orchestrated the development of low-income housing. He worked very closely with African Americans to make the housing affordable. Porter argues that businessmen typically do not understand the nuances of minorities as sociologists do. In mortgage banking and real estate, he is sensitive to minorities. However, he recalls one man who said, "Dr. Porter, I love you, but you are the landlord." Hence, "no matter what you are [a sensitive sociologist], the role [of landlord] defines you," said Porter.

When real estate development waned in the late 1980s as a result of the economy and deficit, Porter shifted to real estate training. Six years ago he initiated a school of real estate. Porter notes that "it is very unusual for non-lawyers to be teaching real estate." There are few doctorates of any discipline, let alone sociology, in the field of real estate training. This is what makes Porter's school unique.

Likewise, continuing his social change theme, Porter's unique approach in real estate training is to emphasize the sociological imagination. He encourages his students to view real estate in the tradition of C. Wright Mills. Porter feels that his approach humanizes students to the ethics of real estate, especially in fair housing discrimination, redlining, and block-busting. Ethics are important to Porter.

According to Porter, students love his approach. Compared to other training programs, Porter's attracts a wider range of students. According to him, 50% of his students are minorities, both foreign-born and native-born. Without minorities, Porter says that he could not continue his school.

Largely, all of Porter's students are attracted to the small tutorial seminars. More important, through Porter, they are engaged in the sociological imagination. If you are interested in a career in real estate, you may write to Jack Nusan Porter at The Spencer School of Real Estate, 79 Walnut St. #4, Newtonville, MA 02460, or call him at 617-965-8388.

Harold and Jameson Brown of The Hamilton Company

I don't know why, but it took thirty-six years before I hooked up with Harold Brown and his son Jameson and started to build. But once again, God laughed at my plans, and again, I ran into bad luck. We had a builder who turned out to be a hustler; costs went up; and Harold and Jameson decided to "flip it," to sell the permits and the land. I would get a percentage of the profits from the sale plus a nice commission. I sold it for six hundred thousand dollars.

Happily, the new owner and his broker promised me they would put up that plaque and a bench in honor of the Wilson brothers. It would be a fitting tribute to the brothers and the end of a strange and seemingly endless project.

Porter of The Spencer Group Ltd. brokers $600,000 Sale of 2,236 S/F of Land in Roxbury

[full details]

By Todd Larson

This past summer, papers were passed for the sale of 17 Centre St. and 234 Roxbury St. in Fort Hill, Roxbury. The sale price was $600,000 for the 2,236 s/f parcels and the city permits to build a five-story condominium of three floor-through units including a garden parlor duplex, with an underground garage and a common roof deck with a city view.

The seller was Center Hill Associates LLC of Allston. The buyer/developer is Celiberti Realty LLC of Medford. The listing broker and co-owner of the property is Dr. Jack Porter of The Spencer Group Ltd. The buyer's broker is William Laferriere of Coldwell Banker Residential Brokerage, Boston. Designed by Hacin + Associates of Boston in a contemporary style with "a big splash of windows," the two-bedroom, two-bath units will range from 1,230 to 1,800 s/f, according to Laferriere.

"We can sell an inexpensive product with a lot of space, which you can't get in the South End or South Boston," he said.

Centre Hill Associates LLC comprised the late Harold Brown, his son Jameson Brown, and Dr. Jack Porter, who had owned the land since 1984 and had held it for 35 years. "Before I bought the land from Larry Loffredo, George Dimsey, Jesse Balerdi, and David Stanley back in June of 1984, it consisted of three small houses," Porter said. "But a fire was set by arsonists and they burned down. The owners were charged for the cost of tearing down the homes and did not have the money, so I was able to buy all three parcels for the unbelievable price of $3,000."

The area is very historic, Porter added. "There is the Spooner-Lambert House, an Underground Railroad passage for runaway slaves nearby, and the historic Eliot church, going back to Colonial times. Back then, the only whites living in this area were artists, hippies, gays, and other 'street people' not worried about the school system. It was an interesting area."

The development itself occupies a historic site as well. "It sits on top of the Underground Railroad," said Laferriere. "It's timely with the release of the new movie *Harriet*, about Harriet Tubman."

Porter had initially thought of building a park on the parcels and donating it to the City of Boston. "I hired the renowned African-American architect Theodore Johnson to design it," he said. "It was to be called 'The Porter-Wilson Memorial Park' and dedicated to the 'celebration and preservation of the African-American/Jewish Connection,' the only one of its kind in the country. The Wilson brothers lived next door and had marched with Martin Luther King Jr., and the Porters, my parents Irving and Faye Porter, were Holocaust survivors."

When the land became too valuable for a park, Porter decided to build on it instead. "At one time I even got permission to build six units, but funding fell through," he said. "That plus other factors led to it being vacant for a long time. I am happy it will be built through Mr. Celiberti's and Mr. Laferriere's efforts. But I hope we can have a bench or a plaque dedicated to the Porters, the Wilsons, and Dr. King somewhere on the property. The Wilson brothers especially should not be forgotten. They were wonderful people, and old-time civil rights workers."

Chapter 21

The Landlord: Dealing with Weirdoes (Crazy Tenants), Wise Guys (Italian, Russian, African American), and Community Organizers (Chuck Turner, Mel King, Ray Flynn)

———————

Introduction

To be a landlord is a difficult job, and especially so for a socialist like me. Here is a flavor of that dilemma:

When a Socialist Becomes a Landlord
[Jack Porter, *Jewish Currents*, April 1991, 28–29]

I should title this, "When a socialist becomes a landlord." For many years, I considered myself a democratic, perhaps even a scientific, socialist. Then about a decade ago I started accumulating property—land, apartment buildings, even a prominent hotel. I had a net worth of over a million dollars, maybe several million dollars. I thought I was riding high, borrowing hundreds of thousands of dollars, spending, planning, developing, and then just as suddenly, all the play money was taken away and my empire collapsed.

All this time I still thought of myself as a progressive guy, but my tenants didn't think so. I was the best landlord in the world, but not to them. It is very simple. The system itself, the very structure of capitalism, makes it very difficult, if not impossible, to be the "good guy." People confused the role of landlord with me the person. A tenant once said, "Jack, you're a nice guy, but I gotta fight you—you're the landlord!" And as Proudhon once said—"Property is theft." Even though the state or city is even a worse landlord than a private owner, the structure makes it difficult to be seen as a benevolent landlord. Not that leadership by committee is always netter. Barney Rosset once tried to run Grove Press according to socialist principles with committees and votes and democracy, and what happened? The publishing company almost went under. You can't run certain things by committee; you need a leader, a boss, someone to make a decision instantly.

I think that's the very heart and soul of the dilemma of socialism—who leads? Who follows? Who makes decisions? And how are they made?

Textbooks call socialism "a command economy" and capitalism "a market economy." There is a bias here ("command" is a biased and powerful word that conjures up Hitlerism as well as Stalinism), but the point is well taken. Socialism is usually seen as a "command" society—someone is directing a five-year plan, often with disastrous results. Can we institute market, Adam Smith-type mechanisms into these command societies? I feel we must if we want socialism to survive, and that is exactly what is being done today in Eastern Europe.

A second point: twenty years ago, I edited a book called *Jewish Radicalism: A Selected Anthology* with Peter Dreier. Today, I am (or was—I'm selling off most of my property) a landlord in Boston, and Dreier, still a socialist, is director of housing for the entire city of Boston! This is one of the most powerful positions that a socialist can have in America, and Peter is still a "Jewish radical" trying to help the poor and homeless, building homes for the working class, and raising up the impoverished. He's trying to work within a system that is totally stacked against his kind of mission, and yet he continues to do good work. I sometimes joke that Peter became more radical and I became too Jewish!

We need people like Peter Dreier in positions of power; we need socialists or progressives in places where they can at least *try* to inject some humanity into a system that has very little. It is a struggle. Perhaps it cannot be done. Perhaps being a progressive landlord is an oxymoron. Perhaps owning an apartment building in Roxbury and calling yourself a socialist is a contradiction in terms. Perhaps I will have to sell and give up all my property before I can be truly liberated, but then I think about all the *mamzers* (bastards) out there who own property. Why don't *they* have any guilt? Why am *I* the only tortured one? And again I plaintively ask—who shall lead? I have no answers.

Before I tell the tale of Hank Johnson in "The Landlord," I'd like to describe some other characters: Weirdoes and Crazy Tenants; Wise-Guys and Mobsters; and Community Organizers.

Weirdoes, Con Artists, and Crazy Tenants

I have already discussed some of the weirdoes in previous chapters, but Hank Johnson's tale tells it better. I even hired at one time "mob guys" to collect rent or evict tenants back in the 1980s. I hired one guy for two hundred dollars to threaten a tenant who was not paying me rent, but the guy went to the wrong apartment and choked a woman. I told him he choked the wrong person and I wanted my money back. He said, "Good luck. It will cost you another two hundred dollars to choke the right guy."

Wise Guys and Mobsters: Lending Money

- I had a small mortgage company in the 1980s in Newton Highlands, and I already told the tale of Don Rivers coming to me for money for the Ocean House, but I had many other people. There was the case of a guy from Attleboro, Massachusetts, who needed money to set up a nightclub. I am certain he was with the Mafia. Sometimes they look for legal money to buy or build things. There were gamblers and other addicts like spendaholics or shopaholics who could not stop buying things. We lent money only if they had collateral like a house, or sometimes a car or boat. Otherwise, we had no recourse and would lose the money.
- I worked for First Federal Mortgage, a company run by Glenn Polansky and his brother. Glenn was an unethical man, charming but unethical. He worked hard, but he never paid his staff. Maybe the profits went "up his nose," as they say—cocaine.
- I had various students who might have been minor "wise guys," associates of organized or, better yet, "disorganized" crime. Real estate is a good way to launder money. I also got to know people who knew relatives of victims of James "Whitey" Bulger. At an auction I bought some of Whitey's tools—flashlights, locks, knives, and other items—and then sold them to a "mob museum" in Las Vegas and made a good profit. I also knew Whitey Bulger's famous and influential brother, William "Billy" Bulger, as well as relatives of other minor gangsters.

- I had minor "brush-ins" with the local Russian mob that came up from New York (Brighton Beach), and I had a relationship with a beautiful Russian woman, who I will call Valentina, who could not stop spending money. I lent her three to five thousand dollars at a time, since I knew she received alimony payments of twelve thousand dollars every four months. I charged her the legal state usury rate of twenty percent. However, one time I lent her three thousand dollars, and she was late with the payment. I called her, and she sheepishly told me that her alimony had run out and that she had no money. That's the risk you take when you are a private lender and have no collateral backing up the loan. I still see her and love her. I also lent money to restaurant owners for liquor licenses and other expenses, but I got out of the business because of the risks involved, and also, since I usually lent to friends, I didn't want their not paying me to jeopardize our friendship. I am still friends with all of the people I lent money to.

Community Organizers

- Community organizers and politicians are not thieves (though some might think so), but I add them here as colorful characters whom I met while a landlord in Boston. Ray Flynn was first an activist in South Boston before becoming the mayor of Boston. He is a great guy. (See photos.)
- The co-editor of my book *Jewish Radicalism*, Peter Dreier, was also a community organizer but officially worked for the City of Boston.
- And the charismatic Harvard-educated African American community organizer and later Boston City Councilor Chuck Turner also became a good friend. Though he had some trouble later in life, his impact on Roxbury was great, and the memorial in his honor brought out not only Mayor Walsh and the police commissioner, but also hundreds of ordinary citizens touched by his life. (See photo)

The Landlord

Sgt. Schreiber called me back as promised. "Jack, he wasn't in. We went in Sunday morning and a second time late Monday night, and he still wasn't there. Maybe he's dead?

But at least he was gone. There was a warrant on him in two counties, Suffolk and Middlesex, and he was easy to recognize—a psycho-escapee from a mental hospital with long graying red hair down to his shoulders, a large white streak down the middle, a dilapidated leather briefcase full of legal briefs, tools, towel, toothbrush, putty, screwdrivers, drugs (medicinal and otherwise, everything he needed in court to "win" his case.

He drove the Boston legal system crazy. One day he stole five hundred FedEx applications and sent out five hundred subpoenas. Staff members from Joe Kennedy's office, Senator John Kerry, the US Attorney General's Office all arrived wondering what the hell this was. It even made the *Boston Globe*. My lawyer had never met anyone like him. Hank Johnson, alias Richard Moore, alias Tim Hallissey, wanted in three states and two counties for general craziness, just happened to be my tenant, and he was driving *me* crazy inch by inch with his writs, show-cause summons, and threats of lawsuits, attachments, and judgments. In short, he wanted my apartment building in Mission Hill, Boston, near Roxbury.

Dammit, it started with Leslee. Rabbi Blatt of Brighton didn't want her anymore, but he didn't tell me why. I admit: she was sexy, very attractive in a hard-bitten sort of way, and I was attracted to her. But she was crazy as well as sexy. She was a fantastic painter, but she only painted variations of the Madonna. I should have guessed then, but no, I was Mr. Nice Guy, so I let her stay in the apartment on Fisher Avenue in return for painting the house, and she was, like I said, a great painter—walls or madonnas.

Alone, she was fine, but soon the place began to fill up with weird street people: Barbara, a crazed Mormon whose husband had fled with the kids and who was deathly afraid of sex and touch; and then there was John, a psychotic on leave from Met State and a lover of Leslee's, who gave fantastic back-rubs; and the craziest of them all—Marilyn from Toronto, who became super Orthodox Jewish, and who made phone calls all over America to rabbis asking for a *shidduch* (a matchmaker) to fix her up with some other loony bird.

She also had a bad habit of playing with matches. I personally had to throw her out. But Hank Johnson was by far the most volatile and dangerous, not in any physical sense, but in a legal sort of way he was super-intelligent and dangerous. Leslee was right. Hank Johnson wanted my building.

When we finally entered his barricaded room, we discovered the phantasmagoric universe of his crazed mind, debris nearly two feet high: empty milk cartons, newspapers, tools, legal papers, ephemera, and of course a wide assortment of drugs and ointments for Hank's irritations, hair oil, buffered aspirins, antacids, stomach, painkillers, and many bottles of tranquilizers like chlorpromazine my attorney said is used by schizophrenics to maintain a semblance of sanity. Personally, Hank Johnson never posed a threat to me, but as his craziness increased, that would change.

I returned from work one day and saw four cop cars, and my wife and kids huddled outside our four-bedroom suburban Colonial. "No bomb down there, ma'am. You can go back in," Lt. Kelly told my wife. Curious neighbors offered us their homes for the night, but we decided to brave it in our own house.

Suddenly, the police radio crackled: "Come on over to the Water Department as soon as you're finished." I got into the cop car and sped over to City Hall. "Some nut telephoned in a bomb threat to the town waterworks. Can you identify his voice?" I listened to the tape-recorded message. "Yeah, it's Hank Johnson."

Hank Johnson wasn't my only problem. Colette, a young lady from Haiti, had kicked her Black Muslim common-law husband out and wanted to party. In the process, she conveniently forgot to pay her rent for nine months. It was a long party—but just enough to get on welfare and move to Lawrence. She wasn't a bad person if you ignored the often obscene messages she left on my answering machine, but she had some friends who began to use voodoo to threaten me from evicting her. To this day, even a discussion of voodoo makes me uncomfortable.

Then there was Patricia. Pat's husband was a very nice guy but had a drinking problem. He was also common-law. She sent him down to Georgia to recover. She was a policewoman—well, not exactly a policewoman; she worked in the dispatch room of the Boston Police Department, and she chose my apartment because it was the safest street in the area. I'm sure she has changed her mind with all the break-ins, fights, and general *meshigas* (Yiddish for "craziness"), but she's still there because she, too, had a good hustle.

It seems that the previous owner had not registered the building with Rent Equity. There was an unregistered basement apartment, thus the building was technically under rent control, and the rents plummeted from $900 to $384 or less, some as low as $264, which is pretty good for a four-bedroom apartment in Boston, but since I had a $250,000 mortgage on the property and no one paying rent, I was slowly headed for foreclosure land. I knew it; they knew it; and the banks knew it.

Pat was not only not going to pay me the $384 instead of her usual $900, but she was suing me for the "overcharges" from previous months when she had paid $900, plus she was adding up damages for alleged code violations, legal fees, court fees, and interest. In the ghetto, one knows all the tricks to beat you down and survive.

So, let's add it up: I was facing voodoo in Apt. 1B; bomb threats from Apt. 2; and a hefty lawsuit from Apt. 1. Well, at least the nice people in Apt. 3 were paying rent. Well, with my luck, the wonderful lady from Barbados dies, leaving three lovely children.

But wait, there's more. When Hank Johnson and his menagerie were finally evicted (a legal process that can take over nine months), my wife and I got taken by another "friend." George needed a place to stay for "only one month." He was an ex-con for whom I had testified in court as a character witness to reduce his sentence. His crime: gun-running.

But this time I was smart. I had him sign an agreement that he was there only as a security guard, not a tenant. Thank God I had the agreement. Three weeks into his tenancy, there was a break-in and a TV and VCR were stolen. This happens almost every day in Roxbury, but no, big macho George felt this could not happen to him. He had to find a scapegoat. Guess who? Whitey from the 'burbs—he brings charges against my wife and I for breaking and entering!

My dear readers, you see, life in the suburbs is very boring. So, for divertissement, my wife and I go into Roxbury and steal VCRs. It's very lucrative, even better than real estate investments.

PS In January 1991, we lost our building at a foreclosure sale—or at least we think we did. Do we still own it? No, God, noooooo . . . !

1992

Part Four

1991–2020—THE STABILIZING YEARS

Chapter 22

The Death of My Mother

My mother died at nearly 101 on December 3, 2009, and was born on March 15, 1909. She lived through almost the entire twentieth century, and, boy, what she lived through! She was the sole survivor of her entire family in Europe—the sole survivor! I have written about her family, her escape from the Nazis, and even about her life in America, and have still not captured her essence.

She was what we call a *tzadekis*, the female version of a *tzadik*. "Righteous woman" is itself inadequate to describe her essential goodness. Not that she was a "push-over"; she could be tough, but she had a heart of gold, as did so many of the women survivors we knew in Milwaukee—Mrs. Cyla (Tzila) Sztundel, Mrs. Baum, Mrs. Ertel, Mrs. Lichtman. I have added several stories and obituaries about her. Several were written after her death. She continues to inspire young men and women with her story, plus my sister Bella was a reincarnation of her life.

I was in Israel when my mom died—or rather, on the West Bank, in a small town near Bethlehem called Beit Sahour, visiting a wonderful Christian Arab family, the Rishmawis, an ancient family going back to the time of Christ. I had told my cousin Idkeh Shuster that I was staying there, and that turned out to be a good idea, since I may have missed my mother's funeral in Milwaukee otherwise. In fact, I came late.

The Rishmawis got the call and contacted me. I was on a tour of Herodian, the ancient home of King Herod, when I was told about mom dying. I called my brother Shlomo and told him I needed forty-eight hours, not the twenty-four that most *frum* Jews use to bury the dead. I needed more time, since it would take me some time to cross the checkpoints back into Israel. I managed to cross over into Bethlehem, and then I took a taxi to Ben-Gurion Airport. The Israeli officials took the change in plans in stride and did not charge me extra; death is a common experience in Israel, and people need to come or return at a moment's notice. I took the El Al to Newark and landed the next morning jet-lagged. There I had to wait for a direct flight to Milwaukee.

Because it was at the last moment, the US airline was not so accommodating. The ticket cost over seven hundred dollars one-way, three times what it would cost today. Luckily I had the money in my credit card. I arrived in a few hours to General Bill Mitchell Field. I was "early," and the funeral had not yet started. People were waiting for a huge crowd from Baltimore and Philadelphia, including Shlomo and his wife Shushy's family and friends.

I probably should have taken a taxi directly to the funeral home, but instead I waited for the Baltimore plane to arrive, and we all went together in a van. The reason why I should have come earlier was that, when I arrived, they had shut the coffin, and I would not see my mother ever again. I was upset, but also relieved, that my last image was of her alive and well and not in a coffin. So it was okay.

I had prepared my eulogy on the long flight from Israel, and, being a practiced public speaker, I was ready. It would be fine despite eulogies coming from some of the finest and most erudite rabbis in the country, people like Rabbi Michel Twerski, who had also eulogized my dad. (See "The Death of a Father" in this book.) My most memorable line was the tale of the seven "twigs": individually each can be broken, but together they are impossible to break, and so we must keep *shalom bayis*, just as Momma would want.

Momma was right. Stay strong. Stay together. Keep the faith. Here are more stories about my extraordinary Momma Feygeh.

* * *

How does one contemplate and explain the death of one's mother? My father's death in 1979 thirty years ago at age seventy-three was more powerful for me, hit me harder for some reason. My mother's death was easier, yet here's this gnawing feeling in my soul, and I miss her terribly. Even though she lived a long life—we even got a note from Michelle and Barack Obama on her 100th birthday in March 2009—I still can't believe she's gone. Even though we thought she'd live on like the Eveready battery bunny until ... who knows ... 105, 107, even 110, she died suddenly on December 1, 2009, with little warning.

I was in Israel and on the West Bank, visiting with a Christian Palestinian family, the Nimeer and Shama Rishmawi family and their son George in Beit Sahour, near Bethlehem. I knew she was not feeling too well and had stopped eating, and I knew she might die while I was there, but I hoped I could return in time.

She died 2:30 p.m. December 1, a day before my birthday. In fact, my hosts in Palestine, the Rishmawi family of Beit Sahour, near Bethlehem, were planning my birthday party when I got a call from my cousin Idkeh in Tel Aviv that she had died. I still had the party and left the following night, along an arduous trip via El Al Israel Airlines back home, one of the most difficult trips I have even taken, in order to make it to the December 3 funeral in Milwaukee, Wisconsin. I made it, and what a celebration of her life. Over a hundred people showed up, including all of her twelve grandchildren and numerous friends and relatives.

I had a special relationship to my mother, and now I am an orphan, totally alone. I'd always been alone; now even more so.

She was one of the last remaining Soviet Jewish partisans left in the USA, though there are few in Israel and Canada and Europe, part of the Kruk-Max *otryad* (Soviet fighting force) from 1942–1944 in northwest Ukraine, Volynia region. She was a cook and the family nurse, and under her no one died of natural causes; she nursed many back to life in the woods. There were about 150 fighters—Russians, Poles, and Ukrainians—and a family camp of about two hundred Jews. All survived the war. She was the sole survivor of her family, out of twenty-five killed by the Nazis and their Ukrainian collaborators.

My sister Bella was the real *tzadekis* I said at the funeral. She unselfishly took care of our mom for fifteen years in that assisted living center. What a sacrifice.

I worried that we would all fall apart, bickering and fighting. I told the audience the story of the "branches," a story my mom told me—how, if you take one branch, you can easily break it, but if all of the children take a branch and bind together, you can't break it.

My mom was the last matriarch of her community to die—Mrs. Richt, Mrs. Bankier, Mrs. Zimmerman, Mrs. Weidenbaum, Mrs. Sztundel, and Mrs. Lande in just the past few months—all had died. She was the "last of the Mohicans," so to speak, the last member of her partisan group, the "last survivor" of the Shoah, in a way.

A truly righteous and saintly lady, I will miss her terribly.

Beside her son, Dr. Jack Nusan Porter of Newtonville, Massachusetts, and his children, Gabe and Danielle, and sister Bella Porter-Smith of St. Louis Park,

Minnesota, she leaves behind another son, Rabbi Shlomo Porter of Baltimore, Maryland, and numerous grandchildren and great-grandchildren. Burial was in Milwaukee, Wisconsin, on December 3.

Sources

Forward. Obituary, December 10, 2009.

JSOnline.com, December 19, 2009. See link to obituaries under "Porter-Arenzon Escaped Nazi Massacre."

Milwaukee Journal Sentinel. Obituary, Saturday, December 19, 2009.

Porter, Jack Nusan, ed. *Jewish Partisans of the Soviet Union during World War II.* 2 vols. Lanham, MD: University Press of America, 1982; repr. 2002; 3rd ed. in progress.

Steven Spielberg Foundation interview, 1998.

Wisconsin Jewish Chronicle. Obituary December 20, 2009. See it online in January 2010.

Where Are They Now? Ex-Partisan Faye Porter Turns 100\

[*Wisconsin Jewish Chronicle*, April 3, 2009, 8–9]

By Leon Cohen

Faye Porter now lives in a Jewish assisted living facility, Menorah Plaza, in a suburb of Minneapolis.

But when she marked her 100th birthday at a party held on March 15, among the nearly 100 celebrants were many friends from Milwaukee, according to Porter's daughter, Bella Porter Smith of Minneapolis.

Their presence testifies to the nearly 50 years that Porter lived in Milwaukee, her qualities as a person, and the story she lived, according to her daughter and to her son, Jack Nusan Porter of Newtonville, Mass. (Her third child, Rabbi Shlomo Porter, directs the Etz Chaim Center in Baltimore.)

As they tell it, Porter (*née* Merin) with her husband Irving (originally Srulik) survived the Holocaust in Ukraine by living in a forest with a partisan group for two years (1941–43). Her husband was one of the fighters in the group, while she was a cook and nurse.

The German Nazis murdered everyone in her immediate family, including her two children who were born before the war. The couple had three children afterward.

Nevertheless, "She didn't let the Holocaust turn her into a sad and angry woman," said Jack Porter, a sociologist and Holocaust scholar. "I don't know how she did that."

In fact, "she has a very optimistic personality," said Porter Smith, a teacher at a Jewish day school. "She has told me" that she thinks she has lived so long "because she was always kind to other people."

And while Faye found it difficult to speak with a Chronicle reporter, as she couldn't hear a telephone voice well, she was able to say through her daughter that she did not believe that she really was 100 years old, but "I'm satisfied with how I am."

Faye and Irving moved at first to Chicago, where Irving couldn't find work. They moved to Milwaukee in 1946, where they had cousins, according to Porter Smith.

However, Irving had a difficult time finding work in Milwaukee because he insisted on observing the Sabbath, while all the factories insisted that he work on Saturdays, Porter Smith said. Eventually, he became a scrap metal peddler and Faye was a homemaker.

They lived in the orbit of Congregation Beth Jehudah, and Faye was "very close" to Rebbetzin Leah Twerski, the mother of Rabbi Michel Twerski.

Apparently, Faye still has fond memories of that aspect of her life. Milwaukee "was the best city to live around and around," she said. And the Twerskis were "special people. They kept Shabbes and took care of everybody," she said.

To this day, Rabbi Michel Twerski calls her every Friday to wish her a good Sabbath, said Porter Smith.

After her husband died in 1979. She later married Judah Arenzon, with whom she lived for about six years, until his death.

She continued to live on the west side until about 15 years ago, when Porter Smith brought her to the Minneapolis area. At first, she had a vegetable garden and did some baking, but she can't do those things now.

But she still visits with people, said her daughter. And her son maintains that she has a reputation as a "tzadikis, the Jewish equivalent of a saint and a holy lady."

"Even at the birthday party, mothers brought their children to her for blessings," said Jack Porter. "I can still feel blessed to have a holy and righteous mother."

Porter-Arenzon Escaped Nazi Massacre in Ukraine

After She Moved to Milwaukee, She Raised a Family, Lived to 100

[The *Journal Sentinel*, December 18, 2009]

By Amy Rabideau Silvers

Everything in Faye Porter-Arenzon's life was measured by what happened Sept. 24, 1942.

She could not save her family—two young daughters, her parents, all her siblings, other relatives—from massacre by Nazi SS officers and local Ukrainian police.

But she survived, later rescued by her husband, a partisan with the resistance movement in the Ukraine. Together they lived in a partisan community in the forests of their homeland and began a family again. Together they came to America.

And she became the matriarch of a new family in a new land.

"It was a miracle," said her son, Jack Nusan Porter, a Holocaust and genocide scholar. "She survived to produce all these generations."

Porter-Arenzon—she married again after the death of her first husband—died of natural causes Dec. 1. She was 100. She last lived in St. Louis Park, Minn., where she moved to be near her daughter after the death of her second husband. Services have been held.

Born Faygeh Merin, she married Srulik Puchtik in 1937. They lived in Maniewicz, a small town in northwestern Ukraine. Later, they took the more American names Faye and Irving Porter.

By 1941, however, the Nazis had taken away most of the town's Jewish men.

"Luckily, a good Polish man gave my father a rifle and 150 bullets," Jack said. "My father started the nucleus of a mostly Jewish fighting group—the majority were Russian Jews—with other Polish and Ukrainian and Russian fighters."

On Sept. 23, 1942, the Nazis and police began rounding up all the remaining Jewish residents of the town.

"They took us out, put us in the middle of a road and counted everyone," she later recalled in a news article. She was then a thirty-two-year-old mother, holding the hands of her daughters, ages 4 and 2.

The situation was still fluid. She tried to get people to do something, anything, saying they should burn the town and run for the forests. People were too afraid to try.

"So she told her mother and sisters and daughters, 'Let me try to find a place for us to hide,' " Jack said.

A policeman stopped her as she left the area. "Why waste a bullet on me now?" she argued. "You're going to kill us all tomorrow."

He let her leave.

She found a barn and tried to go back for her family, but by then there were too many guards. Even if she managed to get back to her family, there was no way they could escape together.

"She went back to the barn," her son said. "And the next morning she heard the shots."

Twenty-five members of her family and her husband's family were killed.

"Three-hundred-eighty Jews were rounded up and taken to the edge of town, shot and buried in a mass grave," said daughter Bella Smith.

Nazis began searching the countryside, including the barn where she was hiding. She was grazed by a bayonet as a Nazi stabbed the hay pile. That night, she crawled into the forest, alone for months.

"She didn't know my father was alive," her daughter said. "He didn't know she was alive. He heard there may have been survivors and found her. She was down to 80 pounds and he carried her back to the partisan unit."

The partisan group, which became known as the Kruk-Max Otryad, grew to include 150 fighters and more than 250 civilians in a family camp, the third-largest such group in Europe, Jack said.

"Mom was the nurse and a cook with the fighter group," Jack said. "Theirs is like the story of the movie, 'Defiance,' about the Bielski Otryad."

After liberation by the Russians in 1944, they lived at the Bindermichel displaced persons camp near Linz, Austria. There they were a rare married couple who survived the war, becoming surrogate parents to young people who had lost their own.

"They would walk these girls down the aisle when they married," Jack said.

His father's brother, in the US since the 1920s, heard they were alive. He sent $100, enough for steerage tickets for the couple and son Jack. They first lived in Chicago, but soon settled in Milwaukee in 1946.

Irving Porter became a scrap dealer. Faye Porter took care of her family, becoming the mother of another son, Shlomo, and daughter Bella, and later a grandmother and great-grandmother.

Her husband died in 1979. Porter took in young women boarders, always interested in trying to find everyone a marriage partner.

She also played matchmaker for herself.

"Do you know someone who wants to get married?" she asked a nice man at a neighborhood senior center.

"Yes," said Yehuda "Judah" Arenzon. "Me."

They married in 1980. He died in 1986.

She remained warm and giving, hopeful and kind.

"She was a *tzadakis*, a righteous person," Jack said. "People actually came up to her and asked her to bless their children and themselves."

"Don't be stingy with a blessing," she would say. "It doesn't cost anything."

As Porter-Arenzon got older, her blessings took on special meaning.

"She would say, 'God should bless you that you should come in my age and be healthy,' " her daughter said.

Faye Porter-Arenzon, z'L: A Life Full of Miracles

[*Jewish Family Magazine*, 25, no. 8, January 29, 2014]

By Devora Schor

In 1989, when a journalist interviewed Mrs. Faye Porter-Arenzon—the mother of Rabbi Shlomo Porter, director of Etz Chaim Center for Jewish Studies—she told him about the many miracles that saved her life during the war. He asked her, "What about all the other people whom G-d did not save? Why didn't He do miracles for them?" She answered, "That's a good question. I don't know." He asked, "So, how can you still believe?" She answered, "I don't know. I believe in G-d, and that's all. I believe." Although she did not have the answers, she could live with the questions.

Faye Porter-Arenzon left this world on December 1, 1909, at the age of one hundred. To most observers, her advanced age and the fact that she survived the Holocaust at all can clearly be attributed to miracles. But it could be said that the biggest miracle was her own recognition of the miracles, her unusual ability to live with complete faith in G-d, even though she had ample reason to lose that faith. Could that be the definition of *emunah peshuta*, the simple faith that eludes so many of us today?

* * *

Mrs. Porter-Arenzon was born Faygeh Merin, around March 15, 1909, in a small town called Horodok, which is today part of Belarus. It was a very small town, with only about 100 Jewish families. With the outbreak of World War I, the whole town moved hundreds of miles away. Faye's father was a *melamed*, who would teach in the house. Faye listened to what he was teaching the boys and knew all the *parshios* of the Chumash very well because of her memories of that time. She married the boy next door, Srulik Puchtik in 1937 and moved in with her in-laws in Maniewicz. They soon had two daughters.

Srulik's brothers had left for South America and the United States, but he stayed in Europe to support his sisters and earn money for their dowries. (Some of the sisters did get married, but they all died during World War II.) In 1941, the Nazis came and tried to kill all the men—at that time they weren't killing the women and children—so Srulik ran away. Because of his connections with non-Jews, he was able to hide in the cemetery of Horodok for six weeks. During that time, he sent flour home to his wife and children. A woman whose husband had been killed came to Faye's house and saw that she was making dough for bread. The woman said that she had no food, so Faye gave her half of the dough. Faye would later say that she thought she survived the war in the merit of this act of *chesed*.

When Srulik returned, he and Faye lived for a year under German rule. When people realized that the Nazis were coming back, this time to kill everyone, Srulik wanted the family to run away to the forest, but Faye was afraid to go with the two little children. He ran away by himself, and with the help of a Polish forest guard named Slovac, was saved. "Every Jew who escaped from the dead," Faye said, "Slovac took them to his forest and took care of them." When Srulik got to the forest, Slovac gave him a rifle, 150 bullets, and two grenades.

That a Jew from a small *shtetl* knew how to use firearms was a miracle in itself. Srulik had learned how to handle a gun and shoot because he had been drafted into the Polish army 20 years before. At that time it seemed like a tragedy, but in the end it saved his life. Srulik told Faye that if she should escape, she should come to the forest and Slovac would know where he was hiding.

* * *

On Sept. 23, 1942 (Elul 23), the Nazis began rounding up the Jews of the town into a ghetto. Faye was staying with her children at her parents' home. That evening, she went across the street to her cousins' house to figure out how to escape. When she got there, it seemed no one was there, so she went back into the street. A Ukrainian soldier put a gun to her head and was about to kill her. She said, "Why waste a bullet? Anyway you are going to kill all of us tomorrow." Miraculously he let her go.

She tried to return to her family, but by then there were too many guards. She saw that even if she could reach them, they would not be able to escape. She ran into a barn and hid in the straw. The next day, the Nazis went from house to house rounding up all the Jews and taking them to the edge of town. Faye heard the shots as they killed them—380 people in all, including 75 members of her family and her husband's family—and buried them in a mass grave. The Nazis searched the barn and even bayoneted the pile of hay where she was hiding, but they did not find her. Another miracle.

That night, Faye ran away to the forest with her cousins, who had hidden in the ceiling of their house. They survived by eating berries. She did not know if her husband was alive. She went to Slovac's house, but only his wife was home, and she had not seen Srulik. After six months, Srulik found Faye in the forest. She was down to 80 pounds, and he carried her back to live with the partisans. A miracle.

The partisan group included about 150 fighters and more than 250 civilians in a family camp. The majority of them were Russian Jews, but the Russian army controlled the group. Srulik became commander; he blew up train tracks and eight Nazi trains and attacked Germans command posts, killing many Nazis.

Faye and Srulik were one of the few couples among the partisans. Faye became the nurse and cook for the partisans. She was always kind and giving, even at the risk of her own life. One night someone came to her in terrible pain from stomach cramps. It was strictly forbidden to light any kind of fire at night; despite the danger, she warmed up milk for him. That man later lived in Milwaukee near the Porter family. His son was the one who convinced Rabbi Porter to go to yeshiva as a teenager. A physical kindness was returned with a spiritual kindness.

In 1943 the partisans dictated that only fighters were allowed in the camp, no women and children. Srulik decided to separate from them, and took responsibility for the entire civilian group. It fell upon him to find food and protect them. Every night he and his helpers went out to look for food. They dug potatoes out of the peasants' fields and stole chickens from their hen houses, killing them on the spot by twisting their necks. Once, the people waiting for him in the forest thought he had gotten killed. Men were already lining up to marry Faye, but she said, "Let's wait and see if he comes back." Two weeks later he returned.

By October 1944, the war was over on the Eastern front. Faye was pregnant, and her son, Jack Nusan, was one of the first Jewish boys born after the war, on December 2, 1944. Srulik and Faye decided to do the *bris* on the eighth day. There was no *mohel* to be found, and they agreed to have the son of a *mohel* do the bris, even though his only experience was watching his father.

At the *bris*, Srulik saw a Jewish Russian soldier, who had just returned from the war front. He asked the soldier if he would be interested in meeting his cousin, a woman who had survived the war with them in the partisan camp. The soldier answered, "Why not." Then he asked the cousin, an older single, if she would like to meet the Russian soldier. She also agreed. Suddenly, Srulik banged on the table, to get everyone's attention, yelling, *"Mazal tov."* Everyone was astounded. What was the *mazal tov*? "We have here a *chatan* and *kalla*," he announced. Srulik told the *mohel* to set up a *chupa* right away, and the *mohel* married them. Their marriage lasted for 40 years. Of course, the newlyweds moved in with Faye and her husband, together with the other 20 people who lived in the one-room apartment.

* * *

Faye and Srulik wanted to move to Israel, but they decided to go to America first, hoping to go to Israel from there. They put a photo of themselves in *The Forward*, and a brother of Srulik recognized him and sent them an affidavit and a ticket to America. In America, Faye had to learn a new language and adjust to a new world. First they lived in Chicago. They later moved to Milwaukee, where their son Shlomo was born. Srulik worked as a scrap metal dealer. At age 44—despite the doctors' warnings not to have another baby—Faye gave birth to a daughter, Bella Yenta, named after both their mothers.

Faye and Srulik's home was *shomer Shabbos*, even when most jobs required one to work on Shabbos. Says their son, Rabbi Porter, "Our Shabbos table was full of Torah, *zemirot*, songs, and stories, which filled our hearts with joy, happiness, and meaning." Faye and Srulik's tradition of kindness, optimism, and faith continued as they raised a family in America. Rabbi Porter remembers coming home from public school and telling his mother that the lunch served that day smelled really good and he wanted to eat it. His mother went to school to see what it was that smelled so good, and reinvented the dish at home so that her son would be happy with a kosher lunch.

The Porter home became the *hachnasas orchim* of Milwaukee. They took in anyone who needed a place to stay: *meshulachim*, rabbis, people who came for medical treatment, and hobos. Faye fed them all.

After her husband Srulik died, in 1979, Faye took in girls who were becoming religious and became like a mother to them, including doing her best to find them a *shiduch*. At age 75, Faye married a wonderful man, Yehudah Arenzon, and they had a great marriage for nine years until he, too, passed away. She met him at the senior center, after asking this nice man sitting next to her if he knew of someone who wanted to get married. "Yes," he said, "I do."

Yehudah had been a *Gerrer Chasid* in Warsaw and learned in yeshiva until he was 15. He left it all and went to South America before the war. In the last years of his life, through Faye's influence, he became a complete *baal teshuva*.

* * *

At her *levaya*, Rabbi Porter said, "Mama, you were so real and uncomplicated, and only now can I begin to comprehend your greatness . . . Everyone I know has self interests, except you, Mama. You never asked for anything for yourself. If my wife, Shushy, would complement you on a beautiful object in the house, she would say, 'You like it? You can have it. *Ich vil geben alas mit varama handt*—I want to give everything away while my hands are still warm.'

"You had every right to be negative, after losing your children, but you chose to see only the good. You had every right to forsake *Hashem* and *Yiddishkeit* . . . but you chose *yiras shamayim, ahavas torah*. Mama, you showed so much honor to every rabbi. You had the right to become withdrawn after losing Tata 30 years ago and then Yehudah Arenzon 16 years ago, but you chose to love and to give to others. You could have given up on life, but you chose life. You chose to care about others."

* * *

For the last 15 years of her life, Faye lived in Minneapolis in an assisted living facility near her daughter. Although she had dementia towards the end of her life, it was a "good kind of dementia," according to Rabbi Porter, "in the sense that she remained positive. Because she did not remember things, every moment of her life was new and fresh."

Her *emuna* was very strong and never faltered. As Bella said at the funeral, "My mother was a very wise woman. A month ago she was quite weak, so I decided to spend the night with her, to make sure she was okay. My mother asked me to lie down next to her. We both fell asleep for a short time; in the middle of the night my mother woke up, fully alert, and turned to me and asked, "Why do we suffer so? Why do the goyim hate us?" I said, "Mama I don't know. What do you think is the reason?" She said, "I think it's because we don't do enough *mitzvot*." My mother, with dementia, was so, so wise."

Rabbi Porter talked about the last few months of his mother's life: "About a month ago my mother stopped eating and was losing weight. My sister and I talked about putting in a feeding tube. When the gastroenterologist heard that a one-hundred-year-old woman wanted to schedule a feeding tube, he came by to meet her with the intention of talking her out of doing it. When he met my mother, she said to him. 'You should come in my age and be healthy—G-d should bless you, because you are helping this old lady. Do you know how old I am?' He said yes. She said, 'You should come in my age and be healthy.' Then he asked her, "Why not until 120?' As it turned out, he was a Russian Jewish doctor, and he proceeded to encourage my mother to do the procedure. She told him, 'Lucky will be the girl who you will marry, because you are so kind.'

"Before the procedure my mother was with a gentle nurse, from India. My mother was saying, 'Aron, Sender, Zisa, Elka, Rivka.' The nurse asked me if she was naming her children. I said, 'No, she is naming her brothers and sisters who were killed in the Holocaust.' The nurse said in awe, 'She is the first survivor I ever met.' My mother worked to be able to not forget them—even as she was forgetting so much."

Most of us in Baltimore did not have the privilege of knowing Faye Porter-Arenzon, but hearing about her life is truly inspiring.

Top 10 Things I Learned from Bubby

1. To raise children is like lifting a heavy stone.
2. *Malbish B'Kavod.* ("Dress with honor.")
3. *Eat on time and sleep on time.*
4. Don't be stingy with a *brocha* [a "blessing"], it doesn't cost anything.
5. Listen and remember so that you remember what you learned.
6. Your parents are your best friends.
7. Love yourself.
8. *Torah is der besta s'chora.* ("Study is the best business.")
9. Make yourself like home.
10. Take care of yourself—mentally and bodily.

Chapter 23

Running for Office—Skakes, Fitzie, and Other Kennedys

—————

I have always loved politics—arguing about it, writing about it, but never running for it. Until in 1999, when I decided to run for office in my home town of Newton, Massachusetts, first for School Committee, then for Alderman twice (later called City Councilor), and then, for the biggest prize of all—US Congress. I lost in all three races. My best turnout—ironically, my first run—was for School Committee. I got over four thousand votes, but my opponent, a popular man named Rodney Barker, got six thousand.

I did quite well for a first-time run, they told me, mostly because I garnered support from the Right—people who opposed sex education in school and other conservative issues. That was how I learned lesson #1: you can get a lot of votes for being "against" something rather than "for" something. I really wasn't "against" sex education; I just had the guts to run against a liberal who was for all these liberal issues. Those four thousand people just wanted to defeat a liberal; they didn't care who beat him.

But it was a tricky balancing act, being a non-liberal—actually a radical, but also not being a conservative. It's funny: I had better friends among the Newton conservatives like Tom Mountain than I had among the town liberals. I have always wondered why that was true. Did I instinctively understand working-class conservative people? Did I unconsciously distrust liberals? The answer was probably yes to both those questions. Or was I really turning more conservative in a kind of populist libertarian kind of way? However, in many ways, running for local office does not mean you have to take up liberal or conservative issues. Is class size or MCAS examinations (exams testing acquired skills) liberal or conservative? One can also see how my sociological and real estate background came in handy.

"Without a Vision, the People Perish"—from the Talmud

Dr. Jack Nusan Porter for School Committee has that vision!

At Issue: Strategic Thinking

* <u>Dr. Porter has the sociological imagination</u> to see the system-wide view and to implement it; Dr. Porter can halt the decline in quality and bring leadership to the schools; Dr. Porter can help unite the North and South sides, upper class and working class; giving all citizens a voice.

Dr. Porter will help get <u>more state aid</u> for education *<u>reduce class size</u> *begin acquiring more buildings and more real estate to ease the student crunch *<u>provide innovative ideas</u> *increase morale *question "sacred cows" as to effectiveness such as the DARE program *take the pressure off our children and parents *reexamine MCAS.

Dr. Porter believes not in micro-management but in providing <u>wisdom and vision</u>. Recent polls have shown that between 33–41% of US citizens do not think that kids are getting a quality education in this country, and the same is true for Newton.

Dr. Porter has been around: *eighteen year resident of Newton *Parent of two children who went to Zervas, Brown, and Newton South High School; one is in Newton South now *Co-chair of Newton 2000 Educator and Youth Leader both here and in Israel; Adjunct Prof. of Sociology at UMass-Lowell; Former Asst. Prof. of Social Science at BU; Former Research Associate at Harvard University; Editor and Curriculum Builder; textbooks and study guides in sociology, the Holocaust, and comparative genocide use world-wide; author or editor of 30 books and over 500 articles; BA in Sociology from University of Wisconsin; MA and Ph.D. in Sociology from Northwestern University; Businessman; Real Estate educator and Consultant; Spiritual Leader, Temple Emmanuel, Chelsea, Mass.

<u>Endorsed by over 150 citizens of Newton. Vote on November 2. Vote for Dr. Jack Porter for School Committee.</u>

He has the Vision and the Wisdom to lead us into the 21st Century!

For more information on how you can help call (617) 965-8388; fax 964-3971; or email: jacknusan@aol.com

Ward 6 September 10, 1999

DR. JACK PORTER

A NEW FACE*A NEW VOICE*A NEW VISION FOR SCHOOL COMMITTEE

Dear Friend:

My name is Dr. Jack Porter. I am a candidate for the Newton School Committee from Ward 6. I have been a resident of Newton for the past 18 years. I would like to tell you a bit about myself.

I was born in the Ukraine and raised in Milwaukee, Wisconsin. My childhood there inspired me to focus on the field of the social sciences. I received my doctorate in Sociology from Northwestern University. I have published several books and numerous curricula guides used worldwide. I am currently the Spiritual Leader of Temple Emmanuel Synagogue in Chelsea and Adjunct Professor of Sociology at UMass, Lowell.

I chose to become a candidate for School Committee for several reasons.

- I am passionate about the quality of life in Newton
- I am concerned about the status of our school system
- I owe it to my children to make the Newton school system better for their children
- I am qualified to develop new solutions for the challenges facing our school system
- I am a new face with a new vision to voice your concerns

I ask for your support. JOIN ME in bringing Newton's schools into the new millennium. EVERYONE NEEDS A FRESH START. WE CAN MAKE A DIFFERENCE.

VOTE FOR DR. JACK PORTER
A NEW FACE
A NEW VOICE
A NEW VISION
FOR SCHOOL COMMITTEE

Paid for by The Committee to Elect Dr. Jack Porter
40 Hartford Street, Newton Highlands, MA 02461
Phone: (617) 965-8388 e-mail: jacknusan@aol.com

The second time I ran for office was for Newton City Council. The first time, I got four thousand votes; the second time, four hundred. Why? First, because I did not have a strong campaign director, nor enough money. But the real reason was I didn't put in the effort. You have to want to win: I also learned that you need four things to win:

1. strong ideas;
2. a strong team;
3. lots of money;
4. a strong commitment to win.

You must have at least two of these for a credible run. But I learned a lot. In fact, running for office is a great learning experience. You should try it.

But the most fun was when I decided to run for US Congress for the seat held by the liberal, even radical, Barney Frank, or, as he put it, the "only left-handed, gay, Jewish Congressman in the history of the United States." (I guess there must have been a right-handed Jewish and gay guy once.)

Here is my story, and what follows is my profile in *The New Yorker* (a total surprise, by the way, as are most good things; when you least expect them and do not "push" for them, they come your way). Again, the *New Yorker* made me "quasi-famous." That is the power of this magazine, second only to the *New York Times*, and maybe, in some circles, more prestigious. I learned that fact when I started to receive feedback from all over the country. Some people were even jealous of me for getting that profile.

Two things helped me. One, I had a wonderfully supportive and very attractive wife, Raya, a beautiful Ukrainian woman who loved American politics. Two, I hired a real campaign manager and paid him. It was fun making signs and cards, going out to events, and traveling the state, or part of the state, since the Twelfth District was in southeastern Massachusetts.

I also found that my politics were not really liberal like Joe Kennedy's, but radical on one side and even "conservative" on the other. Thus I found support from young (and some old) lefties and, more importantly, from the smaller towns in the district, like Wenham or Waltham. Not a few were turning away from liberalism. (See my campaign card below.)

Porter for Congress

A New Kind of Democrat: Liberal on Social Issues, Conservative on Money Matters, and Radical on Foreign Policy and Immigration

Dr. Jack Porter is running for US Congress, 4th District, stretching from Brookline to Fall River, Barney Frank's former seat.

To help, call Dan Cross, Campaign Director at (617) 894-1801 or email at <danieliancross@gmail.com>. Also, follow Jack Porter on Facebook and Twitter and soon at the <PorterforCongress.com> website. Contributions can be mailed to Porter for Congress, 79 Walnut St., Suite 4, Newtonville, MA 02460-1331 or call (617) 965-8388.

The Kennedy name helped Joe get the female voters, especially older Jewish and Catholic women, or Latinos, who made up a large vote in the southeastern area of the district and who remembered his grandfather and grand-uncle. If I were running in another state, I might have beaten him. Only in Massachusetts is it difficult, but not impossible, to beat a Kennedy. (As I speak, Kennedy is in the run of his life against Ed Markey for US Senate, and I hope Markey wins.)

The problem in 2012 was with the media. They choose who is important and who is not. There were many times I would show up at an event and be talking to a reporter, and then Kennedy would show up, and they would say, "Sorry, Jack, but my editor wants a quote from Joe. I'll get back to you." But, of course, they never did.

Or you're out fundraising, and a donor would say, "Jack, I'd give you money if you were running against someone else, but you know you can't beat Joe."

Well, I may have received only one percent of the vote, but I got that profile in *The New Yorker*, and Joe didn't. That's politics.

But my encounter with the Kennedys goes back many years before that run. When I was teaching real estate classes downtown, one of the firms, R.M. Bradley, was considered a kind of "Kennedy front," meaning that any Kennedy-owned real estate in Boston would be managed not by well-known Kennedys directly but by close family friends and some distant relatives.

One such relative was Robert Fitzgerald, known as "Fitzie," but the other was much more infamous—Michael Skakel, known as "Skakes." Skakel was Ethel Kennedy's nephew, the son of her brother, and Ethel Kennedy was Bobby Kennedy's wife. You don't get much closer than that. (Incidentally, the brokers at R. M. Bradley had a running joke about Skakel, who briefly worked there: "Keep Skakes away from the golf clubs!")

We became friends; he even came over to my home in Newton Highlands. I had to tutor him personally in order for him to pass the state real estate exam, because he had dyslexia or some other learning disability. He was very likable, a roly-poly, slightly chubby charmer.

Later, at his trial in Bridgeport, Connecticut, over his alleged killing of Martha Moxley, I drove down and was often interviewed by media—national and international, shows like *Entertainment Tonight*, *Access Hollywood*, and other "quasi-news" shows. Kennedys were always hot property. The media circus was interested in me because I was Skakel's teacher and they wanted to know what he was like as a student or if he talked to me about Martha Moxley. (He never did.) I also had a copy of his exam certification, signed by never taken.

I remember a tense scene during the trial in a local restaurant where in one room was Dominic Dunne, writing a book about the trial; Mark Fuhrman, the cop at the O. J. Simpson trial, who was also writing a book about "killers," and several media people, plus Martha Moxley's mother and son. Wow, that was something to watch! This trial was as close as I would ever get to a major event. I didn't make it to the O. J. Simpson trial in LA, but I was at this trial every day.

But my encounter with the Kennedy family actually goes back to my first years in Boston in 1975 when I taught sociology at a private women's school, Pine Manor Junior College. I had several students who were dating younger Kennedys like Christopher Lawford (his father, Peter, had married a Kennedy gal), plus a beautiful blond from Texas whose equally beautiful older sister was dating Ted Kennedy. I begged them to invite me to some of their parties, but they never did.

In any case, the next chapter has the famous *New Yorker* profile of me running against Joe Kennedy in 2012.

Chapter 24

The *New Yorker* Article

This story also caused a bit of a sensation. It was my first (and hopefully not my last) time in the famed *New Yorker*. Like everything in life, if you don't plan on it, it happens. The "hook" was that I was running against a Kennedy and for some reason that excites *New Yorker* people. However, I thought the profile made me look a bit dilettantish, but, hey, it's the *New Yorker*. Eight years later, Joe Kennedy is in a tough fight for the US Senate race against incumbent Ed Markey and he could lose. Now, *that* is a story that *New Yorker* readers want to hear about—a Kennedy losing!

The Campaign Trail: Write-In

[Ben McGrath, "The Talk of the Town," *New Yorker*, April 9, 2012]

J ack Porter opened the trunk of his Volkswagen Jetta the other day, at the Vince Lombardi Service Area, on the New Jersey Turnpike. "I feel like I'm doing a drug deal," he said, as he pushed aside a suitcase and an old Louisville Slugger and reached into a duffelbag to fetch something— books, it turned out. They were his latest: "Happy (Freilich) Days Revisited: Growing Up Jewish in Ike's America," "Milwaukee Memories," and "Sexual Politics in Nazi Germany: The 20th Anniversary Edition." Porter, a sometime sociologist, rabbi, and real-estate consultant, was wearing a khaki jacket over a tan sweater and khaki pants. He was on his way from Boston to Baltimore, and had been making good time. "I'm flabbergasted," he said, noting the lack of traffic. "So, do you want to sit here for a while?" He climbed back into the driver's seat. Underneath his feet was a rubber mat featuring a large image of Tweety Bird. Nearby, a hearse idled. "I think it was Michele Bachmann who said, 'This is a series of humiliations,' and she's so right," Porter said. He was referring to life on the campaign trail.

Porter, who is sixty-seven, is one of several "total unknowns," as he says, running as Democrats for the Massachusetts congressional seat soon to be vacated by Barney Frank, after thirty-two years. Joseph Kennedy III, Robert F.'s grandson, is also running, and is heavily favored, in spite of his having been born just a year before Frank took office. "I mean, the rest of us are just chopped liver," Porter said. "The main reason I'm running—well, there's two or three. One: Look, I'm a Holocaust survivor. I was born in Ukraine during the war. I came to this country in 1946. How many chances do I have to run for Congress—an open seat and, especially, against a Kennedy?"

Two: "Massachusetts is changing," he said, and he forecast the death of small-town New England liberalism. "In ten years, it's almost like—it's not going to be completely a red state, but it's going to be balanced. Whenever you step a mile outside of Newton, it's a totally different attitude that you get now." A former S.D.S. member, Porter now favors a "third way" that he characterizes as "radical-libertarian-progressive." He styles himself a blend of Ron Paul and the independent Vermont senator Bernie Sanders: an environmentalist deficit hawk.

Three: "I'm almost running against Romney, too," he said. "What I would say to him is 'You're going to lose, Mitt. I just want to tell you that.' And I already know his response. He'd be like anybody in the Mormon sect: 'Have a nice day.' You see, I'm an expert in cults and sects." Porter is the author, also, of "Kids in Cults," "Jews and the Cults," and "Handbook of Cults, Sects, and Self-Realization Groups." In 2000, he took a tour, led by Tagg Romney, Mitt's eldest son, of the new Mormon Temple in Belmont, near Boston, before it was consecrated and rendered forever off limits to nonbelievers. "I told him I come from a long line of rabbis," Porter said. "Right before me, Ted Kennedy was given a special tour. It was a friendly meeting of Kennedys and Romneys."

In January, in advance of the New Hampshire primaries, Porter drove his Jetta north, to Manchester, and got himself on CNN, posing as an independent voter with an "Anybody but Romney" sign. Several weeks ago, he had a letter published in the *Boston Globe*, complaining about the occasional Mormon practice of baptizing Jews posthumously. "In doing some genealogical research some years ago, I came across my mother's name, and I realized that the Mormons baptized her," he said. He added, "I've even sent money to Rick Santorum."

Porter was planning to visit his brother, another rabbi, in Baltimore, and from there he would continue on to Washington, D.C., to meet with the Federal Election Commission. "It's gotten really hard to set up a campaign bank account," he said. "You just go with the flow or else you go under the wheel."

"I'll show you a picture of my wife," he said, retrieving a photo album from the back seat. "That's our wedding—which, of course, none of my family attended, 'cause she hasn't converted yet." Raya, Porter's wife, is Ukrainian. ("I know now that not every Ukrainian is an antisemite.") Another picture showed Porter smiling at a pizzeria, in Newton, next to Tom Mountain, the chairman of a local Republican organization. "He and I are best buddies," Porter said. "I've discovered that at Republican clubs you find a lot of independents and people who are really quirky. Maybe they'll vote for Jack Porter as a protest vote."

Chapter 25

The Lost, Confused, and Yet Somehow Productive Years of 1990–2010 (Divorce, Stress—the Mallory-Weiss Syndrome—Death of Second Wife, Alienation from Family yet Traveling the World Lecturing on Genocide and Its Prevention)

These years were confusing for me. It was the beginning of the end of my marriage to Miriam, and there was lots of stress: from the breakup, from tenants, from making money—or rather, not making enough money for a growing family. The kids were entering their teens. There were soccer, baseball and basketball games, Hebrew school at Temple Emanuel in Newton, and it led almost to my death from the Mallory-Weiss syndrome, which I will describe in my last chapter.

Stress will do that. It will kill you. But, luckily, I survived that near-fatal event and got through the divorce. I felt that the children should not move, so Miriam kept the house and I got a cash settlement. I would be in the children's lives, moving just a few blocks away.

The Talmud says that when you divorce your *first* wife the heavens cry. It is the most difficult divorce of all, because children are involved. I still remember what her lawyers told me: "Do you want to send *my* children to college, or *your* children?" meaning, "Let's settle this quickly and painlessly and not spend so much money on attorney fees."

I agreed. Most likely our marriage broke up due to my selfishness: I put my career, my ego, my writings, and my being on the media ahead of my wife's needs and desires. She was a private person, and I wasn't.

I was single for a long time, nearly ten years, but I remarried in 2009 to Rona Vogel in a loving yet bizarre marriage. Rona was disabled; she was born with a heart defect and felt she would not live long (she lived to age sixty-two), but her parents were wealthy and set up a trust fund of hundreds of thousands of dollars to help her. However, she had a sister who was an alcoholic and totally out of control—a mental case. But she was an excellent cook. I was invited to her home in 2005 for Passover. It was a semi-disaster emotionally, but I met her lovely sister, and she fell in love with me and wanted marriage.

I put it off for a long time, but she begged me. She was being abused by her sister physically, and her trust fund was being drained. The only way to save her was to marry her. So, in October, soon after the Red Sox played in the World Series, we married at Newton City Hall.

She moved in. Her sister, however, would come to my window and pound on it. We had to call the police. It was very stressful, but Rona was happy to be with me and to be away from her sister. But then disaster struck. On a trip to New York, after we had picketed the ADL offices for the Armenian community, she died in my arms in a hotel room. The Armenians were aghast that Abe Foxman, ADL's director, would not recognize the Armenian genocide due to Turkish pressure on Israel and America.

After we had picketed the ADL headquarters, we returned to our hotel room, and Rona complained of chest pains. Early in the morning, she died. I didn't know what to do, but I saw, outside my window, a church. So I walked across the street and asked to speak to the priest.

"My wife died, and I don't know what to do," I told him.

"What religion are you?" he calmly asked.

"Jewish," I said.

"Well maybe we should call a rabbi."

And he called a Rabbi Hausman, who was a rabbi for a *shul* catering to Broadway actors and dancers. She came right over. We held Rona's hand and then looked at each other. There was nothing more we could do. She was dead, and we had better call the police. I would have loved to have put her in a car and driven to Boston, but that is against the law. You can't transport a dead body across state lines without a permit.

The NYPD, just like on TV, came over, and they were very professional. They first checked her medicine bottles and verified that her pills backed up my story that she had died of heart failure. They also called her doctor in Newton. His name was on the pillbox. And then they called me back:

"Jack, her doctor says you're not her husband. Can you explain that?"

"Well, we were only married nine days, and he would not have known."

That satisfied the detectives. But then they had another question: "Mr. Porter, when we first arrived you told us, 'She wanted to die.' What did you mean by that?"

"I meant that she wanted to die in Boston. She wanted me, while she was in pain, to take us back to Boston. She didn't want to die in Manhattan."

That also satisfied the detectives, so they released the body to a funeral home, and I returned to Boston by bus, and she returned by hearse. It cost over eight hundred dollars to transport the body. Rona, as usual, the smart girl that she was, wanted to save us a lot of money. God bless her.

Her family, of course, blamed me for her death, and so I needed police protection at the funeral (a police car was posted near the gravesite), plus I had three to four strong Armenian men acting as bodyguards. They would never forget our coming to New York to support their cause, and they *never* forget their friends.

I buried her at Hand-in-Hand Cemetery off Centre Street in West Roxbury. Little did I know that my third wife, Raya, would be buried right next to Rona, and one day in the future I will be buried next to them.

But my career flourished despite these horrible events. I became a major leader in genocide studies and attended many international conferences. (I explain this in chapter 22.) But I was still not finished searching for a "career," because in the year 2000 I became a rabbi. (That story, my short rabbinical career, I tell in the next chapter.)

I was still searching for love, and found that as well with Raya.

Chapter 26

Rabbi in Paradise ("Key West Rabbi")

This was one of the most fascinating periods of my life and yet so short—only three months. I saw an ad in the Jewish *Forward* with the title "Looking for a Rabbi in Paradise." I answered it and got hired. The story appeared in several places—the *Forward* of New York, *Moment Magazine*, the *Boston Globe*, *Boston Magazine*, and several local neighborhood papers like those in Chelsea, MA, as well as Key West newspapers. (I also added some stories about my pulpit in Chelsea, MA.)

"Key West Rabbi" was quite a tale and made me a "celebrity." The picture of me and entertainer Randy Roberts was itself a sensation. Here is the story.

LIFESTYLE, LIFESTYLE, LIFESTYLE IN KEY WEST, FLORIDA

Congregation B'Nai Zion is a 114 year old, 65 family, Conservative synagogue looking for all of the qualities every other congregation wants in a Rabbi: good judgment, good people skills, the ability and desire to teach adults and children as well as good Torah skills. What we uniquely

have to offer is the opportunity to live in what we consider paradise. Key West is a small (35,000 permanent residents), diverse community of interesting people that also has great weather, fishing and boating. The people are friendly, cooperative, tolerant and easy-going, but don't mistake us for any sleepy fishing village. We also have world-class culture; theater, symphony, art, writers and much more. We offer a $110,000 annual package to the right Rabbi. If you're eager to be as creative and inspiring as the congregants you'll encounter here, please mail resumes to our President, Dr. Fred Covan, 1809 Seldenberg Ave., Key West, FL 33030.

New Career for New rabbi at B'Nai Zion

[*Key West Citizen*, Saturday, August 25, 2001, front page and 12A]

By Terry Schmida
Citizen Religion Editor

B'Nai Zion Synagogue's new rabbi, Jack Porter, is a Russian-born "post-denominational" Jew, considered one of the world's foremost scholars on the Holocaust and the modern sociology of Jewry.

"I'm what you'd call a mid-career rabbi," said Porter, who started his duties at the United Street synagogue last week, succeeding Rabbi Sol Landau. "Before I became a rabbi, I was a college professor, writer and real estate developer. Basically, I started on a spiritual path towards God during my separation and divorce five years ago."

But if he's something of a neophyte as a rabbi, Porter has devoted much of his life towards learning and teaching about the history of his people, as a college professor and the author of more than 30 books on the subject.

A committed socialist, Porter, 56, moved with his Holocaust-survivor parents to Milwaukee from an Austrian refugee camp shortly after he was born.

Influenced by his parents' struggles, he grew up a political activist, campaigning against the war in Vietnam and the ROTC and campaigning for civil rights as a leader of Students for a Democratic Society in the Midwest.

At 17, he went to Israel to work on a kibbutz, picking bananas in the sub-tropical south of the country.

He remains concerned about the fate of the Middle East and sees intransigence on both sides of the conflict.

"Religious fundamentalism has taken over on both sides," the outspoken Porter said. "If Islamic fundamentalists looked at Jews and Jewish fundamentalists looked at Arabs, they'd really see how similar they are. They're mirror images."

Though he only became a full-fledged rabbi last year, Porter was a spiritual leader at Jewish temples in Marlboro, Mass., and Chelsea, Mass., for three years, before deciding to head south to Key West, a city he'd never even visited.

"This really is the friendliest synagogue in Florida," said Porter of the synagogue's 150-or-so members. "We're very open to everybody. I have to give them credit for keeping this place going for more than 100 years, through some tough times."

Now that he's here, Porter is eager to get to work on his goals for the synagogue.

"We want to expand the Hebrew school and the congregation itself and reach out more to the community, and improve the image of Jews here," said Porter. "Right now, the relationship between B'Nai Zion and Chabad is one of mistrust and competition. It's my job to bridge that trust and work to build more tolerance of each other."

The Chabad Jewish Center of the Florida Keys is a second Key West synagogue, located on Eisenhower Drive.

Cabaret Nights: Tales of One Rabbi's Short-Lived Pulpit in Paradise

[publication details]

By Jack Nusan Porter
For a month before and a month after the September 11 terrorist attacks, I was the southernmost rabbi in the continental United States or, as my brother liked to say, the *"Key Vester Rebbe."*

My memories of those days resurfaced recently when I read "Drag Queens at the 801 Cabaret" (University of Chicago Press, 2003), by two University of California at Santa Barbara sociology and women's studies professors, Leila J. Rupp and Verta Taylor.

The 801 Cabaret—at 801 Duval St., on Key West's main drag, excuse the pun—is a place whose inner walls I once knew well.

It all began when I answered an ad—interestingly enough, it had appeared in the Forward—that announced "Rabbi Wanted in Paradise." For a rabbi with only three years of experience, it was a great opportunity, especially in light of the ennui that ensconced me then, a side effect of my divorce. Key West did indeed sound like "paradise," especially when one factored in the $50,000 salary—and the free apartment.

I was hired by the nondenominational B'nai Zion synagogue to do outreach to Key West's citizens, be they Cuban exiles, "snowbirds" from the North, Jews who "immigrated" from Miami, gays, lesbians or drag queens.

While I had briefly attended the interdenominational Academy for Jewish Religion in New York City, I was ordained by an Orthodox rabbinic court in Manhattan. Basically, I'm a Conservative rabbi with nondenominational feelings, that comes from an Orthodox family background. All of this means that I'm a fairly radical rabbi, maybe even too radical for Key West, but forgive me for getting ahead of myself.

Known alternately as the "Conch Republic" (after those fibrous mollusks), "the Rock" (as in "I need to get off the Rock") or simply "Paradise," Key West is closer to Cuba (90 miles) than to Miami (154 miles). For years, it has provided a haven to writers, kooks, smugglers, artists, intellectuals and tourists.

It's not perfect, of course, but it does come pretty close. Even so, I only lasted two months there.

My mandate from the synagogue board was to try to increase *shul* membership, and one great untapped source—the synagogue and I agreed—was the gay and lesbian community. One way to reach out was to do *kiruv* to the heroes of that community—the drag queens.

To Rupp and Taylor, drag queens are not simply gender-benders; they are social protest personified. Every night, on stage at the 801 Cabaret they educate the public about what it means to be a man or a woman in our society. To be a drag queen is not for the fainthearted; as some say, it takes "balls."

My goal was to reach out to these men, or at least to the Jews among them—and to get them into synagogue. As jobs go, it wasn't unpleasant. It was certainly colorful.

At the 801, there were Inga (Roger), Kylie (Kevin), Sushi (Gary), Milla (Dean), TV (Timothy), Scabola (Mathew), Gugi (Rov), Desiray (Joel) and Margo (David). Other Key West favorites include Lady V, Mama Crass, Baby Drag, Krystal Klear, Raven, Mr. Randy Roberts and the Bitch Sisters. Of them, only Margo, Mr. Randy Roberts and possibly the Bitch Sisters were Jewish.

At first, there was some confusion on my part. But the folks at the 801 were more than happy to clarify for me.

"Jack, I could go to *shul* as Margo," David told me, "but what would be the purpose? It would be a bit of a shock at first, and B'nai Zion would accept me, but I would most likely go to *shul* as David, not Margo. Margo is my stage act. It would serve no purpose except for entertainment value to go as her. I'd go as David." But in the end, he never came.

I got into trouble with Mr. Randy Roberts when a *Boston Globe* reporter writing about my outreach efforts ended up calling him a "cross-dresser" in the article. He is an entertainer and a female impersonator, he told me, and don't you forget it.

I was told that I was the first rabbi to come to a drag show. While that is not entirely true, I was pleased and honored. At one show, I was a "victim" of Randy's humor, no matter that I was a rabbi. I had gone to the bathroom during his act; when I returned, he asked me in front of the entire audience: "Did you wash your hands, rabbi?" Dutifully, I responded, "Yes, I did."

While dressing in drag goes against the halachic prohibition of men dressing in women's attire, drag queens could certainly bring some much-needed energy and spirit to synagogues and schools. Plus, they could teach lessons about tolerance, diversity and sexuality.

However, it would take a very liberal congregation indeed to have drag queens teaching Hebrew school. Despite its tolerance, I doubt even B'nai Zion would allow men in drag to teach Sunday school, although out of drag would be a different story—albeit one that never came up.

Well, this rabbi may have been too radical or simply just too "inexperienced" for Key West; I was fired after two months. It turns out I'd become too involved in Key West's nightlife, neglecting my duties. Among the side projects I poured myself into instead was a screenplay: "Key West Rabbi."

That's Key West for you.

Jack Nusan Porter is the author of "The Jew as Outsider" and "Sexual Politics in Nazi Germany," and editor of "The Sociology of American Jewry" and "Jewish Radicalism," among other books, and an adjunct professor of sociology at the University of Massachusetts in Lowell.

Rabbi's Real-Life Screenplay Is Too Hot for Fla. Synagogue

[Nathan Cobb, Names & Faces, Boston Globe, Saturday, March 30, 2002]

Consider **Jack Porter's** screenplay, which he calls a work in progress:

Boston-area rabbi rejects snow shovel, takes job at a Key West synagogue in Florida. Rabbi befriends transvestites, money launderers, the homeless, and assorted other characters. Rabbi is sent packing by synagogue. Rabbi re-embraces snow shovel.

Porter, who lives in Newton, says the script is actually the latest chapter in his nomadic professional life. His resume includes college teacher, real estate developer, sociologist, and, most recently, rabbi. Last year he answered an advertisement for a position at Congregation B'Nai Zion in Key West. He lasted three months by his own account, six weeks by the synagogue's. "I got caught up in the fantasy of Key West," Porter muses. B'nai Zion president **Fred Covan** won't comment, except to say, "My mother told me that if you can't say something nice about someone, don't say anything at all."

Porter says he spent a great deal of time interacting with Key West's population of cross-dressers. "My job was outreach," points out the fifty-seven-year-old divorced father of two. "I was trying to reach out and get Jewish transvestites to join the synagogue. But, actually, none of them did." ("There are exactly two Jewish transvestites down here that I know of," Covan counters.)

In any case, Porter began to write the script he calls "Key West Rabbi." He says his congregation was not amused. "They said, 'Rabbi Porter, we didn't invite you down here to write a screenplay about transvestites and bums.' So I lost my job."

He's still writing about it. He's completed an outline, he says, and he's looking for a co-writer. Meanwhile, he's also looking for a new pulpit.

Spiritual Leader Jack Nusan Porter Wants to Revive Chelsea's Once-Thriving Jewish Community.

[*Boston Globe*, September 26, 1999]

By John Laidler
Globe Correspondent
CHELSEA—When Temple Emmanuel first began operating out of a converted church building 60 years ago, Samuel Silberstein recalled that it was sometimes difficult to find a seat.

During holiday services and even some regular ones when a special speaker was featured, Silberstein said, "There wasn't enough room in the sanctuary itself for everyone, so we used the vestry to seat the overflow." On those crowded days, nearly 800 people might turn out. On routine weeks, two hundred would attend.

Today, the problem faced by the congregation is not a shortage of seats but of people. Only about 35 regularly show up for services at the synagogue in a white building about 150 years old at the corner of Cary Avenue and Tudor Street. On high holidays, attendance is about 175.

The plight of Temple Emmanuel, whose membership has fallen from as many as 800 families in 1939 to about 150 today, mirrors that of the city's Jewish community as a whole. In the 1930s, Jews made up as much as forty-eight percent of Chelsea's population, or roughly 25,000 people, according to Silberstein, the Temple Emmanuel treasurer who is a local expert on the history of the city's Jewish community.

Today, he estimated, there are about 2,300 Jews left in Chelsea, most of them elderly. Only two working synagogues remain—the Conservative Temple Emmanuel and the Orthodox Walnut Street synagogue.

According to Silberstein, Jews, most of them escaping persecution in Russia, Latvia and Poland, began arriving in large numbers in Chelsea in the 1880s. At the peak of the Jewish population in the 1930s, there were 14 synagogues in the city, he said.

But by the 1930s, Jews began migrating out of the city. "Those that became comfortable started moving to the Brooklines and the Newtons," Silberstein, 83, recalled. "Then another small migration occurred right after the Second World War to Swampscott and Marblehead, and after the Korean War, a migration to Medford and Malden. What is left are all the older people."

But if its heyday seems a distant memory, Temple Emmanuel may still have a future. That at least is the earnest hope of its new spiritual leader, Jack Nusan Porter.

Assuming his post this month, Porter succeeds Rabbi Benjamin Rodwogin, who presided at the temple from 1945 until he died earlier this year. Although not ordained as a rabbi, as a spiritual leader Porter can carry out the duties of a rabbi.

At first blush, Porter would seem an unlikely choice to lead the congregation. A one-time 1960s radical, he has spent much of his later years as a sociology professor and author. But in recent years, Porter has taken a renewed interest in spiritual matters, leading to his decision to commute to New York last year to study at the Academy for Jewish Religion. During that same year, he also did a stint as spiritual leader at Temple Emanuel in Marlborough.

The fifty-four-year-old Newton resident, whose brother, Shlomo Porter, is a prominent Baltimore rabbi, said he is thrilled by the chance to breathe new life into a venerable synagogue. He said he relished the idea of working with an urban congregation—particularly an older one—something he says is a rare opportunity.

"I come from a working-class background, and I've always been very happy with older people. And that's what Chelsea is . . . Probably the last Jewish working-class neighborhood in the Boston area," Porter said.

"I think it's a wonderful city," he said of Chelsea. "It reminds me of Milwaukee, where I grew up, a working-class town with a lot of ethnic groups."

Although he said he especially enjoyed working with older people, Porter recognized that recruiting young people is essential for Temple Emmanuel to survive.

"The real challenge for me is to maintain the shul, to bring in speakers, to keep it up as it is, not to have it decline. And then the challenge beyond that is to get younger people to come, which is harder," he said.

Porter said he will look for a variety of ways to recruit new members such as putting up signs and mailing flyers, and organizing Torah study groups and other special programs that might appeal to younger people.

While it began in 1939, Congregation Emmanuel was an outgrowth of an earlier Conservative congregation, Beth El, which was organized in 1927. According to Silberstein, Congregation Beth El worshipped in a temple it constructed on Crescent Avenue. But the congregation went out of business when a bank foreclosed on its building in 1936 or 1937. Many of its former members regrouped and in about 1938 formed Congregation Emmanuel. In 1939, the new congregation purchased its present building, which had formerly served as the Cary Avenue Baptist Church and later the First Methodist Episcopal Church.

Born in a rural town in Ukraine in 1944, Porter is the son of Faye and the late Irving Porter. Before the war, his father ran a flour mill. After the German occupation of Ukraine, his parents and other Jews hid in the forests to escape the German special police force and its Ukrainian collaborators. Porter's father fought as a commander in a special Jewish brigade that eventually became part of the Soviet partisan movement fighting the Germans and the Ukrainian nationalists.

Following the war in 1946, the family—minus Porter's two sisters, who had been killed by the pro-Nazi Ukrainians prior to his birth—immigrated to the United States. They settled in Milwaukee, where one of Porter's uncles lived.

Immediately following his graduation from high school in 1962, Porter spent a year in Israel, where he worked on a kibbutz and studied in Jerusalem.

Enrolling in the University of Wisconsin at Milwaukee in 1963, he became actively involved in the civil rights movement. At one time, he joined a march in Chicago led by Martin Luther King Jr. He also heard King speak at his campus.

After graduating from college in 1967, Porter spent four years at Northwestern University, obtaining a master's degree in 1969 and a doctorate in 1971, both in sociology. During those years, his political focus shifted to the antiwar movement. A leader of the radical Students for a Democratic Society, he was caught up in the drama of the times, including taking part in the protests outside the Democratic National Convention in Chicago in 1968, where he was tear-gassed. He later attended the conspiracy trial of the "Chicago Eight" to show support for the defendants.

Since 1971, Porter has taught sociology and Jewish theology and history at a number of colleges. He has been an adjunct professor of sociology at the University of Massachusetts at Lowell for 22 years, specializing in genocide studies. Over the years, he has written books and articles about the Holocaust and other topics. Porter also has a real estate investment business and teaches real estate. And he has dabbled in electoral politics as a campaign volunteer and this year as a candidate for School Committee in Newton.

Porter said he is only one of a number of Jewish radicals from the 1960s who have followed spiritual paths in recent years.

"I think [it is] because the answers of the millennium are not all political, but spiritual. There is an exhaustion of political answers," he said. "And also you have to grow as a person. And as you grow, you get older, the approach the end of your life, the middle of your life. You begin to ask certain questions—What is the meaning of life? What is the meaning of God? What is the meaning of evil?—and you can't get that from political tracts. You have to turn to the spiritual texts."

Chapter 27

Finding Love Again, with Raya, 2011–2017

_____

In September 2011, it had been two years since my second wife, Rona, had died in New York, and I was lonely again. Then *mazel* (luck) struck, and one needs *mazel* in life. I had a next-door neighbor who rented an apartment in the home of the Cheses family, a *frum* family, who would later make *aliyah* to Israel. Mila and her husband were Ukrainian non-Jews, and they had a friend who was single and looking for a husband.

One Friday evening they invited me over to meet her. I walked in the door, and I saw the most beautiful woman in the world—a tall blond with a friendly smile and curvaceous body. I was dumbstruck. I sat down next to her, and immediately we were holding hands like old friends, and the drinking started, and the food, two very traditional Ukrainian customs.

To make a long story short, two months later, on November 18 (a lucky number, in Jewish tradition), we were wed in Newton City Hall. Rayisa (Raya for short) was a physician in Kiev, but her husband began fooling around with nurses at the hospital where they both worked, and it hurt Raya so much that she not only got divorced but also left for America on a tourist visa. But tourist visas are only good for six months, so she entered, like so many illegal immigrants, into the underground economy.

You get a job, you get money; your employer is happy to pay you a lower wage or even room and board, and you get to stay in America. One problem: you're illegal, and technically you could get deported. But it was a different world back then. No one was looking to deport a good-looking five to ten blond. Police and immigration officials were more interested in illegal workers from Central America, especially if they had a criminal record.

Once, Raya told me, she was stopped for a minor traffic violation and showed the cop her passport and visa. The cop noticed that it was past due and said, "You should get it renewed." That's it. That's all they did. Just a warning. I wonder if they would do that today. So, you may have been safe in some ways from deportation, but still your situation was precarious.

There are only three ways to get a green card in America and be assured that you might stay: (1) be a political prisoner, or be in danger politically back home; (2) have an occupation that is needed by the American government; or (3) marry an American. Since Raya did not qualify for the first two criteria (though being a physician should have qualified her, the American Medical Association made it almost impossible to get a license), the fastest and most effective route was to marry.

Raya's job was very common for Ukrainian or Russian non-Jewish women. Jewish women and men for some reason came under a different category and could easily get green cards. (This was political and going back to the time of the *refuseniks* in the late 1970s who came here as political and religious refugees.)

Raya worked for a Russian Jewish family in Newton who had two children, and since both husband and wife worked, they wanted a Russian-speaking nanny. That's what Raya did for several years, but it was not only a difficult job with long hours, but since she lived in the attic, she was always "on call." She desperately wanted out.

Several of Raya's friends had married Americans. Tatyana married Wayne, Ola married Tony, and Raya was about to marry Jack Nusan Porter. True, it was no easy task. You had to show pictures from your wedding as proof that you were going to live together, and letters from Clergy or other prominent people in the community. As a rabbi, I also wrote letters for other couples.

We had a good lawyer, and it was surprisingly inexpensive and efficient. As long as you followed the rules, you got the green card. However, people might ask: Did people marry out of love, or for money? There was a nightclub in Randolph called Vincent's, and the Ukrainian women would go there to meet American men, and what's not to love? Beautiful, delightful women, great cooks and housewives, good workers—just love them and provide for them.

Most of the relationships were love matches. Yes, one heard of some women paying money to men; even of scams. One Chinese guy told me he had received twenty thousand dollars each from five different women to marry him (and, of course, to divorce each of them), but I didn't believe him, plus that could land you in jail. It was not easy to fool the immigration officials. They knew all the tricks. Just be honest. While some of the couples may have been split apart by the death of a spouse, in all cases the people we know are still together. I also found it ironic, given the prejudice about them, that our final interview was with a Muslim woman!

But my biggest obstacle was not immigration officials but my own family. They were *frum*, and it was taboo to marry outside of the faith. But Raya really wanted to become a Jew. (See her wonderful letter she wrote for the rabbis.) So we embarked on a conversion process of study. It culminated in a *mikveh*, a ritual dunking in holy water and your immersion as a new Jew. Three rabbis officiated (see document).

It was a wonderful ceremony, and Raya attended services and kept the Sabbath. She had always wanted to be a Jew, and I believed her. The problem was that the conversion was not done under Orthodox supervision, so it was not acceptable to my brother, who is an Orthodox rabbi. But my sister Bella and her husband Mitch accepted Raya into the house. In fact, their relationship with her was very warm, almost as if Bella had a sister her own age. But my brother and some people in the religious community did not accept her. For example, I would get wedding invitations that pointedly would have *my* name on the envelope but not hers. Still, she did attend several weddings within our own family.

Raya worked hard to learn English, to learn about American history and culture, and she loved American politics. When I ran for US Congress in 2012 against Joe Kennedy, she was right there with me, just like Melania Trump and her husband, the President—both of them tall, beautiful, confident Eastern European women.

After we married, she wanted to better herself, and so she studied for a position in the medical care field. The obstacles for her becoming a doctor were immense, and that is a tragedy when we have such a shortage of physicians. But while she studied, she also had jobs caring for seniors in their homes, also a difficult job.

And then, sadly, through bad luck and bad genes she "contracted" colon cancer. She fought it bravely, just as my sister had for two years, but it had metastasized too quickly, and after a short stay in a hospice, she died on November 24, 2017, almost exactly six years after we had first married. (See her obituary.)

Raya was buried next to Rona, my second wife, and I will be buried next to Raya, a fitting place to not just one but two wonderful women whom I dearly loved.

What follows is the letter she wrote on why she wanted to become a Jew. I found it after she died, and I find it enormously moving.

Why I Want to Become a Jew

March 8, 2013

I was born in Kiev in 1960, and my mother is Ukrainian, and my father was Russian.

I came to America eight years ago to work as a nanny. Now I work as a health care aide.

I began studying Judaism before I met Jack Porter. I studied books like Rabbi Donin, *To Be a Jew*, and Herman Wouk, *This is My G-d: The Jewish Way of Life*. Later I studied Rabbi Israel Meir Lau of Israel, *Yahadut Halacha Lema'aseh*—all in Russian.

Plus I worked for several Jewish families, some *frum*, so I know Kashrut and Shabbat laws. Also *Taharat Hamishpocho*.

I met Jack Porter, my husband, through a friend, and we fell in love, and we are very happy. My first good thing was to marry Jack; the second thing was to become Jewish.

I love Judaism very much. I like Passover, Sukkot, Chanukah. I like to eat food in Sukkah and feel close to God. I want to be in the *mikveh* and feel very clean and very close to God. And I like to make latkes for my husband. I light candles every Shabbat.

I have a daughter married in Kiev and a mother living in a town near Kiev.

I am a medical doctor by education and experience. I worked for many years in hospitals.

Now, I will study to be a nurse. I work with older Russian women at this time, several of them Jewish. I wash them, feed them, and listen to them. They teach me also how to be a Jewish woman.

Sincerely,
Raya Porter

Dr. Raya Teshena & Dr. Jack Nusan Porter

November 18, 2011

[*Boston Sunday Globe*, January 1, 2012]

Dr. Raya (Rachel) Teshena of Kiev, Ukraine, and Dr. Jack Nusan Porter of Newtonville, MA, were married Friday morning, November 18, in a civil ceremony at Newton (MA) City Hall. City Clerk David Olson performed the ceremony. Another ceremony and reception was held December 4, 2011, at the Women's Club in Newton Highlands, MA.

Mr. Porter, 66, is the son of the late Irving and Faye Porter (Puchtik), both Soviet partisans during World War II. Mr. Porter senior was a scrap metal dealer in Milwaukee, and his wife was a housewife.

Ms. Teshena, 51, is the daughter of the late Vasilii Teshen, a pharmacist in Kiev, and Katarina Teshena, an economist, living near Kiev.

Mr. Porter is an internationally known sociologist, writer and human rights activist. He is the former treasurer and presidential candidate of the International Association of Genocide Scholars, the largest organization of genocide scholars in the world. His many books include "Genocide and Human Rights," "The Sociology of American Jews" and "The Genocidal Mind."

He is a former Research Associate at Harvard University's Ukrainian Research Institute and a former professor of social science at Boston University's College of General Studies. He attended Northwestern University, where he obtained his PhD in sociology, and the University of Wisconsin–Milwaukee.

He is also Director of The Spencer School of Real Estate in Newton and a real estate consultant in the Greater Boston area. Porter met Raya (Rachel) Teshena a few days before her birthday, October 4th, 2011. They were fixed up by her girlfriend, Mila, Porter's next door neighbor. Porter turned out to be her "birthday present." It was instant love and admiration. She is a tall, green-eyed blond, and a former doctor, and Porter is a slightly shorter, balding sociologist, and though born in Rovno, Ukraine, was raised in Milwaukee, Wisconsin.

OBITUARIES

Raya (Rachel) Porter, 57

[*Jewish Advocate*, December 6, 2017]

Raya (Rachel) Porter Raya (Rachel) Teshena Porter of Newtonville, formerly of Kiev, Ukraine, died on Nov. 24, 2017 after a long battle with metastasized colon cancer. She was 57.

Raya graduated Kiev University Medical School and worked as a gynecologist in Ukraine. She immigrated to the US in 2004, becoming a citizen a year later; in Newton, where she lived, she worked as a nanny and home healthcare aide. Raya met her husband-to-be a few days before her birthday, Oct. 4, 2011, when her girlfriend Mila fixed her up with her next-door neighbor, Jack Porter. He turned out to be her "birthday present." It was instant love and admiration between the 5 foot, 10 inch blonde and the balding, slightly shorter sociologist.

"She was a wonderful person, beautiful both inside and out, and she will be terribly missed," noted Jack, a research associate at The Davis Center for Russian and Eurasian Studies at Harvard University.

Raya was the beloved wife of Dr. Jack Nusan Porter for six years; the adored and loving mother to Sveta (Roman) Kogut of Kiev; the loving grandma to little Vanya; and the devoted daughter of Katarina Teshena, an economist, of Borispol, near Kiev and the late Vasilii Teshen, a pharmacist.

Raya leaves legions of grieving friends. Her warmth, her concern for others, and her excellent advice will be missed. The family would like to thank the doctors, nurses and social workers at Dana Farber, Brigham and Women's, St. Elizabeth's Hospital and the Stanley Tippet Hospice in Needham. Donations to them would be appreciated. Raya donated her body to the Harvard Medical School. A memorial service was held at a private home in Newton on Nov. 26 and shiva was held later in the week at the Porter home in Newtonville. Condolences can be left on Jack's Facebook page.

Chapter 28

Back to Harvard and Stability, 2011–2020—Renewed Productivity, Especially with Help from World-Famed Designer and Cousin Allen Porter, Support from My Mentor and Genocide Guide Greg Stanton, and Spiritual and Communal Support from My Sephardic *Shul*)

———————

I returned to Harvard in 2013, not to the Ukrainian Institute but to the Davis Center for Russian and Eurasian Studies, and I have been there ever since. Maybe I had an "angel" on the nominating committee who liked me, or maybe it was my massive 660-page tome on the Jewish partisans of World War II—my magnum opus, I call it—but I was accepted and welcomed. It is a fine place to be. I do my work, and I don't get involved in "politics." I try to be nice to everyone and grateful to be there. Maybe maturity has been a factor. I have to stop battling, and I am now considered an "elder" with some wisdom and experience.

The Davis Center has changed. It is a far cry from the fierce and brightening anti-Communist McCarthy era of the late forties and fifties, when people like Talcott Parsons, for whatever reason, brought Nazi collaborators to fight the

"Red Menace." (See the sources section for details of that struggle, which is beyond the scope of this short memoir.)

It was also a time that saw the impact of the many émigré intellectuals, scientists, and writers who came to America in the 1930s. Sociologists like Werner Cahnman, Ernst Borinski, Louis Wirth, and Lewis Coser; mathematicians like Albert Einstein; and scientists like Wernher von Braun.

Werner Cahnman in particular made a deep impression on me. A member of that German Jewish "aristocracy" of scholars and teachers who escaped Nazism, they had a deep impact not only on the American Jewish community but also on the African American, especially in the Deep South.

Borinski, for example, taught for many years at traditional Black colleges like Tugaloo College. A wonderful book and documentary *From Swastika to Jim Crow*, details the impact that these Jewish survivors had on their African American students and in fact mentored them to become the civil rights leaders of the future.

Today, the Davis Center is much more diverse than it was in the '50s. It is supportive of the people who fought for Soviet human rights—Andrei Sakharov, Aleksandr Solzhenitsyn, and others less well known. The Center deals with not just politics but also culture, film, cinema, and especially sex and gender issues, women's roles, and transgender and gay rights in Russia and beyond. It is also much more attuned to the Jewish aspects of Soviet history and culture. One can thank people like Alexandra Vacroux, Maim Shrayer, Josh Rubenstein, and Rochelle Ruthchild for this.

I was also one of the first to deal with sexual issues regarding Nazi Germany and the Shoah, so I am comfortable with these issues. True, at times political correctness comes into play and can be annoying, but overall these new perspectives are refreshing.

My newborn confidence led to not only leadership in various intellectual fields—genocide studies, modern Jewish studies, radical studies, predictions of genocide, terrorist acts, and extreme evil—but also in my personal life. This is not surprising: when one is happy in one's work, it leads to success in one's social life, and vice versa. So, after a decade alone, I found a fascinating woman in Rona Vogel. Though short-lived in courting and only nine days (true) of marriage, it was an amazing relationship. She died in November 2009.

Two years later, in November 2011, I married another great woman, Rayisa (Raya) Evashko, whose relationship I have described earlier. I am so sorry Raya is not alive to share in my success.

I also was lucky to be mentored in genocide studies by several important people, mostly Greg Stanton but also Israel Charny and Kurt Jonassohn.

And in the area of photography, architecture and design, and in broadening my own horizons, I have to thank my first cousin, Allen Porter, who sadly died of the coronavirus on April 28, 2020, at age ninety-four in Evanston, Illinois. Allen was a tough taskmaster with high standards who pushed himself and his people to attain new heights. He was in many ways a bit of a genius when it came to design, and, as I pointed out earlier, in the Bauhaus tradition you must learn to design everything—from perfume bottles to book covers. There is no elitism of high culture versus low culture. In short, he helped me see the "sociology of space."

What did I accomplish in this decade, 2011–2020?

A lot—even a Nobel Peace Prize nomination for my work in genocide prediction, plus a *New Yorker* profile. But my biggest accomplishment was seeing my son get married and have a wonderful life with his wife Jessica and their two sons Luke and Nate, plus seeing my lovely and accomplished daughter Danielle have a successful career in a stressful field—as an immigration attorney. I am lucky to have such fantastic kids. And also to have an "adopted son" like Andy Turpin, who has been by my side in tough times and in good times.

As the articles that follow show, I have had an interesting life and have made an impact. What else can one ask for?

Jack Nusan Porter—Journey through the Woods

[Aliza Danielson, "title," *Lifestyle Magazine*, date]

It started when I thought a purported Holocaust survivor looked too young and too good to be one. The confrontation lasted about 15–30 seconds, but was enough. He backed off, telling me I attacked like a tigress and what was my problem? Well, we both decided that assumptions are dangerous, and that "assume" is spelled the way it is for a reason (because assumptions makes an "ass" of "u" and "me"), and then we decided to be friends. The man was Jack Nusan Porter, and the incident took place in Washington, D.C., at a conference sponsored by the US Holocaust Memorial Museum. Then we began to correspond, and what came out is an interesting story.

Jack Porter started life in Rovno, Ukraine, in December 1944, just as the Russians liberated the city from the Nazis. He was known as the "Partisan Baby"—his mother, Faygeh, conceived him in the forests, where she and her husband, Yisroel, fought against their oppressors: the Ukraine fascists and the Nazis. His birth, the first one after the liberation, came after 25 immediate members of his parents' families, including two older sisters, were killed in Maniewicz, just north of Rovno.

And so, his parents imbued him with a sense of being special, of having special obligations. As he says, "Much was given and much was asked." Like many other children of Holocaust survivors, he had a sense of mission, of saving the world, of working on *tikkun olam*, to ensure that never again would such events take place.

B y the time the 1960s rocked and rolled around, Jack was in college at the University of Wisconsin when the labs in Madison were blown up. Although he was a leader in what is considered by some to be the "notorious" Students for a Democratic Society (SDS), he never believed in the use of violence to get the message across, and quickly left when violence became its main tactic.

Instead, he channeled his energies into becoming part of the burgeoning Jewish students movement, part of a general movement across the country. There were two aspects to this: one was the self-empowerment of Jewish students with proud ethnic identity—which was the same that was manifesting itself in the black community and in the women's liberation movement—and the other was as a defense group which protested antisemitic acts and anti-Zionism.

"Then," says Jack," it was time to grow up, get married, have children and be responsible." He became a sociologist who taught at Northwestern University and later at Boston University. In 1974, he married Miriam Almuly, a Sephardic woman he met in Brookline, Mass. Today they have two children, Gabe and Danielle.

"While raising your family you put all those idealistic notions on the back burner, and then one day you wake up and realize, Hey, whassup? This is no life."

At first, he stuck it out. Why give up a marriage? Why give up the big house in the burbs? But he was spiritually bereft. He hadn't begun to meet the expectations laid upon him by the special circumstances of his birth.

For 10 years he had been studying the Native American lifestyle among the Wampanoags in New England and the Lakota Sioux in the Dakotas. He studied with Slow Turtle, Sly Fox, Wildcat and Crow Dog—spiritual leaders of their tribes. Wildcat preached that every individual has his own spiritual journey that he must complete. What surprised Jack was that Wildcat was Jewish as well as Native American. Wildcat was a Jew by choice who joined a community and synagogue in Providence, Rhode Island and then, toward the end of his life, returned to his original ways.

What Wildcat taught Jack to do was to go into Nature, to seek a connection to the Power of God. He taught him the Indian ways of cutting oneself off from the material world and renouncing egoism. No rabbi had ever been able to connect Jack to God. Then Wildcat asked Jack to go among his own people and become a teacher and a Jew.

It was Wildcat who convinced him to get beyond the bar mitzvah lessons into the core of Judaism and the seeking of God.

In 1997, Jack and his wife, who had grown apart and gone down different paths, separated. Jack began to commute to New York City, where he pursued Jewish studies at the non-denominational seminary, The Academy of Jewish Religion. He was joined there by many fellow travelers on a similar journey. Most of them were in their 40s and 50s, men and women who decided to become rabbis as a second or third career. Many were doctors and lawyers and successful business people who wanted more out of life than money.

Jack received *smicha* (rabbinic ordination) from the Orthodox Board of American Rabbis in New York, under Rabbi Menachem Friedman. Today he is ready to hit the bricks and search for a pulpit. He feels he has an important message to bring to young Jews (and old ones, too) that may have a slightly different cast: "Throw away the labels, but come back to spiritualism and tradition. Be a *mensch*, that's what counts. The rest is commentary."

Jack brings the joy of the Stolener Hasidim from his parents' past into the present. He brings traditional Yiddish to his flock, with a taste of Habonim, the Labor Zionist movement. He loves the notions of kibbutz and summer camps, the speaking of Hebrew, and social democracy with tolerance and justice for all.

The hippie is a rabbi. The rabbi is a hippie, and that's good thing. He is fulfilling the special obligations of the special circumstances of his birth and, as of last month, his dream has come true: He's the chief rabbi of Key West, FL, one of the hippiest havens in the world.

Never Again . . . For Anybody

Genocide Scholar and Fighter for Human Rights

[*Community Magazines*, October 2008]

By MacKenzie C. Kimball

The Newtonville home of Dr. Jack Nusan Porter, sociologist, genocide scholar and all-around Renaissance man, is filled with books. The spines that sit on his shelves boast a variety of human rights topics and represent his dedication to protecting the persecuted. Porter's mission to educate others about the systematic destruction of groups throughout history, as well as prevent future atrocities, is one he has been carrying out since day one.

Porter's life has been forever shaped by events that occurred before he was born. On September 25, 1942, in Maniewicze, Ukraine, during the reign of the Nazi regime, Ukrainian police and the SS Einsatzgruppen shot and killed 25 of Porter's relatives. They were buried in a mass grove they had dug for themselves. Among them were the sisters he would never meet—murdered at the ages of four and two. Miraculously, his parents were able to escape the fate that would be inevitable for six million others.

Two traumatic years later, on December 2, 1944, Porter's parents welcomed him into the brutal and merciless world they were forced to accept. His mother referred to him as "a special baby with a special purpose in life," and one look at the extensive list of his accomplishments and genocide prevention endeavors confirms her prediction.

Continuing the Tradition

Porter was not the first human rights activist in his family. Both of his parents were Soviet partisans, and his father, Irving, was instrumental in the opposition to the Nazi power. "My father was helped by a Polish friend," explains Porter, "who, in a very great act of generosity, gave him a rifle and 150 bullets, which automatically made him leader of the resistance, in a way."

Working as a laborer before the SS began rounding up Jews, Irving established relationships with many German civilians, which proved beneficial during wartime. "My father was able to talk to Germans and not be killed," Porter recalls in awestruck admiration. "It was unbelievable. He asked one of them, 'Who will live and who will die?' The German replied, 'The best of you will be the last of you to die.' The tragic fate of European Jews was determined before anyone had the chance to protest; the only option was to fight. The resistance grew out of this hopelessness," claims Porter, who spent a year with his parents in a Displaced Persons (DP) camp in Austria before coming to the United States on the second refugee boat to leave Europe after the war.

His family settled in Milwaukee, Wisconsin and, despite all they had endured, Porter's parents raised him to be tolerant of others. "My father would tell me to treat everyone equally. He also taught me that you have to care about the Palestinians; you have to care about the Ukrainians and the Polish; you have to care about the people you might think are antisemites." Armed with this unconditional compassion, Porter has spent a large portion of his 63 years fighting for the victims of genocide.

"We all have prejudices," states Porter matter-of-factly. "I was on a baseball team with another guy from Newton; he played short and I played second. I can still remember the Irish guys saying 'Wow, those Jews can play ball.' They were surprised." He laughs. There is no anger in his voice, only understanding. Unlike many child survivors of the Holocaust, Porter harbors no resentment. He refuses to believe that all prejudice stems from hatred. "People's reactions—you are very complicated," he continues. "Maybe it's ignorance, maybe it's just ethnic differences, maybe that's why I became a sociologist."

A Unique Approach

After receiving a Ph.D. in 1971 from Northwestern, Porter brought his extensive knowledge of genocide studies to the Ukraine Institute at Harvard University and, later, to the young minds of Boston University and the University of Massachusetts at Lowell.

Dr. Greg Stanton, president of the IAGS and founder of Genocide Watch, the Cambodian Genocide Project and the International Campaign to End Genocide, had nothing but remarkable things to say about Porter. "He is considered by many to be the leading expert in the world on gender aspects of genocide," Stanton confidently declared. "He's responsible for important pioneering work on the social and psychological causes of mass destruction and persecution. I find his approach refreshing."

Porter's unique approach is evident in his book, *The Genocidal Mind* (2006), which looks at the issues of mass destruction from a different angle. His cover-to-cover attempt at explanation is multi-faceted and traverses the realms of post-modern theory to psychological and social analysis. "You have to have a comparative, cross-cultural approach," says Porter while, once again, humbly giving credit to his father for this idea. "You can't just see this issue as the Holocaust, by either saying that it was ineffable . . . or that our pain was so special that it can never compare to anyone else's pain."

Lifework through the Local Lens

While the Holocaust and issues of Jewish genocide are important to Porter, his efforts reach far beyond his religious group. It is no secret that the Anti-Defamation League (ADL), a national civil rights organization, has yet to acknowledge the killings of 1.5 million Americans in Turkey between 1915 and 1923 as genocide. However, the group's refusal to do so has recently inspired the active opposition of many and, among the morally conscientious contenders, stands Porter. According to Newton resident David Boyajian, the man responsible for calling attention to the ADL issue with his July 6th letter to the Watertown Tab, Porter has been instrumental. "Jack is very helpful because he's not only a genocide scholar and treasurer of the IAGS, but he's an inside tie to the Jewish community," says Boyajian. "At a Newton town meeting he even pushed the Human Rights Commission to make a decision."

Porter's latest book, *Is Sociology Dead? Social Theory and Social Praxis in a Post-Modern Age* (2007), steps away from the issue of genocide and focuses on aspects of human study through a series of short essays. While sociology suffered during the 1980s and early 1990s, it has since rebounded and become a popular academic field in colleges across the nation. "Sociologists make jumps from the personal problems to the public issue," explains Porter, "which may be why some people are afraid of us." Within the pages of this book lies an article titled "Two Newtons or One? One Affluent, One Not," which deals with the stark financial and ethnic contrasts between Newton North and Newton South. Whether he topic is genocidal atrocities or his neighbors, Porter's work is unabashedly controversial.

As if writing or editing 30 books and over 600 articles and essays was not enough, Porter is also the director of the Spencer Institute, a think-tank for genocide studies, and the Spencer School of Real Estate. He is a former rabbi and is currently providing historical background for two potential made-for-television movies, *Partisans* and *Key West Rabbi*.

Possible Solutions

Many people find our war-torn world disheartening, but Porter, dedicated to protecting human rights, has kept his hope alive. "I believe person-to-person diplomacy is where we have to start," states Porter. "A lot of activist groups work in a vacuum . . . They ask: Why, as a major world power, don't we get involved? The answer is because places like Dafur or Rwanda don't mean anything to us geopolitically. Groups need to understand the power structure."

Porter feels that the best way to combat and prevent genocide is to travel to violence-engulfed areas and educate people. Recently, the success of an experimental program that sends anthropologists and other social scientists to war zones in the Middle East has piqued Porter's interest. The belief is that social scientists will be able to teach our soldiers about the culture and decrease unnecessary violence. Porter volunteered for the program. "Sure, it will be dangerous," he says, "But if it will help a soldier survive because he'll have a better understanding of tribal culture, I'll do it."

At the age of 63, Porter, genocide scholar, human rights activist and author, has accomplished more than many could hope for. His history suggests that he will stop at nothing to share his knowledge with the world in hopes that, one day, it will help end persecution and mass murder. "Never again," says Porter, "means never again for anybody."

Porter: One of the Last Local Jewish Radicals

Resident's Parents Provoke Memories as He Strives to Instruct Others

[*Newton TAB*, January 28, 1997, 10]

By Kristen Lombardi
TAB Staff Writer
To sit across from Dr. Jack Porter is to witness energy.

On a given morning at Baker's Best in Newton Highlands, this fifty-two-year-old resident will sip coffee as he ponders the importance of his life so far. As he runs through a list of achievements, Porter will pick up, then rearrange the items on the table—a few ballpoint pens, two coffee cups, a stack of papers.

Porter will readjust these items over and over.

He talks of his life growing up as an Orthodox Jew in Milwaukee and his hands move to the pens. He talks of his experience being the child of Holocaust survivors and his hands move to the cups.

"I have been an outsider all of my life," said Porter. He is a short, balding man with a smile that shoots across his face. "I am the conduit of my parents' story. They saw me as a special child with a mission. This has made me what I am."

He would describe himself as one of the last Jewish radicals in Newton.

Others might describe Porter as a man of many trades, fueled by various passions. He teaches sociology and genocide studies at the University of Massachusetts at Lowell. He charts the lineage of New England "rabbinical dynasties."

Porter is also working to convince Jewish students at both Harvard and Brandeis universities to organize a march and boycott Swiss chocolate, watches and other goods. Choosing these universities because of their international visibility, Porter said he hopes a boycott of goods will compel the Swiss government to hand over money deposited by—or stolen from—victims of the Holocaust to their families.

"I would like the Jews to get about $25 million. I want [Swiss government] to make reparations and put the money into a cultural fund," he explained.

As if these activities weren't enough, Porter has joined the editorial team at "Jewish Family & Life!", an online magazine devoted to "changing the face of American Jewry, one family at a time," according to the magazine's mission statement. The magazine's address is http://www.jewishfamily.com.

Several weeks ago, Porter accepted the position of deputy publisher at the magazine. In this role, Porter will both raise funds through individual and organization contributions, and strategize with the staff on the magazine's future.

"Yosef [Abramowitz] is the premier young Jewish journalist," said Porter, speaking of the magazine's founder and current editor, who has written countless articles for Jewish newspapers. "He's charismatic, brilliant and youthful. He knows what young people want, and he knows the [editorial] direction to go in."

Since Jewish Family & Life! went on the World Wide Web this past year, the Webzine has grown in popularity. Now, about 250 people visit the site on a daily basis. They might click on articles on Jewish opportunities in the Girl Scouts, on doing Disney the Jewish way, or on the Holocaust.

"With the Internet, the audience reach-out is endless," said Porter.

All of Porter's interests stem from a desire to forward the Jewish tradition. It is a desire Porter seems to have carried with him for a lifetime. A desire rooted in memories of his upbringing, of his days at the only Jewish day school in town. And how his joy dissipated when the school rabbi absconded with all the money.

"There wasn't much [community] support for another school," he said.

Later on, Porter's drive took on revolutionary shapes. Embracing the student radicalism of the 1960s, Porter joined the Student Democratic Society. He began hanging out with the likes of Jerry Rubin and Abbie Hoffman, championing a world view based on social and civil justice, free speech and anti-oppression.

For Porter, his radicalism seems an extension of his Jewish heritage.

"As a child of survivors, I feel guilty about poverty and oppression," said Porter, as he rearranged the pens before him. "You want to do something to change society."

Porter may spend his days as deputy editor for an online magazine, but his radical impulses have hardly died down. In fact, according to Porter, activism in the 1990s is family-oriented. Activism now is about helping parents raise moral children in a society of decay. It's about helping parents raise active, involved kids of the future.

"The biggest thing is keeping the family together," said Porter, explaining that many baby boomers are clueless on how to parent in today's society. "Parents are caught between the freedom of the '60s and the conservatism of the '90s."

It seems that with everything Porter does, he satisfies his self-proclaimed desire to "spread the gospel on what it means to be a Jewish radical." Quite simply, he continues to think of working towards a mission, of contributing to society.

He continues to hear his parents' whispers of his special place in the world.

If he did not, Porter might "just get lost, spinning around alone," he said.

Sources

Fleming, Donald, and Bernard Bailyn. *The Intellectual Migration: Europe and America, 1930–1960.* Cambridge, MA: Harvard University Press, 1969.

Gerhardt, Uta. *Talcott Parsons on National Socialism.* New York: Aldine de Gruyter, 1993. The book that set the Talcott Parsons controversy aflame.

————. "Scholarship, Not Scandal." *Sociological Forum* 11, no. 4 (1996): 623–630. Her response to me and to Martin Oppenheimer.

Messina, Adele Valeria. *American Sociology and Holocaust Studies.* Boston: Academic Studies Press, 2017. Messina spends over twenty pages analyzing my work and research on Talcott Parsons and National Socialism and my role in Holocaust studies as a sociologist. See xx–xxiv and 44–57.

Oppenheimer, Martin. "Footnote to the Cold War: The Harvard Russian Research Center." *Monthly Review* 48 (1997): 7–17.

————. "Social Scientists and War Criminals." *New Politics* 6, no. 23 (1997).

————. Letter to the editor. *Sociological Forum* 12, no. 2 (1997): 339–341.

Pipes, Richard. *Vixi: Memoirs of a Non-Belonger.* New Haven and London: Yale University Press, 2003. An excellent book full of insights into the academic and political world.

Porter, Jack Nusan. "Toward a Sociology of National Socialism." Review of *Talcott Parsons on National Socialism* by Uta Gerhardt title of book. *Sociological Forum* 9, no. 3 (1994): 505–511.

————. "Talcott Parsons and National Socialism: The Case of the 'Ten Mysterious Missing Letters.'" *Sociological Forum* 11, no. 4 (1996): 603–611. I question why Parsons wrote nothing about National Socialism after 1946. Did the killing in Germany of his colleague Edward Hartshorne have anything to do with it?

————. *Jewish Partisans of the Soviet Union during World War II.* Newton, MA.: The Spencer Press, 2013 (originally published in 1982).

_____. *Sexual Politics in Nazi Germany.* Newton, MA: The Spencer Press, 2011.

_____. *The Genocidal Mind: Sociological and Sexual Perspectives.* Lanham, MD: University Press of America, 2006.

Weiner, Jon. "Talcott Parsons' Role Bringing Nazi Sympathizers to the US." *The Nation*, March 6, 1989, 305–309.

Wrong, Dennis. "Truth, Misinterpretation, or Left-wing McCarthyism?" *Sociological Forum* 11, no. 4 (1996): 623–630.

Chapter 29

Toward the Future / Miracles / Mormons / and Mahayana Meditation / Finding Peace and Love Again

———

I have seen in my lifetime various miracles and mysteries. I can't rationally prove any of them; either you believe in miracles or you don't. Here they are:

1. The miracle of my life being saved from the Nazis in 1944.
2. The miracle of our surviving the Holocaust and escaping from the Communist Soviet Union in 1945.
3. The miracle of our surviving the ocean voyage to America in 1946.
4. The miracle of my getting out of the Vietnam War military draft because of a blessing from the Bobover Rebbe in 1966.
5. The mystery of angels and other phenomena at my father's death in 1979.
6. The miracle of surviving Mallory-Weiss syndrome in 1991.
7. The mysterious phenomena I felt after the funeral in Rome of Pope John Paul II in April 2005.
8. And the miracle of life itself being tested during the 2020 coronavirus epidemic.

How does one analyze an ongoing life? I can see why some write two, three or more memoirs. There have been so many memorable times in my life that it has taken me several books to describe them. As Hemingway once said, "A well-lived life is the best revenge" (against death). With that, I'd like to talk about the miracles in my life that have helped me survive, plus some ideas, in these terrible times, on how to cope with death.

The year 2019 proved particularly painful, sort of like God telling me, "As you begin your seventy-fifth year on earth, I'm going to test you, Yankele." I lost nearly ten people in 2019, including my billionaire real estate business partner, Harold Brown; my accountant, Jewish War Veteran Post Commander George Marshall; the "kissing sailor of Times Square," my buddy George Mendonza; and several others. Plus, it was the second anniversary (*Yahrtzeit*) of my late wife Raya, who died in November 2017.

Yet 2019 would prove nothing compared to 2020 in terms of death. I was under a lot of stress at the end of December 2019 and January 2020, and so I went to the emergency room at St. Elizabeth's Medical Center in Brighton, Massachusetts, for mysterious pains in my side and shortness of breath. I took a lot of tests, but luckily they found no heart, kidney or lung problems. It was simply stress. But just maybe it was an early version of the coronavirus.

This all came several months before the global onset of the disease in March and April 2020. My sister was rushed to the hospital around Purim, March 8, for serious health problems, and we prayed for her. She was making a slow but steady recovery, but then she suddenly died on April 14, 2020. At the same time three of my nephews, her son Aryeh and my brother's two sons Meir and Nosson, all came down with the virus but recovered.

I searched my own religion for answers but found very little at first on material dealing with the afterlife, the soul, resurrection, and coping with death and dying. That is because Judaism stresses *this* life and *not* the afterlife as Christianity does. But I found comfort in two surprising places: Mormonism and Mahayana Buddhism. My good friend and high-school schoolmate Wayne Hilbig was a helpful guide to the world of Mormonism. Ever since one of our class reunions in Milwaukee, I always wanted to visit Wayne, and in the summer of 2019 I took a plane and a train out to Salt Lake City to see him and his lovely wife Susan.

His warm welcome was overwhelming. I was treated like a foreign dignitary. A special envoy greeted me—John Fillmore (yes, he was related to former US President Millard Fillmore) and his wife met me with gifts, brochures, lunch, and a grand tour of the Mormon Temple, capped off by a Sunday concert of the famed Mormon Tabernacle Choir. They even wanted to announce my presence to the crowd and over the radio across the country and overseas!

What did I learn from Wayne and Susan? The most important thing was that all Mormons are bonded with their families on this earth and in the afterlife *forever.* There is no fear; you will be reunited with your departed sisters, parents, grandparents and cousins, and you will live in a celestial Garden of Eden forever.

The second source of comfort was the writings of the great Zen teacher Thich Nhat Hanh. In fact, in the summer of 2018, when I went to Kiev to visit Raya's daughter and husband, I also wanted to take a grand tour on the Trans-Siberian Railway from Moscow to China and from there to Vietnam, where Thich Nhat lives in a monastery, but I became ill from the extreme heat and had to turn back.

His form of Zen Buddhism is a form of Mahayana Buddhism, and his books on meditation and acceptance of the present have helped me. They quelled my fear of flying (even though I have traveled to nearly forty countries) and helped accept whatever life throws my way, including death.

His series of books—*How to Sit, How to Eat,* and *How to Love*—are all forms of meditation. But the basis of Mahayana Buddhism is really Hermann Hesse's *Siddhartha,* which is the name of the Gautama, the Buddha. In this novel, Siddhartha, a young man, leaves his family for a contemplative life, and then, restless, discards it for one of the flesh. He conceives a son, but, bored and sickened by lust and greed, moves on again. Near despair, Siddhartha comes to a river, where he hears a unique sound. The sound signals the true beginning of his life—the beginning of suffering, rejection, peace, and finally wisdom.

It is the sound of enlightenment. Just reading this book can calm you.

But then I looked to my own faith. One book, suggested by my dear sister Bella, and one that we studied together, was *Living Emunah: Achieving a Life of Serenity through Faith* by Rabbi David Ashear.

Basically, what Rabbi Ashear is saying is that complete faith in God will bring tranquility and happiness. Just believe in Ha-shem, in God, and it will work. In fact, soon after studying with my sister, she herself suffered life-threatening events before and during the coronavirus, and, with all our prayers, another miracle happened and she recovered, but sadly, a few weeks later, she had complications from her colon cancer and died of pneumonia on April 14, 2020. Two weeks later, my first cousin, Allen Porter, the eminent designer and photographer, died at age 94 from the coronavirus in Evanston, Illinois.

There are works, especially in the Zohar and the Kabbalah, that deal with the afterlife, plus a book by Simcha Paull Raphael, *Jewish Views of the Afterlife,* that ties it all together.

I have had several events in my life that one could call miracles. One of my earliest was with the Bobover Rebbe, Rabbi Halberstam, in 1966 when he came to visit his sister, the Rebbetzin Leah Twerski, wife of the famed Chernobyler Rebbe Jacob Twerski of Milwaukee and mother of Rabbi Michel, Shia, Motel, Aaron, and Shlomo Twerski and their wonderful wives and children. I was about to go to the Selective Service Center for a physical and mental evaluation in order to be inducted into the army and possibly go to Vietnam.

My mother pleaded with the Rebbetzin for him to see me and give me a *bracha* (a supplicative prayer) in order that I not go to Vietnam. I entered the Rebbetzin's dining room, very nervous, with my mother and sat next to Rabbi Halberstam. I remember his beautiful face, white beard, and silver cane, his eyes sparkling, as he put his hand on mine, closed his eyes, and went into deep thought: "Ergesht nit tzu Vietnam," he exclaimed. "Mir gehen." ("He will not go to Vietnam." And "we must go" to catch the plane back to New York City.)

Armed with that prayer, I entered the induction center the next morning, very tense but hopeful. And the prayer worked! I flunked the physical and was given a high number to be called later, but I was never called for induction. The next day, my friend Shelly Bankier also went, but he had no prayer, and he was inducted into the army. (However, he played sick mentally and was released, so he, too, never went to Vietnam.)

Such is the power of the Rebbe!

Then, in 1979, there were the angels and images we saw when my father died in St. Joseph's Hospital in Milwaukee near our home. (See my essay "The Death of a Father" in this book.)

The third miracle/experience was Mallory-Weiss syndrome, which sent me to Newton-Wellesley Hospital in 1991 with internal bleeding. Again, it was induced from stress form my tenants in Roxbury. I collapsed at home. Luckily, my little daughter Danielle was there and called out, "Mommy, something's wrong. Daddy fell down." I was immediately rushed to the hospital. There they asked many strange questions, including: "Are you an alcoholic?" "Do you vomit a lot?"

I answered no, I was not an alcoholic, but I had been vomiting a lot, because my mother said that if I stuck my finger down my throat and vomited it would relieve the headaches I was getting from the stress. The problem was that it also twisted the esophagus and could cause internal bleeding. This is the Mallory-Weiss syndrome. I had fainted in front of my children from lack of blood. But, given transfusions and fluids (I lost four pints of blood), my life was saved by doctors, and I was nursed back to health by my wife and children. I had survived.

The fourth mystery was in April 2005 at the funeral of Pope John Paul II in Rome. I decided on a whim to go to Rome. I arrived to find that four million people had come to Rome, one million of them Polish citizens, some driving for thirteen hours straight to attend and then thirteen more for the drive back.

I vividly remember everyone around me on their knees except the camera crews and me. Jews do not bow; the event was so intense. Later that night in my hotel room at the Hotel Florida, I had an epiphany. I saw angels and celestial beings climbing a ladder, and I was calmed. I promised God I would become a good person and do good in this world.

So, you see, I believe in miracles and I believe in God speaking to us in mysterious ways, and thus I will find hope and love and happiness as I enter the last stages of my life.

Sources

Ashear, Rabbi David. *Living Emunah.* Brooklyn: Art Scroll Books, 2017. Very useful in coping with illness, dying, and everyday stress.

Encyclopedia Judaica. s.v. "Afterlife." 2 vols (1971).

Hanh, Thich Nhat. *How to Sit.* Berkeley: Parallax Press, 2014. He is one of the greatest Buddhist monks of all time.

Hesse, Hermann. *Siddhartha.* New York: Bantam Books, 1981 (originally published in 1951). The classic text of our time. Reading it will calm you.

Raphael, Simcha Paull. *Jewish Views of the Afterlife.* 3rd edition. Lanham, MD: Rowman & Littlefield, 2019. The most complete book on its subject.

"Miracle." *Celebration* [a Chabad/Lubavitch magazine], March 9–10, 2020.

Michie, David. *Buddhism for Busy People.* Ithaca, N.Y.: Snow Lion Publications, 2008.

Paulson, Michael, and Charles M. Sennott. "A Hero for the Ages: Pope John Paul II, Catholics' Dynamic Leader, Dead at 84." *Boston Globe,* April 3, 2005. Front page article.

Sonsino, Rabbi Rifat, and Daniel B. Syme. *What Happens after I Die?* New York: UHAC Press, 1990.

Spitz, Elie Kaplan. *Does the Soul Survive?* Woodstock, VT: Jewish Lights, 2000. Sensitive and useful.

Photographs

Family in Maniewiecze, Ukraine. My father at top, age twenty-one; his parents, Yaakov Puchtik and Bella Singerman Puchtik, sitting below him; his fifteen-year-old younger brother Boris to his left; and his sister to his right, either Chasia (b. 1908) or Zelda (b. 1910); the young boy could be the son of another sister Rachel (b. 1900).

My grandparents, Maniewiecze, 1939. Grandpa Yaakov Puchtik (b. 1870) and Grandma Bella Singerman Puchtik (b. 1875). They were sixty-nine and sixty-four, respectively. This picture was taken just a few months before WW II began in September 1939.

The famous "Partisan Baby" photo, Rovno, Ukraine, Spring1945. Notice: my father's uniform, boots, and Partisan First Class Medal; my mother's sadness and swollen feet; my dyspepsia.

A rare photo of my relatives, my father's sisters, and their husbands and children, in our shtetl in Maniewicze, Ukraine, before the war. Everyone was killed by the Nazis.

Pictures of the displaced persons camp in Bindermichel, Linz, Austria, 1946. Mrs. Blasberg and friend are in front of the building that housed the camp.

Me (the cute kid) and my dad (center/left) with other fathers and their young children; American GI in the background; Mr. Sender Lande and his daughter Leah on the right.

Group of partisan friends outside Camp Bindermichel. My dad is on the lower left, Moshe Kramer is on the lower right.

Displaced persons waiting with their luggage.

Group portrait of passengers.

Old neighborhood, Tenth and Garfield, Milwaukee, WI. "Boys in the Hood." Our home is on the right. Picture courtesy of Harriet Spicer, née Cox.

Lonny and Anna Cox, owners of the sandwich and BBQ restaurant that stood in front of our home on Tenth Street. Picture courtesy of Harriet Spicer, née Cox.

The Greater Galilee Baptist Church, formerly Congregation Beth Israel, home of the Milwaukee Hebrew Academy.

Picture of Mom, Dad, Sol, and Bella, 1963.

Beth Am Center, possibly a bar mitzvah, late '50s. Larry Weidenbaum and wife, back-right; my mother second from right; Mr. Rosman on right; Mrs. Rosman, in front-left; Mr. and Mrs. Sender and Edith Lande on left; and back-left Mr. and Mrs. Ziggy Singer.

Cousin Allen Porter, designer and photographer, with his business partner, in their Chicago office.

From left: Uncle Morris, Aunt Betty and cousin Allen Porter, in Los Angeles, in the 1950s.

Washington High School.

Golda Meir visiting Milwaukee; ambassador to the United States Yitzhak Rabin is on her right; Milwaukee's Mayor Maier is on the far right with Milwaukee leaders.

Golda Meir reception at airport. My sister is in the center of the crowd.

Father Groppi leading marches.

The police guarding the march that I was on.

Barney Rosset and Fred Jordan, Grove Press offices, c. 1970.
Photo by Bob Adelman.

Native American leader Wild Cat and me.

Photo of Joseph (Yotza) Almuly.

Mom and me.

Me, with Raya, running for US Congress in April 2012, in front of Newton (MA) City Hall.

MEDITATION
Sri Swami Satchidananda

Swami Satchidananda.

Me and Jerry Rubin, radical '60s leader at Abbie Hoffman's funeral, Worcester, Mass. Courtesy *Lifestyles* magazine.

With my brother and sister.

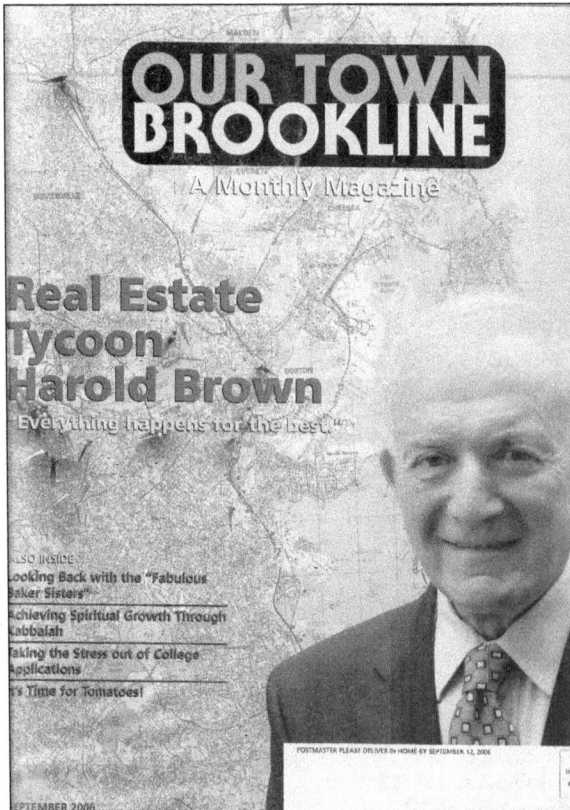

Harold Brown, my mentor in real estate.

Glossary of Terms

Afula: A city in the Jezreel Valley in the Northern District of Israel, often called the "Capital of the Valley."

agora (pl. *agorot*): A monetary unit of Israel, equal to one hundredth of a *shekel*.

agun: "Chained husband."

agunah: "Chained wife."

ahavas torah: "Love of Torah" (Hebrew).

ahavat avodah: Love of work and the land of Israel (Hebrew).

Alei U'vnei: "Arise and Build" (Hebrew)., the motto of Habonim (see below).

aliyah: Moving to Israel.

Aliyah Bet: The illegal voyages to Palestine, especially of children from Europe, before the state of Israel was established.

apparat: An administrative system of the Communist Party, particularly in a Communist nation.

apparatchnik: A member of a Communist apparat.

avodah: "Work, worship, and service" (Hebrew). May refer to agricultural work, business-type activities, and serving God.

baal tesuva or *baal teshuva:* a secular or Reform Jew who has become Orthodox. Yiddish, lit. "returnee to the faith," or "master of repentance" according to the Talmud.

balagan: Chaos or fiasco (derived from modern Hebrew).

Beersheva or Be'er Sheva: The largest city in the Negev desert of southern Israel.

beit midrash: House of study (Hebrew).

Bi'lin or Bil'in: A Palestinian village in the Ramallah and al-Bireh Governorate, twelve km west of the city of Ramallah in the central West Bank, with a mostly Muslim population.

Bindermichel or Bindermichl: a Displaced Persons (DP) camp near Linz, Austria, where the Porters lived for a short time before their coming to America.

Blitzkrieg: German for "lightning war," the lightning-fast invasion of Poland by Germany on September 1, 1939, official beginning World War II.

B'nei Akiva: The world's largest Zionist youth movement, established in 1929 in Mandatory Palestine and now boasting more than 125,000 members in forty-two nations.

B'nai B'rak: A city on Israel's central Mediterranean coastal plain just east of Tel Aviv; a center of Haredi Judaism.

boyova: A fighting unit (Russian), for example, of the Kruks partisan group during World War II.

bracha: Prayer (Hebrew and Yiddish).

Breicha **(or B'rikha):** The illegal movement of Jews from Europe to Palestine after World War II.

Breira (full name: "Breira: A Project of Concern in Diaspora-Israel Relations:"): An organization founded to express a left-wing position on Israel, lasting from 1973 to 1977.

bris: The Jewish ceremony of circumcision.

brit: Circumcision.

brocha: Blessing (Hebrew).

Chabad: An Orthodox Jewish Hasidic movement; an acronym formed from the Hebrew words *Chochmah, Binah, Da'at,* meaning "Wisdom, Understanding, and Knowledge."

chalutziut **or** *chalutzic:* Pioneering (Hebrew).

Chasid **or** *Hasid:* a member of a Jewish sect founded in Poland in the eighteenth century by Baal Shem-Tov, emphasizing mysticism, prayer, strict adherence to ritual, religious zeal, and experience of the joy of communion with God.

chasunah: Wedding (Hebrew).

chatan: Bridegroom (Hebrew).

chaushis: Disaster (Yiddish).

Chaverim **or** *Chaveirim:* An umbrella name for Orthodox Jewish volunteer organizations providing free roadside assistance and other non-medical emergency aid.

chavurah or *havurah*: A small group of like-minded Jews who assemble to facilitate Shabbat (the Sabbath) and holiday prayer services, share communal experiences such as lifecycle events, or facilitate Jewish learning.

Chayyim (also *Haim, Hayim, Chayim,* or *Chaim*): Life (Hebrew).

chazir schmalz: *Pig fat.*

chesed: Grace, benevolence, or compassion (Hebrew).

Chevra Kadisha: A Jewish burial society (literally "holy society")

Choroshoy: "It's okay" (Russian).

chugim: Elective courses or activities in a Jewish/Hebrew education program or camp.

chupa (or *chuppa* or *chuppah*): The canopy under which a Jewish couple stand during their wedding ceremony (Hebrew).

Cossacks: A fierce Soviet tribal group, noted as cavalrymen and warriors.

Devekut, debekuth, deveikuth or *deveikus*: Closeness to God, which may be in the form of a meditative trance experienced during prayer, Torah study, or performance the 613 mitzvot.

D.P. or DP: Displaced Person or camp; stateless refugees.

Eilat: A southern Israeli port and resort town on the Red Sea, near Jordan, noted for its calm beach waters.

Einsatzgruppen: Schutzstaffel (SS) paramilitary death squads of Nazi Germany, responsible for mass killings during World War II in occupied Europe.

eishes chayil: A woman of valor or exceptional courage (Hebrew); named for a portion of the Proverbs 31:10–31 traditionally sung before the Friday night Shabbat repast.

emuna or *emunah*: Faith (Hebrew).

emunah peshuta: Simple faith (Hebrew).

Eretz Yisroel: Land of Israel (Yiddish and Hebrew).

Erev: The day before (e.g., *Erev Yom Kippur*, "the day before Yom Kippur") (Hebrew)

Farband: An American Jewish Labor Zionist fraternal order, founded in Philadelphia in 1908.

Finjan: An Arabic term for a special coffeepot Israelis use to make black coffee.

The *Forward*: A popular national Yiddish newspaper.

frum: Religious (Yiddish).

frumer shul: An Orthodox synagogue (Yiddish).

Gan Eden: The Garden of Eden; heaven.

Gan Hazikaron: A garden of remembrance.

garin: Seed (Hebrew).

gefilte fish: A popular food made from fish balls (Yiddish).

Gehinnom: Hell; purgatory.

genizah: An area in a Jewish synagogue or cemetery for the temporary storage of worn-out Hebrew-language books and papers on religious topics prior to proper cemetery burial.

glatt: "Smooth" (Hebrew), referring to an animal's lungs with no adhesions; commonly used in *glatt kosher.*

Geonim: Jewish leaders.

greeneh: Newcomers to America; greenhorns (Yiddish).

Habima Theatre: The national theater of Israel.

Habonim (later Habonim/Dror): The Labor Zionist youth movement.

hachnasas orchim: Hospitality, welcoming guests (Hebrew).

Haftarah: A series of selections from the books of Nevi'im of the Hebrew Bible that is publicly read in synagogue, following the Torah reading on each Sabbath and on Jewish festivals and fast days.

Haganah: A Zionist paramilitary organization created in 1920 to defend Jewish communities from Arab attacks, such as their 1920 attack in Jerusalem, and the Great Arab Revolt of 1936–1939 in Mandatory Palestine. The Haganah was integrated into the Israeli army in 1948 upon Israel's establishment as an independent state.

hagshamat-atzmi: Self-realization (Hebrew).

halachic: Of the *Halakha*, the collective body of Jewish religious laws derived from the written and Oral Torah based on biblical commandments and subsequent Talmudic and rabbinic law.

hamsin: A dry, hot desert wind.

handlen: Action, or engagement in a trade (Yiddish).

Hanoar Hatzioni: A youth movement (full name: Histadrut Halutzit Olamit Hanoar Hatzioni, or HH for short) established in 1926, with its head offices now in Israel. Its three main pillars are Chalutzism, Pluralism, and Zionism.

Hashem or *HaShem*: A casual term for God; Hebrew lit., "the name."

Hashomer: "The Watchman" (Hebrew); a Jewish defense organization in Palestine founded in April 1909 in Palestine but disbanded after the founding of the Haganah in 1920.

Hasid or *Hassid* (pl. *Hasidim* or *Hassidim*): Devotees of Hasidism (or Hassidism, Chassidism, or Hasidic Judaism), a Jewish religious group that arose as a spiritual revival movement in the territory of contemporary Western Ukraine during the eighteenth century and spread rapidly throughout Eastern Europe, emphasizing devotion to one's *rebbe* (rabbi) as a channel to become closer to God.

Hillel: The Foundation for Jewish Campus Life (aka **Hillel International** or **Hillel**): The world's largest Jewish campus organization in the world, with chapters at more than 550 colleges and communities worldwide. Named for Hillel the Elder, a Jewish sage who moved from Babylonia to Judea in the first century, known for his formulation of the Golden Rule.

hofesh: Free time (Hebrew).

Horodok: Faye Porter's birthplace (sometimes called **Grodok**) in Ukraine, now in Belarus.

Ichud Habonim: Jack Porter's Labor Zionist youth movement group at the time of his 1963 visit to Israel.

ir: City (Hebrew).

irbutz: An urban collective, like a commune in a rented apartment building (Hebrew).

Joint: The Joint Distribution Committee, an international organization that helped refugees in Europe.

Judenrat: A World War II administrative agency imposed by Nazi Germany on Jewish communities across occupied Europe, mainly within the Nazi ghettos. The Germans required Jews to form a Judenrat in every community across the occupied territories.

Judenrein or *Judenfrei*: A Nazi term for an area "cleansed" of Jews or excluding Jews during the Holocaust.

Kabbalah: A set of esoteric teachings in Jewish mysticism meant to explain the relationship between God, the unchanging, eternal, and mysterious *Ein Sof* ("The Infinite"), and the mortal and finite universe (God's creation).

Kach: A radical Orthodox Jewish, ultranationalist political party in Israel, founded by Rabbi Meir Kahane in 1971, based on his Jewish-Orthodox-nationalist ideology, dissolved in 1994.

kaddish: An ancient Jewish prayer sequence regularly recited in the synagogue service, including thanksgiving and praise and concluding with a prayer for universal peace.

kalla: Bride (Hebrew).

Karnei Hittin: The Horns of Hattin, an extinct twin-peaked volcano overlooking the plains of Hattin in the Lower Galilee, Israel.

kashrut (or *kashruth* or *kashrus*): The body of Jewish laws governing the suitability of foods, for example, for Pesach (Passover) (Hebrew).

Kedoshim, *K'doshim*, or *Qedoshim* ("Holy ones" in Hebrew): The thirtieth weekly Torah portion in the annual Jewish cycle of Torah reading, and the seventh cycle in Leviticus 19:1–20:27.

Keriah: The rending of clothes.

keter: Crown.

Kfar Hittim: Israel's first *moshav shitufi* and tower/stockade settlement, located in northern Israel on a hill 3 km west of Tiberias.

Kfar Vitkin: A *moshav* in central Israel, named for Labor movement leader Yosef Vitkin.

kibbutz: A communal settlement in Israel, typically a farm.

kibbutznik: A kibbutz dweller.

kiddush or *kidush:* Literally, "sanctification," a blessing recited over wine or grape juice to sanctify the Shabbat and Jewish holidays (Hebrew).

kiruv: "Bringing close" (Hebrew); an act of bring Jews closer to God, each other, and their Jewish heritage in fulfillment of the Biblical principal, "Love thy neighbor as thyself."

Knesset: The unicameral national legislature of Israel, responsible for passing all laws, electing the President, Prime Minister and State Comptroller, approving the cabinet, and supervising the Israeli government's daily functions.

kosher: Clean or fit to eat according to Jewish law and customs, e.g., for Pesach (Passover).

Kruk: Nikolai Kanishchuk, the Ukrainian Communist leader of the partisan band that the Porters fought in. He was killed after the war by Ukrainian family members.

kumsitz or *kumzits:* A musical gathering that Jews partake in.

kupah: Communal sharing (Hebrew).

lamed vovnik: A "thirty-sixer," one of the thirty-six chosen few who can save mankind from destruction, according to Hebraic tradition.

landsmanschaft: A mutual aid society, benefit society, or hometown society of Jewish immigrants from the same European town or region.

levaya: Funeral (Hebrew).

Lishnifkeh: Irving Porter's birthplace.

Machon: Short for **Machon L'Madrechei M'Chutz L'Aretz**, or the Institute for Youth Leaders from Abroad.

madregot: Steps; stages.

madrich: Leader (Hebrew).

malchut: Kingdom.

Malenka: The *nom de guerre* ("raspberry") of Bert Lorber, one of the most important commanders in the Kruk-Maks Group.

Malbish b'kavod: "Dress with honor" (Hebrew).

Maniewicze, Maniewicz, Manievitch or **Manevitz:** A small resort town in northwestern Ukraine, where all of the Jews from the surrounding areas were taken and killed; the site of the massive "Maniewicz massacre."

Marine Perch: The American ship that took the Porter family to America in June of 1946.

maskirut: Headquarters (Hebrew).

mazel: Luck (Hebrew).

mazel tov: A Jewish phrase expressing congratulations or wishing someone good luck.

Megilat Esther: The scroll of Esther, a firsthand account of the events of Purim, written by Esther and Mordechai.

melamed: A religious teacher or instructor.

meshigas: Craziness (Yiddish).

meshulach or *meshullach*: "Messenger" (Hebrew and Yiddish); an emissary of rabbis, sent to collect funds for charities (Hebrew).

middurah: Campfire (Hebrew).

mikveh or *mikvah*: A bath for the ritual immersion of a Jew to enable that bather to achieve ritual purity (Hebrew).

minyan: A group of ten men.

Misnagdim: The Jews of Eastern Europe who resisted the rise of Hasidism in the 18th and 19th centuries, primarily concentrated in Lithuania

mitzvah (pl. *mitzvot*): An act of righteousness; religious duty; or precepts and commandments ordained by God (Hebrew).

Mogen Davids: Star of Davids (Yiddish and Hebrew).

mohel: A person who performs the Jewish rites of marriage and circumcision (Hebrew).

moshav: A cooperative Israeli agricultural community of individual farms pioneered by the Labor Zionists during the second wave of *aliyah*.

moshavnik: A *moshav* dweller.

moshav shitufi: A cooperative Israeli village in which farm and agricultural production services are handled collectively but consumption of the goods are determined by individual households.

Mount Tabor: A mountain in Lower Galilee, Israel, at the eastern end of the Jezreel Valley, the site of the Battle of Mount Tabor between the Israelite army under Barak's leadership of Barak and the army of the Canaanite king of Hazor, Jabin, under Sisera's command, and the site of the transfiguration of Jesus in Christian tradition.

nekamah or *nekumah*: Revenge. (Yiddish)

New American Club: The local group that Jewish refugees organized to help them acculturate in America.

oblava: An action by the Germans to surround an area, or to clear out the partisans by raiding the forests and burning the encampments. (Russian)

otryad: A partisan fighting group, for example, the civilian section of the Kruks partisan group during World War II. (Russian)

Palmach: The elite fighting force of the Haganah, the underground army of the Jewish community during the British Mandate for Palestine from 1941 to 1948.

Parshiot or parshas: Portions, or parts, of a Biblical text.

Petach Tikvah or **Petach Tikva:** A city in the Central District of Israel, 10.6 km east of Tel Aviv, founded in 1878 primarily by Orthodox Jews of the Old Yishuv (Jewish community). Also known as Em HaMoshavot.

Po'alei Zion: Workers for Zion, a movement of Marxist-Zionist Jewish workers founded in various cities of Poland, Europe and the Russian Empire shortly after the Bund, a Jewish socialist and secular movement founded in the Russian Empire in 1897, rejected Zionism in 1901.

Pollacks or **Polacks** (pl. **Polakim**): Yiddish for Polish citizens, sometimes derogatory.

Rabbi Meir Baal HaNes: A Jewish sage who lived in the time of the Mishna, considered one of the greatest of the Tannaim of the fourth generation.

rabbonim: Rabbis (Yiddish).

Ramat Gan: A city in Israel's Tel Aviv District, east of the municipality of Tel Aviv. Established as a *moshav* in 1921, it is now home to one of the world's major diamond exchanges and numerous high tech industries.

Rambam: An acronym for Moses ben Maimon, also known as Maimonides, a medieval Sephardic Jewish philosopher, astronomer and physician who was one of the most prolific, influential Torah scholars of the Middle Ages.

Rehovot: A city in the Central District of Israel, about 20 km south of Tel Aviv.

Rephual: "God will heal" (Hebrew).

rikud: Israeli dancing (Hebrew).

rosh: Leader (Hebrew).

Rosh HaNikra: A kibbutz in northern Israel on the Mediterranean coast near the Lebanese border.

Rosh Yeshiva: the title given to the dean of a *yeshiva* (see below).

Rovno: The large city in Ukraine where Jack Nusan Porter was born.

ruach: Spirit, *esprit de corps* (Hebrew).

Savyon: A local council in the Central District of Israel, bordering the cities of Kiryat Ono, Petah Tikva, and Yehud.

schnorrer: Beggar, sponger, scrounger, layabout (Yiddish); one who asks for small handouts without offering anything in return.

sefer Torah: A scroll containing the Torah or Pentateuch (Hebrew).

Shabbat or **Shabbos:** The Sabbath (Yiddish).

shalom: Peace, used as a greeting upon meeting or to wish someone well upon parting (Hebrew).

shalom bayis or *shalom bayit*: The Jewish religious concept of domestic harmony and good relations between husband and wife. It is the Hebrew term for "marital reconciliation" in a Jewish court of law.

shadchenta: Matchmaker(?).

shecht: To slaughter meat according to the rituals of *kashrut* (Yiddish).

Shema Yisroel: "Hear, O Israel" (Hebrew); a prayer said when a Jew is in great danger.

shidduch: Matchmaker, a Jewish arranged marriage, or a system of matchmaking in which Jewish singles are introduced to one another in Orthodox Jewish communities for the purpose of marriage (Hebrew).

shiksa(s): A Gentile woman (or women); sometimes derogatory.

shira: Singing (Hebrew).

Shiva: The seven days of mourning.

shmatte: An article of clothing, or a rag (derived from Yiddish).

shmira: Guard duty (Hebrew).

Shoah: The Holocaust (from the Hebrew *HaShoah*, "the catastrophe")

shochet: Someone officially certified as competent to slaughter cattle and poultry as prescribed by Jewish law (Hebrew).

shomer: Guard (Hebrew).

shtarker: A man of great physical strength (Yiddish).

shtetl (pl. *shtetlach*): A small Jewish village or part of a village where Jews live.

shul: Synagogue.

shvartzes: Blacks (Yiddish); sometimes derogatory.

sicha: Discussion (Hebrew).

Sim Shalom: A blessing recited at the end of the morning Amidah and the Mincha Amidah during fast days in the Ashkenazic tradition, or at all prayer services in the Sefardic, Chasidic-Sefardic, and Nusach Ari rites.

smicha: Rabbinic ordination.

Stollener Hassidim: A band of ultra-Orthodox Jews.

tahara: The ritual washing and dressing of the body in preparation for the afterlife.

Tateh: "Daddy," an affectionate Yiddish term.

tchukkralneys: Fiber processors.

Tehillim: The Book of Psalms, the first book of the *Ketuvim* in the third section of the Hebrew Bible.

tikkun olam: The overcoming of all forms of idolatry, or a general aspiration to behave and act constructively and beneficially.

tiyul: Hike (Hebrew), usually in the country or the woods.

tofim: Clay drums.

toranut: Cleanup (Hebrew).

Tza'adah: Celebratory march.

tzadekis: "Holy Woman"; a saint, or a caring, helpful woman (Hebrew).

tzadik: "Holy Man"; a saint, or a caring, helpful man (Hebrew).

tzedakah: "Justice" or "righteousness" (Hebrew) in the form of charity or charitable giving, as an ethical obligation.

tzitlach: Receipts for money paid or donated.

tzrif: A bunk or cabin at a camp.

ulpan: An institute or school for the intensive study of Hebrew for adult immigrants to Israel. Meaning "studio," "teaching," or "instruction" in Hebrew.

Vatik: A veteran Israeli.

viorst or *voyrst*: An uncertain Slavism for distance measurement, perhaps longer than a kilometer.

wadi: A valley, ravine, or channel that is dry except in the rainy season.

Wandervogel: A movement of German youth groups from 1896 to 1933, protesting against industrialization by hiking in the country and communing with nature.

yellow patches: The yellow stars or patches that Jews had to wear in Nazi-occupied Europe.

yeshiva (pl. *yeshivot*): An Orthodox Jewish seminary or place of study, focusing on the study of traditional religious texts, primarily the Talmud and the Torah, and *halakha* (Jewish law).

Yiddishkeit: Jewishness; the quality of being Jewish; the Jewish way of life or its customs and practices.

yiras shamayim: Fear of Heaven, fear of God (Hebrew).

Yohanan ben Zakkai: A Jewish sage in the era of the Second Temple, and a main contributor to the core text of Rabbinical Judaism, the *Mishnah*.

Yom Ha'atzmaut: The annual celebration of Israel's Independence Day toward the end of April, commemorating the Israeli Declaration of Independence in 1948.

Zalonka: The *nom de guerre* ("green") for Irving Porter; it means "green" in Russian.

zemirot: Jewish hymns or songs, often sung during *Shabbat* and Jewish holidays.

zemlonka: A bunker, lean-to, hut, or makeshift shelter that hid partisans in the forest.

z'man sikum: Culminating sessions.

Appendix

My Contribution to
Knowledge

————

I.   Contributions to Jewish Thought—since 1967

Influences: Morris U. Schappes, Yuri Suhl, Moshe Kerem, Label Fein, various Jewish-Socialist or Socialist-Zionist thinkers such as Tzvi Bisk and Moshe Zedek

- Jewish radicalism / Jewish Left / Jewish Counterculture / Marxism and Judaism
- Black-Jewish relations
- Self-hatred Among Jews
- *The Jew as Outsider*—book
- "The Jewish Student"—the YIVO Annual article on Yale and Northwestern University students
- The Jewish woman—Rosa Sonneschein
- The Jewish homosexual—Magnus Hirschfeld
- Neo-Nazism—several articles
- The sociology of American Jews
- How to be a rabbi
- The *Agunah* (the "chained wife") and the *Agun* (the "chained husband") in a divorce

II.   Contributions to Holocaust Studies—since 1971

Influences: Yuri Suhl, Yehuda Merin, Erich Goldhagen, Yehuda Bauer, Omeljan Pritsak, Magnus Hirschfeld, George Mosse

- Resistance to Nazism in general
- Soviet partisan resistance
- Jewish "family-camps" in the forest
- Jewish women fighters
- Ukrainian-Jewish relations
- Sexual and other deviance among Nazi leadership[37]

III.   Contributions to Holocaust Studies—since 1971

Influences: Helen Fein, Kurt Jonassohn, Vahakn Dadrian, Steve Katz, Israel Charny, Adam Jones, Dirk Moses, Greg Stanton

- Definition of genocide and misapplications of term
- Sex and gender aspects of genocide
- Resistance to genocide
- Denial of genocide
- Predicting genocide
- Mathematical models to predict genocide
- New directions for genocide research—new "postmodern" theories
- Bridging the gap between Holocaust and genocide studies

IV.   Contributions to Sociology and Anthropology— since 1968

Sociological Influences: Howard S. (Howie) Becker, Bernie Beck, Charlie Moskos, Irwin Rinder, Lakshimi Barawaj, C. Wright Mills, Alvin Gouldner, Marcello Truzzi

Anthropological Influences: Sidney Greenfield, Robert Silverberg, Paul Bohannon, the guy at UCLA

---

37 See my book *The Genocidal Mind: Sociological and Sexual Perspectives.*

- The Theory of "middlemanship" (triadic coalition, situational theory, the urban middleman)
- Conflict and conflict resolution
- Radical sociology
- Cults and religious movements
- The culture of Kurds, Armenians, Azidis, Palestinians, and Ukrainians
- "Soft" methods; unobtrusive methods
- Culture: new approaches
- Off-beat sociology (the work of Marcello Truzzi)

V.   Contributions to Media, Film, Design, and Networking—since 1968

Influences: Allen Porter, Marlon Porter, Steve Samuels, Malcolm Gladwell, Ty Burr, Richard Snyder, Jessica Lipnack, Robert Schwartz, Frank Lloyd Wright, the Bauhaus School of Design

- Rebellion and revolution in film
- LBGQ reviews of film. For example, *The Cake Maker, Tom of Finland*
- The Ahimsa Project of Networking
- Film reviews
- Film noir
- Critique of the media
- The sociology of architecture
- Design, LA, Chicago and Bauhaus

VI. Contributions to Prose, Poetry, and Memoirs—since 1967

Influences: various English teachers at Washington High School and the University of Wisconsin–Milwaukee, also Milwaukee Raconteur John Allschwaung

- Memoirs of Milwaukee, Maniewicze (Ukraine) and Milford (Massachusetts)
- Radical poetry and prose
- Hollywood screen treatments

VII. Contribution to Political Activism—since 1965

Influences: Jerry Rubin, Abbie Hoffman, Lee Weiner, Steve Buff, Father James Groppi of Milwaukee, Saul Alinsky, Chuck Turner, singers Steve Goodman, Bob Dylan, Judy Collins; Crosby, Stills, Nash, and Young; Country Joe McDonald and the Fish; Jefferson Airplane (Marty Balin, Paul Kantner, et al.)

- Civil rights, specifically open housing for African Americans in Milwaukee and Chicago; marched with Martin Luther King Jr. and Father James Groppi, 1967
- Anti-Vietnam war march on Washington, 1969
- Pro-Palestinian rights, marched and was tear-gassed in Bi'lin on the West Bank, 2011
- Protested the Turkish and US and the ADL regarding the Armenian Genocide, 2007
- Trip to Northern Iraq in 2007 for Kurdish and Azidi rights
- Fighting for Ukrainian Freedom against Russia and Putin, 2012
- Fighting anti-Zionism since 1967
- Fighting antisemitism my whole life

Famous People I Have Met or Who Have Influenced Me

————————

In my over seventy years on this planet (I was seventy-five on December 2, 2019), I have managed to meet quite a few interesting and famous people, some very briefly (Jackie Kennedy Onassis), some from afar (John F. Kennedy), some for as much as a half-hour (David Ben-Gurion), and some over many years.

I am sorry that I never met Hitler or Stalin (I'd probably be dead if I did) or Karl Marx or Charles de Gaulle or Winston Churchill, or Jean-Paul Sartre or Simone de Beauvoir, though I have met people who knew them—Claude Lanzmann, for example, knew Sartre and De Beauvoir, and may have been her lover. Also, I never knew Albert Memmi or, most of all, Marilyn Monroe, Elvis, or James Dean, though I do fantasize that I saw and dated Marilyn in New York City in the late '50s when I visited there as a teenager; but it was, sadly, just that, a fantasy. I know people who knew Elvis and James Dean, though. Yes, I do.

I also include people who were one or three degrees away from me. It's unbelievable that, no matter how famous and influential they are, one can eventually get two or three degrees from anyone in history. Hitler, however, is the only person to whom I could not find someone close enough and who lived to talk about it, but if I try hard enough, I think I could find someone who at least *saw* him. I knew people who were two degrees away from Stalin. Really. But Hitler was difficult. Here's my list:

Joseph Stalin

My father, Irving Porter (Srulik Puchtik), after World War II met a man taking notes and copying the writings of Jews who died in the Shoah. The place was a school or a public building where they were held before being put on trains and killed. During the time that they waited, they often left written notes or wrote on the walls, sometimes with their own blood, one last goodbye. The name of the man who took those notes was Soviet writer Peretz Markish, and he had met Stalin with a large group of intellectuals.

Stalin later killed him, Solomon Mikhoels, and members of the Jewish Anti-Fascist Committee plus other Jewish intellectuals in a fit of antisemitic rage in the early 1950s. As I've said, anyone who met Stalin or Hitler probably died. Luckily, my dad met Markish in 1945 after the war, somewhere in Ukraine.

Sigmund Freud

I never met him, since he died in 1939, six years before my birth, but I "knew" him through not one but two people. The first was my former "aunt-in-law" Lea (Leytza) Almuly, my former wife Miriam's aunt, a sister to her father Joseph Almuly, whom I have described elsewhere in these memoirs, and sister-in-law to Reli Almuly, Joseph's wife. Leah was born in Yugoslavia to a wealthy upper-class Sephardic family—the "Grandees," Stephen Birmingham would call them, the elite of world Jewry.

My aunt-in-law Leytza (Lea) Almuly, a funny, quirky spinster who was my father-in-law Joseph (Yotza) Almuly's sister, was one of the first to go into therapy with Wilhelm Stekel (1868–1940), an Austrian physician and psychologist who became one of Freud's earliest followers and most eminent students. She never told me the details of her psychotherapy, but she had come from the upper class and suffered their neuroses. I believe the therapy took place when Lea lived in Vienna.

She must have been sensitive, suffering from, what they called in the *fin-de-siècle* era, "hysteria"—what we would call today a "nervous breakdown"—depression, suppressed anger, phobic activity, an obsessive behavior. Her parents sent her to Stekel for psychotherapy in the 1930s.

I am not sure what impact the new science of "psychoanalysis" had on Laytza, but she never married, had a strong attachment to her brother, almost in competition to Reli, his wife. But she was a fascinating and loving person, and I am glad I knew her. Her tales of life in Vienna and Belgrade in the 1930s were rare and valuable. She died in Newton, Massachusetts, at age 89.

The second person I knew briefly was Sophia Lowenstein Freud, Freud's grandniece, who was a professor of psychology and social work at Simmons College in Boston. I traveled to her home in Lexington, Massachusetts, and I told her about Laytza and her analysis. Sophia was a lovely woman.

Edward Bernays

Ironically, Freud left behind many surviving relatives. One of them was an early sociologist and marketing guru named Edward Bernays, a relative of Freud's wife, a Bernays. My connection to Bernays was threefold.

First, his work was influential in my field of "applied sociology." He actually used sociological methods to sell products and was arguably the first mass marketing expert.

Second, I knew his daughter, Ann Bernays, a middling successful novelist and "book leader" in Boston as the long-time head of New England PEN, the writers' "club" in the '80s and '90s. I found her very domineering and arrogant and not a very nice person. Example: In 1986, Elie Wiesel won the Nobel Peace Prize, and I asked Ann if I could invite him to speak to a PEN meeting. She said, "He won for 'peace,' not literature. He's not really a serious writer." Actually, several New York critics like Irving Howe said the same thing: that Wiesel was not a very good writer of fiction—essays perhaps but not fiction—and *Night*, his most famous book, was not fiction but based on a true story and was considered nonfiction. Later, however, in New York, if not Boston, Wiesel was recognized by PEN.

Finally, I attended a bizarre trial in probate court when late in life, in his nineties, Edward Bernays took up with a younger woman in her fifties, and his two daughters, Ann included, went to Probate Court to make sure the woman would get nothing from the estate. What was odd is that John Silber, then president of Boston University—where Wiesel taught, by the way—took the stand to defend the paramour and said she was a fine, upstanding person and did not marry Bernays for his money. The woman lost the case, and the estate rested firmly in the hands of his daughters. I attended the trial, and I don't think Ann Bernays was happy to see me there, even though I was just a curious bystander.

Wilhelm Reich

My connection was my very short-term therapy with one of Reich's students, Myron (Mickey) Sharaf. He lived in Newton Highlands at 18 Dunklee St., just a few blocks from my house. It was in the mid-1990s, and I met him at a coffee house. He had written a well-received book about Reich (*Fury on Earth*, 1983). He even had an Orgone box in his back yard, a kind of upright outhouse with a wooden chair and different kinds of wood and metal inside which supposedly helped the body to get rid of toxins. (Reich developed all kinds of contraptions, most of them useless. In fact, he was jailed, in part for selling bogus health equipment in Maine.)

The therapy, called bioenergetics, consisted of my laying down on a mattress in Myron Sharaf's attic and his pushing and squeezing the muscles in my back and chest. It hurt. I never returned for a second session, and Sharaf died soon afterward, a strange yet charismatic man like Reich himself. But who has the Orgone box?

Since I was into psychoanalysis and other therapies, going back to my days when I had suffered from a nervous breakdown in 1969 while in graduate school in Chicago at Northwestern University, I was curious about Reichian therapy. I have described my forays into the therapeutic world in an earlier chapter, from my first encounter with psychoanalysis in Chicago with Dr. Edward Rubin to my escapades on the West Coast with Esalen to my later psychotherapy with the eminent Harvard psychiatrist Dr. Robert Ravven.

Reich had theories of "body armor" and "sexual energy." One had to massage the chest and shoulders and loosen up that "armor," and out would spring all kinds of suppressed feelings, usually of a sexual nature. The Orgone box would accelerate such therapy.

But one can see why this was controversial, especially with women. Could it lead to arousal and sex on that mattress? And what would the good doctor say about that? That sex was healthy? Actually, yes. Sexual or orgasmic release was crucial for therapeutic breakthroughs. This influenced the entire hippie "free love" and "open marriage" movements of the '60s and '70s. However, it was quickly suppressed by a combination of factors, mostly the feminist movement, which viewed any sex with a therapist as a form of "rape" or at least of sexual "harassment."

Reichian "orgone therapy" moved to Europe, and even Israel, and is very popular in the Scandinavian countries, Holland, and Germany. The Orgone box and Reichian therapy has gathered dust, but it did influence a generation or two of therapists who utilize "body" therapy, usually male-on-male and female-on-female. Reichian therapy and its offshoots—Gestalt therapy, Reiki, and psychosynthesis, remain influential yet controversial.[38]

---

38 Sources: Mickey's book; other books on Reich; books on "Third Force" therapies; psychoanalysis (Freud) being first, behavior modification (B. F. Skinner) being the second

Fritz (Frederick S.) Perls

Perls was one of the most charismatic figures in psychotherapy and the man who developed Gestalt Therapy. He was also one of the sexiest figures, even into his seventies.[39] I met him briefly in the hot tubs of Esalen, California, at the famous Esalen Institute. What an experience!

John F. Kennedy

I saw him from the sidewalk in Milwaukee, while he was on a visit campaigning, probably to help Democratic Governor Pat Lucey, on May 12, 1962. It was my last year at Washington High School. I have "proof" of it: I wrote it down in my calendar. I was seventeen years old, and I was downtown in the street cheering him on. (There may even be a rare film of me somewhere in the archives.)

Robert Kennedy (via his son and grandson)

I never met Bobby Kennedy himself, but I did meet his son Joe Jr. and Joe's son Joe III. In fact, I ran against Joe III in 2012 when he first ran for US Congress. I lost, but *The New Yorker* did a profile of me about my run that was quite humorous ("Talk of the Town," April 19, 2012).

Jackie Kennedy Onassis

I met her at Harvard University at the John F. Kennedy School of Government. She had a high, girly voice but a very strong presence. I remember her telling someone: "You don't have to do that (asking for an autograph). Just talk to me." She disliked being treated like a movie star. I just said hello. I was still star-struck. But in the pre-selfie age, I had the presence of mind and got someone to take a photo of us.

---

force. There have been several movies and documentaries on Reich, and the Reich museum in Rangeley, Main, plus their publications are further sources.

39 See his book *In and Out of the Garbage Pail.*

Ted Kennedy

I saw him from afar on several occasions, but he always had many bodyguards around him, and even in Massachusetts he was fearful of being killed, so he never stayed too long mingling with the crowds. So I never had a chance to talk to him face-to-face.

Bill and Hillary Clinton

I have a photo of Bill and me. I met them several times, most memorably at the opening of the US Holocaust Memorial Museum in 1993. He was as charismatic and attractive in person as his image was. I saw or heard Hillary several times when she was running for president.

Jimmy Carter

I attended the 1976 Democratic Convention in New York City with a press pass from the *Jewish Advocate* of Boston. I saw many famous people (Warren Beatty, Paul Newman, Lauren Bacall) and heard Jimmy Carter, a great guy if a somewhat weak and ineffectual president.

Al Gore and Joe Lieberman

I met Al Gore at a garden party in Cambridge at John Kenneth Galbraith's home in the 1980s. I met Joe Lieberman at a fundraiser in a Boston hotel when he was Al Gore's vice presidential partner when Gore ran for president.

Donald Trump

I heard him speak and walked by him at a real estate conference. He was the golden boy of New York real estate. He had the Midas touch. This was in the 1980s, long before he became a TV celebrity and, of course, president.

Martin Luther King, Jr.

I saw him in the fall of 1967 at the University of Wisconsin–Milwaukee student union. He may have come to march with Father James Groppi. I still remember several racist trucks outside the speech with "Communist" and "Martin Luther Coon" banners. His killing was no surprise.

David Ben-Gurion

I met David Ben-Gurion and his wife Paula, and I have a photo to prove it, in Chicago at his hotel in 1968 when he was on a fundraising tour of America. Boy, he had charisma, even though his English was broken. What I remember most was his encouraging us to move to Israel to live and his wife Paula calling out to him, "David it's late. You need your rest. Let's go to the hotel room and sleep."

Golda Meir, Yigal Allon, Moshe Dayan, and other Israeli leaders

While I have a chapter in my book about Golda and me, surprisingly I never met her face-to-face. However, in the spring of 1963, while I was on my yearlong trip to Israel, I saw her and the others from a distance. They spoke at Kibbutz Lochamei Hagetaot on Yom Ha-Shoah (a Holocaust Remembrance Day). I did, however, meet Shimon Peres in person over the years, since he came to America quite often.

Malcolm X

I never met Malcolm X, but I knew people in Roxbury (part of Boston) who knew him, and I knew people who lived next door to him there.

Albert Einstein

Nor did I ever meet Albert Einstein. He died in 1955, when I was only ten, but I met several famous physicists who knew him. On a visit to the Institute for

Advanced Studies in Princeton, New Jersey, I visited his home and the institute, to which I had applied for a fellowship.

Abraham Joshua Heschel

Yes, I met him in spring of 1972 at an ADL conference in the Catskills, at Grossingers (wow, those days are gone). He had received an award, and I remember his words to the audience: "Finally, you have awarded this to a plain old Hebrew teacher." Afterwards, most of the guests ignored him except me, his wife, and young daughter Susannah, and a few nuns and priests. I was there on a panel discussing campus radicals and how to deal with them. My book *Jewish Radicalism* was due out soon. He was almost "biblical" in appearance; truly charismatic. Again, sadly, he died shortly afterwards at age sixty-five.

Martin Buber

Yes, I saw him two or three years before he died on June 13, 1965. In the fall of 1962 and the spring of 1963, I was on The Machon Institute for Youth Leaders in Jerusalem, and secular Israelis, *kibbutznikim*, and Israeli intellectuals would come to his home in Rehavia right before Shabbat on Friday evenings and sing and schmooze in front of his door, and he would come out and greet us. He looked as the pictures show him—bent over, white-haired, and smiling.

Isaac Bashevis Singer

I heard him speak at Harvard, where Rabbi Ben-Zion Gold invited him every year to give a talk. He was a white-haired elfin character even back then.

Magnus Hirschfeld

I never met him. He died in 1935, but I have written so much about him I feel I know him. He was truly a fascinating curmudgeon, a leader in the history of sexual and gay rights.

The Swami Satchidananda

I heard him speak on a hill in Sonoma County, near Napa, California, in the late 1960s. I have his tapes, and I meditate to them. I loved his voice.

Henry Kissinger

I met him at a party at a Boston hotel before he was about to speak. I was going to criticize his decision to support the dictator Pinochet in Chile, but felt maybe it was not the best time. He looked very formidable, even in his eighties.

Robert Reich

I worked in his campaign for governor of Massachusetts in the 2000s, but he started too late and could not get enough money to run. But he was very smart and charismatic. And very short. Sadly, short men and women do not win in politics.

Cornel West

Cornel is my buddy. When I ran for office in Newton, Massachusetts, we met at a coffee shop, and he flipped out his wallet and gave me fifty dollars. He is one of the most charismatic speakers one could ever listen to. I am envious. I wish I had his gift and his audience.

Lubavitcher Rebbe

Yes, I met him in 1991 and waited in line along with hundreds of other Hasidim to get one dollar from him. I got two dollars by mistake, but the Hasidim said it was not a mistake but a special gift. I even have a short video of him giving me the money. Charismatic does not begin to describe him.

Bobover Rebbe

I met him several times—the first when I was about to be drafted into the US Army and was going in for my physical. He met me along with my mother at Rabbi Twerski's home in Milwaukee and gave me his blessing "not to go," and I didn't.

Rabbi Twerski and His Sons

I describe their impact on me and my family in my book. A wonderful family. I wish I had gotten to know the *alter rebbe* better, but I was way too young. He was too intimidating.

Elie Wiesel

I have many photos of him. We were close. I loved the guy.

Simon Wiesenthal

I met the famous Nazi hunter in Baltimore when he spoke at a function my brother Rabbi Shlomo Porter sponsored. He was heavily guarded. He spoke poor English, yet was so charismatic.

Primo Levi

I heard him speak once before he died, sadly from a suicide. I wrote about him and other Holocaust writers and poets in a controversial essay called "Holocaustal Suicides." See my book *The Genocidal Mind*.

Rosa Sonneschein

I never met her, but I met her grandson.

Ayn Rand

I heard her speak when I first came to Boston. It was at a famous speakers' series they had. I had no idea she was Jewish and Russian! She was very conservative and hated Communism. She was the first twentieth-century conservative intellectual and influenced most of the conservative thinkers and leaders in the world.

Margaret Mead

I met her at a conference, either a library or anthropology conference, in New York City. We sat on some steps with other acolytes and chatted. She was so special.

Norman Mailer and Norris Church Mailer

I met him around the hear 2000 in Provincetown. I was staying at a time-share in Brewster Green on Cape Cod, and I had left a message for him at this home. I got a call later that evening. "Hello, this is Norman Mailer. You stopped by?" I said, "Yes, I did and left my number. Can we meet tomorrow?" And yes, we met the next day and briefly chatted. I forgot about what. I also met his lovely redheaded wife, Norris Church Mailer. He was easy to talk to. I was surprised, given his image as a tough guy.

George Plimpton

I met him at a famous fundraiser in Mattapoisett, Massachusetts, for the *Partisan Review*, one of those parties right out of a movie set. It should have been filmed. George, a charming man, could put together a party and invite nearly anyone, and they would come. I miss those parties.

Keith Richards

I met him at a Norman Mailer Foundation dinner in Manhattan. We talked as fellow writers—he had just finished his memoir *Life*. Very smart guy, very easy to talk to. The only problem: the "clipboard Nazis," as I called them, came up to us and said, "Sorry, we have to limit Mr. Richards's time with each person."

Tony Bennett

I also met Tony Bennett at the Norman Mailer Foundation dinner party. He was also very easy to chat with. Those dinners for the Mailer Foundation were so special. Everyone went—and I mean everyone! Muhammad Ali, the Clintons, Elie Wiesel, and many other lesser-known stars and bigwigs. They all loved the Mailers and Larry Schiller, the man who organized it.

Noam Chomsky

I met him on several occasions at his office at MIT. He even wrote me letters of reference for jobs and grants and admired my work. He was and is an international idol, but sadly never recognized in his own country. Too radical.

Jerry Rubin

I have a photo of him and me at Abbie Hoffman's funeral in Worcester, Massachusetts. I loved the guy.

Erving Goffman

I met him briefly at sociology conferences. He died much too soon, at sixty. He was one of the few sociological geniuses; others include C. Wright Mills, Robert K. Merton, Talcott Parsons, Alvin Gouldner, Howie Becker, Laud Humphries, and Marcello Truzzi.

Howard S. Becker

He was my professor at Northwestern University from 1967 to 1971. Took classes with him. Loved the guy.

Alvin Gouldner

I met him, I think it was in 1989, on the Boston University campus. I spoke briefly with him as he walked to class. He was a formidable and intimidating figure, but he once told me, "Jack, there is nothing like Jewish, Black, or gay sociology. There is only good or bad sociology." I never forgot that.

C. Wright Mills

I never met him, but I met or talked with his three former wives and two of his three children. I liked his daughter in Boston, but I had a bad experience with his son Nik in Nyack, New York. I liked talking to his wives; one was in a nursing home in Boston, and one I visited in Nyack.

Talcott Parsons

I met him when he came in 1968 to speak to us graduate sociology students at Northwestern University. He autographed one of his books for me. I still have it. He looked like your rotund avuncular uncle, but he was brilliant and stood sociology on its head with his grand theories.

Marshall McLuhan

I always wanted to meet him, so one day when I was in Toronto I took a chance and walked up to his house near the campus of the university and, lo and behold, he invited me in, and we had tea! I also took a course at UCLA with his colleague and co-author Edward Carpenter.

Abram Sachar

I met him several times in the late '70s and '80s when he was founding president of Brandeis University.

Frank Sinatra

I saw his concert at the Boston Garden and got quite close. I also met one of his bodyguards years later in New York.

Gregory Peck

I met him and his lovely wife, Veronique Passani Peck, a French woman, at a homecoming at Northwestern University in 1969. I went to him, said hello, and that's it. He looked exactly as he did on screen—tall and handsome. He was visiting his son, who went to Northwestern University. Sadly, sons and daughters of famous people have tough lives—it's hard to live up to an icon. The son committed suicide later in life. I met him also—also a very handsome man.

While I'm at it, NU graduated many Hollywood stars. I met Peter Strauss from TV's *Rich Man, Poor Man*, as well as Charlton Heston's sister. She was a professor of speech at NU. Ann-Margret, who bedded Elvis, and Meghan Markle, who is married to Prince Harry (fifth in line to the British throne), are also NU graduates. I wish I could have met all three of them.

George Clooney

We met at a genocide and refugee conference in Yerevan, Armenia, during the Aurora Prize Awards in the summer of 2016. We talked for about ten minutes right before a panel that we were on, about my research on refugees. He was a great guy. His words to me were memorable: "Jack, talk quickly, because when those doors open, it will all be over," meaning the crowd of people will enter and they will all rush up to talk to him, and that's what happened. Jack Porter "disappeared." I should have taken a selfie of us, but I didn't want to appear like a "fan."

We also had a connection via my friend, Boston real estate developer and movie producer Steve Samuels, who produced the 2007 *Michael Clayton*, a movie that Clooney starred in. It was the only time that I knew someone who got a "shout-out" at the annual Academy Awards show, when Tilda Swinton won Best Supporting Actress for her performance in the movie.

She thanked Steve publicly from the stage. It was also one of the few times I almost got a ticket to the Academy Awards. I asked Steve if he could snag me a ticket or two (I would have brought my daughter), but he said that, even though he produced the movie, he was given only two tickets, one for him and one for his wife Amy.

Warren Beatty and Lauren Bacall

I met them at Jimmy Carter's presidential nomination at the Democratic National Convention at Madison Square Garden in New York City in the summer of 1976.

Bob Hope

I saw him in performance in the Boston area.

Sid Caesar and Imogene Coca

I saw them, too, in performance in Boston, at the Colonial Theatre.

Tony Curtis

I saw him in Boston, too, and we schmoozed. I was a "stage-door Johnny" outside a Boston theater, where he reprised his role in *Some Like it Hot* in a musical version of the film. He was a very nice guy. I was actually more interested in talking to the beautiful blond actress that co-starred in his play; she had the Marilyn Monroe role. I have forgotten her name.

Al Martino and Jerry Van Dyke

I saw them in Las Vegas walking through a casino. All I remember was that Martino was very rude: "Get out of my way!" Van Dyke was not much better. He was the lesser-known brother of Dick Van Dyke. Some actors are rude. Like this next one.

Tommy Lee Jones

I met him and tried to talk to him at the Brattle Theatre in Cambridge in Harvard Square in 2015. I thought he would be nice, since he was with a Harvard friend and had come back for a reunion. Again, he was quite rude and intimidating.

Ed Asner

I had lunch with him near Harvard Square. He had responded to a letter of mine trying to get a movie made from my *Jewish Partisans* book. I think he had a relative who was a Soviet partisan plus I think in another era he would have been a Communist Party member. He was very "progressive." I loved his parting remark: "Jack, I love the jib of your sails." A great guy, but sadly he could not come up with the money for the project. It costs about twenty million dollars to make a Hollywood movie today. However a film was made with Daniel Craig called *Defiance*, and it was based on Nechama Tec's book of the same name, not my book. That's Hollywood for you . . . it's not easy to break through, but I gave it a good shot.

Jefferson Airplane/Starship

I met them and partied with them after a concert in a small "garage-like" warehouse in East Stroudsburg, Pennsylvania, around 2011. I was driving across country to Milwaukee from Boston and always stopped there to stay overnight. Paul Kantner and Marty Balin were still with the group. Others had left, like Grace Slick. But the young dark-haired singer who replaced her was very good. They were great guys. I have photos of them. Sadly, they passed away a few years apart, in 2018 (Marty) and 2016 (Paul).

Country Joe McDonald

I met him after a concert at a private party in Milwaukee.

Everly Brothers

I saw them perform in Milwaukee in the early '70s. I never saw Elvis, but I saw other rock-'n-roll acts: Dr. John, Country Joe and the Fish, Jefferson Airplane.

Arlo Guthrie

I met him after a concert.

Ted Williams

I met him at an event with Gov. William Weld in a Boston Park and had a great discussion with Ted (over half an hour) all by myself, because I talked to him like a regular guy, not a fan. He was a conservative Republican who supported Bill Weld for governor, and would have likely supported Donald Trump had he lived longer. But we had a great discussion about politics.

Johnnie Logan and Alvin Dark

I met them at a Boston Braves reunion. It was wonderful to finally meet them.

Warren Spahn, Hank Aaron, and Eddy Matthews

All of them were Hall of Famers from the 1950s, and I saw them at the old Braves County Stadium in Milwaukee. I loved the entire team. I can still rattle off every player at every position.

Alan Dershowitz (*Boo . . .*)

I met him several times over the years near Harvard Square and in Boston. I thoroughly disliked him. I thought he actually "increased" antisemitism after he appeared on TV because of his obnoxious, know-it-all attitude. I am writing a book called *Chutzpah at Harvard* that discusses his life and other Harvard professors.

Jack Nusan Porter's Family Tree

1A.   AVRUM **MERIN** (a   ) married CHAYA YUDEL, and they had:

- NUSAN (a *melamed/scholar*) married BAILA SINGERMAN, and they had: Yaakov, Aaron, Elka, Sender, Feige, Zisya, Rivka, and Chana.
- CHANA married YANKEL LEIBERMAN (a   ), and they had: Esther (Frumkin), Morris, Ben, Joe, Freda (*Harry Friedman), Sylvia (*Larry Fuhr)—Dick Fuhr and Bob Fuhr.
- RIVKA married CHAIM LEIB BARON (cleaning and tailor), and they had: Esther (–> Jack Fisher), Nathan, Sidney, and   ?   (–> Molly: Kenny).
- YOSEL (blacksmith) married MINDEL GOODMAN (Abe Goodman's sister), and they had: Berel, Baila, Yehuda (–> Luba: Yossi and Mina), Leah, Pessel.
- SOSSI married ITZIK LEIB BRONSTEIN (   ), and they had: Velvel, Berel, Motel, Avrum (–> Celia: Billy and Susie), Leyka, Zlota, and Shaya.
- LEAH married MOSHE HASKELL (tailor)—he was a Stoliner Chassid.
- HERSHEL (a butcher) married CHUMKA PUCHTIK (Avrumchik's sister), and they had: two daughters.

2A. SHLOMO **SINGERMAN** (   ) married ELKA, and they had:

- BAILA married NUSAN MERIN (Melamed), and they had: Yaakov, Aaron, Elka, Sender, Feige, Zisya, Rivka, and Chana.
- MENUCHI married last name WOOL, and they had: Mordechai, Elka, and two more sons.
- MORDECHAI married girl, last name SHPIELBERG (Hinda Porter's cousin): no children.
- CHUNI married SHIFKA, and they had: Baila, Esther, two daughters, and two sons.

3A. NUSAN **MERIN** (Melamed) married BAILA SINGERMAN, and they had:

- YAAKOV (a butcher) married Sosi, and they had: Malka and four more children.
- AARON (   ) married SOSSEL ZELTZER, and they had: Shmulik, two girls, and Aaron (named after their father, who died of an infection after an appendix operation).
- ELKA married MORDECHAI WOOL (grocery) (mother was Menudi Singerman), and they had: Chuni, Sissel, Shlome, and a daughter.
- SENDER (   ) married CHAVA, and they had: two children.
- FEIGE married YISROEL PUCHTIK, and they had: Chaya Yudel, Pessel, Yaakov Nusan, Shlome Sender, Baila Yenta
- Zisya |
- Rivka |—Single
- Chana |

4A. AVRUM **KLEIGER** married PESYA, and they had:

- ESTHER YENTEL married YAAKOV PUCHTIK, and they had: Chaim Moshe, Michla, Ruchel, Yisroel (Srulik), Chasya, Zelda, Leon, Velvel, Baruch Leib (Boris).
- SOSI married SAM YUGER of New York.
- HERSHEL married NECHI, and they had: Jack Klieger (–> Elaine: Jackie), Minnie Klieger, and Sam Klieger(–> Charlotte: Douglas, Chris, and Judy)
- YANKEL married ESTHER MALKA SINGER, and they had: Bessie (–> Harry Sokol: Shirley), Ruchel/Rae (–> Morris Lieberman:

Sidney, Leonard, and Donald), Rose (-> David Kaufman: Brenda and
Judy), Sophie (-> Lou Kaplan: Phyllis and Edith), Lottie (-> Arthur
Magidson: David, Judy, Isabel, Eddie, and Bobbie), Paul (-> Miriam:
Debbie) and Schnooksie* (-> Harry Schoenfeld: Howard, Linda,
Susie).

*Mother was E. M. Singer, Father was Rev. Rosenblith (   )

5A.   CHAIM MOSHE **PUCHTIK** married MICALI, and they had:

- A married   ?   , and they had: Chika (-> Hershel Merin), Michla,
  Brucha, Avrumchik (-> Chaua: son and Yitka), Fruma (-> Walter
  Hustein: Joe and Helen) and two more sons.
- ANSHEL   ?   married GREENBERG, and they had: Ben Porter, who
  married Sheindel Barg and had George (-> Leila: Carol, Gail, Ann);
  Joe (Frances Aisenberg: Richard Porter); Barney (Florence Giraloma:
  John Porter).
- YAAKOV married ESTHER YENTEL KLEIGER, and they had:
  Chaim Moshe (Morris), Michla, Ruchel, Yisroel (Srulik), Chasya,
  Zelda, Leon, Velvel, and Boruch Leib (Boris).

6A.   YAAKOV **PUCHTIK** married Esther YENTEL KLEIGER, and
they had:

- CHAIM MOSHE (MORRIS), businessman, tobacco, married Betty
  Friedman, and they had: Allan (-> Sylvia: Marlon)
- RUCHEL married AVRUM BENIS (artist), and they had: three
  children.
- MICHLA married Hershel Leib Seigel (blacksmith), and they had:
  three children.
- LEON (   ) married   ?   , and they had: son and daughter.
- VELVEL—Single, died during WWI of hunger.
- YISROEL married FEIGE MERIN, and they had: Chaya Yudel, Pessel,
  Yaakov Nusan (Miriam), Shlome Sender (Shoshana: Esther Malka &
  Elka Chava), Baila Yenta (Mitchell Smith: Sruli, Avi, Aryeh (Nosson,
  Sruli, & Meir), Shragai, & Mindy
- CHASYA married ITZIK (shoemaker), and they had: 3 children.
- ZELDA married BEREL SCHVARTZBLATT (builder), and they had:
  2 children.

- BORUCH LEIB (BORIS) married HINDA ZELTZER, and they had: Sam (–> Judy: Adam, Mason and   ), Abe (Joy: Scott), Jack (Myra:).

Sources and Permissions

Articles

1. *Jewish Advocate*, "My Days and Nights in the JDL."
2. The *Forward*, "Cabaret Nights: Key West Rabbi."
3. *Wisconsin Jewish Chronicle*, "Porter-Arenzon Escaped Nazi Massacre in Ukraine," December 2009.
4. The *New Yorker*, "Write-In" by Ben McGrath, April 9, 2012; permission granted by Conde Nast.
5. *Newton Magazine*, "Never Again—for Anybody" by McKenzie C. Kimball, October 2008—permission granted by publisher.
6. The *Boston Globe*, "Key West Rabbi" story.
7. *Boston Herald-American* (now the *Boston Herald*) for the Nazi hunting articles.
8. *New England Real Estate Journal*, "Porter of The Spencer Group brokers $600,000 deal," January 31–February 6, 2020.
9. *Jewish Family Magazine*, story on my mother.
10. The *Key West Citizen* for story on my being the rabbi there.
11. *ASA Footnotes* for the sociologist in real estate story.
12. The *York Weekly* (Maine).

13. Jeanette Friedman from *Lifestyles*, "Journey through the Woods," Fall 2001.

14. *Chelsea* [MA] *Times* for the story of rabbi in Chelsea story.

15. *Davka Magazine* in LA, "Zalonka: Interview with a Partisan Leader."

16. Interview of Faye Porter; permission of Prof. William Helmreich.

About the Author

Jack Nusan Porter was born on December 2, 1944, in Rovno, Ukraine. He is the son of a Soviet partisan commander, Srulik Puchtik (Irving Porter), who fought under the *nom de guerre* "Zalonka" in the forest resistance in northwestern Ukraine during World War II. Jack Nusan Porter's mother was a nurse and cook in the same fighting unit, called the Kruk-Maks Group, from 1942–1944.

He came to America from Bindermichel DP camp in Austria in July 1946 and was raised in Milwaukee, Wisconsin. He graduated from the University of Wisconsin–Milwaukee and received his PhD with honors in sociology from Northwestern University in 1971 at the age of twenty-six. He was a research associate at the Ukrainian Research Institute of Harvard University and was an assistant professor of social science at Boston University.

He is considered one of the founders of contemporary genocide and Holocaust studies, having taught the first course in the sociology of genocide in the United States in 1976 at the University of Massachusetts–Lowell and compiled the first anthology in the field *Genocide and Human Rights* (1982). He has been elected both treasurer and vice-president of the International Association of Genocide Scholars, and ran for president four times, more than anyone in history.

Two of his books have been nominated for National Jewish Book Awards. In 2015, his work in genocide was nominated for a Nobel Peace Prize.

He has published more than forty books and anthologies and more than seven hundred articles and reviews, including *Student Protest and the Technocratic Society, Jewish Radicalism* (with Peter Dreier), *The Study of Society* (contributing editor), *The Sociology of American Jews, The Jew as Outsider, Confronting History and Holocaust, Kids in Cults, Jews and the Cults, Sexual Politics in Nazi Germany, Conflict and Conflict Resolution, Jewish Partisans* (two volumes), *Genocide and Human Rights, Women in Chains: On the Agunah,* and *Holocaust and Genocide.* He has made many contributions to reference books and journals including the *Encyclopedia Judaica, Encyclopedia of Sociology, Encyclopedia of American Jewish Women, Handbook of Pastoral Care, The YIVO Annual, Judaism, Jewish Social Studies, Contemporary Jewry, Society, Midstream, Sociological forum,* and the American *Journal of Sociology* (book reviews).

He was the founder and editor of the *Journal of the History of Sociology* and was a contributing editor to the *Encyclopedia of Genocide.* He received the John Atherton Fellowship from the Bread Loaf Writers' Conference and fellowships from the Memorial Foundation for Jewish Culture and the World Jewish Congress. He is listed in *Who's Who in America* (50th Golden Anniversary Edition), *Who's Who in Israel and Friends of Israel, American Men and Women of Science,* and *Contemporary Authors.*

He has lectured widely on American social problems and political/religious movements and has testified before several government commissions. He has edited a curriculum guide *The Sociology of Genocide/The Holocaust* (1992) for the American Sociological Association.

Jack Nusan Porter was a student at the Academy of Jewish Religion in New York City, studying for the rabbinate, and later received his *s'micha* (rabbinical ordination) from an Orthodox Va'ad in the year 2000. He is presently affiliated with the Davis Center for Russian and Eurasian Studies at Harvard University and resides in Newtonville, Massachusetts. He can be reached at porter_jack@comcast.net. His website is www.drjackporter.com.

Books by Jack Nusan Porter

Student Protest and the Technocratic Society (1971)
The University and the Community (1971)
Jewish Radicalism: An Anthology (1973)
The Study of Society (1974)
Kids in Cults (1977; 1985; 1994)
The Sociology of American Jews (1980; 1982)
The Jew as Outsider (1981; 2014)
Jews and Cults (1981; 2014)
Handbook on Cults and Sects (1982; 2014)
Conflict and Conflict Resolution: A Historical Bibliography (1982)
Genocide and Human Rights (1982; 2002)
Jewish Partisans of the Soviet Union, 2 vols. (1982; in process of being reprinted
    by Academic Studies Press in one volume, 2020)
Notes of a Happy Sociologist (1983)
Confronting History and Holocaust (1983; 2014)
With Ruth Taplin, *Conflict and Conflict Resolution: A Sociological Introduction*
    (1987)
Since Solomon and Sheba: Black-Jewish Relations from Biblical to Modern Times
    (in progress)
Sexual Politics in Nazi Germany (1991; 1995; 2000)
The Sociology of Jewry (1992; 1999)
The Sociology of the Holocaust and Genocide (1992; 1999)
The Sociology of Business (1992)
Women in Chains: Handbook on the Agunah (1996)
With Rudiger Lautmann and Erhard Vismar, *Sexual Politics in the Third Reich:
    The Persecution of the Homosexuals during the Holocaust* (1996; 2000)
L'Matara: Partisan Poetry and Prose (forthcoming)
Rabbi Joseph Mayer Jacobson and Boston Jewry (1998)
21 Screen Treatments for Hollywood, TV, Broadway, or as Graphic Novels (2018)
With Gerry Glazer and Sandy Aronin, *Happy (Freilich) Days Revisited: Growing
    Up Jewish in Ike's America* (2010)
Milwaukee Memories/Milwaukee and Hollywood/Small Town Secrets (2011)
Encyclopedia of Genocide (contributing editor, 2000)
The Holocaust and Comparative Genocide: Cases, Theories, Legacies (in process)
The Genocidal Mind: Sexual and Sociological Essays (2006)
Is Sociology Dead?: Social Theory and Social Praxis (2008)

Mathematical Models to Predict Terrorism, with Trevor Jones (2022)
Genocide: An Introduction (2020, in progress)
Anti-Semitism: From Deicide to Genocide (in progress)
The Making of a Spiritual Leader (in progress)
The Journal of the History of Sociology (founding editor; editor 1977–1982)
What is Culture? (in progress)
Introduction to Western Civilization (in progress)
Like Sheep to Slaughter: Essays on Jewish Resistance During the Shoah (in progress)

Awards and Memberships

Bread Loaf Writers Conference, John Atherton Fellow, 1976
Fellowship from the National Jewish Memorial Foundation, 1978–1979
Fellowship from the Institute for Social Research, London, 1982
Research Associate, Ukrainian Research Institute, Harvard University, 1982–1984
Two of my books were nominated for National Jewish Book Awards, 1982 and 1983
Consultant in nonfiction awards National Book Critics Circle Awards, 1997–1998
Judge, Holocaust Books, National Jewish Book Awards, 1993–1995
Finalist, Haskell Teaching Award, University of Massachusetts at Lowell, 1999

www.ingramcontent.com/pod-product-compliance
Lightning Source LLC
Chambersburg PA
CBHW071728270326
41928CB00013B/2596